The Spy Novels of John Le Carré

The Spy Novels of John Le Carré

Balancing Ethics and Politics

Myron J. Aronoff

St. Martin's Press
New York

PR
6062
.E33
Z56
1999

THE SPY NOVELS OF JOHN LE CARRÉ

Library of Congress Cataloging-in-Publication Data

Aronoff, Myron Joel.
    The spy novels of John le Carré: balancing ethics and politics /
Myron J. Aronoff

        p.   cm.
    Includes bibliographical references (p.) and index.
    ISBN 0–312–21482–0
    1. Le Carré, John, 1931—Criticism and interpretation.
2. Politics and literature—Great Britain—History—20th century.
3. Le Carré, John, 1931—Political and social views.
4. Political fiction, English—History and criticism.   5. Didactic
fiction, English—History and criticism.   6. Spy stories, English—
History and criticism.   7. Le Carré, John, 1931—Ethics.
I. Title.
PR6062.E33Z56 1998
823'.914—dc21   98–43405
                                                                              CIP

Internal design and typesetting by Letra Libre

First edition: January, 1999
10   9   8   7   6   5   4   3   2   1

For Rita, Miriam, Matt, Yael, Eric, and Maya

Contents

Preface/Acknowledgments

Robert McNeill: "Is spying an honorable profession?"
John le Carré: "I am sure it can be, yes. I think it probably can be."
(McNeill-Lehrer Report, May 1989)

This book examines the spy novels of John le Carré, focusing on key ethical dilemmas that confront citizens, particularly of democracies, when their states engage in espionage. Le Carré's unique ethical critique, a kind of ambiguous moralism, and his skeptical outlook are firmly grounded in his liberal political temperament. This book is written for a broader audience than just my fellow academics—it is for le Carré buffs as well as for those who may not have read many (or any) of his novels.

Readers unfamiliar with the main characters may need to occasionally refer to the *dramatis personae* I have provided as a reference. For avid le Carré fans, they are old friends. I have provided only enough plot summary in each chapter to put into context the examples I draw for the discussion of a specific topic. Those who are only interested in the main discussion may wish to ignore the notes, which are for readers who wish to check my sources and to pursue the finer points of argumentation. The same goes for the bibliographical references. I sincerely hope that readers who decide to follow this suggestion will have pleasure in reading the main text and suffer no guilt from ignoring the rest.

The genesis of this book was a series of seminars I taught in the Rutgers College general honors program and one that I taught aboard the *S.S. Universe* for the University of Pittsburgh's Semester at Sea program. I thank my students in these seminars, whose enthusiastic reactions and comments stimulated me to write "Intelligence and the Dilemma of Democracy: Themes in the Work of John le Carré," a paper I delivered at the 1994 annual meeting of the American Political Science Association. I am grateful to the discussants of the panel in which this paper was presented, Michael Zuckert and Barbara Allen, as well as to Kathleen Gerson, Irving Louis Horowitz, Richard Lau, Carey McWilliams, Gerald Pomper, and Joseph

Romano, for their comments on this paper. Their generally positive reactions reinforced my determination to expand the paper into a full-length book.

I acknowledge my debt and my gratitude to the two institutions and the many individuals who contributed to making this book possible. A key individual in each institution that supported the research and writing of this book is an avid reader of le Carré. My personal thanks to Richard Foley, dean of the Faculty of Arts and Sciences of Rutgers, the State University of New Jersey, and to H. L. Wesseling, rector of the Netherlands Institute for Advanced Studies in the Humanities and the Social Sciences (NIAS), where I was a fellow in residence for the academic year 1996–97, for their personal interest and support. My profound gratitude goes to the institutions they represent, particularly to the staff of NIAS (especially librarian Dinny Young), who provided an ideal environment for living in the wonderful Netherlands and working in a stimulating intellectual environment. I thank collectively those many colleagues with whom I interacted during my year at NIAS, particularly the participants in the Philosopher's Group, to whom I gave presentations of the first two chapters of this manuscript for their useful comments.

I especially wish to express my sincere gratitude to two colleagues who have read and commented on drafts of the entire manuscript. Where their suggestions provided a new insight or line of analysis, they are also credited in the notes. Gerry Pomper's careful reading produced particularly insightful comments. I owe a very special debt to Richard Trahair, whom I met only once many years ago. Through the wonder of e-mail, from Australia to the Netherlands he has been my secret sharer on this project. As a devotee of le Carré, a good soul, and a collegial intellectual, he has provided ongoing commentary and encouragement as this book was being written. I am especially grateful to him.

I wish to also express my sincere thanks to my editor at St. Martin's, Karen Wolny, both for her enthusiastic support and her thoughtful reading and many helpful suggestions. I have never had an editor who made so many valuable recommendations for revision. The book is much better for her assistance, as well as all of the other suggestions I received from the meticulous copyediting of Wendy Jacobs and those named here. I also appreciate Rick Delaney's assistance during the production of this book.

Although David Cornwell (John le Carré) declined my request to interview him, he kindly answered questions I raised in several letters over the course of a year. I wish to express my gratitude for his thoughtful and graciously handwritten personal replies and for the untold hours of reading pleasure and intellectual and moral education his novels have provided me over the past 35 years. The time spent rereading, contemplating, and writing about his work has been an exceptionally stimulating and enjoyable experience. Although the writing of this book might be called a labor of love, it has been too much fun to call the writing of it labor. Since Cornwell claims never to read anything written about him, I hope that if someone close to him reads this, they will pass on this expression of my thanks.

This project was very much a family affair. My spouse (and best friend) Rita, my daughters, Miriam and Yael, my sons-in-law Eric Wallach Aronoff and Matthew Cohn, and my sisters, Aida Berenson and Marcia Aronoff, all contributed by searching for books and articles, and/or by reading and commenting on drafts of the manuscript. They all, but especially Rita, encouraged me to carry on the project at times when (because of many obligations and obstacles) it seemed as if I would never succeed in completing it. Rita, Miriam, Yael, and Eric made numerous helpful comments that were incorporated into the book. Words are insufficient to express my gratitude to them for their help, support, and most important, their love. I therefore dedicate this book to Rita, Miriam and Matt, Yael, Eric, and Maya (the first of the next generation of our family) as an expression of my deep love for them.

Introduction

Now that the cold war is over and the Communist tyrannies are largely done for, our country still awaits a real national debate on the means and ends—and the costs—of our national security policies. [Aldrich H. Ames, former CIA officer and convicted Russian spy][1]

Introduction

E spionage has been called the world's second-oldest profession.[2] That spying has a venerable legacy is well documented. The Bible describes Moses, following the Lord's instructions, sending spies to make a reconnaissance of the land of Canaan (Numbers: 13).[3] John G. Cawelti and Bruce A. Rosenberg (1987:3, 37) cite spying in the *Iliad* and in the *Odyssey*. They also mention Delilah and Judas as archetypal spies in the Judeo-Christian tradition. Certainly since ancient times and in every civilization, rulers have used spies to gather intelligence on foes and friends alike. Even (or perhaps especially) after the end of the Cold War, we can expect the business of espionage to continue to thrive.

The primary goal of this book is to illuminate and evaluate key political and ethical themes raised in the novels of the preeminent spy writer of our time.[4] Perhaps more than any other contemporary novelist, John le Carré confronts important personal and collective dilemmas that arise when liberal democracies engage in spying, counterspying, and covert operations. Le Carré's exploration of central political ethical dilemmas of our time elevates the significance of his work well beyond the limitations of the conventional spy genre. I interpret le Carré's world of espionage both on its own terms and as a metaphor for much larger moral problems and political issues, an approach consistent with le Carré's intent. As he told Melvyn Bragg (1976:90), "at the moment, when we have no ideology, and our politics are in a complete shambles, I find it [the espionage novel] a convenient microcosm, to shuffle around in a secret world and make that expressive of the overt world."[5]

Although there is clearly a political tone to his work, le Carré's political message is deliberately ambiguous. His moral message, if possible, is even more ambiguous.[6] The tension between ethics and politics, central to le Carré's work, constitutes the focus of my analysis. Like James Boyd White (1994:271; emphasis in original) *"I am trying to work out a set of questions that will connect texts, and their readers, across the lines of professionalism."*[7]

Because many current trends in literary criticism tend to treat almost every novel as political,[8] I clarify my approach to the analysis of the political importance of le Carré's novels as distinct from others who have analyzed his work.[9] I use the term *political novel* as an approach to interpretation, not as a means of categorization. From this perspective, the political novel does not constitute a fundamentally distinct literary form. A political novel is characterized by internal tensions between the immediacy of human experience and the general inclusiveness of the underlying political ideology.[10] The conflict between the two constitutes the drama of the political novel. Irving Howe (1992:21) suggests that "at its best, the political novel generates such intense heat that the ideas it appropriates are melted into its movement and fused with the emotions of its characters . . . to create the illusion that they [the ideas] . . . seem to become active characters in the political novel." This perfectly describes le Carré (although Howe never wrote about him).

The political novelist sets his own ideas and fantasies against opposing opinions and against the imperative of political necessity: "In the political novel, then, writer and reader enter an uneasy compact: to expose their opinions to a furious action, and as these melt into the movement of the novel, to find some common recognition, some supervening human bond above and beyond ideas. It is not surprising that the political novelist, even as he remains fascinated by politics, urges his claim for a moral order beyond ideology; nor that the receptive reader, even as he perseveres in his own commitment, assents to the novelist's ultimate order" (Howe, 1992:24). Abstract ideology confronts the rich diversity of human experience and motive. The imperative of politics confronts the temptation of the apolitical, a pastoral element, which provides the polarity and tension of the political novel. In le Carré, the pastoral elements are personal sentiments and relationships of love and hate, loyalty and betrayal. The imperative of politics is *raison d'état* (political necessity or expediency).

John le Carré is one of our most preeminent contemporary political novelists. He deals with very serious ideas—including the consequences of the dominant international political myth of our era, the Cold War, and more recently with the sense of disorientation in the aftermath of its demise.[11] Perhaps one reason why critics like Howe ignored le Carré is because of condescension toward the spy genre which is considered not sufficiently "serious."[12] This book strongly argues against such judgments. Although le Carré is a great story teller, his novels constitute more than mere "entertainments," as Graham Greene (self-deprecatingly) labeled his own novels dealing with intrigue, to distinguish these from his so-called more "serious" fiction.[13] Another reason is that le Carré's political ideology is subtly understated and ambiguously presented. In contrast to novelists like Orwell, Malraux, Koestler, and Solzhenitsyn, who articulated clear political positions,[14] Tony Barley (1986:22–3; emphasis added) notes, "Le Carré's political novels depart from this convention by refusing to make ultimate evaluations on their readership's behalf. The political in le Carré's fiction inheres not in 'message', . . . nor even in the presence of political statements, but in the *enactment* of political encounter, and enactment which involves readers as much as characters."

Studies of le Carré

Although several studies of le Carré's work were published prior to this one, the approaches differ significantly from this one. Peter Lewis (1985:112) notes that the Schillerian distinction between the naïve and the sentimental, "between trusting the impulses of the heart and complying with the dictates of the intellect" is a central motif in le Carré's work. Similarly, David Monaghan (1985) makes the impossible goal of the human aspiration to realize complete humanity by seeking to resolve this tension between the poles of nature and art, and feeling and reason (or reflection) the central theme in his analysis *The Novels of John le Carré:* "The central problem in all le Carré's novels is how to be fully human in a society whose institutions have lost all connection with human feeling"(11).

Cawelti and Rosenberg (1987:183) point out that this "underlying theme of le Carré's portrayal of the aforementioned human dilemmas of the mid-twentieth century is stated most obviously in his one novel without espionage as an explicit theme, *The Naive and Sentimental Lover"* (1972). They suggest that this tension between reason and emotion is a problem that le Carré has personally deeply experienced:[15] "he yearns to unite in himself the naive-sentimental division, yet as a product of modern experience he is keenly aware of the impossibility of establishing a lost harmony between man and nature" (186). None of these critics focus on the uniquely political form in which le Carré poses the modern dilemma, nor do they stress its ideological undertones and implications.[16] Where they are interested in style as it relates to genre and other literary influences, my interest in style is confined to its relation to le Carré's ideological temperament.

Style and Ideology: Ambiguity
and the Liberal Temperament

Many of le Carré's readers are confused by this indirection and ambiguity in his novels. It has also led to contradictory critical interpretations of the meaning and significance of his work. This book clarifies and explains the pattern and the significance of le Carré's ambiguity and elucidates the vague and sometimes seemingly contradictory political or ideological undertones of his work.

Le Carré's ambiguity serves various purposes and can be understood from three different vantage points: ideological, personal (psychological), and stylistic. Le Carré's political teaching is indirect, ambiguous, allows the politics to emerge from an encounter between the confrontation of protagonists, and reflects a sense of humor, sadness, and sympathy for the human condition.[17] It shares many of the properties ascribed by James Boyd White (1994:40) to Plato's *Crito:* "The effect of this dialogue . . . is not to offer the reader a system, a structure of propositions, but to disturb and upset him in a certain way, to leave him in a kind of radical distress." According to White (1994:42), Plato's literary technique reflects his philosophical stance: "This text offers us the experience of incoherence partly resolved, then, but resolved only by seeing that in our own desires for certainty in argument, for authority in the laws—or in reason, or in persuasion—are self-misleading; that we can not rest upon schemes or formulae, either in life or in reading, but must accept the responsibility of living, which is ultimately one of establishing a narrative, a character, a set of relations with others, which have the kinds of coherence and meaning it is given us to have, replete with tension and uncertainty."[18] Le Carré's use of this literary style reflects a similar stance.

It is a feature of his liberal temperament. In fact, high tolerance of ambiguity is one of the defining features of the liberal temperament. Wilson Carey McWilliams (1995) discusses the ambiguous relation between temperaments as "dispositions of the soul" and ideology as doctrines. Although there is an affinity between the two, they are not identical. Among other traits, McWilliams suggests, liberal temperaments presume open minds; they are giving, generous-spirited, prone to look for the possibility of improvement and therefore embrace change, deprecate form in favor of substance, and are inclined to see most social relationships in terms of their utility to the individuals.[19] Their greatest vice is a tendency to love mankind but to neglect their own.[20] At the same time that le Carré, through central characters like George Smiley, expresses a revulsion against doctrines and ideologies, this disposition actually reflects his underlying liberal temperament.[21]

Although a liberal, le Carré subjects liberalism to considerable criticism. Politics in le Carré's fiction are not conveyed overtly through ideological statements but are expressed through the actions and inactions of the characters. The ideal of liberalism is tested against political realities. Therefore, the reader must extrapolate le Carré's vision from his portrayal of the contradictions between ideas expressed and actions. Barley (1986:24–5) observes: "Despite his own preference for a liberal worldview—he nonetheless treats this ideology to severe dissection which glaringly demonstrates its inadequacies when confronted by the reality of political events and by more hard-headed ideologies. . . . Morally attractive and completely untenable, liberalism and individualism are dramatized as contradictory, confused and feeble—'flabby' is the adjective Smiley chooses to describe his liberal behaviour."

Moreover, the shaping of the author's personality and character also helps to explain the chameleon-like quality through which he appears to change political colors and reveals a variety of frequently contradictory viewpoints. Le Carré, in interviews and essays, frequently refers to his own fragmented personality and that of other artists.[22] Le Carré told Miriam Gross (1980:33); "If I knew exactly where I stood I wouldn't write." He told Thom Schwarz (1987:20); "When you have done all your thieving and put your character together, you've got fill him with your own breathe. That's what makes the character play . . . you speak through him and give him life, which is the narcissistic part of writing. When you really hear the right voice speaking through him, you know you have another fragment of yourself moving through the book."

Finally, in addition to reflecting ideological temperament and a personality trait, ambiguity is also an effective literary technique to disguise a moral critique or a political message. Without ambiguity, le Carré's art would appear to be much more polemical.[23] Barley (1986:22) notes that politics in le Carré's novels are the reverse of propagandistic. Whereas he sees this "ambivalence as problematic,"[24] I interpret this ambiguity as emblematic of a liberal temperament. Le Carré's literary style relates to the liberal temperament, which clearly informs his work and makes it particularly well suited for political interpretation.

Le Carré reveals to James Cameron (1974:68; emphasis added) that "there's one thing the books have in common. They almost all begin and end at odd hours of the night. That's to say—it all never began and it never finished. After the resolution comes the resumption. Just as every revolution leaves a prerevolutionary condition. The whole thing is a continuum. It's *open-ended*."

The political significance of le Carré's work, because it is subtly embedded in actions that apparently lack political implications, must be extracted and interpreted by the reader. This ambiguity is a challenge, but it does not mean that le Carré finds all options equally valid. Le Carré does not condescend to his readers. Rather, he expects them to think independently. He told Pierre Assouline (1986:60), "I am convinced the reader likes to work a little and at the end is happy to have resolved a somewhat complex story."

My political interpretation of le Carré's novels builds on yet expands in significant areas the analyses of my predecessors. For example, the two scholars who have written most extensively on political aspects of le Carré's work disagree in categorizing it. Having identified the underlying liberal nature of le Carré's novels, Eric Homberger (1986:14) suggests that "it would be misleading to call him a political novelist; he is rather a novelist for whom meaningful experience and moral life are not disengaged from politics." Barley (1986:25), however, opines that "political novels" is the more appropriate term. Rather than debating the appropriate label for le Carré, in the spirit of Howe, I clarify the political nature of his literary art.

Because certain aspects of le Carré's biography are essential to understand his viewpoint, I compare key events in his life with the alter-ego he created in his most autobiographical novel. This brief comparison provides a context for interpretations of the author's work.

David Cornwell and Magnus Pym

John le Carré was born David John Moore Cornwell on October 19, 1931 in the coastal town of Poole in Dorset, England. The younger son of a Nonconformist (Protestant, but not Church of England) family, Cornwell was raised in a religious, extended family and a chaotic and unstable nuclear family. The many parallels between the lives of Cornwell and his fictional surrogate, Magnus Pym, reveal important insights into le Carré's formative years. Tom Maddox (1986:161) observed that "if, in a heartless mood, one were to design a life for a writer of spy fiction, one might create Cornwell's." In 1986 he published his most autobiographical novel, *A Perfect Spy* (hereafter referred to in this chapter as *Spy*).

Magnus Pym, in a testament written to his son before committing suicide, begins his story six months before his birth, when his father, Richard (Rick), marries his mother, Dorothy (Dot), in order to avoid being prosecuted by her father, a minister (justice of the peace and Liberal member of parliament) from whose church Pym senior has embezzled funds. He traces the parallel lives of his father and himself: both spend their lives trying to put right pivotal betrayals to significant others in early adulthood that result in lives characterized as chain reactions of multiple betrayals.

Cornwell's father, Ronnie, served his first prison term for fraud in 1936—the same year his mother, Olive (nicknamed Glassy), deserted her family. David only learned of his father's imprisonment when he was eighteen and was reunited with his mother at twenty-one. Rick Pym was also a con man who served time in prison. Both fathers (real and fictional) ran unsuccessful campaigns as Liberal candidates for parliament in an attempt to escape active military service during World War II.

Psychological profiles dispersed throughout the text of *Spy* produce composite portraits of the highly disturbed mother, who is institutionalized in a mental hospital when Pym is young, and of the pathological father and son. "I have one photograph of her and there have been times—though no longer, I swear it, she is dead for me—when I would have given my soul for just one more" (2:29). Given the similarity in their backgrounds, one can only surmise that some of the personal anguish of the author is reflected in the pathos of Pym's recollection of his mother. David Cornwell eventually located his mother, bought her a house, and still visits her.[25] Pym, later in life, arranges to meet his mother. When he sees her and she fails to conform to his image of her, he leaves without having spoken to or made any contact with her.

Pym remembers discovering coloring books used by his mother, in which the faces of the religious figures were scribbled out with crayon. Pym interpreted the act as symbolizing her inability to identify with normal people and to live in the real world. His summary portrait of his mother, Dorothy Watermaster, reads: "An abstraction. Mine. An unreal, empty woman permanently in flight. If she had her back to me and not her face, I could not have known her less or loved her more" (2:30). This portrait is a psychological projection by Pym of his personality onto that of his mother. It may also be interpreted as an aspect of the author's self-portrait.

In different interviews, le Carré has characterized himself as a "bolter" who attached himself to individuals and institutions only to feel trapped by them, so he abandons them:

> I was by nature a defector . . . a bolter . . . I come from bolting stock. . . .
> My mother bolted from her home in order to marry my father, bolted again
> when I was five, and stayed bolted for the rest of my childhood. My father
> bolted from his orthodox but repressive upbringing and, as what is politely
> known as a financial adventurer, kept bolting of necessity for most of his life,
> often from the arm of the law, and sometimes unsuccessfully. These things
> are catching. I myself bolted from an English public school . . . at 16; from
> the burdens of bachelorhood at 23; from the twilight world of British intel-
> ligence at 33; and from a first marriage at 36. An instinct simultaneously to
> engage in life and escape from it is not unusual in creative people. . . .
> But . . . I have it in spades. While the patriot and child in me rushed to em-
> brace one great institution after another, so the would-be artist was already

secretly packing his bags, tunnelling under the castle walls, and testing the depth of the moat. (*Johns Hopkins Magazine* [1986]:13, hereafter cited as *JHM*)

Ironically (and self-referentially), le Carré has Pym write, "A writer is King. He should look down with love upon his subject, even when the subject is himself" (4:69). Pym's great love, after his mother, is his nanny, Lippsie: "Life began with Lippsie. . . . Before Lippsie all Pym remembered was an aimless trek. . . . After her everything seemed to flow in the one un-stoppable direction. . . . From Lippsie to Poppy, from Rick to Jack, all one jolly stream. . . . And not only life but death began with her as well, for it was actually Lippsie's dead body that got Pym going, though he never saw it" (4:69). Annie (Lippsie) Lippschitz, a German Jewish refugee who was his father's mistress, became an adoring surrogate mother to Pym. The novel is so replete with moving references to her, including his last thought before Pym ends his life, that this reader wondered whether there was a person who played such a pivotal role in the author's life. David Cornwell confirmed my hunch, explaining that he and his brother had a German Jewish nanny "around 1937–38" (which would have been when he was six to seven years old). He reports that she returned to Germany during the war and that he searched in vain to discover her fate when he served in the British army in Austria after the war (1949–50), where he interviewed many refugees.[26] Both experiences might partly account for the empa-thetic treatment of the large number of Jewish characters in his novels.

Lippsie's suicide was driven by guilt at having survived the Holocaust, by her guilt about her relationship with Pym's father, and by her guilt over having given in to the pressure from Rick to steal checks from the school where she was employed and where Pym was a student. Her suicide rep-resented for Pym betrayal and abandonment by a second mother. Lippsie's death confirmed "his knowledge that women were fickle and liable to sud-den disappearances" (4:99). Betrayal is a major theme in Le Carré's work in general and especially in his treatment of women. He has admitted: "I find it hard to write about women; although I can understand intellectu-ally why they act as they do I find it difficult to imagine myself acting in that way" (Wakeman, 1975).

In addition to feeling responsible for her death, Pym blamed his father, who had cynically used her and pushed this already psychologically frag-ile woman over the brink, as he had done to his wife, Pym's biological mother, as well.[27] Pym's two mothers were but two of the many victims of Rick's betrayal. His son, Pym, was yet another.

Ronnie Cornwell was the single most important influence on David's life.[28] Similarly, Rick Pym plays an overbearing role in his son's life and in this novel. "All he demanded was the totality of your love. The least you could do in return was to give it to him blindly. And wait for him, as God's Banker, to double it over six months" (2:45). Pym's resentment against his father is so great that he refuses to allow Rick to meet his grandson. His ambivalence is conveyed by the combined "loathing and devotion" he feels at remembering the touch of his father (2:33). Pym is literally haunted by Rick's ghost (6:127). He refuses to visit his father on his deathbed and is racked with guilt because he had fervently wished him dead (6:127, 10:270).

Vivian Green (1988:33), who has known David Cornwell since his youth, states: "There was in fact no real escape from the father's consuming affection and pervasive influence." Although he paid for the cremation and memorial service of his father who died in 1975, Cornwell refused to attend the service.[29]

Mary, the second wife of Magnus, blames Rick for her husband's situation. She speaks of his empty look—"Like an actor without a part" (3:60). She realizes that "all his life he's been inventing versions of himself that are untrue. Now the truth is coming to get him and he is on the run" (5:120). On another occasion she says, "I sometimes think he is entirely put together from bits of other people, poor fellow" (4:382). All these are descriptions le Carré has used at various times to characterize himself.

If the family backgrounds of the author and his fictional alter-ego are virtually identical, so were their educational backgrounds. Cornwell attended St. Andrew's Preparatory School and Sherborne School, which he left in 1949 to spend a year studying German at the University of Berne. Pym followed an identical path. Both author and his fictional character began their careers in intelligence during their respective year in Switzerland as students by reporting on the activities of their peers.

In an early biographical statement in John Wakeman (1975:841), le Carré denies having belonged to the Secret Service. But, after many credible reports contradicting him were published over the years, he finally admitted to having been in the Secret Service. In response to a direct question from George Plimpton (1997:55), he related that he was "first picked up when I was a young student in Bern, having run away from my first school, I retained a reporting responsibility."[30] This directly corresponds with Magnus Pym's career.

He also told Plimpton that he was engaged in espionage while serving in the army intelligence corps in Austria. "That was a very formative time, because one of my jobs was trolling through the displaced-persons camps, looking for people who were fake refugees, or for people whose circumstances were so attractive to us from an intelligence point of view that we might consider returning them, with their consent, to the countries they came from." Pym also served in military intelligence in Austria.

Just as Pym was recruited by British internal security while at Oxford (where he, like Cornwell, graduated with first honors in modern languages, majoring in German), Gelber and Behr (1983) cite an intelligence source who claims that upon entering Oxford, from which Cornwell graduated in 1956, he compiled reports on left-wing student groups. In response to a direct question from Joseph Lelyveld (1986:79) whether he had done so, le Carré replied: "I don't think it would have been a respectable thing to have done." Lelyveld says, "He replied on a note of such exquisite, not to say hilarious ambiguity that the truth of the matter, I thought, stood out clearly."[31] Pym also spies on his peers at university.

Cornwell taught German at Eton, England's most famous "public" school, from 1956 to 1958. After leaving Eton, he worked as a freelance illustrator before entering the Foreign Service. Gelber and Behr cite former British intelligence sources who claim that in the two-year gap between his taking the Foreign Service exam and his Foreign Office posting to Bonn, Cornwell served under Maxwell Knight in MI5, after which he transferred to Secret Intelligence Service (MI6) under cover as a junior diplomat.[32] Magnus Pym also transfers from MI5 to MI6 after graduating from Oxford.

Cornwell spied from 1959 to 1966, first under cover as a second secretary at the embassy in Bonn and subsequently as a consul in Hamburg. He was serving in Germany during the erection of the Berlin Wall, which is the central symbol in his first major successful novel *The Spy Who Came in from the Cold* (1963). Le Carré told Plimpton (1977:55) that "after teaching at Eton, I went into the cold-war setup properly. In all I don't supposed that I spooked around for more than seven or eight years, and that's forty years ago, but that was my little university for the purposes that I needed later to write."[33]

Both Cornwell and Pym were married twice. Cornwell has three sons (Simon, Stephen, and Timothy) from his first wife, Alison Ann Veronica Sharp, whom he married in 1954 and divorced in 1971. He has one son (Nicholas) from his present wife, Valerie Jane Eustace, to whom he has been married since 1972. Pym had only one son.

Cornwell became the successful novelist John le Carré, whereas Pym became a double agent and a suicide. Le Carré has suggested on several different occasions that had he not found a creative outlet through literature, he might have become a neurotic or possibly even a double agent. Comparing the similarity of his background with the infamous Cambridge spy Kim Philby, he told Plimpton (1997:66) that "there could have been a time when I, if properly spoken to by the right wise man or woman, could have been seduced into some kind of underground act of revenge against society."

Major Themes

Chapter 1 examines the role of George Smiley, le Carré's most intriguing and enduring character, who appears in eight novels. Smiley symbolizes the dilemma of the liberal in confrontation with more dogmatic foes. Smiley's moral conscience constantly questions the price paid by democracies for attempting to protect political freedoms through the covert world of espionage. He consistently questions the assumptions that those around him take for granted. The exploration of Smiley's role in chapter 1 highlights le Carré's position on several issues, particularly the confrontation between the individual and institutions. This characterization of Smiley develops the notion of the liberal sentiment and introduces the concept of a skeptical balance.

The discussion of Smiley also examines contentions by other authors, such as whether Smiley should be regarded as a developing character, whether Smiley resolves the modern dilemmas that haunt le Carré's mature work,[34] whether le Carré resolves the liberal dilemma,[35] and whether le Carré's political vision develops in the course of his writing career. Their conclusions are the point of departure for my exploration of the nature and implications of le Carré's ethical and political stands.

Chapter 2 explores the theme of loyalty and betrayal. In a variety of contexts, le Carré explores the chronic ambivalence of notions like loyalty and duty, showing that "loyalty can be disloyalty and duty a crime" (Lewis 1985:33). He poses the dilemma that betrayal of either an individual or institution is the inevitable result of to loyalty the other. Loyalty to class provided protection for the infamous Cambridge spies on whom le Carré modeled the Soviet "mole" (double agent) in *Tinker Tailor, Soldier, Spy.* An analogous phenomenon helped protect Aldrich H. Ames, the convicted Moscow spy, and second-generation CIA officer, who spent most of his adult life in the agency.[36] The conflict between personal and institutional loyalties, which I introduce in chapter 1, is further elucidated in this chapter. I also introduce the notion of ambiguous moralism.

Deception is the basic tool of the spy, just as the creation of illusion is a key instrument of the novelist. The discrepancy between appearances and reality, a central motif of le Carré's work, I explore in chapter 3. With great artistry, he reveals the processes through which actors create collective myths to imbue their lives with meaning and, simultaneously, by which they deceive and are deceived. Le Carré indicates that self-deception is a trap to which members of the intelligence community are especially susceptible. The attraction of the "tradecraft" of intelligence can be enthralling. Therein lies one of its great dangers, however, because enchantment with the means may cause loss of sight of the ends.[37] The scenario of a masterful espionage deception becomes a metaphor that speaks to much broader and more universal phenomena, such as the mythical aspects of the Cold War and of the new world order. This central theme is uniquely appropriate for analysis from the phenomenological approach I employ in this chapter.[38] In addition, I clarify the notion of skepticism.

Le Carré's novels reveal the major moral and political dilemmas confronting contemporary Western democracies, especially the conflict between liberal democratic principles and political necessity (or expediency). The preliminary background for the discussion of this issue first presented in chapter 1, is more fully explored in chapter 4 where I examine the relationship between means and ends. Le Carré asks how far a democracy can go in protecting itself against the aggressive espionage efforts of a relentless, nondemocratic foe. If it must resort to means identical to those of a nondemocratic opponent, does it not threaten to undermine the values and principles that it is attempting to protect?[39] The threat, however, goes beyond the viability of democracies. "Do the ends of human survival and peace require such means that humanity will be destroyed in its effort to save itself?" (Cawelti and Rosenberg 1987:183). This chapter explores the limits of *raison d'état,* or political expediency.

Eschewing the possibility of ever fathoming the mystery of human motivation, le Carré explores in elaborate detail the confluence of biography, socialization, culture, and happenstance that lead his characters to reveal their flawed humanity. Le Carré's unique approach to the complex confluence of personality and politics—the tension between the private and the public (or political)—provides the theme of chapter 5: the inherent ambiguities in personalities and the inherent problems of human communication and mutual understanding. Michael J. Hayes (1990:115) even suggests that "David Cornwell's [John le Carré's] novels explore the awful possibility that to use language is inevitably to deceive."

Le Carré depicts British intelligence organizations in the context of and as a metaphor for the decline of Great Britain as a major world power and the rise of the United States as the new hegemon, which is the focus of chapter 6. In the developing relations between the two, bureaucratic politics and interagency rivalries, both within and between each state, play significant roles. The larger international political environment and the more specific micropolitical settings of cooperating and competing intelligence agencies frame my analysis of these themes.

Chapter 7 explores the culture and craft of espionage as seen through le Carré's work. I discuss the recruitment, training, and handling of agents, the attributes of an effective case officer, and techniques of interviewing and interrogation. Discussion of such examples of tradecraft helps to establish the credibility, if not the authenticity, of le Carré's fictional world. Chapter 8 examines the relationship between fiction and the real world of espionage. Some current problems of American intelligence as the United States attempts to adjust to dramatic changes in international politics are compared with le Carré's fictional treatment of the United Kingdom in analogous circumstances.[40] The activities of intelligence agencies (including, but by no means exclusively, covert operations) raise serious questions, the implication of which go to the heart of the core democratic values of Western democracies. Openness, the essence of democratic government, blatantly contradicts secrecy, upon which espionage depends.

The concluding chapter articulates the need to strike a *balance* between ethical and political imperatives. Through this work, I hope to generate greater awareness and general public discussion of these themes. The political and ethical implications for Western democracies of the enormous power of the secret world of espionage has received inadequate attention in the scholarly literature.[41] Such discussion has been even more conspicuously absent from public debate.

The high expectations raised in anticipation of a peace dividend that failed to materialize in the aftermath of the Cold War has led to considerable public disappointment. Gross incompetence bordering on criminal negligence allowed the Russian mole in the CIA, Aldrich Ames, to do incalculable damage to U.S. national security. The failure of the director of the CIA to swiftly undertake serious steps to reform the agency make conditions particularly propitious for public discussion of these issues in the United States.

Such discussions are no less important, however, for other democracies—especially for the nations of Central and Eastern Europe, which are struggling to overcome the legacies of their recent past and to find their new democratic forms and practices.[42] I sincerely hope that this analysis of major themes in the work of John le Carré will contribute to informed public debate as well as to scholarly discussion of these and related issues.

Chapter 1

George Smiley: Liberal Sentiment and Skeptical Balance

> *It was a peculiarity of Smiley's character that throughout the whole of his clandestine work he never managed to reconcile the means to the end. . . . Once in the war he had been described by his superiors as possessing the cunning of Satan and the conscience of a virgin. (A Murder of Quality, 1962:9:73)*[1]

> *Personal integrity drives us to make sense of our moral world, to demonstrate and feel the connection between our personal lives and deepest values and what we do." (J. Patrick Dobel, 1988:196)*

Introduction

Le Carré relates how he came to create George Smiley, by "putting him together from various components—either real or imagined—of my own situation, and adding the solvent of my own filial affection and admiration" (*JHM*, 1986:14). He suggests that he and Smiley were alike in more ways than the differences in their age and appearance might suggest. Among the qualities that he shares with Smiley are shyness, a desire for anonymity, and the fact that they were both intelligence officers and German scholars. Although le Carré had a turbulent childhood, Smiley had none. "You do not have to be a genius to guess that Smiley as a father-figure in my imagination was the very antithesis of everything that my own erratic father had been in reality" (*JHM*:14).[2]

George Smiley,[3] le Carré's most fascinating character, makes an appearance in eight of his fifteen novels published to date dealing with espionage.[4] He serves as an exemplary role model for the heroic struggle to achieve a balance between conflicting ethical and political imperatives, competing loyalties, dreams and reality, ends and means, optimism and pessimism. Decency, integrity, kindness, sympathy, and compassion are

Smiley's most outstanding character traits. He is an intellectual whose chosen profession has forced him to become a man of action, thereby causing a constant struggle to maintain his personal integrity. Smiley is a humanitarian whose actions ultimately cause harm and even death to innocent people, including some for whom he greatly cares. Smiley, whom Alan Bold (1988:21) calls "one of the great creations of modern literature," has received more commentary from literary critics than any other le Carré character.[5] Although a spy, Smiley remains a *mensch* (a very decent human being). Le Carré told George Plimpton (1997:55–6) that Smiley was modeled on Lord Clanmorris (a.k.a. John Bingham), with whom he worked in MI5, and on an Oxford don (almost certainly Vivian Green).[6]

Through the analysis of Smiley's role in le Carré 's novels, I introduce the themes that are elucidated in the following chapters. Lars Sauerberg (1984:51) observes:"In le Carré's stories plot structure and ethical dilemma are two sides of the same thing, provided that Smiley's point of view (in the stories in which he appears) is accepted as the central one." Therefore, my focus here is on Smiley's personification of key dilemmas, contradictions, and ambiguities that both frame and are expressed in the action of the novels—especially the individual's struggle to maintain personal and professional integrity in an institutional context, which makes this mission nearly impossible. Because le Carré has admitted to speaking through Smiley, he is also key for understanding the author's point of view.[7]

Description by Le Carré

Le Carré introduces Smiley in his first novel, *Call for the Dead* (1961).[8] His wife, Lady Ann Sercombe Smiley, in the first sentence of the novel calls him "breathtakingly ordinary." One of her pet names for him is "toad."The narrator states:"Short, fat, and of a quiet disposition, he appeared to spend a lot of money on really bad clothes, which hung about his squat frame like skin on a shrunken toad" (1:7).Viscount Sawley (an in-law) declares at their wedding that "'Sercombe was mated to a bullfrog in a sou'wester.' And Smiley, unaware of this description, had waddled down the aisle in search of the kiss that would turn him into a prince" (1:7).[9] In addition to the amphibian metaphors, Smiley is also described as a mole because of his constant blinking behind his thick glasses, which he habitually cleans with the end of his neck tie.[10] His secretary refers to him as "my darling teddy-bear" (13). David Caute (1980:209) calls him "a Winnie the Pooh with brains." In a later novel, he is described as tubby, hopelessly unassertive, and naturally shy. Smiley "smiled seldom, though he was by no means humourless."[11] In the same novel his agent calls him an "owl."

Smiley Is Socially Nondescript[12]

And so Smiley, without schools, parents, regiment or trade, without wealth or poverty, traveled without labels in the guard's van of the social express, and soon became lost luggage, destined, when the divorce had come and gone, to remain unclaimed on the dusty shelf of yesterday's news. (1:7)

He attended both an unimpressive school and an unimpressive Oxford College (which, for the uninitiated reader, might sound like an oxymoron) where he hoped to make an academic career. Although he married an aristocrat, Smiley belongs to an unrespectable club. In an interview with Miriam Gross (1980:62; emphasis added), le Carré revealed: "I wanted to create someone who didn't belong to any social class but who did belong to a *specific generation*—the generation that believed you had to be politically committed either to one camp or the other, with no middle ground." He told James Cameron (1974:55), Smiley belongs "to the wrong time. There's a sense that their [his and Alec Leamas'] thing is running down."

As his creator, David John Moore Cornwell,[13] would be later, Smiley was recruited in 1928 through his professors to the intelligence service while contemplating pursuing advanced study of seventeenth-century German literature at Oxford. We are told that Smiley's profession, among other things, "provided him with what he had once loved best in life: academic excursions into the mystery of human behaviour, disciplined by the practical application of his own deductions" (1:8).[14] Smiley served under cover as a university lecturer in Germany during Hitler's rise to power, an experience that made him more withdrawn and strengthened his love of England and his hatred of fascism. Leroy Panek (1987:35) points out that Smiley essentially remains a scholar and teacher throughout his intelligence career and emphasizes his teacher-student relationship with several agents and younger colleagues.

Smiley, recalled from the field in 1943, marries Lady Ann Sercombe (the secretary of his boss Steed-Asprey). Released from the Service after the war, they return to Oxford. By the time we meet him, Smiley is a cuckold who died a little inside when his wife left him after two years of marriage, and he dies each time she returns and leaves again.[15] He is a *solitary* man.[16] He is the champion of lost causes in his marital relationship (the childless marriage to an unfaithful wife) as well as in his efforts to restore lost honor to his (once loved) department and to England.[17]

Smiley realizes "he had entered middle-age without ever being young, and that he was—in the nicest possible way—on the shelf" (1:12). The intellectual amateur spies who had recruited Smiley and with whom he worked during the war were replaced by bureaucratic politicians ("espiocrats," in le Carré jargon) like Maston, the minister's adviser on intelligence, described by Steed-Asprey as "the Head Eunuch."[18] Smiley transferred to Counter Intelligence in 1951 and returns to Maston's section ten years later.[19] "The low morale, the internal feuding, and the red tape that ties an agent's hands even while his chiefs are deceiving him have all killed his belief that intelligence work can influence the clash between good and evil."[20] Caute (1980:209) calls him "a pro, a player, all his life yet at heart an amateur, a gentleman."

A more striking contrast to James Bond could not have been created if that had been the author's intention. Andy East (1983:170) suggests that "le Carré's Secret Service protagonist, George Smiley, signified a contemptuous revolt against Bond." Le Carré has denied that this was his intent. Le Carré says that the character, James Bond, as literary champion from the early period of the Cold War, "was an absolute travesty of reality; it was an absurdity and a vulgarity."[21] Le Carré has written, "Bond himself would be what I would describe as the ideal defector. . . . Bond, you see, is the ultimate prostitute. He replaces love with technique."[22] In an interview with Leigh Crutchley (1966:548), le Carré contrasts the tradition of escapism in the spy genre with what he calls the literature of involvement. He contrasts the Bond type of hero of the former literature, "who has developed a pretty hard-nosed cynicism towards any sense of moral obligation," with his attempt "to remake a figure who was involved in the dilemma of our time: . . . We are sacrificing the individual in our battle against the collective." Le Carré considers this moral cynicism a reflection of one of the worst aspects of contemporary western society.

Aspects of Smiley's Role in the Early Novels

In the dramatic conclusion of his first novel, Smiley confronts his former student, agent, and friend, Dieter, a German Jew who had worked for the British against the Nazis and at the time of the novel was running an East German espionage network in England. Dieter is holding a pistol as Smiley rushes at him. They fight on a bridge and Dieter, a cripple, falls into the river and drowns.[23] Smiley is overcome with guilt and remorse at having caused the death of his former friend. The worst part was that he knew: Dieter had let him do it, had not fired the gun, had remembered their friendship when Smiley had not. . . . Dieter, mercurial, absolute, had fought to build a civilization. Smiley, rationalistic, protective, had fought to prevent him. 'Oh God,' said Smiley aloud, 'who was then the gentleman?'" (16:145).[24]

This note of moral ambiguity, which questions whether the means (killing a former friend) justified the ends (protecting British democracy from the threat of East German communist subversion), is the most consistent theme in le Carré's work. Dieter was no angel.[25] Yet despite the blood on his hands, he remained loyal to his friendship with Smiley and refrained from killing him when he had the opportunity to do so. Smiley had acted in the "national interest" but at a considerable price to his own conscience, even though he did not intend to kill him but merely to stop Dieter before he could shoot him. Le Carré asks the reader (and possibly himself) whether such costs in terms of human lives and the compromising of ethical values is worth the gains in national security.[26]

Smiley resigned from the Circus (le Carré's name for the branch of the British Secret Service for which Smiley worked) rather than agree to cover up the so-called suicide of one of its employees in order to save the Foreign Office public embarrassment. David Seed (1990:144) observes a major ironic theme in le Carré: "The search for truth is usually conducted against an official insistence on secrecy which is designed to avoid administrative embarrassment." This was an act of personal and professional integrity, for Smiley resigns on a matter of principle. (He is later forced to resign twice as a result of power plays within the Circus.) Smiley also turned down an offer to rejoin the Circus after he successfully exposed the East German espionage network operating in the United Kingdom. Therefore, in le Carré's second novel, *A Murder of Quality* (1962), he was officially retired when he responded to a personal request of a former colleague to go to Carne School to investigate the charge (written in a letter to an advice columnist in a church-affiliated newspaper) that her husband, a teacher at the school, planned to kill her. By the time Smiley arrived at the school, she was already dead.

For my present purpose here, the most important contribution this novel makes is to further sketch in aspects of Smiley's character, which is most graphically illustrated by the first epigram of this chapter. Smiley's inability to reconcile the means to the end is discussed in this chapter and is elaborated in chapter 4. His possession of the cunning of Satan is illustrated by the manner in which he solves what has become a double murder at the school. His tradecraft (professional techniques) and particularly his ability to empathize with, and put himself in the shoes of others, are well illustrated. Smiley's virginal conscience is displayed by his concern about the likely execution of the thoroughly unsympathetic murderer. Whereas one can identify with his remorse at the death of his friend Dieter in the first novel, one finds it difficult to generate much sympathy for the demise of Terence Fielding. That he is the brother of a former colleague is sufficient to activate Smiley's sympathetic conscience.[27]

Le Carré's third novel, *The Spy Who Came in from the Cold* was his first major success.[28] Smiley plays a limited and ambiguous role in this work. According to his ex-boss, Control, Smiley "isn't with us any more," yet

Control suggests that Leamas, the central character, look Smiley up for background on the case (2:25). Control, who meets Leamas in Smiley's home, explains Smiley's absence. "He doesn't like the operation . . . [to protect a British mole in East German intelligence by throwing suspicion on his assistant who suspects his treason]. He finds it distasteful. He sees the necessity but he wants no part in it. His fever . . . is recurrent" (6:61). The fever to which he refers is Smiley's conscience. When Leamas remarks about his cool reception by Smiley, Control again affirms: "Quite. He wants no part of it" (6:61). Control explains, "He is like the surgeon who has grown tired of blood. He is content that others should operate" (6:62).

Nonetheless, Smiley's few appearances throughout the novel are critical to the success of the operation.[29] His personal moral distaste for the means used were overcome by his concern for the welfare of Liz Gold (Leamas's girlfriend), by his loyalty to the agency, and by his patriotism. Ironically, Smiley's genuine feelings of concern for Leamas and Liz indirectly contributed to their deaths. Le Carré offers this as an illustration of the maxim that the road to hell is paved with good intentions. Unpredicted consequences are endemic to covert actions.[30]

Once again, in spite of Smiley's sincere humanitarian concerns, the price paid for success is human lives. This time, the victims included the innocent Liz, Leamas, another sympathetic character, and an entire British network in Berlin—all to protect and promote the career of a ruthless anti–Semite named Mundt, who is a British double agent in the East German secret service (the executioner in the previous novel whom the British have captured and "turned"). Le Carré makes Jens Fiedler, the East German counterintelligence officer on the trail of the double agent (a Jew, who is the primary victim of the British plot), a very sympathetic character. Liz Gold (also Jewish) is a childlike innocent who is sacrificed: "The central character in the book loves two people and both are Jews: by indulging his decent instincts, he destroys them both. I used Jewish people because I felt that after Stalin and Hitler they should particularly engage our protective instincts."[31] Such literary characterizations dramatize the difficulty of the moral dilemmas and the gravity of the consequences of such covert actions.

In *The Looking-Glass War* (1965), Smiley has returned to the Circus. His superior, Control, enables a rival agency operating out of the British Ministry of Defense to carry out a disastrous operation in East Germany that discredits defense intelligence and costs the life of their agent in the field.[32] Smiley accuses Control of complicity in the fiasco, which probably put the rival agency out of business. Feigning shock, Control cynically denies the charge: "Run along. And preserve the difference between us: your country needs you. It's not *my* fault they've taken so long to die" (21:227).

Smiley, dutifully following orders, flies to Germany to close down the operation before defense intelligence can warn their doomed agent. Although he clearly disapproves of the role Control played in giving military intelligence sufficient rope to hang itself, as a good soldier Smiley allows himself to be used by the government to handle the mess. In this case, Smiley's loyalty to his department causes him to become an accessory to the betrayal of a rival department. Once again, his personal morality is sacrificed to his institutional loyalty.[33]

Smiley's Quest for His Unholy Grail: The Karla Trilogy

After leaving Smiley out of *A Small Town in Germany* (1968), Le Carré made him the linchpin for his trilogy *Tinker, Tailor, Soldier Spy* (1974), *The Honourable SchoolBoy* (1977), and *Smiley's People* (1979). Smiley is introduced in the first of the three novels in the trilogy as having been in forced retirement for a year in consequence of his being on the losing side of a power play.

Unlike most writers of the spy genre, who focus on direct action in an attempt to build suspense, le Carré appears to digress with subplots that introduce extraneous themes or characters. Invariably, however, the subplots contribute to the portrayal of the complexity of the characters and the moral dilemmas they confront. For example, Smiley is convinced by his solicitor not to divorce his wife (who had run off with yet another lover): "George, how can you be so vulgar? Nobody divorces Ann. Send her flowers and come to lunch" (2:19). The use of the term *vulgar* signifies the aristocratic disdain for divorce (as opposed to infidelity).

George's complex relationship with Ann symbolizes (among other things) steadfast loyalty despite betrayal by the object of one's loyalty— one's spouse or one's country.[34] Beene (1992:25) claims, "Smiley with Ann lives, albeit in emotional collapse, but without her he wanders a no-man's land." Holly Beth King (1987:68) suggests that while his love for Ann is his "greatest vulnerability," it is also "what preserves him as a hero in a world of ultimate betrayal." Although Smiley rebels against the hypocrisy of her class, his loyalty to her symbolizes his attachment to traditional British values and a tradition he still cherishes. Panek (1987:37) suggests that Ann also represents Smiley's "pathetic quest for love," which he defines as "Sisyphean." Panek also contends that she (and other women for other characters) represents Smiley's "striving for the spontaneous, human side of life" (45).

Following a particularly unpleasant encounter with an obnoxious aristocratic Foreign Office bureaucrat (whom le Carré portrays with the satiric bite of Jonathan Swift), a depressed Smiley views his loyalty as a form of weakness. "Weakness . . . and an inability to live a self-sufficient life independent of institutions . . . and emotional attachments that have long outlived their purpose. *Viz.*, my wife; *viz.*, the Circus [British intelligence]; *viz.*, living in London" (3:25). With typical paradox, le Carré implies that such "weaknesses" constitute the core of Smiley's moral strength and decency. Yet, for the sake of his loyalty, he has been forced to sacrifice other deeply held moral principles.

Ironically, Smiley, who was "retired" because he was convinced that there was a Soviet mole operating at a high level of the British Secret Service, is called back to the Circus to find the mole. In so doing, he is forced to confront many of the ghosts of his past. First and foremost is Karla, the head of Soviet intelligence.[35] A reissued edition of the trilogy published in a single volume is entitled *The Quest for Karla* (1982), an allusion to the Arthurian legend. Indeed, Smiley refers to Karla as his unholy grail.

In chapter 23, Smiley recalls to his protégé, Peter Guillam, his first personal encounter with Karla in a hot Delhi jail. Smiley tells how Karla never said a word. He explains how, putting himself in Karla's shoes, he conducted an interrogation with himself.[36] Smiley gave Karla his favorite brand of American cigarettes, and as Karla rose to go, without having said a word to Smiley, he took Smiley's lighter from the table. It had been a gift from Ann and was engraved with the words "To George from Ann with all my love." Smiley explains, "I thought it thoroughly appropriate that he should take her lighter; I thought it—Lord help me—expressive of *the bond between us*" (209; emphasis added). Smiley spends a sleepless night in a fevered delirium in which he reflected his own insecurity through his dreams of Karla.

When Smiley returned for his last visit with him, Karla was holding Ann's lighter in his hands. "I believed, you see, that I had seen something in his face that was superior to mere dogma, not realizing that it was my own reflection" (211).[37] Smiley concludes: "I behaved like a soft fool. The very archetype of a flabby Western liberal. But I would rather be my kind of fool than his, for all that. I am sure" (23:213). He tells Peter that "Karla is not fire-proof, because he's a fanatic. And one day, if I have anything to do with it, that lack of moderation will be his downfall" (23:215). This prediction has an ironic denouement in the third and final part of the trilogy.

Smiley's musing about self-delusional aspects of love while he waits to ensnare the mole in a trap hints at a connection between the theme of loyalty and betrayal and the theme that there is frequently a discrepancy between appearances and reality. Le Carré suggests that one type or aspect of love may be understood as a form of self-delusion. He does not say that all forms of love should be so characterized. He clearly illustrates in his work that without love, life is not worth living. By way of analogy, we might say that without the collective illusion that we all share the same cultural meanings, when in fact we interpret them differently, human sociability would be impossible.[38]

Smiley is torn between anger over the tragic consequences of the multiple betrayals of the mole and his humanitarian feelings. "I refuse. Nothing is worth the destruction of another human being. Somewhere the path of pain and betrayal must end" (36:345). Ann describes Smiley as "deceived in love and impotent in hate" (36:346). Yet his loyalty and inability to sustain hatred toward those who have betrayed him and his resolve to act despite serious reservations about the consequences of his actions are precisely what make Smiley a tragic, flawed, but heroic figure. Andrew Rutherford (1987:25) contrasts Smiley, who "lives in practice by a code of loyalty, of fidelity, of obligation," to the mole and suggests that they "emerge as representatives of integrity and corruption in a world of crumbling values, which can be sustained, it seems, only by bleak courage and loyalty without much faith. Yet the novel itself implies a faith—not so much in a country or political system (though le Carré 's preference is clear), as in man himself—in his capacity to live humbly, yet heroically and sacrificially, a life of service."

In spite of his doubts, Smiley acts characteristically and sets out to capture the mole, whom he plans to trade for British agents behind the Iron Curtain who were betrayed by the mole. Smiley grieves over all the betrayals and writes letters to Ann that he never mails. In his final interrogation of the mole, Smiley learns that Karla had put the mole (a bisexual, a characteristic that further symbolizes his duality and mythical godlike qualities) up to having an affair with Ann ("the last illusion of the illusionless man" 38:364), in order to throw Smiley off the mole's track. This knowledge intensifies Smiley's obsession with Karla.

In *The Honourable Schoolboy,* Smiley is put in charge of the demoralized and politically weakened Circus. Roddy Martindale, the effete Foreign Office wit, says: "Only Smiley . . . could have got himself appointed captain of a wrecked ship" (40). Now that Smiley is in charge, there is no Control to cajole him or behind whom his conscience can hide. He acts far more resolutely in pursuit of his goals. He separates from Ann—an act symbolizing his resolution not to be encumbered by the ties of sentimentality, which have always constrained him. Smiley relentlessly plots the downfall of Karla. As a humanitarian, Smiley is seen valiantly trying to save networks of agents and weeping at the news of their loss. But a more resolute Smiley is revealed during an interview with a field agent, Jerry Westerby, of whom Smiley asks whether he still has the will to act:

A lot of people haven't these days. The Will. Specially in England. A lot of people *doubt* as a legitimate philosophical posture. They think of themselves in the middle, whereas, of course, really they're nowhere. No battle was ever won by spectators, was it? We understand that in this service. We're lucky. Our war began in nineteen seventeen, with the Bolshevik Revolution. It hasn't changed yet . . . I still feel strongly that I owe. Don't you? I've always been grateful to this service, that it gave me a chance to pay. Is that how *you* feel? I don't think we should be afraid of . . . devoting ourselves. Is that old-fashioned of me? (5:104–5).[39]

The changes in Smiley in this trilogy may be rooted in his moral sense, but they also reflect his changing positions in the intelligence service, from outsider to top executive responsibility, and a consequent tilt in the direction toward institutional loyalty and justification of the means by the ends.

Smiley was probably laying it on a bit thick to motivate the unsophisticated Westerby to come out of retirement.[40] Also, his new role did not allow him the luxury of playing the devil's advocate as he had formerly done. Even so, it appears that Smiley is considerably more single-minded than previously—deliberately suppressing his inclination to doubt, question assumptions, and second-guess policies and decisions. Le Carré reveals the reason: "Beyond the expressed sense of obligation, loyalty and patriotism, however, there is also his obsession with Karla. He called it Karla, and it was true that somewhere in him, like a leftover legend, there burned the embers of hatred toward the man who had set out to destroy the temples of his private faith, whatever remained of them: the service that he loved, his friends, his country, his concept of a *reasonable balance in human affairs*. . . . But hatred was really not an emotion he could sustain for any length of time, unless it was the obverse side of love" (5:109; emphasis added).

To get vital information, Jerry is ordered to "burn" (blackmail) a Hong Kong banker named Frost, who is later tortured and killed for divulging information to the English. In assessing this unexpected outcome, Smiley forces his intellect to overcome his emotions, refuses to engage in self-deception, and accepts full responsibility. His colleague, Connie Sachs, moralizes, "Karla wouldn't give two pins. . . . Not for one dead Frost, not for ten. That's the difference, really. . . . We're fighting for the survival of Reasonable Man . . . That's who we are: reasonable. . . . We're not just English. We're reasonable" (14:322).

Smiley's Dilemma

Peter Guillam contemplates Smiley's Dilemma: "One day . . . one of two things will happen to George. He'll cease to care or the paradox will kill him. If he ceases to care, he'll be half the operator he is. If he doesn't, that little chest will blow up from the struggle of trying to find the explanation for what we do. Smiley himself in a disastrous off-the-record chat to senior officers, had put the names to his dilemma, and Guillam with some embarrassment recalled them to this day. To be *inhuman in defense of our humanity,* he said, *harsh in defense of compassion.* To be *single-minded in defense of our disparity"* (19:460; emphasis added).[41] Le Carré invites the reader to consider whether it is reasonable to engage in such activity in the name of Reasonable Man. One can imagine how Smiley's "chat" would be received by senior civil servants in any department, much less an intelligence agency. No wonder Peter is embarrassed to recall it. Le Carré leaves it to the reader to decide whether he is embarrassed for Smiley (his mentor) or for the senior officials. Depending on the reader's own values, temperament, and ideology, Smiley's struggle to resolve such paradoxes can be viewed as either absurd, heroic, or both—that is, quixotic.[42]

The formulation of Smiley's dilemma forces the reader to ask serious questions. Do not inhumane acts threaten to destroy the humanity one is defending? Can harshness protect compassion without one hardening one's heart? Does not single-minded, not to say obsessive, anticommunism undermine the very freedoms on which liberal democracy depends? These questions underlie the creative tension of the actions of this trilogy in particular and le Carré 's work in general. Although le Carré appears to hold and express multiple and sometimes contradictory points of view, and subjects liberalism to a particularly severe critique, ultimately his position is rooted in a liberal disposition. As mentioned in the introduction, I follow Wilson Carey McWilliams (1995) in distinguishing between liberalism as a temperament—a disposition of the soul—and as an articulated ideology. For Beene, "Smiley is a liberal humanist who endures only as long as he can question this humanism" (1992:8).[43]

In his relentless pursuit of this case, Smiley becomes embroiled in interagency politics and is deceived by intrigues and an alliance between his main rival in the British Foreign Office and the CIA. The Americans end up with the Russian Chinese mole, Smiley's rival ends up in charge of the Circus, and Smiley is back in forced retirement. In a letter to Ann, Smiley writes his own professional epitaph: "I chose the secret road because it seemed to lead straighter and furthest toward my country's goal. The enemy in those days was someone we could point at and read about in the papers. Today, all I know is that I have learned to interpret the whole of my life in terms of conspiracy. That is the sword I have lived by, and as I look round me now I see it is the sword I shall die by as well. These people terrify me, but I am one of them. If they stab me in the back, then at least that is the judgement of my peers" (22:533). Even the reader predisposed to sympathize with Smiley can lose patience with his allowing himself to be so manipulated. Perhaps lack of concern for personal position is admirable. But, he betrayed ideals and persons loyal to him by failing to put up a fight.[44]

In the third and final volume of the Karla trilogy, Smiley is once again reluctantly called back from retirement as a kind of consultant, ostensibly to cover up the death of one of his former agents in order to save the government from public embarrassment. In contrast with *The Looking Glass War,* where Smiley reluctantly but dutifully carried out his orders, and *The Honourable Schoolboy,* where as chief he resolutely sets policy within the political and bureaucratic constraints of his office, in *Smiley's People* he considerably exceeds his brief and takes great personal initiative in order to finally ensnare his arch rival and nemesis, Karla.

Smiley is reminded by Oliver Lacon, identified as Whitehall's Head Prefect to the intelligence services, "We are *pragmatists,* George. We *adapt.* We are *not* keepers of some sacred flame. I ask you, I commend you, to remember this!" (4:56). Whether or not he remembered it, Smiley certainly did not act on this advice:

> Even five years ago he would never have admitted to such sentiments. But today, peering calmly into his own heart, Smiley knew that he was unled, and perhaps unleadable; that the only restraints upon him were those of his own reason, and his own humanity. As with his marriage, so with his sense of public service. I invested my life in institutions—he thought without rancour—and all I am left with is myself. And with Karla, he thought; with my black Grail. (12:152)

Sauerberg (1984:201) suggests: "To Smiley, communism, Russia, Karla and Haydon are interchangeable names for the power in his own mind which is irreconcilable with his deep sense of human decency."

As he contemplated Karla's absolutism, Smiley wonders: "How can I win? . . . alone, restrained by doubt and a sense of decency—how can any of us—against this remorseless fusillade?" (17:245). But Smiley discovers Karla's weakness, the last remnant of his humanity—his love of his psychologically disturbed daughter, whom he has institutionalized in Switzerland. Smiley is described as "hunter, recluse, lover, solitary man in search of completion, shrewd player of the Great Game, avenger, doubter in search of reassurance—Smiley was by turns each one of them, and sometimes more than one" (20:277). In this sentence, le Carré compresses the contradictory impulses and traits that constitute part of Smiley's humanity.

Le Carré presents Smiley through the eyes of others to reveal both his determination and his vulnerability. His determination motivates his action, whereas his vulnerability is due to his moral sensibility. Before springing the trap on Karla, Smiley is described by his friend Mendel, a retired policemen, as "pacing himself before his big fight"—saying "he needed movement in order to escape himself" (20:278). His landlady said he looked bereaved. A colleague observed: "George always bruised easy. . . . You see a lot—your eyes get very painful. George saw too much, maybe. . . . George has got too many heads under his hat" (20:279). We also get a rare glimpse of a self-reflective Smiley. While going through files at the Circus, Smiley encounters an old photograph of Karla, whom he sees as his mirror image: "He read into his own past as into Karla's, and sometimes it seemed to him that the one life was merely the complement to the other; that they were causes of the same incurable malady" (20:281).

In an earlier visit (in the same novel) to Connie Sachs, an aged, ill, former colleague whom he verbally bullied to get information vital for trapping Karla, Connie remarked: "Twin cities, we used to say you were, you and Karla, two halves of the same apple" (15:205). Most uncharacteristically, Smiley lost his temper: "He was standing over her, incensed by her cheap and unjust comparison, knowing that neither Karla's methods nor Karla's absolutism were his own. He heard himself say "No, *Connie!*" and discovered that he had lifted his hands to the level of his chest, palms downward and rigid, as if he were pressing something into the ground. And he realised that his passion had scared her; that he had never betrayed so much conviction to her—or so much feeling—before" (15:206).

This is the most passion Smiley had ever displayed in any of the novels.[45] His overreaction[46] may have reflected an awareness that in order for his trap to work, he and Karla would have to reverse roles. Smiley was only able to blackmail Karla into defecting to the West because Karla's compassion for his afflicted daughter gave him the opening. But in so doing, Smiley resorted to Karla's abhorrent tactics.

Nevertheless, Smiley retains his capacity to empathize with his enemy. This characteristic prevents him from demonizing the enemy, which, as I argue later, is a primary step in moral disengagement and leads to the abuse of power. Peter Guillam knew why Smiley insisted they get to the border crossing two hours before Karla was scheduled to cross: "Because we *owe,* Smiley would have said if he had been in a talking mood. Because we owe the caring and the waiting, we owe this vigil over one man's effort to escape the system he has helped create. For as long as he is trying to reach us, we are his friends. Nobody else is on his side." But when Karla began to cross, Smiley has second thoughts: "*Don't come,* thought Smiley. *Shoot,* Smiley thought, talking to Karla's people, not to his own. There was suddenly something terrible in his foreknowledge that this tiny creature was about to cut himself off from the black castle behind him" (27:366,370).

As Karla crosses through the liminal point between East and West, the narrator describes Smiley:

> an unholy vertigo seized him as the very evil he had fought against seemed to reach out and posses him and claim him despite his striving, calling him a traitor also; mocking him, yet at the same time applauding his betrayal. On Karla had descended the curse of Smiley's compassion; on Smiley the curse of Karla's fanaticism. I have destroyed him with the weapons I abhorred, and they are his. We have crossed each other's frontiers, we are the no-men of this no-man's-land. . . . he did not want these spoils, won by these methods. (27:370–1)[47]

But, despite his moral anguish, Smiley makes no effort to stop Karla from crossing over. Once they face each other, Karla drops the cigarette lighter that had been given to Smiley by Ann, which Karla had borrowed from Smiley the interview in a Delhi jail and which Karla had kept over the years since then. "They exchanged one more glance and perhaps each for that second did see in the other something of himself. . . . Smiley . . . stepped quickly out of the halo, passing very close to Ann's lighter on his way. It lay at the halo's very edge, tilted slightly, glinting like fool's gold on the cobble. He thought of picking it up, but somehow there seemed no point and no one else appeared to have seen it" (27:373). The last line in the novel is Smiley's response to Guillam's statement that George had won. "'Did I?' said Smiley. 'Yes. Yes, well I suppose I did.'"

This last scene, the denouement of both this novel and the trilogy is, I believe, the most moving that le Carré has written. Like a narrative laser beam, it poignantly fuses the themes in a concentrated drama. Smiley's reply to Peter expresses his questioning of whether the means that he used to entrap Karla justified the end. Smiley's exploitation of Karla's love for his daughter mirrored Karla's earlier exploitation of Smiley's love for Ann, symbolized by the lighter that glittered like "fools gold."

Smiley's failure to pick up the lighter after Karla dropped it is a rich, multilayered symbol. It might be interpreted as a gallant gesture in refusing a symbol of defeat (like the sword of a defeated general) or a chivalric gesture of the knight refusing to reclaim the token of his faithless lady after the successful completion of his quest.[48] Yet it also (and perhaps more clearly) symbolizes Smiley's loss of his last illusion—in refusing to be fooled (deluded) by a love in which loyalty was not reciprocated.[49] In that context, his stepping out of the "halo" of light symbolizes this loss of innocence, as well as that which he lost when he resorted to emotional blackmail to ensnare Karla. It is an extremely effective scene.[50]

Critical Evaluations of Smiley

Smiley and Karla, who were initially portrayed as opposites, change places and are transformed into aspects of the other. Karla's only illusion—love of his daughter—led to his betrayal of his life's work and his country. Tom Paulin (1980:60) reminds us, however, that "Karla is saving his own skin by defecting." Brady (1985:286) suggests that Smiley and Karla are "psychic doubles . . . Jungian shadows of each other . . . one in emphatic unity." The price Smiley had to pay for "victory" made it a very bitter, if not pyrrhic one for him.[51] J. Patrick Dobel (1988:206) observes that le Carré's books "often reach a critical denouement when Smiley acknowledges the costs of his own actions without moral balances to exonerate him." He reminds us that Karla is given away initially not by love but by his fanaticism, his signature of violence in having Smiley's former agent brutally murdered: "George Smiley does *not* become Karla. Smiley never kills his lover or his agents. Nor does he kill to cover his tracks. His agents are not destroyed for errors and he still abhors violence. His goals to the end remain reactive and specific. He accepts responsibility for his actions" (Dobel, 1988:210; emphasis added).

Beene (1992:109–10) suggests that the trilogy "unites Smiley's halves and terminates him. Through eight novels Smiley professes an undying be-lief in the power of Western democracy, in the superiority of moral means over questionable ends, in the permanency of intellectual ideals, and in the salvation possible through love. Yet at every step he fears these decencies are illusions. . . . By succumbing to Karla's methods, Smiley damages (if not defeats) the beliefs he seeks to ratify.[52]

Panek (1987:33) says that in the world of opposites portrayed by le Carré, his heroes find it is "an unbearable strain to live an uncommitted, undefined existence . . . [so] they act, they engage themselves to one of the alternatives and pass out of the world of flux. They all do it except George Smiley . . . who . . . repeatedly attempts to find a human path between clashing extremes." Le Carré implicitly compares other characters to Smi-ley to highlight different responses to the human condition. Although Smiley is very unusual, he is neither as unique nor as devastated as Panek implies:

> Smiley . . . is the only character in le Carré who can stand between two worlds and, if not reconcile them, live with the opposites thrust upon him by life. In the last two novels [*The Honourable Schoolboy* and *Smiley's People*] le Carré shows the dissolution of Smiley's abbey. . . . In *Smiley's People*, George moves from the multifaceted human being to the single-minded one. . . . In so doing this Smiley cuts himself off from Ann . . . He wins Karla's defection, but loses himself. . . . Smiley in *Smiley's People*, moves from

between two worlds, but in so doing he loses the humanity which he possessed. All he is left is his painful consciousness. (Panek, 1987:38)

Robert Lekachman (1980:505), calling Smiley the "incorruptible instrument of corrupt politicians and solitary upright man in a universe on the take," concludes that the denouement of the trilogy represents "the disintegration of antique virtue in an unprincipled society." Abraham Rothberg (1987:50–1) defines "Smiley's decline and fall . . . as the downfall of those virtues in British life for which he stands, and by implication demonstrates the causes of the decline and fall of British power and prestige. . . . Smiley shifts from approval or at least forgiveness of personal and political betrayal to an inability and refusal to forgive and forget such treachery; he moves from his contingent and ambiguous loyalties to institutions to a loyalty only to his own standards and ideals."

Bold (1988:22) concludes that Smiley remains a vulnerable man in a vicious world, who, though he is "contaminated by the deception that surrounds him, he is not entirely destroyed by it. He retains his essential decency. For all his faults, he seems genuine though that is another illusion, for he is a fiction, albeit an immortal one and one made in the image of a real man."[53] Lewis (1985:164–5) refers to "Smiley's triumph over his Moriarty, George defeats his dragon." Yet "Smiley's quest ends not with simple affirmation of unambiguous, permanent truths but with a resigned acceptance of the paradoxical contradictoriness of human experience, the impossibility of certainty."[54] Monaghan (1983:581) says, "Smiley is usually able to keep a delicate balance between his duty to the Circus and his obligation to be human. . . . In *Smiley's People,* however, George Smiley experiences such a complete sense of betrayal in his betrayal of others that the delicate balance seems to have been finally lost." The soul-searching in which he engages leads Monaghan to conclude: "That Smiley can still think in such moral terms implies that his corruption is not absolute." Sauerberg (1984:63) suggests, "Karla becomes a symbol to confirm that Smiley's quest, after all, has been the right one. The proof of its rightness lies not in the circumstances that Karla defects, but in the circumstance that Karla defects because he too nurses a last illusion of love. Karla paradoxically becomes the ultimate confirmation of Smiley's beliefs."

Smiley Returns Reborn (Not Born Again)

Smiley returns (probably for the last time) in *The Secret Pilgrim* (1990).[55] George has bought a cottage in North Cornwall—where Ann sometimes stays with him—and has a sinecure at Exeter University.[56] It is most significant, particularly in light of the symbolic meanings analysts frequently attach to Smiley's relationship with Ann, that he retains this relationship, when so many concluded after *Smiley's People* that the relationship was over for good. In an ironic commentary on the post–Cold War era, Smiley is brought back from retirement once more to chair the Fishing Rights Committee, composed of officers from Moscow Centre (le Carré's term for Soviet intelligence) and the Circus to identify intelligence targets of mutual interest to both services.

Smiley speaks to a graduating class of British spies, and his remarks spark in his protégé, Ned, memories of Ned's thirty years of service in the Circus. Although Ned's stories occupy the bulk of the novel, Smiley articulates the ideological motifs that constitute its core message. In the introduction, I indicate the important reasons why le Carré is such an ambiguous and elliptical writer and explain why he confronts his reader with many different and even contradictory perspectives. Like the Japanese director Kurasawa's classic film *Rashamon,* le Carré's technique creates multiple and complex realities. In Smiley's lecture, however, he comes closer to articulating a clear ideological position than in any of his other novels. This is why "Smiley's credo," as expressed in this novel, is so important.

The scene is set with Ned's observation of George's good humor and vigor. He characterizes Smiley as "reborn." When Ned introduces Smiley as "a legend of the Service," the latter replies, with characteristic self-deprecation, "I think I'm just a rather fat old man wedged between the pudding and the port" (1:7). Smiley speaks directly to Ned's "heretical heart" as the "secret questioner," raising questions that Ned has asked himself throughout his career. Ned calls Smiley "the iconoclastic prophet of the future" (1:9).

Smiley repeatedly warns the young spies of the high price their job will cost them—the truncation of their natural feelings leading to the death of their own natures that results from the manipulation of their fellow men. These are the consequences of what he terms *a life withheld:* "The end may justify the means—if it wasn't supposed to, I dare say you wouldn't be here. But there's a price to pay, and the price does tend to be oneself. Easy to sell one's soul at your age. Harder later" (1:10).

Smiley disassociates himself from those who are discomfited by the dramatic changes in world affairs because his life was dedicated to bringing about these changes. He first claims, then questions—thereby qualifying—victory by the West: "We won. Not that victory matters a damn. And perhaps we didn't win anyway. Perhaps they just lost. . . . What matters is that a long war is over. What matters is the *hope*" (2:12; emphasis added).

Above all, he warns them against *self-deception,* which, he concludes, was the greatest negative consequence of the Cold War. "If I regret anything at all, it's the way we wasted our time and skills. . . . All the *delusions* we had about who we were. (2:12; emphasis added) Sometimes I think the most vulgar thing about the Cold War was the way we learned to gobble up our own propaganda . . . when our enemies lied, they lied to conceal the wretchedness of their system. Whereas when *we* lied, we concealed our virtues. Even from ourselves . . . And we scarcely paused to ask ourselves how much longer we could defend our society by these means and remain a society worth defending" (6:116).

Smiley insists that "it is essential in a free society that the people who do our work should remain *unreconciled*" (10:246; emphasis added). He decries *expediency:* "All I'm really saying, I suppose, is that if the temptation to *humanity* does assail you now and then, I hope you won't take it as a weakness in yourselves, but give it a fair hearing" (10:247; emphasis added).

Smiley's humanitarian liberal credo is summed up in the following passage. "I only ever cared about the *man*. . . . I never gave a fig for the ideologies. . . . I never saw institutions as being worthy of their parts, or policies as much other than excuses for not feeling. *Man,* not the mass, is what our calling is about. It was *man* who ended the Cold War in case you didn't notice. . . . Not even Western man either, as it happened, but our sworn enemy in the East, who went into the streets, faced the bullets and the batons and said: we've had enough. It was *their* emperor, not ours, who had the nerve to mount the rostrum and declare he had no clothes" (12:321).

Smiley continues with a major critique of ideologies: "And the ideologies trailed after these impossible events like condemned prisoners, as ideologies do when they've had their day. Because they have no heart of their own. They're the whores and angels of our striving selves" (12:321). He concludes with a blistering critique of the State: "It's the over-mighty modern State we've built for ourselves as a bastion against something that isn't there any more. We've given up far too many freedoms in order to be free. Now we've got to take them back. . . . So while you're out there striving loyally for the State, perhaps you'll do me a small favour and *lean on its pillars* from time to time. It's got a lot too big for its boots of late. It would be nice if you would cut it down to size" (12:324; emphasis added).

Concluding Interpretations

Le Carré cautions us against the persistent unreliability of the artist. He warns that tomorrow he will disagree with everything he says today. Using interviews of the author and essays by him to frame my interpretations of his central fictional character, I further elucidate the relationship between le Carré's style and his ideological disposition. Anthony Masters (1987:242) notes that "it is in his political views that Smiley most clearly resembles Cornwell, as he explained to *The Observer* in February 1980: 'I think he stands where I stand; he feels that to pit yourself against any "ism" is to strike a posture which is itself ideological, and therefore offensive in terms of practical decency. In practice almost any political ideology invites you to set aside your humanitarian instincts.'" So, despite le Carré's warning and the prevailing fashions in literary criticism, I shall take him at his word and interpret Smiley's liberal temperament as expressing that of his creator. Interviews with le Carré and his nonfictional essays and editorials support this interpretation. For example, he told Thom Schwartz (1987:20): "We had a lot of the same characteristics, as well as sharing a lot of experiences in Middle Europe just after the World War II. We'd both seen the ghosts in the rubble, if you will; knew what the true cost of war was. We'd both been witnesses to the seamless transition from the hot to the cold war, and the almost unconscious realignment of political alliances. . . . Those Orwellian leaps from quite early on in my life left scars, and I put them on Smiley's soul rather than on my own."

Beene (1992:12) claims that Smiley reflects Cornwell's real father, Ronnie. The passages cited above appear to contradict her interpretation. But, as Richard Trahair suggests: "Idealised people often take their origins from selected aspects of one's parents—not ALL of one's parents."[57] In this sense, I suggest that Ronnie Cornwell was primarily a negative role model for his son in the creation of Smiley's character just as he was the direct model for Rick Pym, father of le Carré 's self-parodied alter ego, Magnus Pym, in *A Perfect Spy.* As he told Schwarz (1987:20): "I had a very mucky childhood. . . . So I made Smiley a guy with no childhood and no parents. My father's moral concerns were nonexistent, and I heaped all of mine into Smiley. I think I made a bit of a new father out of him."

Vivian Green was chaplain at Sherborne School when David Cornwell was a student there. Later, he was Cornwell's senior tutor at Oxford and knows him well. He is one of the two main models for Smiley. Le Carré is quoted by Miriam Gross (1980:35) as saying, "When I first invented Smiley he was based to some extent on my mentor at Oxford. . . . whom I admired very much, and partly on somebody I once worked with." He had previously mentioned that "Oxford was my salvation, and it was mainly brought about by the former Chaplain of Sherborne who became Senior Tutor at my College."[58] Green (1988:38) himself suggests:

> In his earlier novels le Carré had created a father figure in George Smiley, a man of impeccable integrity, shrewd, silent, at times sad, cuckolded by the world but loyal to his ideals. Yet le Carré seems to have been unable to put

out of his mind his real father for whom George Smiley was merely a substitute, and basically the legacy of his inheritance from Rick [Ronnie Cornwell], in its moral subjectivism, its stress on material wealth and comfort, its egocentric objectivity. Magnus [David Cornwell a.k.a. John le Carré] discovers in himself reflections as in a distorting mirror of Rick, not of George Smiley, and so became the Perfect Spy.

He created in Smiley a reluctant team player, the bearer of paradoxes in the interest of the greater good, a romantic who reluctantly serves established Western society, an individual whose private morality constantly confronts institutional necessity, a committed doubter, and a disgusted patriot. It is not unreasonable to assume the author shares some and perhaps many of these traits. But le Carré also questions whether they deserve our admiration. He told Schwarz (1987:20–21): "Another reason for my impatience with George Smiley is that I am no longer able to resolve his excuses. There is something specious to me now about his moral posture. . . . We Empire Babies were brought up thinking that we messed with things so that others could have clean hands. But I believe that someone who delivers up responsibility for his moral conscience is actually someone who hasn't got one."

The author claims that his argument with Smiley was over whether what Smiley did with his life was really heroic. He questions whether the sacrifice of moral conscience was really noble. Had Smiley the right to sacrifice his individual moral conscience for a perception of the public good? One might also ask whether Smiley's anguished soul-searching mitigated the consequences of his actions? Is it preferable to withdraw from the arena and leave unsavory activities to those who lack moral scruples and who are therefore untroubled by the ethical implications of their actions?

Le Carré argues (characteristically with himself) that rather than the dissenters, mavericks and traitors, or even the pragmatists, it is the loyal men who bring havoc to the world. He suggests: "The greatest threat to mankind comes from the renunciation of individual scruple in favor of institutional denominators. . . . Real heroism lies, as it always will, not in conformity or even patriotism, but in acts of *solitary moral courage*. Which, come to think of it, is what we used to admire in our Christian savior" (*JHM*:16; emphasis added).

Le Carré suggests that he might have shelved poor old George because he tired of his resigned attitude. "Perhaps I had reached some point of growing up, and wanted my choices to be unmediated by his owlish and increasingly elderly presence hovering over me. Perhaps age had liberated me from the stifling conventions of youth out of which Smiley had originally been born" (*JHM*:15). He claims that "it was only when I took leave of Smiley in my own mind that I was able to address myself to my real father" (Lelyveld: 40). Having dealt with ambivalent feelings toward his real father in *A Perfect Spy*, he no longer needed his surrogate fictional father.[59] Le Carré told Tony Chiu (1980:30), "He [Smiley] and I have grown up a lot since the first book. I might someday go back to write about other of his experiences, but I think I have rounded off the character. Certainly, he cannot progress."

Yet Smiley "reborn" returns for his last hurrah, resurrected by his creator from the status of a secular Christ figure, who "would sacrifice his own morality on the altar of national necessity. For you and me" (*JHM*:15). He has been transfigured into an elderly prophet prodding young spies to become subversive Samsons by leaning on the pillars of the Philistine temple of the all-powerful modern state.

Ned observes his students' faces "lift and relax and light to him as they gave him first their attention, then their trust and finally their support" (1:7). This is also a good description of the effect of le Carré's style on the reader. It is also strikingly similar to Howe's description of the effects of the successful political novel quoted in the introduction. "It is not surprising that the political novelist, even as he remains fascinated by politics, urges his claim for a moral order beyond ideology; nor that the receptive reader, even as he preserves his own commitment, assents to the novelist's ultimate order" (Howe 1992:24).

Le Carré claims, "I never knew a writer yet who saw himself as reconciled or finite" (*JHM*:16). He cites Scott Fitzgerald's suggestion that the trick was to hold two opposing opinions on any one subject and still function. Le Carré is a master at holding contradictory opinions. Like Shakespeare in *Richard II* as analyzed by James Boyd White (1994:77), he seems to be on both or all sides: "He seems incapable of articulating a position, or expressing a feeling, without instantly, or at the same time, expressing its counter or contrary."

Le Carré seems to work on the principle that White (1994:50) attributes to Shakespeare:[60] "The truth cannot be said in any single speech or language, but lies in the recognition that against one speech or claim or language is always another one. In this sense its life is that of voice speaking against voice; this life is what ultimately holds out as authoritative; not the crown or the usurper, but its own performances." White (78; emphasis added) calls this "the principle of controlled and progressive *countersaying*" which he contrasts with "the principle of noncontradiction"—the doctrine of modern exposition.

The most extreme form this countersaying takes with le Carré is the paradoxical statement that appears to contradict itself. Examples of this include Smiley's dilemma: "To be *inhuman in defense of our humanity, . . . harsh in defense of compassion . . ."* Such oxymoronic statements may be interpreted by the reader either literally or ironically. They may be interpreted as expressions of cynicism or idealism, naïveté or sophistication, sophistry or wisdom.[61] They frame for the reader key dilemmas that confront citizens of democracies when evaluating the appropriate role of espionage and politics in general. They lead the reader to consider the alternatives and possibly even come to at least tentative conclusions—including the possible synthesis of opposites. Le Carré plays with the idea that just as apparently opposite characters can exchange places or even fuse (e.g., Smiley and Karla) so apparently may opposite phenomena merge to constitute a new reality.[62] Just as quantum physics and much of the modern social sciences assume that all things are indeterminate, le Carré assumes that there are no definitive solutions to life's perennial dilemmas.

Le Carré blames his childhood for his profound sense of displacement and paradox as well as the perception of the world through an eye "which sees around it a sense of chaos clamoring to be reconciled, or merely dramatized, but never explained away" (*JHM*:13). Whereas le Carré may remain unreconciled, in editorials he seems to have articulated clearer (although not necessarily final) positions. For example, he wonders "whether the 40 years of cold war have bred a silent affinity between the forces of intolerance on both sides."[63] His arguments preview Smiley's speech to the graduates of the spy school. Sounding like the reborn Smiley on that occasion, he suggests that we live in a unique moment of history in which "to be a realist it is necessary to be an idealist."[64]

Another essay rephrased Smiley's speech to British spies for American lawyers: "The difficulty is realizing that we are shorn of all our old excuses for not addressing the real problems of the earth, that *we can no longer put our humanity on hold in order to defend humanity.*"[65] He argues that the fight against communism diminished us, dulled our love of dissent, and our sense of life's adventure. He calls on us to break out of our orthodoxies. "We no longer need to clip the wings of our humanity. It is time we flew again" (Ibid.).

To paraphrase Jerry Westerby's observation of George Smiley (when George gave him the patriotic pep talk cited above), there's a bit of the failed priest in John le Carré. Green (1988:39) playfully suggests: "It would be too sophisticated to advance the theory that le Carré is a moralizer without a message. Yet moral his novels are." He is certainly one of the foremost, if not *the* foremost political moralist among contemporary writers of fiction. He has sustained an ongoing commentary on and critique of the cold war and its aftermath for more than thirty years.[66]

Many layers of political meaning can be drawn from le Carré's depiction of conflict between personal values and public obligations, particularly in

the claims the state makes on the conscience of both its servants and victims. Le Carré's moral vision demystifies certain contemporary myths of
state and stresses the importance of individual human agency in making difficult choices while confronting complex moral dilemmas and puzzling,
problematic, political paradoxes. Stewart Crechan (1988:104) argues "that le
Carré's ultimate aim is not to unsettle but to reassure, and that the 'interaction of perspective', . . . is not open-ended and dialogic (at least not in the
sense in which Bakhtin employs that concept), but moves toward a resolution; and that these perspectives are textualized with a view towards their
assimilation, liberal dilemmas and internal debates notwithstanding."[67]

Le Carré critically dissects but simultaneously reflects the liberal
dilemma. Smiley's passionate denunciation of ideologies in the name of
humanity is an expression of his liberal humanism.[68] Le Carré told Pierre
Assouline (1986:60; emphasis added): "All I desire is that *humane* values be
maintained in our institutions, codes of conduct and systems of thought. It
is probably nothing more than old-fashioned *liberalism*."[69] Such a liberal
temperament is characterized by a high *tolerance for ambiguity*.[70] Judith Shklar (1984:249) concludes, "Liberalism imposes extraordinary ethical diffi-
culties on us; to live with contradictions, unsolvable conflicts, and a
balancing between public and private imperatives which are neither opposed to nor at one with another."

Le Carré's exhaustive examination of the liberal dilemma never arrives
at a satisfactory resolution because, as in the real world, it is irresolvable.[71]
This is essentially Monaghan's explanation of why Smiley changes very little, although he frames it differently.[72] Le Carré (1979:340) insists, "I think
Smiley changes very much from book to book." Whereas critics argue over
the point,[73] I suggest that Smiley's changes reflect his differing positions
within and outside the Circus, maturation, and his constant pursuit of a
balanced skepticism. Smiley's skepticism, akin to what Max Weber
(1946:126–27) called "trained relentlessness in viewing the realities of life
and the ability to face such realities and to measure up to them inwardly"
(see chapter 4).

Skeptical balance is the essence of Smiley's humanism. As Sauerberg
(1984:62) points out, Smiley's balance is rooted in something outside
himself—in Western tradition and values, in restraint and common sense.
Despite all that Smiley endures, his liberal temperament remains a constant. Rather than rejecting individualism and liberal humanism, le Carré's
critical examination of their limitations in the fires of espionage, where
they are most fiercely tested, appears, if anything, to have strengthened his
commitment to them.[74]

Le Carré offers neither solutions for moral dilemmas nor resolutions
of political paradoxes but attempts to heighten his reader's awareness of

the ethical dilemmas inherent in the contradictory tensions generated when democracies engage in espionage. In so doing, he hopes that we, like Smiley, will attempt to come to terms with the moral implications of the policies of our governments and the actions of their agents. Le Carré uses Smiley (and characters who play a similar role in those novels in which he does not appear) to illustrate an approach to cope with (not resolve) these dilemmas.[75] This approach is characterized by the effort to achieve a skeptical balance; one that teeters between the demands of competing loyalties, between dreams and realities, between means and ends, and between idealism and realism. In sum, Smiley, the liberal hero, exemplifies the struggle to achieve a skeptical balance between competing ethical and political imperatives.

Chapter 2

Ambiguous Moralism: Loyalty and Betrayal

Unfortunately there are many kinds of loyalty, and we cannot serve them all at once.[1]

I hate the idea of causes, and if I had to choose between betraying my country and betraying my friend, I hope I should have the guts to betray my country. (E. M. Forster, 1951:78)

Introduction

Le Carré's characterization of the relationship between loyalty and betrayal (or disloyalty) is particularly expressed through his perception of the tension, if not contradiction, between personal and institutional loyalty.[2] As a motif that runs through le Carré's work, it is both a deeply felt personal issue for the author and inherent in the very nature of espionage and of politics in general. Le Carré's poignant concern and self-division results in a fairly unique form of ambiguous moralizing that is similar to the seventeenth-century Dutch artist Jan Steen, whose moralizing and self-parody are visual analogues of le Carré's novels.[3]

E. M. Forster's oft quoted declaration (the second epigraph of this chapter) stands in dramatic contrast to Jeremy Bentham's reputed statement that no matter how great the merits of a friend, "he would always sacrifice his friends to the public good,"[4] and with George Eliot's insistence that "there is no private life which has not been determined by a wider public life."[5] Given that Forster wrote these words in 1939, the implications of the betrayal of many other friends by betraying his country while it was at war evidently did not occur to him. Obviously, a nationalism that blindly sacrifices the individual to the collective is equally ethically questionable. Le Carré's novels portray the moral complexity deriving from the tension between the contradictory pull of individuality and of human sociability.[6]

Le Carré presents the choices as genuine dilemmas. Although he may appear to lean toward Forster's choice of personal over institutional loyalty, he actually shows the disastrous consequences of such choices for the individual who makes that choice as well as for their significant others and, more often than not, for the wider public. If le Carré tends to sympathize with Forster's position, as some critics argue, he is far from dogmatic or simplistic in presenting the choices. His ambivalence leaves doubt in the reader's mind regarding the author's position and makes one question one's own: "More than any other writer of our time, novelist John le Carré penetrates the limits of human loyalty and explores our capacity for betrayal" (Douglas Wallace, 1985:6).

Analysis of the Novels

In *Call for the Dead* (3:25; emphasis added), Smiley interviews the recently widowed Elsa Fennan, who identifies him as the man who interviewed her late husband "about loyalty." Thinking that his interview might have caused Fennan's suicide, Smiley feels sick and cheap and thinks; "*Loyalty to whom, to what*" a question that resonates throughout his work. Smiley wonders how he could explain that he had only been doing his duty. "Duty to *whom* for God's sake" (3:26). Le Carré sees duty as the natural correlate of loyalty, so that establishing which of several conflicting duties (or roles) has priority in a given context is a way of determining one's greatest loyalty. There is particular irony in Elsa Fennan's insinuation that Smiley is responsible for her husband's "suicide," because she is covering up the murder of her husband by East German intelligence in order to protect herself—their agent.[7]

Samuel Fennan, a Foreign Office employee, had written an anonymous letter alleging that he had been a member of the Communist Party when he was a student at Oxford (which was true). Fennan had begun to suspect his wife was stealing confidential information from him and wanted to contact British counterintelligence. It is unclear whether he actually intended to inform on his wife. His actions demonstrated his loyalty to his adopted homeland. (He was a German Jewish refugee who fled to England before the war.) Although he did not do so in their initial meeting, Smiley surmises that it was "*a preliminary to denouncing his wife*" at a later time (17:152). Although Smiley's interpretation is probably correct, because Fennan was murdered before he could meet Smiley in the London suburb of Marlowe, one can't be certain.[8]

Elsa Fennan betrays both her husband and her adopted country by stealing secrets from him, which she passes on to East German intelligence. Le Carré treats Elsa sympathetically, however, by providing her with strong motivation. She survived several year's internment in Nazi concentration camps through her endurance and courage. Her intense fear of the revival of fascism in West Germany was her driving motive.[9] While not condoning her treason, le Carré conveys the complexity of conflicting loyalties and shows, in the case of the Fennans, very different ways in which such dilemmas are resolved by reasonably sympathetic protagonists. Samuel's patriotism was either balanced by, or expressed at the expense of loyalty to his wife (depending on whether he actually intended to inform on her). Elsa betrayed both her adopted country and her spouse out of political conviction.

Smiley is also confronted with tests of conflicting loyalties in this novel. After having run off with her lover, Ann offers to return. "I want to make you an offer no gentleman could accept. I want to come back to you. . . . Let me know"(14:125). Although he is momentarily physically incapacitated by the sight of the envelope even before he opens her letter, and feeling robbed of his courage, his love, and his compassion, at the end of the novel Smiley is on a plane, presumably on his way to Ann, on his "pathetic quest for love." Smiley's love for and loyalty to Ann outweighed societal conventions determining the proper conduct of a "gentleman" or his concern for the opinion of his peers. Ann, an aristocrat, also symbolically represents the traditional order in England to which Smiley is ambivalently and not uncritically loyal.

During his confrontation with Dieter, his former agent whom he kills in a struggle on a bridge, Smiley betrayed personal bonds based on "memories of dangers shared, of mutual trust when each had held in his hand the life of the other" (15:131) out of his sense of duty, patriotism, and revulsion against the principles that Dieter represented. Smiley's "nausea of guilt" (16:145) was the price he paid for his actions. The cumulative effects of such compromises is one of Smiley's main themes in his address to the graduating class of spies (see chapter 1). Rothberg (1987:53), unconvincingly in my opinion, argues that le Carré supports Forster's position because he exaggerates the personal betrayal of Smiley in comparison to the importance of his institutional and national loyalty.[10]

There are ample cases of betrayal from the real world, but not all result in remorse or guilt. For example, Truus Menger was recruited by the Dutch underground at the age of fifteen during the Second World War. She relates a poignant moment when she was ordered to execute a fellow member of her group with whom she was in love, because he had betrayed the group to the Gestapo.[11] She recounted how she secretly emptied the bullets from his revolver. When they were in a secluded spot, she accused him of betraying their comrades and he attempted to shoot her with his empty weapon. Having established his guilt, she shot him dead. When asked whether she felt remorse for having taken the life of another human being, she replied that she did not consider those whose betrayal of trust resulted in the loss of innocent lives to be human. Her dehumanization of her victims (there were more than one) was apparently an effective defense mechanism. She claimed to have felt no remorse for the traitors she executed but to have had dreams of guilt that she had failed to prevent the deaths of her friends caused by the betrayal of such traitors.[12] For her, the utilitarian value of saving more lives of her comrades justified the execution of a loved one.

In *The Spy Who Came in from the Cold* Leamas is devastated by the betrayal of his agents, who, it turns out, were sacrificed to protect a British mole. He struggles with the stigma of treachery while posing as a defector, and he ends up betraying all he knows of Allied intelligence in Berlin. In response to his lover Liz's question as to whether he loves her, he replies that he doesn't believe in fairy tales. But after Liz is shot (in a dramatic act of betrayal) at the Berlin Wall while they attempt to escape, he sacrifices his life in an act of loyalty to and affirmation of his love for her.[13] His act is neither a betrayal of duty to his service nor to his country—both of which he served loyally to the end. Leamas chose not to live with the consequences of this loyalty, which would have meant a betrayal of his love for Liz. He acted out of personal integrity without betraying either personal or institutional loyalties. As Andrew Rutherford (1987:17) notes, le Carré poses the question "whether integrity can ever be preserved in the corrupting world of action." In this case, it could only be preserved through death. Leamas is betrayed by his service just as Liz is betrayed by the communist cause in which she believed.

In *The Looking Glass War* le Carré also questions whether integrity can survive the world of political expediency, and his conclusion is rather pessimistic. The novel is a dark story of the betrayal of one British intelligence agency by another, of an agent by the director of the agency, and of the sense of betrayal felt by the World War II generation, that they have been bypassed and forgotten. It is also a strange love story as well, and a story of love betrayed. John Avery, the young assistant of Leclerc, the director of military intelligence (which in the novel is called the Department), shows more love for his boss and for his agent than he does for his wife, to whom he is unfaithful. None of the men in the novel have loving relationships with their spouses. Just as Avery is manipulated by Leclerc, Avery exploits the bonds of affection of his agent, Leiser, and Leiser's loyalty to the Department and to his adopted Great Britain. Leiser is betrayed many times over before he is ultimately abandoned to his fate in East Germany. Leclerc and the Department are, in turn, betrayed by Control, the head of the Circus, who gives him the rope with which he hangs himself.

A Small Town in Germany contains a full panoply of betrayals, from marital infidelity to foreign policy that betrays fundamental British values. It also pits integrity against political expediency. Alan Turner, the Foreign Office investigator sent to discover the whereabouts of Leo Harting, an employee of the British embassy in Bonn, and to locate top-secret files that have also disappeared, is a cuckold (like Smiley). His investigations reveal that Harting has had affairs with embassy employees, who have betrayed the trust placed in them by giving him access to top-secret documents and areas of the embassy building where he conducts his own research in secret. He has an affair with the wife of the head of Chancery (who betrays her wedding vows) in order to get his contract renewed. Some employees cut off relations with the half-Jewish Harting because "the Germans were getting rather old school again about Leo's kind" (234). Although he became a naturalized British subject, Harting never succeeds in finding an English friend. He is betrayed by his oldest friend to the German secret police.

Because the British are engaged in delicate negotiations over entry into the Common Market and need German support, in deference to German sensitivities they have suppressed conclusive proof that the leader of a neo-fascist movement in Germany is guilty of crimes against humanity during World War II. Turner argues with Bradfield, head of Chancery, that the British are responsible for Harting. "We made him believe in all those promises; Nuremberg, de-Nazification. We *made* him believe. We can't let him be a casualty just because we changed our minds"(272). Turner has come to admire Harting's integrity. "He's not put off by paradox" (272). Harting is sharply contrasted with Bradfield, for whom "it is all doubt. All mist" (273). Whereas Leo remains loyal to memory, history, and fundamental humanistic ideals, Bradfield betrays all of these in loyal service to power and national interest, that is, *raison d'état.* Among other things, A. Norman Jeffares (1976:382; emphasis added) suggests that the novel is also about "the problems of *forgetting,* and about the problems of idealism, innocence, and practical politics."

Le Carré's characters, or at least those who possess a conscience and self-consciousness, constantly confront choices between personal and institutional or ideological loyalties. At one point, he seems to suggest that betrayal is the inevitable result of loyalty. By putting the statement "there is no loyalty without betrayal" (*Smiley's People* 5:66) in the mouth of the adulterous Ann as a rationalization for her infidelities, however, he also subverts the notion. The phrase is repeated in other novels but always by characters who exhibit a lack of integrity. Not only, he suggests, are we caught between the demands of conflicting loyalties, but le Carré also implies there is an inherent conflict between fidelity to persons, to institutions, or ideologies.

This theme is comprehensively explored in *Tinker, Tailor, Soldier, Spy* in which every character is caught in webs of mutual loyalties and betrayals ranging from infidelity to treason. Bill Roach, a new boy at Thursgood's, a prep school, is the only one to observe the furtive arrival of Jim Prideaux, the new replacement for the French teacher who died in mid-term. The friendship that develops between these two loners is a redeeming subplot that balances a story replete with treachery and betrayal. Holly Beth King (1987:65) shows how le Carré uses children like Roach to "reveal to us the rudimentary emotions, motivations and impulses which the adults have learned to suppress, hide and deny. . . . Simultaneously, he reveals the children buried in these so deadly serious adults." King (1987:66) claims that Roach "establishes crucial thematic parallels that reveal the novel's basic moral context for us."

Roach attempts to replace Jim's departed friend, the other Bill—Haydon (the Soviet mole). His devoted and unquestioned loyalty stands in stark contrast to Haydon's cold-blooded betrayal of Jim. As was mentioned in chapter 1, le Carré indicates that Roach is the prototype of Smiley. He therefore supplies the perspective of the child within Smiley, whose devotion to Ann matches that of Roach's devotion to Jim. Like Roach, Jim Prideaux is also the product of a broken home—he was betrayed by parents who broke their wedding vows. Significantly, not a single main character in any of le Carré's work is the product of happily married couple and a warm, loving, supportive family.[14] The implication is that one of the reasons people join the secret world is that is offers a surrogate family. Ironically, the nature of the work makes having a normal family life practically impossible. This reinforces emotional dependence on the surrogate family. Clearly, this is not restricted to the world of espionage.

Through his friendship with Bill Haydon at Oxford, Jim is recruited to British intelligence during the war. He helps Haydon establish networks across southern Europe and fights alongside the partisans in Czechoslovakia. After the war, he retains close contacts with Czech networks. Prideaux is deliberately set up by Bill Haydon as the bait in a plot to discredit Control, who is on Haydon's trail. Prideaux, seriously wounded and tortured by the Czechs to find out how much Control knew about the mole, is eventually traded back to the British.

To dramatize further the depth of Haydon's betrayal of Prideaux, le Carré implies that they were lovers as well as colleagues and close friends.[15] Prideaux follows Smiley as he tracks down the mole. After Haydon has been finally identified and incarcerated, Prideaux breaks his neck in the manner in which he had previously dispatched an injured bird at Thursgood's school. This act could be interpreted either as an act of revenge or as a mercy killing (the allusion to the wounded bird) of someone whose life of intrigue was over and therefore had nothing more for which to live.[16] It is also entirely consistent with le Carré that it was both, because he suggests that individuals act for a multiplicity of reasons—particularly when they appear to be acting without reason. Smiley suspects Prideaux of the murder but ignores his obligation as a citizen to report his suspicions to the proper authorities. Instead, out of personal loyalty to Prideaux, Smiley says nothing, and Jim returns to his new life as a teacher.

David Monaghan (1986:144) points out that "Prideaux's patriotism is both his greatest strength and the source of an intense vulnerability."[17] It limits his critical abilities blinding him (and every one else in the Circus, except, eventually Control and Smiley—both outsiders) to the fact that a fellow Englishman and a fellow aristocrat could be a traitor. Jim's personal loyalties were stronger than his institutional loyalty to the Circus, despite his strong patriotism. He warned Haydon and unsuccessfully tried to warn Smiley that they were under suspicion by Control, before he left on his doomed mission to Czechoslovakia.

Peter Guillam feels not merely betrayed but "orphaned" by Haydon's treachery (36:347). As Mendel, a retired policeman who is one of Smiley's people, said about Peter and those like him, they "lean on grownups who turn out not to be grown up . . . then one day . . . their heroes come tumbling down and they're sitting at their desks with tears pouring over the blotter" (333). He contrasts Peter, who he thinks is likely to crack (although he doesn't), with Smiley: "That one won't crack, though, Mendel decided with approval; one of your flabby oak trees, Smiley was" (334). Peter is torn between his conflicting loyalties to Smiley and to Haydon, between his loyalty to the Circus and his sense of obligation to get to the truth. He reluctantly supplies Smiley with secret documents from the Circus that enable Smiley to identify Haydon as the mole. But Peter is not completely reconciled with his decision and its outcome. "Somehow, for the first time in his life, he had sinned against his own notions of nobility. He had a sense of dirtiness, even of self-disgust" (11:95). As so often is the case with le Carré, the decision that resolves the dilemma fails to bring relief or satisfaction. There always remains a gnawing doubt or sense of guilt, which in the extreme cases, drives the character to self-destruction.

The double agent Bill Haydon, the aristocratic son of a high court judge, is recruited by both Moscow Centre and the Circus while at Oxford. Haydon, a master of deception, is modeled on Kim Philby, the most prominent of the infamous group of Cambridge spies, which included Blunt, Burgess, and Maclean, who also contribute elements to the characterization of Haydon.[18] John Halperin (1980:28) argues that "the resemblance between Philby and le Carré's master-spy Bill Haydon in *Tinker, Tailor* is astonishing."[19] Le Carré told Miriam Gross (1980:62) that in his introduction to Page, Leitch, and Knightley, *The Philby Conspiracy* (1981), he "attempted to prove that Philby was a born deceiver and that his Marxism was nothing but a rationale." He told James Cameron (1974:68), "I feel Philby was essentially dead wrong all the way through and all the time. . . . His consistent objective was to get rid of the values and conditions I hold to be all right; and I don't go along with it." He also said, "Philby was my secret sharer who I never met" (Plimpton, 1997:65). Eric Homberger (1986:74) suggests that le Carré "*Forsterizes* the Philby story" by emphasizing the personal nature of Haydon's betrayals.

Haydon's career, which spans World War II and continues until he is caught and murdered in 1973, does enormous damage to Anglo-American interests and relations.[20] He betrays not only his country but also his class, agency, colleagues, intimate friends, and lovers. By insinuating Haydon's bisexuality, le Carré symbolically conveys another dimension of his ability to be all things to all people and his mythical, godlike aura for those who fell under his charismatic spell. Ned, in *The Secret Pilgrim* (1991:96) suggests that Haydon succeeded in playing on others' emotions "because he had none of his own." Haydon says, "Bugger love" (97). Ned observes: "Bill hated all women and most men, too, and liked nothing better than to turn people's affections inside out" (108).

Loyalty to class and the "old boy" network helped protect Haydon (and the Cambridge spies) from detection until long after coming under suspicion. Doebel (1988:213) notes: "The problems of an ethos leading to a self-protection society and mutual blindness can afflict any institution staffed by a self-perpetuating elite." Among other things, le Carré shows the consequences of the loss of self-confidence of a governing elite. George Blake (1990) contrasts the severity of his 42-year sentence for spying for the Soviet Union while working for the British secret service with the pardon of Blunt and the warning to Philby not to return to Britain, which allowed him to escape prosecution. He claims they received special treatment because they were members of the Establishment, whereas Blake, a half-Jewish Dutch-born British subject, received the heaviest sentence in modern English history. In his introduction to *The Philby Conspiracy* (1968:1–2), le Carré notes: "Hardly a tear was shed for George Blake; Blake was half a foreigner and half a Jew; only the length of his prison sentence excited the public conscience. . . . But Philby, an aggressive, upper-class enemy, was of our blood and hunted with our pack." Judith N. Shklar (1984:157) notes that Forster's credo "says something also about the class and cultural boundaries of his immediate circle, with its passion for exclusion."

Aldrich "Rick" Ames, the Soviet/Russian mole, as a second-generation agent of the CIA, was similarly protected from suspicion by others' loyalty to the exclusive club-like subculture of the "company," which prevented them from drawing obvious conclusions from Ames' behavior. The toll in deaths of agents and political damage to the Circus from Haydon's betrayal is comparable to that caused by Ames to the CIA and to American interests. It will take decades, however, if ever, before the ramifications of the acts of the real Soviet mole in the CIA are made public. The full impact of his treachery on the standing of the CIA and other American intelligence agencies has yet to be either comprehended or registered—if, indeed, it will ever be so.[21]

Haydon, with one exception, seemed incapable of showing any remorse for his betrayals. When Smiley interrogated him and discovered that Jim Prideaux had warned Haydon that he was under suspicion by Control, Smiley detected a "shadow of guilt" cross Haydon's face. Smiley observes with irony that Haydon's disciples were in disarray without him, but "that Bill in turn was also very little by himself. . . . Bill's real trick was to use them, to live through them to complete himself . . . disguising the fact that he was less, far less, than the sum of his apparent qualities" (18:156). This personality type is amplified my discussions of Charlie in *The Little Drummer Girl* and of Magnus Pym in *A Perfect Spy*.[22]

The Hon. Clive Gerald "Jerry" Westerby, *The Honourable Schoolboy,* presents a variation on the theme of the conflict between personal and institutional loyalties. Smiley inquires about Jerry's current (in a long line of failed marriages and affairs) love interest, telling his agent: "We're not necessarily in competition with affection. We simply like to know where it lies." As it ends up, Smiley's concern for Jerry's love interests is well founded. Westerby has become infatuated with Lizzie Worthington and is on the loose, threatening to blow the operation. In a powerful scene in chapter 21, Smiley is confronted by his counterpart from the CIA, who is obviously anxious to take over the operation. As he puts it, Westerby is a "rogue elephant" who is "running amok." The Russian mole in China who is the target of the operation, Nelson Ko, "is the biggest catch you or I are ever likely to land. The biggest of my career, and—I will stake my wife, my grandmother, and the deeds of my plantation—the biggest even of yours. . . . Are we going to let him rob us of the prize, George?" (498–99). Smiley, undergoing one of his periodic bouts of soul searching, "studied himself in his mind, and reviewed his quest for Karla, whom Ann called his 'black Grail.' He thought of Ann and her repeated betrayals of him in the name of her own Grail, which she called love. . . . He thought of Haydon, steered at Ann by Karla. He thought of Jerry and the girl, and he though of Peter Worthington, her husband . . . 'You and I are the ones they leave behind,' ran the message" (499).

Given the untidy record of Jerry's love life, Smiley could have easily dismissed the affection Westerby felt for Lizzie as an adolescent infatuation.

Although it would have made his dilemma easier to do so, he did not. At the same time, he could not warmly espouse Jerry's cause of abandoning all loyalties for love, as Ann would undoubtedly have done. "For a cruel moment nevertheless, as he sat locked in indecision, he did honestly wonder whether Ann was right. . . . *The fact that I am wrong,* Smiley had once replied to Ann, . . . *does not make you right*"(499). This hardly indicates support for a simple Forster position.[23]

Westerby's loyalty to his surrogate father, Smiley, and to the Circus is undermined by the havoc wrought on innocent bystanders by his (and others') actions during the operation and by his infatuation with Lizzie Worthington. He quixotically sacrifices his life for his love for her and out of personal empathy for the love between the Chinese brothers (one of whom is Karla's mole attempting to escape from the People's Republic of China). "Jerry hurled himself forward, not for Nelson's sake, still less for Drake's, but for what linked them, and for what linked him to Lizzie" (524). But, the tragedy of Westerby's death (intensified by Smiley's indirect responsibility for it) is undermined by the ironic manner in which le Carré portrays it. Our sympathy for Westerby is less than it is for Leamas because he betrays Smiley, the Circus, and in a way the woman he loves because his unnecessary death deprives her of the support that she needed and that he could have given her had he lived.

Finally, Smiley is betrayed by a faction of his colleagues led by Saul Enderby. Enderby made a deal with Martello (London station chief of the CIA) in which, in return for the American's support for Enderby's replacement of Smiley as head of the Circus, they get to take the captured Soviet mole. Nelson Ko, who has with his brother Drake's help escaped to Hong Kong, is picked up by the CIA and taken to the United States for interrogation. Although several critics suggest that Smiley gave the order to kill Westerby, the bulk of evidence suggests the contrary. Martello says that rogue elephants should be shot, not Smiley (498). Smiley sends his loyal assistant, Guillam, to find Craw, a fellow journalist and Circus agent who is a friend of Westerby's, to find him (501). Most of the circumstantial evidence points to the psychopathic assassin, Fawn, who had personal reasons to take revenge against him because Westerby had seriously injured him in making good an escape while being guarded by Fawn. Fawn could have also acted out of a misguided sense of loyalty to Smiley as well: "A single figure remained in the open doorway [of the helicopter], looking down, and perhaps it was Fawn, for he looked dark and *mad*. Then an orange flash broke from in front of him, then a second and a third, and after that Jerry wasn't calling any more" (525; emphasis added).

After being deposed in a palace coup, Smiley is called upon by Lacon, a senior adviser in the Cabinet Office with responsibility for the intelligence services, to quietly bury (literally and figuratively) a former agent of Smiley's who has been assassinated in London in mysterious circumstances in *Smiley's People*. Lacon plays on Smiley's loyalty to the Circus, which, like his loyalty to his wife, has been repaid with betrayal. Smiley, in turn, is angry at the service's lack of loyalty to his agent, General Vladimir. As Smiley "launched himself upon the familiar death rites for a departed spy" (81), he remembers Ann's admonition in reaction to his composure at the funeral of a friend. "If you won't grieve for the dead, how can you love the living." He thinks: "You are wrong, . . . I mourn the dead sincerely, and Vladimir, at this moment, deeply. It's loving the living which is sometimes a bit of a problem" (96).

After having discovered his first major clue, which Vladimir had hidden in a tree when he realized he was being followed in a park, Smiley remarks: "It was the first thing Vladimir threw away, he thought: in the spy trade we abandon first what we love the most" (97). Conveying the aura of intrigue and constant suspicion, Smiley thinks, during an interview of a colleague of Vladimir (named Mikhel) in an expatriate organization: "*Enemies I do not fear. . . . But friends I fear greatly.*" Whereas Vladimir had betrayed their friendship by having had an affair with Mikhel's wife, Mikhel betrays Vladimir to the Russians, who brutally murder him. Smiley wonders about Mikhel: traitor, loyal, or both? "*Gentlemen, I have served you both well,* says the perfect double agent in the twilight of his life. And says it with pride, too, thought Smiley, who had known a number of them" (131).

During his investigation Smiley is seized by a profound and vehement fear as a glance at Ann's photograph brings on a Proust-like "surge of memory": "he heard the drum-beats of his own past, summoning him to one last effort to externalise and resolve the conflict he had lived by; and he wanted her nowhere near him. . . . Smiley knew for certain she must have no part in what he had to do. . . . He still knew that it was just possible, against all the odds, that he had been given, in late age, a chance to return to the rained-out contests of his life and play them after all. . . . He had not known his mind till then. But now he knew it" (143). Despite the fact that he desperately wants her, Smiley resolves to resist the temptation to contact her so that he can accomplish the enormous task before him. Smiley consciously evaluates his conflicting loyalties. He ponders "his sense of *civitas* and how much, or how little, he owed to Oliver Lacon" (152). He finally comes to the realization, in the passage quoted at length in chapter 1, that he was unled, and perhaps incapable of being led. The only restraints he was willing to accept were those of his own reason, and his own humanity. Having been betrayed in marriage and by his colleagues in his own service, "all I am left with is myself. And with Karla, he thought; with my black Grail"[24] (152).

Smiley is not exactly alone in his quest. As the title of the book indicates, he is supported by a cast of his most loyal and lifelong friends: Peter Guillam, Toby Esterhase, and a cast of supporting players privately recruited on the basis of their skill and loyalty to Smiley (294). In the final scene, after the drama and almost anticlimax of Karla's defection, Peter Guillam gently touches his mentor's arm. "Come on, old friend. . . . It's bedtime" (374). This penultimate exchange between the two provides emotional balance—movingly portraying loyal friendship in the face of devastating betrayals.

As is frequently the case with le Carré, and as is evident in *The Little Drummer Girl,* the nature of the relationship between the agent and his control is central to the story. For the first time since his first novel, he creates a female agent and a male control. In *Call for the Dead* the relationship was purely professional and the control ends up murdering his agent. A love affair and loving relationship develops between Charlie, the British actress recruited by Israeli intelligence to infiltrate a Palestinian terrorist ring, and Gadi Becker, the Mossad agent who makes the initial contact with her and handles her.

Gadi, who had resigned from the Israeli secret service and had been studying in Germany, was reluctant to participate in the operation. He was persuaded to do so by Kurtz (his former boss and the head the operation), who appealed to his patriotism and to their mutual desire to prevent the hawks in Jerusalem from engaging in a large-scale military operation against the PLO in Lebanon that would result in a significant loss of civilian lives (in addition to the combatants). But, as he becomes more emotionally involved with Charlie, Gadi is torn between his loyalty to Kurtz and to Israel, between his conviction that the operation will prevent an even greater miscarriage of justice and his growing concern for the physical and emotional welfare of Charlie. He repeatedly offers her opportunities to withdraw from the operation. Ironically, as his love for her grows, these gestures seem increasingly sincere, but their involvement makes it impossible for Charlie to quit for fear of losing Gadi, with whom she has fallen in love.

Just as the conclusion of the operation approaches, however, Charlie wants out because she knows she will have to sleep with the leader of the terrorist cell who is the target of the Israeli operation. Although before meeting Gadi she had been promiscuous, she did not want to prostitute herself and betray their love. Gadi's insistence that she go through with the operation results in her emotional near-destruction. Several critics do not qualify this and cite Charlie's statement "I'm dead," as evidence to support their interpretation.[25] Charlie is portrayed as the consummate actress who is always on stage. She is a fantasist who invents her own persona as she takes on roles that others have scripted for her. But her experience in what le Carré calls the "theatre of the real" and the shock and disillusionment of witnessing Gadi's assassination of the leader of the terrorists (who would undoubtedly have murdered Charlie since he had just discovered that she was an Israeli agent) kindled a surviving spark of outrage in her and "gave her back the identity that he had stolen from her" (421).

In the crisis of the conclusion of the operation Gadi chooses loyalty to his service, country, and the success of the operation over Charlie's well-being. However, it also culminated a crisis of conscience that had been developing throughout the novel, leading to a development of his character. At the conclusion of the novel he has made a commitment to Charlie, which holds open the possibility that their love may be strong enough to survive the trauma that they (and especially Charlie) and their relationship have suffered. Le Carré deliberately left their future ambiguously open. Despite Charlie's emotional fragility and Gadi's serious betrayal of their love, le Carré gives them the chance of a future together that is far more optimistic than the conclusions of all his previous novels.

Le Carré's Surrogate:
Magnus Pye—"a Perfect Spy"

Le Carré expands the portrait of what he metaphorically terms the "hollow man" as the ultimate double agent (for which Haydon was a sketch) in his portrayal of Magnus Pym, in *A Perfect Spy*. According to Richard Trahair (1994), "compartmentalized Self," a form of identity diffusion disorder, is the appropriate psychological term.[26] In this novel, which he acknowledges as autobiographical, le Carré attempts to come to terms with his past and particularly with his extremely ambivalent feelings toward his father. He told Charles Truehart (1989: D1) that writing it made it possible for him "to jump over the shadow of my father."[27] Le Carré uses the therapeutically proven medium of humor not only in his portrayal of his father, an outrageous con artist, but even more so in his treatment of the main character, through whom he engages in self-parody in order to avoid self-pity. With betrayal as the leitmotif, this is, paradoxically, one of his funniest and saddest novels.[28] Because Magnus Pym is le Carré's closest fictional representation of himself, I expand the discussion (begun in the introduction) of what Pym reveals about the author.

The first scene introduces Magnus Pym, a man in his early fifties, "in his prime," as he arrives in a south Devon boardinghouse, where he tells the landlady he plans to stay for a couple of weeks to write. We learn he has been using the house for years as a "sanctuary."[29] He has come to write his memoirs, a last testament to his son to explain his life to him before (as we learn much later) Pym kills himself. The novel shifts between flashbacks Pym relives as he writes his life and the present, in which Jack Brotherhood, his mentor in the Firm (the British intelligence agency for whom Pym and Brotherhood both work), the CIA, and Pym's Czechoslovak control (and dearest friend), whom he calls "Poppy," pursue him.

With a shift of scene to Vienna, we learn from his wife, Mary, that Pym, formerly deputy head of station in the British embassy in Washington and now head of station in Vienna, has disappeared (as we learn later, with a "burnbox" full of highly classified documents and a revolver from his station). The news of his father's death has set him "free" to perform his last act. Mary recites the following from what she thinks is a novel her missing husband had been writing. She is speaking to Pym's boss and close friend (her former boss and former lover), Jack Brotherhood: "We betray to be loyal. Betrayal is like imagining when the reality isn't good enough. . . . Betrayal as hope and compensation. As a tribute to our unlived lives. . . . Betrayal as escape. As a constructive act. As a statement of ideals. Worship. As an adventure of the soul" (5:121–2). Such dramatically paradoxical declarations shock and confuse the reader. They also establish a frame for le Carré's moral critique, which is established through the cumulative insights in the formation of the personality of the main character and the betrayals of all the relationships he has had with all other individuals and institutions.

Jack Brotherhood, in thumbing through one of Pym's books, notices an underlined passage: "If I am not for myself who is for me; and being for my own self what am I? If not now when?" (3:62). Neither Brotherhood nor Mary Pym understand the passage. The quotation (not identified by le Carré) is of Rabbi Hillel from the *Pirkei Avoth, the Ethics of the Fathers.*[30] Although the passage is cryptic, Hillel can be understood to stress the need to find a *balance* between one's obligation to oneself and one's responsibility to others in order to live a full and meaningful life. Either extreme of preoccupation with self or of self-denial distorts the personality (or soul, in terms of Hillel's discourse). So interpreted, the passage perfectly fits the context in which it appears.

The conspicuous lack of such a balance in Pym's life from an early age prevented his maturing into a balanced adult and made him the perfect double agent. Pym sees himself as a "blank page" (6:135). One of his women says of him: "He doesn't have affairs. He has lives" (7:181). She calls him a shell into which hermit crabs climb. "Don't look for the truth about him. The truth is what we gave him of ourselves" (7:187). In his attempt to be all things to all people (he learned in Rick's court to be a "pleaser" and "to make himself attractive") (4:75), he was neither true to himself nor faithful to anyone else.

His apparent self-effacement was really a perverse form of adolescent self-ishness because it was based on an obsessive need to win the approval and love of others. "Manhood and maturity beckoned, even if he never made the distance" (6:158). Pym calls himself an "elderly adolescent" still to become a man. Moving from the personal to the cultural, he generalizes, "Who will ever break the genetic code of when a middle-class Englishman's adolescence ends and his manhood takes over?" (16:422). Most of le Carré's spies are elderly adolescents playing dangerous games. A CIA agent, referring to Pym, says all defectors are immature. "It's in and out of the womb all the time" (9:247). Shklar (1984:139–40) stresses the aspect of the experience of desertion, which plays on aspects of the childhood fear of abandonment in acts of betrayal.[31] Le Carré has indicated that he recognized qualities in himself that had he not turned to artistic creativity might have made him a "barking neurotic" (*JHM:* 13).[32] On another occasion he observes: "There were even moments, as I listened to the apologia of the mole Gerald when he is finally unmasked, when I wondered—until I caught my balance again—whether I might have followed in his footsteps."[33]

Pym's insatiable need for approval made him extremely gullible to his father's, and later his surrogate father's, cons and manipulations and taught him by example how to charm and manipulate others. He learned to lie to the police at an early age to protect his father. "Like Rick he was learning to live on several planes at once. The art of it was to forget everything except the ground you stood on and the face you spoke from at that moment" (4:99). Pym is characterized by Poppy as, "the Pym who can't rest until he's touched the love in people, then can't rest until he's hacked his way out of it, the more drastically the better. The Pym who does nothing cynically, nothing without conviction. Who sets events in motion in order to become their victim, which he calls decision, and ties himself into pointless relationships, which he calls loyalty. Then waits for the next event to get him out of the last one, which he calls destiny" (6:147).

If Pym's primary socialization in the court of a con artist shaped his personality and taught him his basic skills of secrecy, manipulation, and intrigue, his secondary socialization as a spy and, eventually, as a double agent solidified his personality and honed his skills to near perfection. At the age of seventeen his hero, Jack Brotherhood, idolized by Pym for his war record, recruits Pym to spy on his friends and fellow university students in Switzerland. It is here that he is befriended by and betrays Axel, whom he later gives the code name Poppy. In his enthusiasm to please Brotherhood, Pym informs on Poppy, an illegal alien with false papers, who is subsequently deported.

Pym characterizes his relationship with Brotherhood and Poppy: "Both were clamouring to occupy the empty spaces of his heart. In return he was giving to each man the character he seemed to be in search of" (8:210). Pym never forgave himself nor Brotherhood for Jack's having induced him to betray Poppy. He writes to Jack, "We reap as we sow, even if the harvest is thirty-five summers in the growing" (8:212). Pym's first wife, Belinda, also blames Jack, the service, and Pym's father for what he became. "You brought it on yourselves, Jack. All of you. He'd have been all right if he'd never met people like you" (12:321). Jack Brotherhood views Pym's betrayal in personal terms. He seems to ignore Pym's betrayal of the service and his country.

Lederer, a CIA agent on Pym's trail, recognizes in Pym what he recognizes in himself: "We're howling psychopaths the both of us" (4:239). Needing to externalize his secret affinity with Pym, he says: "There's a serious strain of controlled instability here. . . . The guy's everywhere. He's all over the place. That English cool of his is just a veneer"[34] (9:244). Lederer speculates that if Pym had ever written the autobiographical novel that he had always aspired to write, "He would have been okay. There's just too much inside him. He has to put it somewhere" (9:246). Consider this in the context of le Carré's speculation, noted above, that he might have become "a barking neurotic" or possibly even a double agent had he not found an artistic outlet.

While at Oxford, on Brotherhood's recommendation, Pym is recruited by British internal security to spy on radical student groups. He quelled the recurrent pangs of guilt that materialized in the form of the ghost of memories of Poppy and denied that it was betrayal by rationalizing his actions. He told himself he did it for England: "For love. To be a good chap, a good soldier" (10:268). Perhaps more seriously for him psychologically, Pym also betrays his father, who was running as a Liberal candidate for parliament in a by-election. He does so in support of a widow whose late husband Rick had swindled out of their farm and life savings. Pym then helps his father turn the situation to Rick's benefit. "He had never adored Rick more" than at that moment[35] (11:301). In his attempt to please everyone he ends up betraying them all. The moral point is that it is impossible to please everyone all the time. One needs to constantly establish priorities in each context.

After graduating from Oxford, with an honors B.A. in modern languages, Pym was drafted and served in military intelligence, where he was actually working for civilian intelligence. While serving in Vienna, at Poppy's initiative, Pym meets him secretly and is tricked into collaboration with Czechoslovak intelligence, for whom Poppy is now working. Ironically, Pym marvels "that it must be a very rare thing indeed to be offered a second chance to prove one's loyalty after failing so miserably at the first attempt" (13:356). It does not even occur to him that in so doing he is betraying his country.

First giving Pym (useless) information, Poppy extorts information from him in return on the pretext of needing it to protect himself from his superiors. Out of naïveté and a sense of guilt and obligation to Poppy for having previously betrayed him, Pym complies and with a sense of exultation thinks: "This is what I was born for, he thinks, not for the first time" (13:363).[36] Although Pym's superior suspected the information they were receiving was fraudulent, out of loyalty to Pym and because the War Office was so pleased with the intelligence, he delayed reporting his suspicions. Poppy failed to meet with Pym's superior after Pym completed his military service. Pym's superior finally reported his suspicions and was fired for his efforts.[37]

After returning from his military service, again at Jack Brotherhood's recommendation, Pym is once again recruited into Jack's service. Pym joins the Firm and marries Belinda with equal detachment. He learns in training camp (as if he needed the lesson) "the ravishment that must be done to truth, friendship and, if need be, honour in the interest of Mother England" (14:407). On his first mission he is sent to Czechoslovakia, where he encounters Poppy. Through intimidation, trickery, and by playing on Pym's sense of guilt, obligation, and friendship, Poppy renews their former collaboration and brings it to a higher level to promote both of their careers as spies. In so doing he analyzes Pym's character and offers him a cause: "Sir Magnus, you have in the past betrayed me but, more important, you have betrayed yourself. Even when you are telling the truth, you lie. You have loyalty and you have affection. But to what? To whom? I don't know the reasons for this. Your great father. Your aristocratic mother. . . . Yet you also have morality. You search. What I am saying is, Sir Magnus; for once nature has produced a perfect match. You are a perfect spy" (15:421). Although Poppy offers Pym a cause, his revolutionary pep talk falls on deaf ears; Pym is no more interested in ideology than he is in money. Poppy captures Pym with these concluding words: "You are a good man and I love you" (15:421).

Pym rationalizes that he serves both Brotherhood and Poppy with "omnivorous loyalty" (16:422). He loves Jack as a surrogate father, the Firm as a surrogate family, and Poppy as his other surrogate father. Pym particularly enjoys being "really well run" by Poppy because it provides structure and purpose to his chaotic emotional life. When Poppy and Brotherhood both advise him to marry his second wife, Mary, because her aristocratic family ties to the Establishment would advance his career, he complies. Pym is shortly thereafter posted to Washington, where he betrays the Anglo-American alliance to Poppy while they express their love for America and the Americans.[38] But, their excesses in America finally catch up with them.

Rick Pym trails his son to America, where he cons him for the last time. As his sick father diminishes in his eyes, he sees himself as having become his father: "All that was left of Pym . . . as I wove my lies and blandished, and perjured myself . . . was a failing con-man tottering on the last legs of his credibility. . . . *Betrayal is a repetitious trade*" (17:454; emphasis added). With ironic understatement he writes to his son "that Pym preferred to test the limits of the tolerance of those he loved" (17:454). His final words, written to his son, are: "I am the bridge. . . . I am what you must walk over to get from Rick to life" (461–2). These words express the hope that his death will end the line of betrayers and make possible a normal life for his son.

Susan Laity (1987:162–3) suggests this novel "represents the latest in a series of attempts to narrate and so control the circumstances of le Carré's life and generation." She observes that in the Smiley narratives, le Carré's father, Ronnie, was displaced into the idealized father, Smiley: "It is noteworthy that in these novels there was no one who obviously was le Carré's surrogates as son. . . . Rather, Smiley himself, . . . is le Carré's double, even as he is his father. For the first time in *A Perfect Spy,* we have a clear, authorial double for the author, a son who is also a father."[39]

In an interview focused on this novel le Carré concluded: "There's a feeling I have very much. . . . I think that many fathers have it, that somehow we are *not* to pass on the things we have inherited from our own fathers" (Lelyveld, 1986:91). David Cornwell has four sons from two marriages. Le Carré confessed himself to be "a soppy father." Stefan Kanfer and Dean Fischer (1977:53) observe that his close relationships with his sons "are an open repudiation of his own deprived childhood—and of the father who died in 1975 without a reconciliation." One of his many purposes in writing this novel, what Laity (1987:164) calls "a kind of alternative suicide," in addition to coming to terms with his feelings toward his own father, seems to have been to break the pattern of duplicity he learned from his father so his sons could live richer and more fulfilling personal lives.

Laity (1987:158) suggests "Pym fails in his narrative search because he cannot find his voice. A divided person may still have a single voice—Rick's is unmistakable . . .—but Pym is a 'mimic.'" She suggests that mimicry is part of the distinctiveness of le Carré's authorial voice, which has become more tenuous "as the nature of the reality he wishes to present appears more ambiguous."[40] Laity (164) cautions: "We cannot trust any one voice, not even the author's, for he is a perfect mimic." She concludes: "For, in the fragmenting of himself into his double, the text, and into his doubles in the text, le Carré throws down the pieces to shore up his defense against, and revenge upon, time."[41]

By the end of the novel, when Pym writes to his wife "Love is whatever we can betray" (16:436), the statement has become completely sub-
verted by the reader's knowledge that it is the ranting of an extremely
disturbed individual.[42] So, too, the initial statements by Pym quoted at the
beginning of this chapter, and others such as, "Love is whatever you can
still betray" (10:270). By now they are understood as a litany of hypocritical rationalizations of a very pathetic and sick person. We cease to suspect
that they may express the views of the author and understand that they can
be more appropriately interpreted as the objects of his moral condemna-
tion—no mater how much he loves the character (who represents an aspect of himself). Le Carré's gift as an artist is to universalize his struggle
with his personal demons, thereby addressing dilemmas we all confront (although in different ways).

Conclusions: Le Carré as an Ambiguous Moralist

Le Carré boldly states: "I have to introduce levels of *moral doubt,* self-
doubt" (Ross, 1996:8; emphasis added). Le Carré is a moralist in the spirit
of the seventeenth-century Dutch painter Jan Steen. Steen frequently portrayed himself in his narrative paintings in an unfavorable light—as a buf-
foon, a lecherous old man whose pocket is being picked by a young
prostitute, a drunkard, and a father allowing his young son to smoke his
pipe. Yet these same paintings symbolically (and sometimes literally
through inscriptions) expressed moral maxims condemning the conduct
being portrayed. Art historians debate the extent to which Steen's self-por-
trayals were true to his real life, just as critics have speculated about how
much *A Perfect Spy* reveals about David Cornwell: "Setting aside the unan-
swerable question of whether he actually behaved like his painted counterpart, it is possible to consider Steen's self-portrayal both as a pictorial
device designed to confuse the line between art and life and as a professional stance through which he defined his artistic identity. Steen's mask-
ing is a strategic comic inversion that worked in complex ways to proclaim
at once the veracity and the theatricality of his images. In this sense, his
persona relates to ideas about art and imitation, specifically about comic art
that imitates ordinary life for the purpose of imparting moral truths" (H.
Perry Chapman, 1996:17).

This blurring of the distinction between art and fiction and real life has
other important functions in imparting ethical evaluations and lessons. For
example, it causes them to be taken more seriously: "The more the bound-
ary between life and art is blurred, and the more the fictive world claims
seriously to be an imitation of reality, the more its values may seem to pro-
pose themselves as ethically valid. Yet paradoxically, this very development

which renders fantasy potentially more dangerous, may also invest it with a higher seriousness" (Rutherford, 1978:141). Consequently, in contrast with the simplistic morality of standard thrillers, Rutherford (144) convincingly argues that "le Carré offers a more complex pleasure by combining psychological release with radical moral concern." Le Carré's moralizing is a form of self-analysis and "self-education."[43]

Another function of the moral ambiguity expressed in le Carré's satirical humor and self-parody, like Steen's, is that it temporizes his moral messages. This softens what otherwise might appear as an excessively judgmental tone in the ethical critique. In other words, this mode of disguise helps prevent the appearance of sermonizing.[44] In addition, by recognizing in themselves tendencies of those whom they criticize and by projecting this into their art, both artists empathetically identify the common humanity they share with those whose foibles they subject to criticism. It is a way of expressing the old maxim that "it takes one to know one!"

Ian Buruma's (1997; emphasis added) description of Jan Steen perfectly captures le Carré's moralism:

> Steen's moralism, then, is too ambiguous to use as proof of his high-mindedness . . . But it was his playfulness, his *moral ambiguity,* more than moralism, that made him so and gave his art its enduring fascination. [9] To take the moral messages in his paintings at face tension value and call him a straightforward moralist is to miss the point. It would be equally perverse to ignore the moral concern altogether, and regard it simply as a joke. It was the *tension* between convention and transgression, art and real life, high and low, that made Steen's art surprisingly close in spirit to our time. . . . Steen was a slippery figure, playing hide-and-seek all the time, *undermining his own moral messages with subversive wit.* De Jongh [1996] assumes that the artist "did not speak his true mind in certain respects, and never will." (11)

Lars Ole Sauerberg (1984:208) defines le Carré as "a moralist who believes in simple virtues like honesty and fairness and who acknowledges his debt to liberal-conservative and pragmatic cultural tradition." Le Carré's "preoccupation with moral values," according to John Kirk (1964:3), "gives his novels their special superiority." Green (1988:39), in the spirit of the paradoxical le Carré, playfully suggests: "It would be too sophisticated to advance the theory that le Carré is a moralizer without a message. Yet moral his novels are." Le Carré's *ambiguous moralism,* which is not the same as moralizing without a moral, is far more forgiving of individual human foibles than he is in his judgement of the institutions which they serve (and betray) and by whom they are exploited (and betrayed).

For example, in *A Perfect Spy* he shows officials more concerned with saving face with the Americans and preserving the Anglo-American alliance than with saving the lives of their agents compromised by Pym's betrayals. In *The Spy Who Came in from the Cold,* entire networks of agents are betrayed by the British to protect their agent in place. Rutherford (1978:146) concludes his analysis of this novel: "Yet the dilemma the book poses remains unresolved . . . our satisfaction comes not from being presented with a neat solution, but from incompatible alternatives so powerfully presented." This statement is equally valid for all of his other novels as well. It is precisely the ambiguity of the moral message that forces the reader to confront the alternatives and to make his or her own choice.

Green (1988:39) ponders whether "le Carré would have agreed with E. M. Forster that affection should take precedence of patriotism I do not know; but the novel's [*A Perfect Spy*] argument points in that direction." I conclude that le Carré does *not* support the simplistic choice of Forster.[45] He does warn, however, that one should never expect loyalty from bureaucratic institutions. As Alan Bold (1988:22) contends, "Taken as a whole, the argumentative thrust of his work is subversive of institutional arrogance. His troubled vision of the world puts him on the side of the victims of the great game." He finds, as Green asserts, a redemptive quality in human relationships to counter the note of pessimism which pervades much of his work.[46] The conflicts of loyalty among individuals and between personal and collective loyalties cannot be resolved in absolute terms by any ideological formula. They must constantly be met, contested, and resolved in the context of daily living. Le Carré's stories convey the complexity of real-life moral dilemmas and make the reader more conscious of the serious implications of the choices one makes in balancing obligations to self, to significant others, and to institutions and collectivities.

Some types of betrayal can be seen as a form of self-deception. As Lockard and Paulhus (1988:1) argue in their introduction to an edited volume on the subject, "The ability to self-deceive contributes to an individual's ability to deceive others." Magnus Pym is a "ideal type" illustration. Shklar (1984:145) reminds us that Shakespeare's Coriolanus, an example of what she calls a pure traitor, "suggests that every traitor is a self-deceiving, self-made alien." The reason why the public traitor is perceived to be a threat to the existence of his society is "because he denies its reality."

Chapter 3

Skepticism: Balancing Dreams and Realities

Where we often fail—and this may be one of the qualities of real tragedy—is in the disproportion between the dream we had and the reality when we meet it. (John le Carré)[1]

Since culture is a collective human artifact, the line between the imagined and the real—as Shakespeare especially shows us—cannot be a bright one. (James Boyd White, 1994:276)

Introduction

My analysis of le Carré's exploration of the interplay between appearances and realities implicitly employs a phenomenological approach, which is based on the assumption that our perceptions of reality are socially and culturally constructed.[2] Le Carré's plots illustrate that appearances are rarely what they seem to be. They show competing versions of reality in which individual and collective self-deception—opposite sides of the same coin—lead to disastrous outcomes for both individual and collectivity. A skeptical outlook, one that critically questions the taken-for-granted assumptions on which all socially constructed depictions of reality are based, is the most successful approach to counter such deceptions and to maintain personal stability and integrity. In chapter 8 I will argue that having skeptical individuals in intelligence organizations is perhaps the most effective means of protecting these organizations from the disastrous consequences of operations based on false assumptions and unrealistic evaluations of situations entailing collective illusions.

Le Carré's plots constitute metaphors for rather than accurate descriptions of the real world of contemporary politics, with special reference to the centrality of the Cold War.[3] In response to le Carré's insistence that the illusions he creates are fiction, Bold (1988:18; emphasis added), however, suggests this disclaimer could be a fiction: "That would be in keeping with the great game where *actuality is illusory,* where *disbelief is perpetually suspended,* where lies are told to preserve a truth—or an ideological abstraction." Le Carré's novels illustrate John Vernon's (1995:12) point that the subject of fiction "is never reality but competing realities." Because le Carré's skeptical position has evolved over his writing career, my analysis of his novels first discusses his early works covering the period of the Cold War. Then I interpret *The Little Drummer Girl* (including conflicting findings of others) as a critical turning point in le Carré's development on this subject. Finally, I discuss the implications of his later novels, which refine le Carré's skeptical outlook.

The Cold War Novels

Le Carré established his reputation with his novels published during the Cold War. Of these, his third novel, *The Spy Who Came in from the Cold,* brought him fame and financial independence. In *Call for The Dead* (1961:70), Samuel Fennan relates to Smiley his disillusionment with "University Communism" and Marxism: "The disproportion between the dream and reality drove him to a close examination of both. . . . He turned his back sadly on it as a treasure he had outgrown and must leave at Oxford with the days of his youth." Fennan appears to have adjusted to this disillusionment as a normal part of his maturation. For many, if not most, of le Carré's other characters, the loss of illusion is much more traumatic and frequently even fatal. Just as the disparity between dream and reality led to Fennan's disillusionment, the disparity between the appearance of Fennan's suicide and Smiley's intuitive reading of his character and other clues enabled him to solve the mystery of his murder by an agent of East German intelligence. LynnDianne Beene (1992:29; emphasis added) notes that, with few exceptions, "The novel's characters unsuccessfully aspire to replace the past's painful realities with illusionary distortions"; still, "grim *realities* replace imperfect *dreams.*" The conclusion of the novel portrays a fellow passenger completely misinterpreting Smiley's character from his physical appearance. The last two sentences read: "He knew the type well—the tired executive out for a bit of fun. He found it rather disgusting" (157). By concluding with this ostensibly irrelevant scene and observation le Carré reinforces the main motif—the deceptiveness of appearances.

In *A Murder of Quality,* because the victim, Stella Rode, had written a letter to a newspaper stating that her husband (Stanley) was planning to kill her, he is the obvious suspect. Le Carré is much too good a writer to be so obvious. But, solving the mystery of the murder is incidental to the exposition of the reality behind the façade of Carne School. This novel is a biting critique of the British class system and of the snobbery and hypocrisy that characterizes it. The mood of gloom, decadence, and death is dramatically established through metaphors.[4] He describes the sons of the rich arriving in sad groups in great cars that shone with mournful purity. Saying that they came to bury poor King Edward (the reputed founder of the school), le Carré describes their suitcases as "coffins," in their black gowns looking like "undertakers' mutes." "They were always mourning at Carne . . . the cloud of gloom was a firmly settled as ever over the grey towers of Carne"(2). Carne represents Britain's imperial past, a mere shadow of its former self, desperately perpetuating a myth in which few, if any, of even those perpetuating it still believe.

The plot of *The Spy Who Came in from the Cold* plays with different representations and misrepresentations of reality. Leamas is recruited, he is told, to set a trap to eliminate Mundt, the head of the East German counterespionage section, who is responsible for the liquidation of Leamas' entire network of agents. Leamas believes that his boss, Control, and Fiedler, Mundt's deputy, are working together to eliminate Mundt because Fiedler is the British mole. Le Carré manipulates Leamas' (and the reader's) sympathies by making Fiedler, a Jew, a sympathetic character and Mundt, an anti-Semite, cruel and hateful. The trial scene is reminiscent of Kafka's work (and of Akira Kurasawa's film *Rashamon*) where it is unclear who is guilty of what crime because contradictory versions of reality are presented. Mundt appears in a prison uniform and is surrounded by police, whereas Fiedler wears regular clothes. Mundt is charged with treason.

But Mundt uses a visit by Smiley to Leamas' girlfriend (who is brought to testify through a deception) and the fact that he paid Leamas' lease to establish a link between Leamas and the Circus after he was supposed to have left the Circus in disgrace. At this point, suspicion of treason is diverted from Mundt to Fiedler, and Leamas realizes that he had been duped into being a pawn in this masterful subterfuge: "And suddenly, with the terrible clarity of a man too long deceived, Leamas understood the whole ghastly trick" (231). Leamas explains to his girlfriend, Liz Gold, their respective roles in the plot. "My job was to let them think what in fact was the truth: that Mundt was a British spy. . . . Your job was to discredit me" (243). Mundt appears to let them escape, however, once Leamas is safely atop the Berlin wall, Liz is shot dead and Leamas climbs back down and is killed, too. As he collapses, he has a vision of a near accident that he had earlier witnessed: on the autobahn "Leamas saw a small car smashed between great lorries, and the children waving cheerfully through the window" (256).

This metaphor lends itself to a number of possible interpretations. The one that seems most appropriate to the theme of the novel and to le Carré's vision is that the lorries ("trucks" in American English) represent the great powers, who are on a collision course. The children represent the naïve and innocent victims, like Liz Gold, whose failure to comprehend the reality of the world makes their victimization inevitable. Leamas, a romantic with greater awareness than Liz, is also duped and manipulated. The only advantage he had over Liz was that he chose to die with her rather than live with the consequences of his actions, which he justified in the name of *raison d'état*. This seems to be small consolation for his awareness. Does le Carré suggest that this is the only advantage there is to be gained from a greater awareness of "reality"? For the answer, one must look further. In doing so one needs to keep in mind Beene's (1992:50) observation: "Rejecting self-imposed ignorance is, in le Carré's vision, the measure of integrity."

The Looking-Glass War (1965) is one of le Carré's bleakest novels. Illusion is the recurring refrain constituting its motif. Barley (1986:48) observes, "These characters bury their heads in dreams and myths of the past and participate in games designed pathetically to revive it." He terms these "fantasies of nostalgia." Andrew Rutherford (1978:19) calls it "a corrupt nostalgia for wartime experiences." Leclerc is the head of a military intelligence agency that has suffered a rapid decline since the end of the Second World War. Through lies, deception, mystification, and the exploitation of nostalgia, he hatches a scheme to try to regain the power, resources, prestige, and glory that the department had during the war. Le Carré vividly portrays the dynamics of collective self-deception through which the members of the department attribute legendary qualities to one another and overlook one another's faults.

When Leclerc informs the wife of a courier who had been killed abroad that he died gallantly, she replied incredulously, "What do you mean, gallantly? . . . We're not fighting a war. That's finished, all that fancy talk. He's dead" (65). In this novel, as well as his others, many women are down-to-earth realists who debunk their men's tendency to live in fantasy worlds.[5] For example, the wife of John Avery, a young member of the department who was recruited after the war, unsuccessfully attempts to question his highly unrealistic fantasies. Avery, on returning from having arranged the return of the courier's body, also expresses skepticism and even contemplates resigning. He correctly evaluates the situation and informs his superiors that they are not competent to deal with investigating reports, which he believes to be unfounded, of new missile bases being erected in East Germany. He contrasts the "dream factory" of his office with the real world "out there," from which he has just returned (100).

He is enticed, however, against his better judgement, by the fabricated illusion of a renewed and reinvigorated department, by the magical amulets of status (like a special ministry pass),[6] and by his desperate need to belong. Beene (1992:61) says, "He trades his scruples for acceptance." Avery is persuaded to take "the second vow," a leap of faith despite his doubts and Smiley's efforts to encourage his nascent skepticism. The novel is replete with similar religious imagery. Like a "doubting cleric," Avery is desperate "to abdicate his conscience in order to discover God" (103).

Just as Avery has been persuaded, he and his colleagues use similar tactics of deception to persuade a former agent, Fred Leiser, to come out of his twenty-year-old retirement and undertake a dangerous mission that costs him his life. They play on his nostalgia for old times during the war, maintaining the illusion that the Department has not changed since the war, that it had unlimited resources and authority, and that it had the full cooperation of the Circus and other agencies. They also play on his strong need to belong to the Department and to Britain (his adopted home). Just as they con their agent, they collectively deceive one another and (in varying degrees) themselves.[7] "All of them in that room—but Avery perhaps best of all—knew the *fatal disproportion between the dream and reality,* between motive and action. Avery had . . . returned from a nightmare journey to see his own experiences remade into the images of Leclerc's world. Yet Avery, like Haldane and Leiser, listened to Leclerc with the piety of an agnostic, feeling perhaps that this was how, in some clean and magic place, it really ought to be" (189–90).

As in the previous case, Avery's perception of the gap between appearances and reality fails to save either Leiser's life or his own "soul" (following the religious imagery of the novel). David Monaghan (1985:18) cites Leiser's description of a man drawing in chalk on the pavement in the rain as the rain washes the drawing away as the "definitive metaphor for the unsubstantiability of the Department's world of illusion." Eric Homberger (1986:64) also sees this as the central metaphor. One cannot help but wonder whether a similar atmosphere prevailed in the CIA (and possibly the White House) during the debacle of the U.S.-sponsored amateurish Bay of Pigs "invasion" of Cuba by poorly trained and armed Cuban exiles in 1961.[8] Le Carré obviously has no doubts: "The Bay of Pigs—that really was the result of men who had generated a collective perception of their own heroism and, drawing from that romantic past, were engaging in something that was almost fantasy."[9]

Whereas *The Looking Glass War* satirizes Britain's unwillingness to face the reality of its diminished role in world affairs, *A Small Town in Germany* traces Britain's loss of political direction in the mid-sixties. Sauerberg (1984:180) suggests "the keyword for a thematic interpretation of the story is *illusion*."[10] Leo Harting, a German half-Jewish survivor of the Holocaust and employee of the British embassy in Bonn, disappears along with forty-three files, including an especially important one. His disappearance appears to be a case of defection. It turns out, however, that Harting has been conducting research in a secret space in the basement of the embassy in order to expose the Nazi past of a rising neofascist German named Karfeld, who leads a nationalist movement with which the British have formed a secret alliance.[11] As in other le Carré novels, the deceptive plot twist is reinforced by the revelation of an even greater deception—in this case the penetration of the activities of the British embassy in Bonn (representing British foreign policy).

As always, metaphors of scenery create an atmosphere that reinforces the theme. Alan Turner, the Foreign Office investigator sent from London, is picked up by an official of the embassy named de Lisle, who describes Bonn as "a very *metaphysical* spot; the *dreams have quite replaced reality*. We live somewhere between the recent future and the not so recent past"[12] (50; second emphasis added). Tony Barley (1986:67) perceptively observes le Carré's use of the past: "To make sense of the present and its ramifications in the future you must first lay bare the past." He calls both Harting and Turner "archaeologists of knowledge." Their investigations attempt to gain a realistic understanding of the past in order to penetrate the fictive appearance of present realities. Harting's goal is to expose the policies pursued by the British diplomats in Bonn in collusion with their allies among the Germans, including Karfeld. Turner's goal is to reveal the true purpose of Harting's actions. Both must penetrate appearances to accomplish their goals.

As he questions Harting's co-workers, it is clear that many of them allowed themselves to be deceived into granting him access to information to which he was not entitled, although they knew they were being deceived. One explained, "I mean you have to really [believe]—*you couldn't live, not without illusions*" (214; emphasis added). On the other hand, Bradfield, head of chancery of the British embassy in Bonn, exchanged his illusions for raison d'état: "Haven't you realized that *only appearances matter?* . . . What else is there when the underneath is rotten? Break the surface and we sink. That's what Harting has done. *I am a hypocrite*. . . . I'm a great believer in hypocracy. It's the nearest we ever get to virtue. It's a statement of what we ought to be. . . . I serve the *appearance* of things. It is the worst of systems; it is better than the others. That is my profession, and that is my philosophy. . . . I expect no more from institutions that I expect from people" (291; emphasis added). David Seed (1990:157) observes, "At issue is not truth but what can be publicly admitted." Like the existentialist who finds meaning by affirming its absence, Bradfield finds purpose, or at least deludes himself that he does, in the service of appearances.

Turner, the hunter, identifies with Harting, the hunted. Beene (1992:67) suggests that because "they share an unfounded idealism and unrewarded patriotism, he and Harting are imperfect mirror images." In a debate with Bradfield about Harting, Turner defends Harting. "He's our responsibility, after all . . .We made him all those promises: Nuremberg, de-Nazification. We *made* him believe. We can't let him be a casualty just because we changed our minds." Bradfield replies: "He should have grown out of it; the rest of us did." Bradfield claims that Harting has offended "against the order that results from chaos; against the built-in moderation of an aimless society." Turner defends Harting by claiming "he's the only one who's real, the only one who believed, and acted! For you it's a sterile rotten game . . . But Leo's *involved!*" (272,292). Bradfield replies that for that reason he is condemned, because there is no longer room for his kind. Bradfield articulates an extremely cynical form of pessimism in the guise of "realism" that denies the ability of individuals and of second-rate powers like Britain to influence events.

Turner protests: "We're *not* automations! We're born free, I believe that! We can't control the processes of our own minds!" With tears showing in his eyes (which may reveal how much he deceives himself) Bradfield replies: "Good Lord, whoever told you that? . . . I have spent half of my life learning not to look, and the other half learning not to feel. Do you think I cannot also learn to forget?" (293); Bradfield is a pathetic example of Smiley's warning to the graduating class of spies of the personal costs of a life withheld.[13] In this debate, Bradfield represents George Bernard Shaw's (1903:238) "reasonable man" and Harting the "unreasonable" one: "The reasonable man adapts himself to the world: the unreasonable one persists in trying to adapt the world to himself. Therefore all progress depends on the unreasonable man." Although le Carré recognizes that politics derives from the tension between the two tendencies, his liberal temperament leans toward a balance between the two defined below in terms of a skeptical outlook.

Although le Carré sympathizes with the "unreasonable" Leo Harting (and with Turner), he is not optimistic about the fate of such uncompromising romantic idealists. Harting ends up lying in the street with a broken neck: "an innocent, reaching beyond the square for a prize he would never find." The final words are presumably Bradfield's. "'Search his pockets,' someone said, in a voice of English calm" (311). Harting has been murdered and his pockets picked to silence him and to prevent him from assassinating Karfeld and exposing the collusion between Britain and the neo-fascist Movement in West Germany. Lars Ole Sauerberg (1984:197) attributes Harting's death and Turner's failure to their "longing for absolutist values." Reason prevails and the illusion of a very different British policy and political reality are maintained. Eric Homberger (1986:64; emphasis added) concludes that Harting is "destroyed by the fatal *disproportion between things as they are and as they might be.*" He suggests that "le Carré presents such figures, whether idealists like Harting, deceived innocents like Leiser, or the limited but essentially virtuous men like Westerby as all in a sense *self-deceived*" (82; emphasis added).

The romantic idealists pay severely for their naïve trust and belief. But the cynical so-called realists pay in different ways for their distrust and lack of faith, as is suggested by the tears in Bradfield's eyes. Both extremes are different forms of self-deception. Le Carré, the liberal, cautions against both extremes. Conspicuously absent from this novel is Smiley, bravely attempting to achieve a balance between the two. Although Turner shares some characteristics with Smiley, he, like Harting, tends toward absolutism and lacks a balanced skeptical outlook.[14]

Tinker, Tailor, Soldier, Spy opens ironically with "the *truth* is," whereas the novel contradicts this certainty by concluding that it was "after all, a *dream.*"[15] Haydon's many betrayals were the catalyst for the traumatic loss of illusions by romantics like Jim Prideaux and Peter Guillam.[16] Jim Prideaux's aristocratic, passionate, public school Englishness (which becomes a nationalism of despair when acted out in the real world) nearly got him killed and left him maimed (physically and psychologically) for life. Peter, aided by his mentor Smiley, manages somewhat better the difficult process of maturing and coming to grip with reality: "Le Carré suggests that it is the public school, this very particular appropriation of childhood, with its definite inscription of gender, race and class, which establishes the values which govern the world-view of so many Englishmen. However, as in Prideaux's case, it is also clear to le Carré that even if these values ever worked, they certainly do not give good service now. Le Carré simultaneously establishes them as values and distances himself from them" (O'Neill, 1988:172–3). Smiley is not a victim of this nostalgia. His disillusionment leads to self-awareness. The novel measures the values of the school and the Circus (linked by the fact that the personnel of the latter were almost exclusively recruited from the former at that time) against the outside world.[17] Smiley becomes aware of the crippling nature of overdependence on both private and public institutions.

The novel turns on the divergence of dream, folklore, and prosaic fact. Despite their contingency, dreams and myths (illusions) are essential, but without awareness of their social construction, they can be dangerous. Smiley's disillusionment leads to painful self-awareness. Through him, le Carré hopes the reader will also be led to greater self-awareness and awareness of dominant political myths.[18] Philip O'Neill (1988:187) interprets Smiley's disillusionment as a statement of "post-modern cynicism." Smiley ponders:

"Illusion? Was that really Karla's name for love? And Bill's?" They are the cynics, not Smiley. Smiley is on his way to Ann. He ponders the notions of illusion and illusionless and at the same time he is thinking about Ann. "He hoped very much that her wretched lover had found her somewhere warm to live. He wished he had brought her [Ann] her fur boots from the cupboard under the stairs" (368). It is true that he sees Ann as "essentially another man's woman," but the point is that after all he has been through, he is standing in the freezing cold and is concerned about her. That is not the behavior of a cynic, post-modern or otherwise. O'Neill's concluding sentence contradicts his application of the term *cynic* to Smiley. "Smiley is doomed to failure but his *blind faith and conviction* is to be congratulated" (187; emphasis added). A cynic with faith and conviction?

The Little Drummer Girl: A Turning Point

The Little Drummer Girl represents an important development in le Carré's work. Because of the novel's complexity, critical evaluations of key characters and of the meaning of the work have been contested. Gadi Becker is the first hero in a le Carré novel in which Smiley does not appear to display the development of a skeptical stance, which is the author's model for coping with the problem of reconciling dreams with political realities.

Shakespeare's well-known metaphor "all the world's a stage," is transformed by le Carré in this story, where espionage is the "theatre of the real."[19] The terms fiction, play, apparition, fantasy, and theater are woven throughout the novel to reinforce a plot that reveals plays within the main play. Charlie,[20] a twenty-six-year-old English actress with vaguely radical tendencies to support desperate causes, is, somewhat incongruously it may appear, recruited by the Mossad to infiltrate a Palestinian terrorist cell.[21] This is in spite of, or more precisely, *because* she sympathizes with the Palestinian cause. The logic behind this seemingly incongruous Israeli choice is that Charlie will therefore be more convincing in her role as a Palestinian sympathizer.

Charlie is recruited by Gadi Becker, an Israeli Special Forces officer with a heroic record of secret operations in Arab lands, with the physical and mental scars to show for it. When Charlie notices him on the beach in Greece where he has been sent to recruit her, she names him Joseph. Gadi has been called out of his retirement from the service by Kurtz, the Mossad officer directing the operation, because of his impressive service record, the fact that he physically resembles the Palestinian captive he has been cast to impersonate, and because "Gadi, he's the best I ever had . . . A lion's heart, a poet's head" (140).[22] Charlie prophetically thinks as she sees Gadi: "He's come to collect my soul" (52).

The scenario plays out. After Gadi succeeds in getting Charlie to fall in love with him, he delivers her to the Israeli team. Kurtz "befriends" Charlie and offers himself as a father figure to her. He successfully exploits her character weaknesses and, with the assistance of his team, consciously and deliberately creates a new reality for her.

> He had appealed to the actress in her, to the martyr, to the adventurer; he had flattered the daughter and excited the aspirant. He had granted her an early glimpse of the new family she might care to join, knowing that deep down, like most rebels, she was only looking for a better conformity. And most of all, by heaping such benefits upon her, he had made her rich, which, as Charlie herself had long preached to anyone who would hear her, was the beginning of subservience. . . . In her whole life, it seemed to Charlie, no group of people had been so attentive, so appreciative of her performance. They understood, she thought. (108, 113)

Le Carré graphically portrays Charlie's recruitment through psychological manipulation and the deliberate construction of a custom-made reality for that purpose. But according to Kurtz's standards, her recruitment fell short of coercion because it had a durable basis of morality. "Volunteers find their own way to persuade themselves" (142). The success of Kurtz's manipulations depended on Charlie's need and willingness to deceive herself. Kurtz uses similar but more extreme psychological techniques to break down the captive Salim, but not physical torture. "If you have to use violence, and sometimes you couldn't do much else, always be sure to use it against the mind, not the body, he said" (177).[23]

Once Charlie accepts the roe that Kurtz has cast for her, Gadi impersonates the captive, Salim, with whom she is supposed to have had a love affair. He constantly steps out from his own persona (or, at least, the one he was playing of himself for her) to that of Salim during their lengthy rehearsal of her role. They literally reenact together the fiction Kurtz scripts of Charlie's activities with Salim. "We are *building a new reality,* a better one" (148; emphasis added). During the lengthy surrealistic period of rehearsal, Charlie asks Gadi: "Do *we* exist as well? . . . Or it is just the other two?" (151). On another occasion, Gadi says: "On the *old reality* we impose the *new fiction*" (155; emphasis added). Charlie remarks on the interplay between the audience's desire to be enchanted and the actor's hope to enchant, which results in the mutual acceptance of the illusion of a new reality. "Theatre's a con trick," says Charlie (161). Le Carré demonstrates, through similar literary devices, how the theater of the real and the writing of fiction are much greater con tricks.

At several critical junctures, before Charlie is sent on dangerous missions, Gadi gives her the choice to quit or to continue. She wants him to make the decision. "Keep convincing me. . . . Do your job" (216). Gadi's show of personal concern for Charlie is interpreted by both of them as a declaration of his love to her. Gadi, like Smiley in a passage cited in chapter 1, sees this as a weakening of his professional discipline. Gadi repeatedly (and prophetically) told her, "*Stay with the logic of the fiction . . . Weaken, and you ruin the operation. Stay with the fiction, and when it's over we'll repair the damage*" (306).

Before being sent on the most dangerous part of her mission, Gadi and Charlie physically consummate their love for the first time. "And she knew . . . that he was doing something outside the script, he was closing the doors on every world but their own" (313). Their lovemaking was a way to "reassure themselves that they were who they said they were" (314). The psychological strain of relating to each other through split personalities threatened the coherence of their sense of reality. By calling "time out," as it were, they could gain a respite in which they could reassure themselves and the other.[24] In response to a question by Melvyn Bragg (1988:140) about a new departure in this novel le Carré responds: "I think it's a far more passionate book, probably the most passionate."[25]

Kurtz, at Gadi's insistence, gives Charlie the opportunity to quit with honor and financial reward before being told her final assignment, which is to locate Khalil (Salim's brother and the mastermind and bomb maker of the cell). Charlie makes her decision calmly and lucidly. She was convinced that Gadi slept with her to hold her back. But she feared that if she did turn back, she would lose his love. Therefore, his attempt to stop her merely strengthened her resolve to proceed.

On arriving in Lebanon, she found how accurate Gadi's statement about the Palestinians was: "*You will find them an easy people to love*" (327). She becomes emotionally involved and identifies with the Palestinian refugees. "As each day passed, the fiction of her pretended allegiance to Michel [Salim] became more firmly based in fact, while her allegiance to Joseph [Gadi], if not a fiction, survived only as a secret mark upon her soul" (337). "In the camp, Charlie experienced at last the sympathy that life till now had denied her" (344). On leaving the refugee camp for a training camp in terrorism, she is told by a friend she had made there: "*We are a love-affair . . . You'll go, and when you've gone, we'll be a dream*" (348). The metaphor of the dream reinforces the blurring of different realities for Charlie. When Charlie is interrogated in the training camp and is asked about Joseph, she responds naturally, without appearing to act a part. She senses "that the difference between life and art had disappeared" (367). This was exactly the goal of her training and psychological conditioning by the Israelis.

Having passed the test, Charlie is sent on her first mission by the Palestinians. At this point she consciously regards Gadi as dead and buried, "a discarded prophet from her adolescence" (374). But, despite her self-denial, by making contact with the Israeli agent at the Zurich airport, she proves her remaining loyalty to him and to them. She had done what they had asked of her. "Part of her has gone over, part has stayed" (383). As Gadi indicates, her actions are more important than words (or lack of them).

Khalil compares terror with the theater. "Terror is theatre. We inspire, we frighten, we awaken indignation, anger, love. We enlighten. The theatre also. The guerrilla is the great actor of the world" (398). Through this metaphor le Carré accomplishes a three-way association among theater, espionage, and terrorism. Espionage and terrorism are the theater of the real. Significantly, the target of the bomb he is preparing for Charlie to deliver is an Israeli professor who is a strong supporter of reconciliation and peace with the Palestinians.[26]

After delivering a booby-trapped briefcase meant to kill the Israeli professor at a public lecture in Freiburg, Charlie finally begs to back out of the operation, but it is too late. She tells Gadi that Khalil intends to sleep with her, but to no avail. As Gadi sends her on her way to meet Khalil, she looks back at him with hatred and thinks, "I'm dead" (409). When she sees the flash and hears the explosion of the bomb that Kurtz and his German counterparts have set off to deceive Khalil, Charlie hears "a distant thud, like a breaking of something *unmendable* deep inside herself; the precise and *permanent* end to love. Well, Joseph [Gadi], yes. Goodbye . . . She was without love and without value to herself. She was where she had started" (410; emphasis added).

Charlie describes the first scene of the final act, a dinner with Khalil before they go to bed, as "the worst play she had ever been in" (415). Discovering that the clock she carried in her purse was working after he had previously removed the batteries (Gadi had replaced it with one containing an electronic homing device so that they could be followed), Khalil demands to know for whom she works and why. "She had reached the end of her invention. All of it, for all time, here and for ever after" (419). She answers him honestly: "It was to save life. It was to take part. To be something. I loved him. . . . I fell in love with the man who looked after me. That's all there is" (420). At this point, Charlie appears to have acquired a level of self-awareness that had previously been conspicuously absent. "Her revelation destroys her spirit but changes her from a manipulated object to a sympathetic character" (Beene, 1992:114).

Gadi's shots blow away Khalil's face, covering Charlie with blood, and her mind snaps. In a scene reminiscent of Smiley's last encounter with Karla in *Smiley's People* (but with a twist), Charlie sees in Gadi the things she hates in herself. "So a sort of exchange of characters occurred, where she assumed his role of killer and pimp, and he, presumably, hers of decoy,

whore, and traitor." As she stared at him, "a surviving spark of outrage kindled in her, and *gave her back the identity that he had stolen from her*" (421; emphasis added).

After receiving psychiatric treatment and recuperating in Israel, Charlie
returns to England and to the stage, where she decides that comedy is "the
better mask for her" (428). During a performance the sight of Gadi in the
audience fails to surprise her, because "the divide between her inner and
outer world had been a flimsy affair at the best of times, but these days it
had virtually ceased to exist" (429). She walks off the stage, out of the theater, and into the street. She tells Gadi, who has followed her, "I'm dead,
Jose. You shot me, don't you remember?" She repeatedly says, "I'm dead."
"But it seemed that he wanted her dead or alive. *Locked together,* they set
off awkwardly along the pavement, though the town was strange to them"
(430; emphasis added).

Interpretations of Le Carré's
Political Sympathies

None of le Carré's novels have received such contradictory reviews and interpretations as has *The Little Drummer Girl.* Part of the controversy derives
from the ideological positions of the reviewers. Arab publishers would not
publish it because they found it pro-Israeli. Nationalistic Israelis and their
supporters condemned it as anti-Israeli.[27] For example, Haim Corney
(1983:6) claims that le Carré started out pro-Israel and ended up "clearly
on the Palestinian side." Writing in the *Jerusalem Post,* he quotes le Carré:
"I count myself an absolutely uncompromising friend of Israel. It may not
sound like it, but it is the case." Corney concludes: "It may also not read
like it." In contrast, Professor Yitzhak Galnoor (1983) wrote a review of the
Hebrew edition of the book in the liberal *Ha'Aretz* in which he refutes
such charges. He concludes that the book might be considered to be pro-
Israeli because only the Israeli characters see a way out of the confrontation.[28] The reality le Carré presents is interpreted through each reader's
critical and ideological prism.

Interpretation of Main Characters

Significant disagreement among scholars in their evaluation of the main
characters and the ultimate meaning of the novel dramatically illustrate the
ambiguity of le Carré's writing—particularly his portrayal of the distortions of reality involved in the world of espionage. These disagreements
highlight le Carré's view of the importance of skepticism as an antidote in
countering the venom of self and collective delusion.

Charlie

Charlie is le Carré's first female title character. Despite her Pygmalion-like relationship with Kurtz and Gadi, Rowe (1988:79) observes, "Charlie has a primacy, a power in the narrative, and le Carré goes well beyond titling in empowering Charlie by making her consciousness the primary filter for much of the action." [29] Although this is true, she is not the moral center of the novel. My interpretation of her role falls between the polar opposite interpretations of Monaghan and Lewis.

Monaghan (1985:13) compares Charlie with Smiley and concludes that "Charlie comes much nearer to achieving personal resolution than any previous le Carré hero." [30] Lewis (1985:210), however, compares Charlie with Humpty Dumpty, who can not be put back together, having been smashed: "Charlie's life since meeting Joseph cannot be unlived: her experiences cannot be erased nor can her profound sense of having become one of the living dead be easily cured." [31] Lewis (1985:211) rejects the romantic interpretation because it might vindicate Gadi Becker, who, he mistakenly claims, represents *the* Israeli position. Le Carré portrays a variety of Israeli positions, including Gadi's developing dovish stand. Consequently, the ending cannot be logically interpreted as a vindication of a nonexistent single Israeli position, much less the nationalist one of the government in power in Israel at the time the novel was written. Lewis finds le Carré's sentimental ending to be inappropriate because this separation between the personal and the political contradicts the reality depicted in this and le Carré's other novels—implicitly rejecting the possibility of the author's development. [32]

Even if one accepts, for the sake of argument, an almost consensual point that le Carré has not fundamentally altered his basic world view, the portrayal of an exception may allow the exploration of the limits of a general rule while providing arguments for its general applicability. This is what, in the social sciences, is called deviant case analysis. I suggest that *The Little Drummer Girl* may be seen either as a deviant case or as a departure for the author, signaling a development in his position. If the former, the question is: What conditions made possible this exception; and what insights does it shed on the general rule? If the latter, as I maintain, one needs to determine the nature of the development in his point of view.

Monaghan's interpretation of the efficacy of the theater of the real for Charlie's development is instructive, although it underestimates the serious psychological damage Charlie suffered. Lewis more realistically recognizes the seriousness of the damage done to Charlie's psyche and of Gadi's culpability (along with Kurtz) for her mental breakdown. But, his reluctance to see the growth of Gadi and the possibility of Charlie's recuperation precludes his recognition of their possible salvation through love. He is correct that, like Humpty Dumpty, people are not easily reassembled, but neither are they eggs. People can be amazingly resilient and live rich and meaningful lives after recuperating from the most unbelievable and unspeakable horrors—even acts of genocide. I agree with Beene (1992:122) who concludes, "Charlie's unsure union with Joseph [Gadi] promises but does not ensure a loving context for her development and a humanistic role for Joseph."

Le Carré's ambiguity encourages such contradictory interpretations. On one hand, Charlie feels an "unmendable" break inside herself and a "permanent" end to her love of Gadi when she "dies" witnessing him kill Khalil. On the other hand, she has gained self-insight (exemplified by the candid and self-revelatory nature of her response to Khalil's final question) and her "identity" through her final disillusionment brought about by the trauma of witnessing the assassination of Khalil. Further confusion is contributed by the narrator's comment that the flimsy divide between Charlie's inner and outer world had "ceased to exist" and by her repeated declarations to Gadi—"I'm dead"—which appear to contradict the commentary that Gadi wants her, "dead or alive," and the image of them walking "locked together."

Kurtz

Strikingly contradictory interpretations are given of Kurtz, the head of the Mossad team who directs the operation. Kurtz is neither as evil, as portrayed by Monaghan, nor is he the Israeli Smiley that Lewis and Bloom suggest. Monaghan (1985:187–91) views Kurtz as the personification of evil: a man for whom hatred and the denial of the humanity of his enemy dominates. Monaghan says Kurtz's life reflects the recent "history of his *race*" (187; emphasis added). Kurtz was a survivor of the Holocaust (since which it has been rather bad form to refer to Jews as a race).[33]

Monaghan claims that the most striking evidence of Kurtz's "dehumanization . . . is provided by his failure to grant independent human status to his long-time colleague and fellow Israeli patriot, Becker," and by his denial of the legitimacy of Gadi Becker's dilemmas[34] (190). The dilemma to which he refers involved Gadi's separation from his wife. Kurtz tried to get them back together. This is hardly a case substantiating a lack of humanity on Kurtz's part. He depicts Kurtz as representing "a damning indictment of Israeli ideology"—ignoring that different Israeli ideologies are presented in the novel and the fact that Kurtz and Becker represent an authentic Israeli position opposed to the government's policies.[35]

In a diametrically opposite characterization Lewis (1985:193–6) claims, "In some respects Kurtz is an Israeli version of Smiley." Le Carré's observation that Kurtz "was too paradoxical, too complicated, made up of too many souls and colours," is highly reminiscent of Smiley (27). Beyond physical similarities, Lewis finds sociological ones. For example, they are both maverick outsiders. They are both patriots at odds with their respective Establishments. Both have contempt for their political and administrative masters. They both are masters of political maneuvering to get backing for their operations. Both assemble teams of loyal followers. In addition, Lewis points out that Kurtz, like Gadi Becker, is strongly opposed to Israeli military intervention against the Palestinians and (mistakenly) sees his operation as a means of precluding such an impending operation. This is an important point ignored by Monaghan.

Sauerberg (1984:63–4, 207) also points out similarities between Kurtz and Smiley, including the way they defend their occupation, the moderation of his dovish position, which differs markedly from the hawkish government, expressing a belief in rationalism as the only alternative to absolutism and in the "redeeming power of a sense of humanity." Harold Bloom (1987:4) claims that "Kurtz is a remarkable success in characterization." Bloom emphasizes Kurtz's "professional ethics, his Smiley-like sense of limits, of a philosophy of restraint, and even of decency, which is after all totally incompatible with counterterrorism"(5). Beene (1992:115–18) gives a balanced analysis that compares their similarities and contrasts their differences, especially Kurtz's lack of Smiley's reflectiveness, angst for individuals, relativism, and perpetual doubt. Beene (1992:116) more accurately captures the essence of their difference when she says, "le Carré never allows Kurtz's conscience to suffer for his actions and hence fails to invest Kurtz with heroic stature." Yet she dismisses this very quality in Gadi Becker as his "degenerating spirit" (117). The exaggerated focus on Kurtz by these scholars prevents them from analyzing important aspects of Gadi Becker's central role.

Gadi

Gadi most resembles Smiley in critical respects and is the key to understanding the ultimate implications of the novel and questions about le Carré's developing position. Of the authors who have written books analyzing le Carré's work, only Homberger (1986:95) mentions Gadi's "inner link with Smiley" and his "complex and paradoxical character."[36] In sharp contrast, Bloom (1987:4) calls Gadi "a failure in representation."[37]

Only Rowe (1988:81) notes that the quest in the novel is Gadi Becker's, not Charlie's. "Whatever the change in Charlie, it comes through

Gadi Becker. The important point that le Carré is making is not about Charlie as a questor but about Becker as moral agent. Becker comes to see Charlie as neither a means to power nor a perk that comes with power; rather, he views Charlie as a moral end in herself." Even if we were to accept the contention that Smiley does not develop as a character (the position argued by Monaghan and by Barley), it is entirely possible that Gadi Becker is a younger successor who displays abilities to learn from experiences and to develop as a character in ways which Smiley (perhaps because of his age) may have lacked.

Before the reader meets Gadi, Kurtz's assistant notes the "big compliment" Kurtz pays to Becker by traveling to Berlin (where he is studying) to see him. Kurtz says: "Gadi made his contribution. . . . No man made a better, according to his ability. He fought in hard places, most of them behind the lines. Why should he not remake himself? He is entitled to his peace" (39). In response to the question why he was then calling Gadi back into service, Kurtz elliptically describes Gadi as the "middle ground" (39). "Because he has the *reluctance* that can make the bridge. Because he *ponders*" (40; emphasis added). In other words, because Gadi (like Smiley) questions assumptions and can empathize with his opponents, he is perfect for the job. Kurtz, claiming Gadi to be the best agent he ever had, praises his courage and his sensitivity (140). Gadi is both a "bleeding heart" and a "red-toothed warrior" (243). Like Smiley, Gadi is described as "legendary" (355).

The narrator refers to Gadi's uneasy conscience (67). Kurtz feels Gadi "haunting me like my own bad conscience" (354). By using "they" with reference to his fellow Mossad team members, Charlie picks up on his ambivalence toward them and possible alienation from them (140). "*They,* she thought. Never *we*" (285). As Gadi convincingly presents the Palestinian case against Israel to Charlie, she marvels at "the paradoxes of a man who could dance with so many of his conflicting shadows, and still stand up" (181). This is strikingly similar to a description of Smiley in *Smiley's People* (279): "George has got too many hats under his head."

Gadi is shown in soul-searching anguish. While viewing his own features in a mirror with distaste, he asks himself who he is. The italics in the original stress that he is a man of feeling: "I *feel* as if I am looking at a dead friend, hoping he will come alive. I *feel* that I am an actor, as you are, surrounding myself with versions of my identity because the original somehow went missing along the road. But in truth I feel nothing, because real feeling is subversive and contrary to military discipline. Therefore I do not feel, but I fight and therefore I exist" (194). Although he continues to fight, Gadi "doesn't like the killing any more!" (204). "*I have killed enough Arabs*" (242). Gadi "was in essence a kind man, of instinctive sympathy for everyone; in battle and in peace, a troubled man who hated causing pain" (314). In response to Charlie's question what he fought for, he replies:"'In '56 because I wanted to be a hero, in '67 for peace. And in '73'—he seemed to find it harder to remember—'for Israel,' he said"[38] (218). He moves from youthful patriotism in the Sinai Campaign to a somewhat more mature form of idealism during the Six Day War, to a growing ambivalence about the Yom Kippur War. At this stage in his battle against terrorism he, like Smiley in a passage cited earlier, feels the cords of his professional discipline loosen as he matures and questions more (219).

While Charlie is undergoing terrorist training in Lebanon, Gadi goes back to Israel on a "journey of self-appraisal regarding the *basic assumptions of his life*" (355; emphasis added). He places flowers on his father's grave, a symbol of Israel's egalitarian pioneering past and recites the mourner's prayer, *Kaddish,* in his father's memory (and perhaps in memory of those values). He visits the village from which Salim and Khalil's family fled in 1967, a symbol of the consequences of Israel's "victory" in that war. He is described as "looking troubled . . . Sick in his eyes and complexion" (356). At the kibbutz on the Lebanese border "where, if anywhere he kept his heart" (356), his friends ask questions that spoke "into the void in his own soul" (357). In his visits to the Lebanese border, to the occupied territories on the West Bank, and to Jerusalem (where he visits the Holocaust museum and memorial), "He seemed to question everything he saw" (358). Kurtz hears of this and recalls him to Europe. Shortly before Charlie's final assignment, the narrator describes Gadi "staring *self-critically* into the gathering dark, like a man *examining all the promises of his past life*—which had he kept? Which broken?" (397; emphasis added). This portrait is of a man far more like George Smiley than is le Carré's portrayal of Kurtz or of any other character in this or any of the other post-Smiley novels. They exhibit the most successful development of a liberal, skeptical, balanced position.

Gadi's character and "ideological" position evolve as he questions basic Zionist assumptions. His role-playing of Salim strengthens his empathy for the plight of the Palestinians and his recognition of their humanity. Beene (1992:119–20), however, would have him go further:"Were he a character of secure moral temperament, Joseph [Gadi] could abandon the Mossad, subvert Charlie's indoctrination to rescue her, and expose his superior's faulty rationale. Instead, his uncertainties about Kurtz's purposes, the validity of war, and his responsibility for Charlie blind him to any emotional consequences. His physical scars from battle and emotional ones from divorce, like Charlie's, leave him another hollow, perfect actor." Beene's failure to either recognize or to respect the depth of Gadi's dilemmas (just as she previously ignores or discounts Smiley's moral anguish when he traps

Karla) prevents her from granting him heroic stature. Gadi cannot abandon the Mossad and subvert the mission because, despite his opposition to his government's policies, he is a patriotic Israeli (just as Goethe in *The Russia House* was a Russian patriot).[39] Although the Israeli government in power at that time (and the one at the time of my writing this book) exploits a sense of national insecurity, Gadi is very aware that Israel has real enemies. Because he was sick of war (he had been fighting his entire adult life), he hoped that with Kurtz, they could prevent an Israeli attack on Palestinian bases in Lebanon by eliminating the terrorist ring. His conflicting loyalties intensified as he began to fall in love with Charlie. He was not blind to the emotional consequences of the operation for himself, for Charlie, or for their relationship. He even repeatedly offered her a chance to get out of the operation, except at the very end, when it was too late. With all of his scars (and moral blemishes) he was *not* a hollow actor.

Critical Interpretations of the Novel

Le Carré does not offer a "solution" to the century old conflict between Israeli and Palestinian nationalism. On the contrary, this novel implies that there is no solution.[40] Through Kurtz's and Gadi's concerns, he presciently anticipates the attack by the government headed by Menachem Begin on the Palestinian forces in the war in Lebanon in 1982. "The deal is that a lot of people in Jerusalem would prefer to charge the windmills of Lebanon than fight the enemy with their heads" (39). Through Gadi, le Carré also anticipates the undermining of the reified mutual demonization of the Other by Israelis and Palestinians that was an essential precursor to political dialogue, which eventually led to the Oslo Accords.[41]

Le Carré's conclusion is deliberately ambiguous because, among other reasons, the real situation is morally and politically ambiguous. That Charlie and Gadi are "locked together" may be interpreted as an act of desperation as well as a sign of hope. They "set off awkwardly," le Carré says, indicating the uncertainty of their venture. The final words, "the town was strange to them," reinforces the notion of the uncertainty of their unknown destination together. At the same time, it offers the *possibility* that Gadi and Charlie may, through their love, help each other overcome their respective traumas. Le Carré hints that Gadi's experience in surviving traumas and that "he listened to the unclear voices of his own inner mind" (426) might give him the strength to overcome this one as well. Charlie's prognosis is more uncertain. But both Gadi's and Charlie's moral development, and the strength he can give to help Charlie recover, leaves the reader with reason to hope but with far less than sanguine certainty of the outcome.[42]

Silver (1987:38) notes: "Charlie's assertion of a new identity, however, proves insubstantial; on her own she is incapable of withstanding the ghosts of the men who dominate her thoughts and actions. . . . Instead, I would argue, the promise of change resides in the acts of exchange, of twinning or merging, that occur between Charlie and Joseph, where le Carré offers what is perhaps the only hope he perceives for a new cultural story of *heterosexual* desire."[43] Israeli and Palestinian Gadi Beckers made possible the mutual recognition by Israel and the PLO, the Oslo Accords, and the interim agreements between Israel and the Palestinian Authority.[44] Although Charlie is not a Palestinian, her "conversion" to the Palestinian side through her experiences may make her relationship with Gadi of wider political significance.

The Post-Cold War Novels

In determining whether *The Little Drummer Girl* is a deviant case or the turning point in le Carré's point of view, one needs to examine how other characters deal with their illusions in confrontation with harsh realities in the later novels. The fate of Magnus Pym (*A Perfect Spy*), whom Rowe (1988:82) terms a "sociopath," was singularly unambiguous. He committed suicide.[45] The most generous possible interpretation of their ends, seen from the perspective of Pym and Poppy, is that they act together to exchange secrets on the high moral ground of furthering the balance between the opposing superpowers to the point at which they dare not take military action. This would make the goal of their betrayal idealism and love. Although the two characters may see it this way, this rationalization appears to be a justification for their more selfish personal motives.

The plot of *The Russia House* (1989) pertains to this theme. A Russian physicist, Yakov Yefremovich Savelyev, a.k.a. Goethe (code-named Bluebird), is anxious to publish in the West top-secret documents that reveal the inadequacy of the Soviet missile guidance system.[46] He chooses an English publisher, by whom he is impressed during an encounter among mutual friends, to entrust with his manuscript. Goethe's intermediary fails to contact this man, Bartholomew "Barley" Scott Blair, because he fails to appear at a Moscow trade fair. Instead, she passes the manuscript to another man, with instructions to give it only to Blair. When this man fails to locate Barley Blair, he passes it on to the British Secret Service. Barley is then recruited by the Russia House, an out-station of the British Secret Service (known as the Circus before it moved to new headquarters), to be the intermediary in contact with Goethe, who refuses to deal with them.

Within both the British Service and the CIA, some doubt the authenticity of Goethe's information and others do not. Similarly, there is disagreement over whether Barley can be trusted. The means used by Clive, the deputy director of the Service, and by his allies in the CIA to authenticate both Barley and Goethe result in Goethe's capture and execution and therefore to Barley's decision to do a deal with the Russians. The only thing that is not clear is whether the exposure of Goethe was an intended or an unintended consequence of these actions. The hawks among the Americans and British had good reasons to have wanted to prevent Goethe's revelations from being known, even by their leaders, much less by the wider public. These revelations would have eliminated the need to maintain at such high levels, much less expand, their own defense establishments, including the inflated top-secret budgets of the intelligence agencies. Ned, the head of the Russia House, explains to Palfrey (the legal adviser) why Goethe's information supported the strategic assumptions of the doves, which did him in.[47]

> So the camps divide. The hawks cry, 'The Sovs are pinpoint! They can knock the smile off the arse of a fly at ten thousand miles!' And all the doves can reply is 'We don't know what the Sovs can do, and the Sovs don't know what the Sovs can do. And nobody who doesn't know whether his gun works or not is going to shoot first. It's the uncertainty that keeps us honest,' say the doves. But that is not an argument that satisfies the literal American mind, you see, because the literal American mind does not like to grapple with fuzzy concepts or grand visions. Not at its literal field level. And what Goethe was saying was an even larger heresy. He was saying that the uncertainty was all there was. Which I rather agree with. So the hawks hated him and the doves had a ball and hanged themselves from the chandelier. . . . If Goethe had only backed the pinpoint boys instead, everything would have been fine. (332–33)

"The greatest danger to mankind is not the *reality* of Soviet power but the *illusion* of it."[48] The manner in which the Western and Soviet strategists target each other, based on each side's assumptions about the other, adds to the surrealistic effect of reflections within reflections within reflections— like the Russian dolls that come apart, with a smaller version inside each one.[49] Similarly, the members of a committee appointed to perform a postmortem on the failed operation, "to impart a sense of ceremony to events that have passed off without any" (340), trade conspiracy theories and engage in contradictory interpretations of whether the Soviet reaction, or lack of reaction, validated or invalidated Goethe's information. Only Ned, accepting blame, consistently argues that both Barley and Goethe were straight: "There was no deception, except where *we deceived ourselves*. It was we who were crooked. Not Bluebird [Goethe]" (341; emphasis added).

Barley ends up in Lisbon awaiting the arrival of his Russian lover (and her children), whom the Russians promised to release and send to him in exchange for the shopping list of questions the Americans had given him to pass on to Goethe. "They don't break their promises," he assured Palfrey (his interrogator) who thinks, "in the face of such trust it would have been churlish in me to contradict him." Palfrey, who is also the narrator, recalls the accusation of his lover: "You think people never change because you don't. . . . You only feel safe when you're disenchanted" (352). As Barley watches for the ship to arrive from Leningrad, Palfrey thinks: "He was believing in all the hopes that I had buried with me when I chose the safe bastion of infinite distrust in preference to the dangerous path of love" (352).

Le Carré leaves it to the reader to determine whether Barley will be reunited with his lover. He told Truehart (1989:D3) that the outcome "depends on who you are when you read the end of the book."[50] The jaundiced eye of the cynical narrator throws doubt on the likelihood of such a happy ending. Le Carré is deliberately ambiguous, however, particularly since the lovers are symbols of possible collaboration between Russia and the West. When the novel was made into a movie, Hollywood, being as much a producer of fantasy and illusion as the secret world and a less subtle one than is le Carré, an unambiguously happy ending was created. In the movie, Michelle Pfeiffer walks down the gangplank and into the waiting arms of Sean Connery. Le Carré's subtlety was evidently lost on the film's producers.

Smiley's reappearance in *The Secret Pilgrim* (1990)[51] indicates the development of greater clarity of his positions, as is suggested in chapter 1: "Oh, there's *some* art to faulting the liar. . . . But the real art lies in recognizing the truth, which is a great deal harder (67). And just occasionally we meet the *reality* we've been playing with. . . . Until this happens, we're spectators. . . . But when the moment of truth strikes—*if* it ever does for you—well, from then on we become a little more humble about what we ask people to do for us" (154; emphasis added). For those who may have mistakenly considered Smiley (or le Carré) an absolute relativist, this passage (and others quoted in chapter 1) clarify that he feels there is a truth that can be recognized only by overcoming self-and collective delusions.[52] The insertion of the phrase "*if* it ever does for you" indicates Smiley's (le Carré's) feeling that the moment of truth does not always strike—especially individuals involved in the secret world. Those involved in espionage operations must realize that they play with reality and with the lives of their agents. Ned, Smiley's protégé who runs the spy school where Smiley is speaking (he headed the Russia House in the previous novel), says, "Very few conspiracies, Smiley once remarked, survive contact with *reality*" (177; emphasis added).

Another story in this novel illustrates the exceptional case when deception can be humane and morally appropriate. Smiley reinforces the illusion of the elderly parents of a criminal (killed by fellow inmates) who had lied to his parents by telling them he worked for the secret service. Smiley "awards" them a pair of gold cufflinks (which had been given to him by Ann) in posthumous recognition of their son's having sacrificed his life for his country. "For once, the mythology of espionage would be used not to disguise another tale of incompetence or betrayal, but to leave an old couple with their dreams. For once, Smiley could look at an intelligence operation and say with absolute confidence that it had worked" (258).

The ostensible hero of *The Night Manager* (1993) is Jonathan Pine, a former member of an elite British military unit who served in Northern Ireland. Pine is recruited by Leonard Burr, the head of Enforcement (a new unit created to end the illegal sale of arms and drugs) to help him trap Richard Onslow Roper, an international dealer of high-tech weapons (which he calls toys) to dictators, revolutionaries, and bosses of drug cartels. Pine and Burr are betrayed by an alliance of corrupt officials of British and American intelligence in collusion with Roper. While being tortured by Roper's goons, Pine contrasts himself with Roper: "You who are so proud of believing in nothing, and me down here with my faith in everything intact" (418). Pine escapes with his life (and with Roper's mistress) through the brilliant scheming of Burr. The tactics Burr employs involve a great bluff. "NO TWO BLUFFS are the same, but one component is necessary to all of them, and that is the complicity between the deceiver and the deceived, the mystical interlocking of opposing needs" (400). Pine ends up living with his lover in a remote cottage, raising horses and painting.[53]

The most idealistic character in this novel is Rex Goodhew, mistakenly described by Sunday papers as "Whitehall's Talleyrand without the limp." Actually, "Goodhew was nothing that he seemed. If there was a separateness about him, it came of virtue, not intrigue." He was "a high-minded Anglican of reforming zeal" with "a pretty wife and clever children who adored him" (47). Yet his naïve belief in the innate goodness of others and the importance of always playing according to the rules of the game led to his defeat and to the failure of Enforcement to foil a major arms for drug operation. Goodhew's minister (a nebulous politician to whom he refers as "my master") regards pure intelligence (the procurement studies group, popularly known as "the river boys") as "realists" and the newer enforcement agency, created by Goodhew under the direction of Burr, as "idealistic" (48). My reading of le Carré is that he uses the term *realist* as a virtual synonym for cynic. Whereas Burr may have been to a certain extent idealistic, I suggest that his idealism was balanced by experience and street smarts, making him what I define as a skeptic.

Burr, who had spent his career with the river boys before taking on his new "underfinanced, underwanted agency," thought otherwise (50). "I've lived with them. Lied with them . . . and I *know* there's more crookery in that shop, more bad promises to keep, more lunching with the enemy, and gamekeepers turned poachers, than is healthy for my operation, or my agency!" When Goodhew informs Burr that his minister wants him to co-operate with Geoffrey Darker, head of the Procurement Studies Group, he responds: "Darker *is* wicked. . . . So why do we have to ponce around pretending Darker's a realist?" (49). Just as Karla is Smiley's Black Grail, so Roper is Burr's "personal Antichrist" (50). Burr shares other Smiley-like qualities, including decency, strong personal concern for the welfare of his agents, integrity, and a skeptical outlook that is premised on strong values but is tempered by the recognition of evil and a willingness to fight when necessary to combat it. He is also a maverick (57). Although Pine is center stage in the novel's action, Burr is the most balanced and mature character and therefore the true hero of the story.[54]

One of the two central characters in *Our Game* (1995), the mercurial double agent Larry Pettifer, fails to achieve such balance. His naïve emotional impulses lead to his death while fighting in a Checheniya-like war against the Russians, presumably with all his illusions intact.[55] His counterpart, former boss, lifelong friend, and rival, Tim Cranmer, pursues him and his own conscience: "Finding himself deprived of both past and future, a dispossessed loyalist, he must grapple with his own leftover humanity as the values he fought to preserve fall away, and the spectre of the reinvented Russian empire begins to haunt the ruins of the Soviet dream."[56] Le Carré economically contrasts the two through the narration of Tim: "Instead we have Larry *redux,* Larry the world-dreamer and Sunday sermoniser, one moment raging against the shameful Western inertia, the next painting treacly visions of altruistic wars conducted by the United Nations strike force empowered to put on its Batman uniform and head off tyranny, pestilence, and famine at a moment's notice. And since I happen to regard such fantasies as dangerous hogwash, it is my luckless role to act the family skeptic" (39).

Characteristically, le Carré ends the novel on an ambiguous note. Larry, the latter-day Lawrence of Arabia, is martyred in the cause of the Ingush. Tim, who had been talking to Larry's former KGB handler and collaborator in the Ingush cause, is left alone as he walks away: "For a moment longer I stood alone, converted to nothing, believing in nothing. I had no world to go back to and nobody left to run except myself. A Kalashnikov lay beside me. Slinging it across my shoulder, I hastened after him down the slope" (302). The implication is that Tim, "up-tight, manipulative, incapable of loving,"[57] has completed a spiritual journey and, if not taking over Larry's extreme romanticism, has at least made a reluctant commitment to the cause of the underdog Ingush. He, after long vacillation (like President Clinton over Bosnia), finally makes a commitment and chooses action over restraint.

Harry Pendel, the Pym-like character for whom *The Tailor of Panama* is named, is a deliberate takeoff on the vacuum cleaner salesman in Graham Greene's *Our Man in Havana*.[58] Both characters invent their reports to please their controllers. As Michael Wood (1996:16) points out, this is a case of "the secret agent as the creator of extravagantly imagined worlds." Harry Pendel has as formidable a talent for invention (which he calls "fluence") as he has for tailoring.[59] "But reality was no longer Pendel's subject, if it ever had been" (275). In an interview with Scott Simon on National Public Radio, le Carré explains that "tailoring is a metaphor for shaping other people's lives and, beyond that again, shaping the intelligence that he later provided to the British when he was recruited as a spy."[60]

Pendel is blackmailed, bribed, seduced, and duped into spying for the British by Andy Osnard, an amoral and corrupt son of lesser gentry. "He had no craft or qualification, no proven skills outside the golf course and the bedroom. What he understood best was English rot, and what he needed was a decaying English institution that would restore to him what other decaying institutions had taken away" (207). He first tried journalism and an animal charity (where he engaged in fraud). He toyed with the idea of a career in the Anglican Church and the BBC, before he found his grail in the Secret Service: "Here at last was his true Church of England, his rotten borough with a handsome budget. . . . Here were sceptics, dreamers, zealots and mad abbots. And the cash to make them real" (208).

The plot hinges on the fact that the United States is scheduled to relinquish the Panama Canal on December 31, 1999. The top-secret Planning and Application Committee, led by the British Treasury, headed by Geoffrey Cavendish (a "freelancer" also known as "Boom-boom Cavendish, arms broker" and "Geoff the Oil") and including a member of parliament and a media baron, plots to revive Great Britain's special relationship with the United States and the power and influence gained through this relationship by persuading the Americans not to abandon the canal. Their contact in the British Secret Service, Luxmore (who is in charge of Iberia and South America), charges Osnard with the task "to provide the *grounds,* young Mr. Osnard, the *arguments,* the *evidence* needful to bring our American allies to their senses" (213). Luxmore instructs Osnard that a born intelligencer "knows what he is looking for before he finds it . . . He intuits. He selects" (214). And he implies that he creatively invents if necessary.

From Harry Pendel, through Osnard and Luxmore, and eventually the British ambassador to Panama and his head of Chancery, to Cavendish and his committee, each actor at every level participates in perpetuating and elaborating the fictive intelligence generated by Pendel and his accomplice, with ultimately tragic consequences. This is perhaps le Carré's ultimate novel of self-deceit and collective deceit. Le Carré is reported to have said, "I would love to know what the CIA has spent on fabricated information. . . . Over the last 25 years it must be half the national debt."[61] He claims that "everyone is using truth as his whore" for their own purposes, which leads to destructive consequences. In this story, the deceptions work, and the United States is "tricked" into invading Panama again with tragic loss of many innocent lives.

Pendel has an apparent epiphany when he realizes how he can use his best friend's suicide to reconcile the pressures from London to provide a smoking gun to justify the American invasion. "In one glorious ray of revelation he saw beyond melancholy, death, and passivity to grand validation of his life as an artist, an act of symmetry and defiance, vengeance and reconciliation, a majestic leap into a realm where all *the spoiling limitations of reality are swept away by the larger truth of the creator's dream*" (384; emphasis added). Pendel, driven by his guilt in recognizing the consequences of his fantasies, ends up walking into an inferno ignited by the invasion in atonement for his sins.[62] His final thought is "certainly in the place that he was headed for, nobody would ever again ask him to improve on life's *appearances,* neither would they mistake his *dreaming* for their terrible *reality*" (407; emphasis added).

Wood (1996:16) points out that Pendel represents "the possibility of the terminal invasion of the material world by rampant fictions." He notes le Carré's observation in *The Night Manager* that for a bluff to work, there must be complicity between the deceiver and the deceived. The real authors of the fiction were those who commissioned Pendel's fantasies because that is what they wanted to believe in order to give them the power they lacked. Wood interprets le Carré's message as "saying that make-believe power is morally one of the most dangerous forms of power there is, and that London is where we find it at home" (16).

Conclusion: Skepticism as a Balance Between Idealism and Cynicism

Le Carré suggests that to a certain degree idealism, faith, and illusion are necessary and desirable, but when the disparity between them and reality is excessive, they lead to tragic consequences, both personally and collectively. Le Carré (1966:549; emphasis added) says "that can come upon any of us who fill in the *gap* between the *dream* and *reality*." The tragedy, as his statement in the epigraph to this chapter indicates, comes from the disproportion between the two. Significantly, this corresponds with scientific findings that self-deception has been beneficial in evolution, and, within limits, is generally psychologically beneficial.[63] In excess, however, it can be self-destructive and socially disastrous.

A strong line of simplistic, wishful, chauvinistic thinking in one or another character, people who, for very Honourable reasons, often . . . their own natural intellectual limitations, are loyal, decent, unashamedly patriotic blokes, like Jerry Westerby in *The Honourable Schoolboy* or Jim Prideaux in *Tinker, Tailor, Soldier, Spy*. People who have almost deliberately foreshortened their critical faculties in order to believe in their country right or wrong, and those chaps ironically, always get the worst drubbing in the story because *you simply cannot cease to criticise,* however noble one's reasons. (Le Carré, 1979:340; emphasis added)

Similarly excessive pessimism poisons the soul as it does the polity. Justifications of *raison d'état* lead to crimes committed in the name of the state. As indicated earlier (see chapter 1), le Carré considers cynicism toward moral obligation a grave danger to society. Sauerberg (1984:193) notes le Carré's concern with "a general human need to create existential significance by reacting against alienating forces" (Note the similarity of this concern and the phenomenological assumptions outlined in the Introduction). The balance between these two extremes can only be achieved through skepticism, "an understanding of life as consisting of facets of many patterns and colours, not all of them equally pleasant" (197).[64]

Just as exceptional paradigmatic heroes like Smiley, Gadi Becker, and Leonard Burr, who struggle to achieve what I term a *skeptical* position, balancing idealism with realism, show the extreme difficulty of the balancing act, they also suggest that it may not be entirely impossible either. The term *liberal temperament* perfectly characterizes my understanding of le Carré's disposition or underlying ideological orientation. The notion of flexibility helps to clarify the notion of balance, the pursuit of which I consider an essential feature of the liberal temperament.[65] I understand balance to be achieved by leaning first one way and then the other, much like a tightrope-walker uses her hands or a balancing pole to maintain equilibrium.[66] The cynic's lack of faith in human sincerity and integrity causes a tilt so far in the direction of excessive realism that she falls from the wire, as does the naïve by tilting too far to excessive idealism. The skeptic, who is inclined to critically question accepted truths,[67] does so as a means of preventing the excesses of self-and collective deception.

The liberal skeptic questions in the hope that a clearer vision thereby obtained can lead to a more meaningful personal and collective existence. Accepting human frailty, he or she expects to make compromises but not of integrity.

The need for skeptical balance in the world of espionage is dramatically illustrated by the self-deceptive arrogance of this excerpt from a directive by George Young, who was vice-chief of SIS at the time it was circulated in 1955: "It is the spy who has been called upon to remedy the situation created by the deficiencies of ministers, diplomats, generals and priests. . . . The spy finds himself the main guardian of intellectual integrity. . . . Men's minds are shaped, of course, by their environment and we spies, although we have our professional mystique, do perhaps live closer to the realities and hard facts of international relations than other practitioners of government."[68] Le Carré's liberal temperament and skeptical outlook, shaped by his own experience and disillusionment with the secret world, directly refute Young's contention.[69]

Chapter 4

Balancing Means and Ends: The Limits of *Raison d'État*

I tried to tickle the public conscience with the issue of raison d'état. I have posed the question: for how long can we defend ourselves . . . by methods of this kind, and still remain the kind of society that is worth defending? (John le Carré)[1]

No ethics in the world can dodge the fact that in numerous instances the attainment of "good" ends is bound to the fact that one must be willing to pay the price of using morally dubious means or at least dangerous ones—and facing the possibility or even the probability of evil ramifications. From no ethics in the world can be concluded when and to what extent the ethically good purpose "justifies" the ethically dangerous means and ramifications. (Max Weber)[2]

Introduction to the Problem

Le Carré has George Smiley directly address the subject of this chapter.[3] "The end *may* justify the means—if it wasn't supposed to, I dare say you wouldn't be here. But there's a price to pay, and the price tends to be oneself" (*The Secret Pilgrim,* 1991:10). Through this warning to a group of young intelligence agents, le Carré poses a key dilemma that runs throughout all of his work. How can democracies reconcile the goal of protecting their openness and the trust on which democratic government depends with the means used by their intelligence agencies, which rely on secrecy, deception, manipulation, and willingness to sacrifice the lives of innocent people, in the name of protecting democratic freedoms?

The paradox expressed by Smiley and by Max Weber in the above epigraphs was also articulated by General Jimmy Doolittle: "It is now clear that we are facing an implacable enemy whose avowed objective is world domination by whatever means and at whatever cost. There are no rules in such a game. Hitherto acceptable norms of human conduct do not apply.

If the United States is to survive, long-standing American concepts of fair play must be reconsidered. . . . It may be necessary that the American people be made acquainted with, understand, and support this fundamentally repugnant philosophy."[4]

A fictional member of the Dutch underground imprisoned by the Gestapo in *De Aanslag (The Assault),* a novel by Harry Mulisch (1982:54) expresses a similar viewpoint: "We have to change a little bit to be like them [the Nazis] in order to fight them, a little bit not to be like ourselves, while they are not bothered by it [hatred]; They can destroy us without a problem. First we must destroy ourselves a little before we can destroy them. Not them. They can remain themselves, that is why they are so strong. But because there is no light in them, eventually they will lose. The only thing is we have to take care that we don't become too much like them, that we don't destroy ourselves too much, because then eventually they will have won."[5]

This paradox is more complex than is implied by the personal dilemmas expressed by Smiley and the Dutch freedom fighter. Although the price paid by those who run the agents (like Smiley) may be high, it is often higher for their agents. (The Dutch agent is executed by the Gestapo). Broad societal and political costs are implied in what Doolittle calls this "repugnant philosophy." "Smiley is talking not only about the soul of the spy, but also about the soul of the country paying the spy."[6] Smiley's statement accepts that all states engage in such activities and even suggests that they have this right. Le Carré (1979:48) has written that "sound and accurate intelligence-gathering is a crucial activity of any modern government."[7] But, unlike the American Revolutionary War patriot and spy Nathan Hale, le Carré would not agree that: "every kind of service necessary to the public good, becomes honorable by being necessary."[8]

Godfrey Hodgson (1977:E6) suggests in an interview with le Carré that the author seems to morally justify intelligence work, which, at the same time, he portrays as useless and pernicious. Le Carré responds: "You are absolutely right. You've nailed the paradox. . . . We are divided. Those of us who have been on nodding terms with these outfits have learned, very seriously, to wonder whether they're any bloody good at all. But if they are good, if they're going to stand up and be counted against the KGB, which without doubt is a ruthless, messy, vile, and very effective organization, are we going to feel safe with them? So that I don't think I'm being slippery when I say that the paradox is one we all share." Eric Homberger (1986:89; emphasis added) reveals another dimension of the paradox: "Buried deep in le Carré's imagination, and at the heart of his troubled humanism, there lies a *horror of manipulation,* a belief that the calculated use of feelings for 'professional' reasons constitutes a violation of personal integrity, trust and the basis for the 'human bond'. Yet manipulation is part of the necessary arsenal of espionage. (Novelists are, in their work the most extravagant manipulators of all.) Manipulation and betrayal are central to the general structure of corruption and falsehood in the world of his novels."

Comparative Background to the Problem

The question of when political necessity may appropriately outweigh values like piety and justice is one of the permanent political dilemmas debated by the ancient Greeks. "More generally the truth of the Athenian thesis raises the nagging question of where (and if) one may draw the line between the demands of necessity and the realm of human virtue and choice."[9] As a perennial problem, it plagues us to this day. It was most succinctly formulated by Max Weber (1946:120), who distinguishes between an "ethic of ultimate ends," in which the goal justifies the means, and an "ethic of responsibility," in which case "one has to give an account of the foreseeable results of one's actions." A decision faced by Prime Minister Winston Churchill and by President Franklin D. Roosevelt (and later President Truman) during World War II is a paradigmatic example of this moral dilemma.

A team of mathematicians and cryptographers working for British intelligence, using a German cipher machine called Enigma, supplied the Allies with a constant flow of intelligence of deciphered German military communications (code-named Ultra). Enigma enabled the British to read intercepted military reports detailing the extermination of Jews by ordinary German police units as early as July 18, 1941. Recently declassified evidence supports charges by researchers that Britain and the United States withheld information about the mass killing of Jews until the discovery of the concentration camps toward the end of the war.[10] An argument might credibly be made for inaction on the part of the Allies in the earliest phases of the war in order to prevent tipping off the Germans that their ciphers were being read, thereby serving the general interest of defeating the fascists.[11] After there was independent corroboration of the Final Solution from other sources later in the war, however, actions such as the bombing of rail links to the camps could have easily been undertaken without jeopardizing Ultra.[12]

Although one can debate the wisdom or ethical implications of such difficult decisions, democratically elected leaders have the authority and even the obligation to make them on behalf of those who elect them. But more serious questions arise when unelected officials in the intelligence community usurp the authority of the democratically elected officials. Those who set themselves up as self-appointed guardians to remedy situations they perceive to have been created by politicians (and others) pose a serious threat to democracy. Imagine if intelligence or military personnel decided to keep the aforementioned information about the Final Solution from the prime minister or president either to protect the secrecy of Ultra or to prevent the diversion of military resources for purposes they deemed not directly related to winning the war.

Significantly, the Soviet mole in British intelligence, George Blake (1990:168), agrees with Young's view cited in the conclusion of the chapter 3. It is precisely such intellectual and moral arrogance that (along with his belief in predestination, determinism, and communism) Blake justified his betrayal of his loved ones, friends, colleagues, and adopted country: "I weighed all this up and, in the end, felt that I should take this guilt upon me, however heavy. To be in a position to render assistance to so great a cause and not do so, would be an even greater wrong" (142). He defended his treason by distinguishing public from private interest: "One would never dream of doing any of these things as a private individual in pursuit of one's own personal interests, but one is quite capable of doing them in one's official capacity when one is acting in what one believes to be the interest of one's country or one's cause. Perhaps *I possess this ability to distinguish and separate the personal from the official to a higher degree* and it was this that enabled me to do my work as a Soviet agent" (147; emphasis added). This is a classic device for disengaging self-monitoring mechanisms in the exercise of moral agency. It is also a form of rationalization and of self-delusion that differs radically from Smiley's self-questioning skeptical stance.

Le Carré's Presentation of the Problem

The intellectual and moral arrogance expressed by Young and by Blake has been put, in various forms, by le Carré into the mouth of some of his most despicable villains.[13] The flamboyant Terence Fielding, senior housemaster of Carne, a self-described dead soul, "Vampire of Carne, Alcoholique et poete" (45), who is revealed to be the double murderer in *A Murder of Quality,* is perhaps the prototype. Smiley finds Fielding "deceitful and perverse" (46) and "the most accomplished liar Smiley had met in a long time" (125). He murdered in cold blood his own student and the wife of a colleague merely to protect his job—morally indefensible means for such a selfish goal. Fielding represents the decadence of the British aristocracy and the means they are willing to use to perpetuate their anachronistic positions and desperately maintain Britain's influence in world affairs. Le Carré clearly condemns the first goal and questions the price paid for the second.

The tone of *The Spy Who Came in from the Cold* (17) is set early by the statement of the central character, Leamas: "Intelligence work has one moral law—it is justified by results." Control tells him that "since the war, our methods—ours and those of the opposition—have become much the same. I mean you can't be less ruthless than the opposition simply because your government's policy is benevolent" (24). The difference is that "we are *defensive*" (23). This is paired with a description of the Russian agent Peters "for whom the end and the means are identical"(88).

The East German counterespionage officer Fiedler tries to engage the reluctant British agent Leamas in a discussion of this theme. Comparing communist and Western intelligence agencies, he concludes: "All our work—yours and mine—is rooted in the theory that the whole is more important than the individual. . . . The exploitation of individuals can only be justified by the collective need, can't it?" (132). Fiedler probes the philosophy and motives of the Circus and concludes: "We're all the same, you know, that's the joke"(184). The refrain is repeated through an important exchange between Leamas and his girlfriend, Liz Gold. Leamas argues that the results justified the means. "It was a foul, foul operation. But it's paid off, and that's the only rule" (244–5). Arguing that *expediency* is the only law in the game, Leamas declares: "What do you think spies are: priests, saints and martyrs? They're a squalid procession of vain fools, traitors too, yes; pansies, sadists, and drunkards, people who play cowboys and Indians to brighten their rotten lives. Do you think they sit like monks in London, balancing the rights and wrongs? . . . It so happens that they need him [Mundt, the British double agent]. They need him so that the great moronic mass you admire can sleep soundly in their beds at night. They need him for the safety of ordinary, crummy people like you and me" (246). Liz is appalled by the exploitation of and contempt for the love and humanity in people: "It makes you the same . . . the same as Mundt and all the rest . . . You're all the same, Alec" (247). In desperation Leamas replies, "For God's sake believe me. I hate it, I hate it all, I'm tired. But it's the world, it's mankind that's gone mad" (247–8). Leamas chooses to die with Liz rather than live with the consequences of his (and the Circus') actions.

Although le Carré equates the methods used by both sides as equally distasteful, he maintains the superiority of Western ends, individualism and humanism, to the absolutism of Soviet communism: "The Western evil is far, far, far less evil than the Eastern one."[14] Le Carré implicitly questions whether the price paid in the violation of the truth and suppression of justice is worth it. Yet despite its critical tone, the story, also seems to defend the sacrifices as sometimes necessary. Le Carré seriously questions the means used while defending the ends of the West at this stage in the Cold War.

If a moral justification can be found for sacrificing innocent lives for the greater good of protecting a way of life in a contest against a determined enemy, there can be no such justification for the cynical sacrifices in *The Looking Glass War,* which were made for the sake of bureaucratic political infighting. Le Carré shows how easy it is, once such methods are justified in the name of protecting the state, to view the general interest through the prism of the interests of one's agency or department. There are four main characters in the novel. The head of the Department (a branch of military intelligence), Leclerc, is so anxious to regain the status and power that he and his department enjoyed during the war that he is willing to sacrifice the lives of his agents in a doomed operation to advance his goals. He becomes so detached from reality that by the end of the operation and the novel, le Carré implies he is insane.

Adrian Haldane, head of research, is completely aware that the operation will be a disaster but cynically goes along with it. John Avery, a young and inexperienced assistant to Leclerc doubts, undergoes a crisis of conscience, and allows himself to be deceived by Leclerc into supporting the operation. He becomes the instrument of Haldane (who heads the operation) in the recruitment and farcically brief retraining of Fred Leiser, a middle-aged agent who had worked for the Department during the war. Leclerc and Haldane manipulate Avery, who, in turn, manipulates Leiser by using his affection for Avery, respect for Haldane, loneliness, and desire to be accepted by English "gentlemen." (He immigrated from Poland.) Leiser is abandoned in East Germany, where he will certainly be executed to save the British government embarrassment and negative publicity.

The main theme of *A Small Town in Germany* is the conflict between the search for truth and the need to suppress it for political expediency. Peter de Lisle, the aristocratic assistant to Rawley Bradfield, head of Chancery (the political section) of the British embassy in Bonn, has much in common with Terence Fielding and with Bill Haydon. De Lisle "expresses, perhaps more completely than any other character in le Carré's novels, the nihilism and despair which such men felt at the national decline."[15] He laments, "I don't know what I'm defending. Or what I'm representing. Who does? A gentleman who lies for the good of his country, they told us with a wink in London. Willingly, I say. But first tell me what truth I must conceal. They haven't the least idea" (124).

As I have already remarked, the British officials in Bonn, in collaboration with their allies in Germany, have no qualms about sacrificing the life of their renegade employee Leo Harting—not to mention their principles—for the sake of political expediency. Harting represents traditional liberal English (and Western) values, which are sacrificed as well.[16]

As the ends become more ambiguous, reconciling the means with them becomes more problematic. Another solid member of the Establishment, Oliver Lacon, senior adviser to the Circus in the Cabinet Office, in a discussion with Smiley in *Tinker, Tailor, Soldier, Spy* ponders the theme of this chapter (and the essence of George Young's memo): "I once heard someone say morality was a method. Do you hold with that? I suppose you wouldn't. You would say that morality was vested in the aim, I expect. Difficult to know what one's aims *are,* that's the trouble, specially if you're British. We can't expect you people to determine our *policy* for us, can we? We can only ask you to further it. Correct? Tricky one, that (70). Le Carré repeatedly highlights the lack of clear principles to guide British foreign policy and the awareness of high civil servants and politicians that allowing espiocrats to make policy is *tricky,* to say the least—especially when there are those who feel they have the moral right and obligation to do so.

But in this case, the goal—to expose the mole who had devastated the Circus—was clear and legitimate. Yet Smiley's conscience responds to the consequences of his capture of the mole Haydon. "Nothing is worth the destruction of another human being. Somewhere the path of pain and betrayal must end" (345). He understands that, in a way, Bill Haydon (another aristocratic member of the Establishment) had been betrayed, too. He remembers a colleague's words:

> Poor loves. Trained to Empire, trained to rule the waves. . . . You're the last, George, you and Bill [Haydon]." He saw with painful clarity an ambitious man born to a big canvas, brought up to rule, to divide and conquer, whose vision and vanities all were fixed, like Percy's, upon the world's game; for whom the reality was a poor island with scarcely a voice that would carry across the water. Thus Smiley felt not only disgust, but, despite all that the moment meant to him, a surge of resentment against the institutions he was supposed to be protecting. (345)

Smiley contented himself with disgust and resentment, whereas Haydon (and the real-world Cambridge moles and others like Blake) felt justified in committing treason.[17]

Whereas in the earlier novels Smiley was more constrained by his conscience, in *The Honourable Schoolboy* as head of the Circus, Smiley abandons his constant questioning and acts resolutely to rebuild the Circus, badly damaged by Haydon's betrayal, and to trap his quarry. Largely because of his structural role, he comes closest in his career, through his actions, to justifying *raison d'état.* He has not abandoned his scruples, but he questions less and acts with much greater resolve than in the preceding novels. Nevertheless, personal factors are also important. Because his patriotism has become distorted by a personal vendetta against Karla, Smiley loses much of the moral high ground that he had until then managed to maintain. Others have interpreted this as his spiritual death or a final change in his moral position. As is elaborated below, it is more appropriately viewed as his most extreme tilt in the justification of ruthless means to achieve worthy ends in his lifelong struggle to achieve a skeptical balance.[18] On the one hand, le Carré implies that in this case the goal—the capture of Karla's high-ranking Chinese mole—did justify the means, which resulted in the deaths of British agents and others. On the other, he frames the story with paradoxes (as I explain in the concluding analysis to this chapter).

Smiley's People contrasts Smiley's doubts and decency with Karla's absolutism and fanatic belief that the grand design justifies all. But in order to trap Karla, Smiley turns the tables and resorts to Karla's methods by exploiting Karla's love for his daughter. Doing so, he is only able to win a pyrrhic victory. This conclusion implies that Smiley (and le Carré) doubt that the end (Karla's capture) really justified the means (Smiley's compromised morality). I disagree with Beene (1992:35), however, who contends that this "completes Smiley's spiritual ruin." She further asserts, "Smiley pays for resolution with his spiritual life. His resurrection, while as hoped for as [King] Arthur's, never happens" (92). Indeed, Smiley is resurrected as a very spiritually healthy prophet in *The Secret Pilgrim*.

The question of whether the use of terror and counterterror is ever justifiable to further legitimate political goals is a of theme of *The Little Drummer Girl*. The exploitation of Charlie by Kurtz and by Gadi Becker was justified by them historically, by reference to the Holocaust, and in the present in terms of preventing a gang of terrorists from continuing to spread their reign of terror at the cost of scores of innocent lives. Gadi, whose character and ideology develop during the novel through his questioning the assumptions and policies of his government, accepts full responsibility for his actions and at the end of the story is seen reunited with Charlie, attempting to repair the psychological damage he and his colleagues had caused her. Le Carré leaves us with a more ambiguous ending than most critics have suggested. Nonetheless, he leaves open the possibility, although not the promise, that their love would enable them to make a life together. Gadi is a Smiley-like character who grows in ways that, several critics have argued, Smiley does not.

In no way can the means used—an endless chain of betrayals—justify the narrow and selfish ends of Magnus Pym. George Young's perspective essentially expresses the pact between Pym and Poppy in this novel. Poppy proposes: "Maybe we can set the world to rights, same as we used to in the old days. . . . Maybe we can put our heads together. We are reasonable men" (353). Pym's response is, "Together we can change the world" (361). Pym further assets, "We are men of the middle ground—we have founded our own country with a population of two!" (363). Together they use their privileged position to betray for a cause they deem higher than that of conventional patriotism or even of ideology. Theirs is essentially a personal pact, however, based on personal affection and mutual self-interest, in total disregard of personal, institutional, and national loyalties and obligations.

The Russia House (1989) is narrated by Horatio (Harry) Benedict de-Palfrey, better known as old Palfrey. He is the legal eagle, law bender, or legal adviser to the illegals (British Intelligence). "For twenty years I have been your humble secret servant, ready at any time to rob the scales of the same blind goddess whom my warm heart was brought up to revere" (29–30). This early passage sets the scene for a plot that mirrors the narrator's readiness to bend the law, unbalance the scales of justice, and remove the blindfold (impartiality) of the law to legitimate the actions of British intelligence and of the CIA.[19]

Set at the end of the Cold War, le Carré appears sympathetic to the justification of the means used by both Goethe and Barley (technically treason) in terms of their ultimate ethical ends (the former political and the latter personal).[20] But Goethe is executed, and Barley may be left waiting at the altar. The relationship between the two mirrors that of Pym and Poppie in several respects but differs in another. Although neither is a professional spy, each betrays his country in the name of a higher purpose. Goethe paraphrases Percherin, who understood that it was possible to both love one's country and hate its system.[21] Goethe quotes Barley: "If there is to be hope, we must all betray our countries" (161). When Barley conveys the Service's offer to smuggle Goethe to England, Goethe replies: "I am not a defector, Barley. I am a Russian, and my future is here [prophetically he adds], even if it is a short one"[22] (210).

Most readers in the West have little problem justifying and even admiring Goethe's actions. He is a man of personal integrity fighting an oppressive political system and attempting to stop an irrational arms race that threatens human survival. He is a man tormented by his creations, who knows that the best he can do in his career is "the absolute worst for mankind."(176). Because of this, he cannot accommodate himself to the reformism of *perestroika*. He "demands action and rejects all cosmetic change" (8). Therefore, his absolutism dooms him to a fate similar to that of the uncompromising Leo Harting, with whose motives most readers can also identify.

Even so, Barley's discovery of "a sacred absolute" to defend his betrayal of both Goethe's trust (by working with British intelligence) and of English security (by doing a deal with the Russians) may appear more ambiguous to the same readers. Barley chooses "the extreme middle ground of which he had elected himself a citizen." "As to his loyalty to his country, Barley saw it only as a question of which England he chose to serve . . . He knew a better England by far [than the old imperial chauvinism], and it was inside himself" (286).[23] "He knew the sacrifice he was prepared to make. He was not their traitor. He was complete" (315).

When he makes contact with the Russian authorities, he trades a shopping list of questions that British intelligence and the CIA wanted Goethe to answer (thereby revealing their areas of ignorance) for the guaranteed protection and eventual release of his lover, her twins, and uncle. The Russians honored at least the first part of the bargain. His lover maintained her job, her apartment, and her privileges. Barley is seen waiting for her arrival in Portugal at the end of the story. In response to a call-in question on the television interview program *Larry King Live,* le Carré replied that he "deliberately left the ending open as if to say to the reader, did they survive together as lovers? Did they make a life together? Was there real collaboration, if you like? It was a little symbolic and I said now read on."[24] In other words, the ambiguity of the ending reflected the unanswered question of whether *perestroika* and Russian collaboration with the West will succeed.

Smiley, in *The Secret Pilgrim,* clearly articulates the dilemma of the relationship between ends and means. He summarizes the nefarious activities of the West during the Cold War and concludes: "*We scarcely paused to ask ourselves how much longer we could defend our society by these means and remain a society worth defending*" (116; emphasis added). That really is the $64,000 question.[25]

In the last story in the novel, the narrator Ned (a protégé of Smiley who heads the Russia House in the previous novel), on his last assignment before retirement, is sent to interview Sir Anthony Joyston Bradshaw. Bradshaw is described by the head of the Service as "one of England's natural shits" who "has HMG by the balls. Your brief is to invite him, very courteously, to relax his grip" (326). Bradshaw speaks in the affected aristocratic speech form known as Belgravia cockney. He has become a multimillionaire, with a peerage purchased with money earned by running guns under the protection of the Service. Ned's attempt to appeal to his conscience angers him because he has none.[26] "I'm Pharaoh, right? If a few thousand slaves have to die so that I can build this pyramid, nature. . . . Think there aren't slaves today? Think capital doesn't *depend* on slaves? Jesus Christ, what kind of shop do you run?" (334).

Ned is silenced in the face of such an expression of absolute cynicism. He thinks of his lifelong battle against an institutionalized evil: "I thought of telling him that now we had defeated Communism, we were going to have to set about defeating capitalism, but that wasn't really my point: the *evil is not in the system, but in the man*" (334; emphasis added). This remark emphasizes an important transition from the Cold War, when evil was institutionalized in the form of political challenge to the West by the Soviet Union, to the threat from non-state actors in *The Night Manager*. The evil represented by the undisguised personal greed of Bradshaw is connected to representatives of the state in *The Night Manager*.

Post-Cold War Good and Evil:
The Night Manager

Bradshaw is the prototype for the more fully developed character of Richard Onslow Roper, the main villain in *The Night Manager*. Le Carré uncharacteristically appears to overdo the evilness of Roper, repeatedly labeled "the worst man in the world," because his callousness and unlimited greed are not balanced by any redeeming virtues. Similarly, the goodness of Pine appears unbalanced by flaws.[27] Burr remarks: "When God finished putting together Dicky Roper, . . . He took a deep breath and shuddered a bit, then He ran up our Jonathan to restore the ecological balance" (53). David Remnick (1993), among others, attributes this aberration in le Carré's writing to his temporary loss of bearings in the post–Cold War transition rather than understanding it as logical response to these changes.[28]

As with *The Little Drummer Girl,* the critics are divided in evaluating the meaning of the happy ending of this novel. Herbert Mitgang (1993) claims, "The author leaves us with the possibility of change. After such a rough but remarkably readable journey through the arms and drug culture, Mr. le Carré deserves credit for keeping the flames of romance and idealism glowing." Remnick (1993:23) more sarcastically notes: "In the end, Pine is victorious—or at least alive—and the credits roll over his return to the pastoral English shoreline where he lives out his life having found love with fair Jed and a new identity courtesy of the British government." It is significant that they focus on Pine ending up happily with his woman and ignore the important inconclusiveness of the outcome of the struggle against the illegal arms and drug trade in collusion with corrupt government officials.

In fact, the forces of darkness, led by Geoffrey Darker, the corrupt head of British intelligence who uses evil means for nefarious purposes, defeat the forces of light, led by Rex Goodhew, the crusading civil servant who fights fairly for a just cause. This obvious play on the names shows the usually subtler le Carré having a bit of fun with his readers. Allowing Pine to live and to have his woman may be le Carré's way of indulging his romantic inclinations. Leaving Roper fully operational, however, and the alliance of the honest and idealistic senior civil servants and agents of Enforcement defeated by the corrupt and cynical officials and intelligence agencies on both sides of the Atlantic, hardly bespeaks a James Bond ending of good always defeating evil (a perspective of political infancy, in Max Weber's view).[29]

One of the main messages of *The Night Manager* is that it takes a great deal more than idealism and good intentions to defeat evil. Only by reverting to the tactics of the enemy is Leonard Burr, a decent disenchanted former member of Darker's ironically named Pure Intelligence unit, able to save the life of his agent. He has to break every rule to accomplish the task. The narrator relays how he repeatedly warns the trusting Goodhew of "the lengths that Darker would go to in order to down a rival—even one as humble as Burr's tin-pot outfit" (52). Poor Goodhew is incredulous when an attempt is made by Darker's assistant to bribe and then threaten him. Only after he is nearly killed by Darker's men does he begin to realize the true nature of his opponents and the extreme means to which they resort to accomplish their goals.

From the perspective of the agents in both British and American enforcement, their own intelligence agencies were almost as great an enemy as the illegal arms traffickers and the drug cartels. "Pure intelligence meant all things bad, whether it resided in Langley or River House. It meant turning a blind eye to some of the biggest crooks in the hemisphere for the sake of nebulous advantages elsewhere. It meant operations inexplicably abandoned in midstream and orders countermanded from on high" (55). Too often, *raison d'état* was used to justify collusion with the targets of enforcement's operations. This was one of the main reasons Rex Goodhew created the new British Enforcement agency and appointed Burr to head it. The intelligence agencies were too willing to turn a blind eye to violations of law and human decency for the sake of stronger political and economic interests.

The end of the Cold War cast a new perspective on the relation of ends to means:

> The story was that after twenty-five years at the Whitehall mast, something inside Goodhew had discreetly snapped. Perhaps it was the ending of the Cold War that had caused it. Goodhew had the modesty not to know. . . . one Monday morning Goodhew woke as usual and decided with no premeditation that *for too long, in the misused name of freedom, he had been sacrificing scruple and principles to the great god of expediency* and that the excuse for doing so was dead. . . . He must mend his ways or perish in his soul. . . . he experienced a silent epiphany. He would crop the secret octopus. He would give away its powers to separate, smaller agencies and make each of them

separately accountable. He would deconstruct, decentralize, humanize. He would begin with the most corrupting influence of all: *the unholy marriage between Pure Intelligence, Westminster and the covert weapons trade,* presided over by Geoffrey Darker of the River House. (59–60; emphasis added)

Burr blames this sinister trinity for allowing Roper to get away with his crimes. "*Goodhew's master puts his telescope to both blind eyes and lets him. If his toys are British, anyone will let him do anything he bloody likes*" (80). He tells Pine, "Today we're talking glut and national bankruptcies and governments offering better terms than their own crooks" (81). When the CIA can't supply arms because of legal restrictions and congressional oversight, British intelligence supplies them through their agents.[30] Palfrey tells Goodhew, "You're too *good,* Rex. It'll be the death of you. . . . Buy British, darling. That's the clue. Don't you understand *anything* bad?" (212). Goodhew is betrayed by his own minister, who serves on Darker's top-secret committee, code-named Flagship. The collusion between politicians and espiocrats makes possible Roper's nefarious illegal business activities. Roper articulates the arrogance of George Young's directive cited in chapter 3. But Roper doesn't even pretend to act in the general interest.

Roper's cynical amoral moralizing is summed up in the following passages, the first of which expresses the assumption that power is based on fear backed by armed threat: "World's run by fear, you see . . . If a bunch of chaps want to make war, they're not going to listen to a lot of wet-eared abolitionists. If they don't, doesn't matter whether they've got crossbows or Stingers. Fact of life. Sorry if it bothers you. . . . Guns go where the power is. . . . Armed power's what keeps the peace. Unarmed power doesn't last five minutes. First rule of stability" (237–38). He complains that powerful nation states are unfair competition for private arms salesmen: "Real enemies were the big power governments. Everywhere you looked, big governments were there ahead of you, flogging anything to anybody, breaking their own rules, cutting each other's throats, backing the wrong side, making it up to the right side. Mayhem. Us independent chaps got squeezed into the corner every time. Only thing to do, get in ahead of 'em, beat 'em to the draw. Balls and foresight, all we had left to rely on. Pushing the envelope, all the time" (245).

Roper claims he isn't engaged in crime, but "politics" (269). He's an amoral moralist. "He *destroys, he makes a good fortune, so he considers himself divine*"[31] (295). He blames the big powers for creating the wars whose arms he supplies (309). In justification of his arms for drugs deal with the Colombian cartels, he cites the precedent of the British opium trade in Canton.[32] Thus le Carré's characterization of the worst man in the world is the mirror image of his portrayal of Smiley's valedictory in *The Secret*

Pilgrim. The post–Cold War pursuit of power and economic gain is no longer disguised in ideological garb that has any credence. The presentation makes clear that the greedy ends—the alliance among corrupt politicians, intelligence officers, and arms traders—do not justify the means—arming the world's dictators and drug lords. The greater clarity of the moral issues involved, not le Carré's post–Cold War disorientation, give this novel a less ambiguous quality than his earlier work.

Post-Soviet Policy and the West: *Our Game*

Our Game portrays a political context significantly changed after the disintegration of the Soviet Union. A former British double agent named Larry goes native among the Ingush neighbors of the Chechens in the Caucasus. In this novel the Ingush (rather than, as in reality, their neighboring Chechans) engage in a separatist war with Russia. Larry collaborates with his former KGB handler (an Ingush) in embezzling Russian funds for the Ingush cause, which he joins and for which he ultimately dies. Tim, the narrator, searches for Larry. Whereas in *The Night Manager* government inaction was condemned for contributing to the illegal arms and drug trade, here government inaction is condemned for allowing a stronger imperial power to suppress a weaker national minority.

Louis Menand (1995:4) contends that "Tim represents the post-Communist West, its head, now that the threat of sudden annihilation is past, buried in its own backyard vineyard while the little people of the earth get trampled on."[33] Larry at first confirms this, claiming that Tim "has been goading me about my indifference to the world's agonies . . . suggesting that I epitomise the shortcomings of the morally torpid West." Tim explains that he plays the role, "but my heart is in none of it" (187). Tim is less one-dimensional than Menand's interpretation implies. Noting le Carré's op-ed essay condemning the West for ignoring the plight of little small nations, Menand suggests, "Though he is too clever a writer not to make the message a little more ambiguous in his novel, he doesn't make it nearly ambiguous enough" (ibid.). His interpretation of le Carré is less ambiguous than the actual characterization warrants. Le Carré's political sympathies are not difficult to determine, however, and they are reflected in a somewhat shallower portrayal of the characters.

Le Carré sympathizes with the Ingush in their struggle against an excessively brutal Russia. He criticizes the tacit support of Britain and the indifference of America.[34] Christopher Lehmann-Haupt (1995) suggests that Timothy's journey "leads him to an understanding of what Mr. le Carré presents as the West's failed response to the changing dynamic within the former Soviet empire." One character refers to post-Soviet

American policy as "planned apathy" that allows Moscow to do pretty much what it wants. If Tim represents the West, he is forced by circumstances to come to a (self) recognition of the consequences of the West's policy of benign neglect during his quest.

Le Carré indicates that the means—i.e., in this case, inaction—are not justified in terms of the end, which is to support, at all costs, the fragile authority of the current Russian leadership. But he also indicates that the alternative is far from risk free. Larry, who rushes in where others fear to, ends up dead and, at best, as one more among the many martyrs to yet another hopeless cause. In the conclusion, Tim slings a Kalashnikov over his shoulder and runs after Checheyev, his former KGB opponent with whom Larry had allied in the Ingush cause. This suggests that Tim has found that he can no longer equivocate and has finally made a commitment to act. It is unclear (as is the belated decision of the United States to intervene in the tragic Bosnian uncivil war) whether his actions will actually make a difference.[35]

When Ends Dictate Means: *The Tailor of Panama*

In *The Tailor of Panama,* the wheels are set in motion by the top-secret Planning and Application Committee, composed of representatives of the British government, parliament, and private enterprise. The committee is chaired by Geoff Cavendish, a dealer in arms and oil, who is the "creature" of Ben Hatry, a great British media baron and fellow committee member. They have close links to their American counterparts (including a general who has the ear of the president, the arms industry, and the "Loony Right").[36] Another member is Tug Kirby, "known as the Minister with the Very Long Portfolio" because of his unrivaled collection of consultancies and directorships, especially on defense companies in Britain and in the Middle East. "Geoff Cavendish . . . produced the first game plan, and Ben Hatry had said fucking do it. . . . Cavendish had struck the deal with Luxmore, encouraged him, bolstered his budget and his ego" (299). Practically everyone along the line plays along by all too willingly believing, or pretending to believe, the imaginary intelligence provided by Pendel—each for his own reason.

Osnard (the British agent who recruits Pendel) is a thoroughly amoral opportunist whose goal is to amass personal wealth.[37] When Osnard asks his superior, Luxmore, to define the British interest in Panama, the reply is that there is none. The goal of the British is to prevent the Americans from fulfilling their commitment to withdraw from the Panama Canal and thereby prevent a power vacuum. The committee wants the Service to give it evidence to accomplish this and to thereby restore the power and influence Britain enjoyed as a benefit of the special relationship with the United States. Dismissing former president Carter's agreement to turn the canal over to Panama, Luxmore says, "*Dangerous diffidence* is what I call it, young Mr. Osnard. The world's one superpower restrained by puritan principle, God help us" (214).

At one point, London accurately concludes "that H. Pendel, superspy, is an overpaid, disloyal, grafting, two-faced con-artist" (231). Instead of firing him, however, Osnard demands that Pendel produce "the grand vision" London needs (233). "Target the Canal. . . . Everything rides on the Canal" (235). He offers to double Pendel's salary if he can recruit his wife, who is secretary to the Panamanian minister dealing with the future of the canal. In addition to bribery, Osnard also resorts to blackmail. Because Osnard was embezzling a percentage of the funds for his agents, the larger the network, the more he made. He also had no trouble convincing Luxmore, who, when Osnard doubts his source's credibility, replies: "Listen to me, Andrew. That's an order. There *is* a conspiracy. Don't lose heart merely because you're tired. Of *course* there is a conspiracy. You believe it, I believe it. One of the greatest opinion-makers in the *world* believes it. Personally. Profoundly. The best brains in Fleet Street believe it, or they very soon will. A conspiracy is out there, it is being cobbled together by an evil inner circle of the Panamanian elite, it centres on the Canal and we shall find it!" (242).[38] Luxmore needed this conspiracy to justify his position, budget, and influence to his superiors. He also shared the nationalistic ideology that coincided with the business interests of the chair and other members of the committee, who spawned and ultimately directed the operation. These most dubious ends were used to justify accepting false intelligence.

Pendel complies by inventing a more complex conspiracy and counterconspiracy carried out by the Silent Opposition, led by his best friend (Mickie Abraxas), and his assistant (and almost lover) Marta, in association with dissident students, his wife and her Christian group, a Masonic-like group of Panamanian businessmen called the Brotherhood, and also by inventing a Japanese plot to take over the canal.[39] A British intelligence analyst named Sally expresses concern over the lack of collateral reports to support the overwritten and undersourced reports filed by Pendel. (Le Carré's women are typically doubters.) Sally (paraphrasing Churchill) "said that never in the whole history of human intelligence had so much been paid for so little"(297). Luxmore is nonplussed, and he rejects the mounting evidence pointing to a scam.[40] In the meantime, Cavendish, the point man, lobbied members of parliament.[41]

The three British members of the committee secretly meet with two "deniable" Americans: Elliot, a columnist for the *Washington Times,* and a colonel named Dirk, representing a general named Van. Hatry tells the colonel to inform the general, "We're all disappointed as fuck he's not running for President" (305). The colonel assures the others that the general will "swing the President." Le Carré satirically describes the scene: "It was five men who cordially detested each other, seated round a well polished eighteenth-century table and united by a great ideal" (306). The Brits coax the Americans to join the plot. The Americans say they would like to but they need a peg, a hook, a condition, or a smoking gun (like the rape of American nuns) to justify their intervention in Panama again. "We have *your* spook reports, unsubstantiated by *our* spook agencies this time, because that's the way we say it has to be" (307). They claim they need "one emotive argument that will play on our television screens" (308).

At no point is there a serious question raised about the validity of the intelligence from Panama. Instead, they bargain over the British right to control "the opposition," the leader of which is made out to be their man. Elliot demands an exclusive scoop on the invasion when it takes place. The Brits demand that their prime minister[42] get something out of this (310). They demand he receive *"credit . . . moral* credit. . . . Morality, their expressions implied was negotiable" (311). They agree the president will pay an overdue visit to London and that the role of British intelligence will be leaked to the "respectable" press. "They parted like unreconciled lovers, worried they had said the wrong things, failed to say the right ones, not been understood" (311). They need not have worried. They had understood one another and the deal had been made. If the British could supply a smoking gun, the Americans would use their clout to persuade American public opinion, pressure groups, pivotal politicians, and the president to invade Panama. Hatry demands: "I want crisis," and Luxmore is sent to Panama to find or to produce one.

Luxmore instructs the British embassy in Panama to aid Panama's Silent Opposition and to take over the students (on a deniable basis): "*How to Oust Your Host Government* or something of the sort" (319). Ambassador Maltby persuades Nigel Stormont, his head of Chancery, to disregard doubts about the operation.[43] The ambassador strikes a deal with London that he and Stormont handle the money (cash and gold) to pay for the operation.[44] Both men are at the end of their careers. Each, for different reasons, needs money.[45] These personal ends become paramount in overriding whatever ethical or professional scruples they had. Stormont, the more reluctant of the two, is persuaded by Maltby.

The embassy personnel with access to Buchan meet and plan their role in the plot. The meeting is viewed through the eyes of Fran, the only woman present, who provides a note of detachment and skepticism. "Men in secret conclave enter an altered state. . . . Men in secret conclave give off a different smell. They are men on heat. And Fran was as excited as they were, though her excitement made her sceptical, whereas the men's excitement made them erect and pointed them towards a fiercer god" (336). The overt sexual references and allusions to the men's excitement is striking given the knowledge that the entire operation is based on fantasy. Political fantasies appear to have an erotic effect.[46] "And the men drinking it in. Swallowing it whole because it is monstrous but secret, therefore not monstrous at all" (337). The secrecy of covert operations exonerate those who take part in them of moral responsibility for their actions in their own eyes.

The smoking gun required by the Americans is ironically supplied by the suicide of Pendel's closest friend, Mickie. Because he had been repeatedly tortured and raped in prison, Mickie was constantly drunk and had repeatedly threatened suicide. He had recently been the object of the attention of the police, which Pendel guiltily attributed to his having made Mickie the heroic leader of the Secret Opposition in his fabricated reports to Osnard. Pendel makes the suicide look like a politically motivated assassination, to provide London with the smoking gun it had been demanding. It is clear that Osnard knew the report was false and was aware of the consequences of passing on this false report.[47]

The report of Mickie's death was the peg that Hatry and Cavendish needed. Hatry's press broke the story under sensational headlines like "OUR MAN IN PANAMA" (an obvious play on Graham Greene's novel) and "CHUBBY BOOZER WAS BRITAIN'S 007." His media reported that Mickie had been "tortured and ritually assassinated" by a special unit attached to the presidential staff. "A hasty refutation put out by three Panamanian pathologists claiming that [Mickie] Abraxas was an inveterate alcoholic who had shot himself in a fit of depression after drinking a quart of Scotch whisky was greeted with the derision it deserved" (396). Hatry's media report that the British coup "saved America's bacon and proved that Britain under a Tory leadership is capable of being a willing and welcome partner in the grand old Atlantic Alliance"(400). They also reported that the participation of a minuscule British token force in the invasion (with the Orwellian name "Operation Safe Passage") was "a cause of national rejoicing" (400).

There are several tiers of moral culpability in this novel.[48] Hatry, who dominates the Committee, is at the apex. With his lackey Cavendish, the pair clearly reflect the spirit of George Young's memo (see chapter 3). In their arrogance, they set themselves above the legally designated authorities and felt entitled to use any means necessary to accomplish their ends. Le Carré does not spare them or their willing tools and accomplices Luxmore and Osnard his bitingly satirical pen, yet they are victorious. As Leo Durocher, a revered American baseball manager, is reputed to have said, "Nice guys finish last!"[49]

In keeping with some of the broadly farcical (and very funny) aspects of the novel, le Carré accounts for the fates of some of the supporting characters, whose moral responsibility lies in either having aided and abetted or not having done anything to prevent the unfolding of events. Osnard, a secondary villain, ends up on the ski slopes of Davos in the company of a "society beauty" (who is twice his age). Ambassador Maltby, who reportedly "came into an inheritance," retires from the Foreign Service, as does Fran (who is half his age). Stormont's wife is admitted to a Swiss cancer clinic. In all, they do not fare too badly. If they are punished, it appears that it will have to be in the next world rather than in this one. This is a strong satirical commentary on how, in the real world, material rewards do not usually correlate positively with virtue. Virtue, conspicuous by its absence among most politicians and intelligence operatives, must be its own reward. The meek tend not to inherit the earth.

In sharp contrast, Pendel sentences himself to capital punishment. In response to seeing the consequences of his creativity, Pendel enters the inferno for which his "fluence" provided the spark of ignition. Pendel is a special case of victim as victimizer. Pendel, the bribed and blackmailed pawn of Hatry, Cavendish, Luxmore, and Osnard, in turn through his fantasies and his suicide betrays and deserts his wife, children, and the only other people he loves, Mickie and Marta, not to mention the countless innocent victims of the invasion. Yet le Carré especially loves him. In response to Norman Rush's (1996) charge that Pendel was "another literary avatar of Judas," le Carré replies that Pendel "was very like me . . . and I thought that I was making a humanitarian appeal even in creating that character and loving him as much as I do."[50] Pendel closely resembles Magnus Pym, le Carré's admitted alter ego, in his autobiographical *A Perfect Spy*. Although these characters are clearly projections of an *aspect* of the author's character, le Carré does not hold them up to his readers as models to emulate—on the contrary. As was argued in chapter 2, like the seventeenth-century Dutch artist Jan Steen, he uses self-parody as a means of making a moral point. By projecting an aspect of himself onto the character, the author identifies his common humanity with the object of his critique.

Through his published work and his interviews, le Carré repeatedly emphasizes (in different formulations) the need to achieve a *balance* between political "necessity" and "moral self-censorship" and acknowledges that "all of us find that very difficult."[51] This balance is not the "middle ground," a phrase frequently used by le Carré to indicate a kind of private no-man's land, as in the pact between Pym and Poppie (*A Perfect Spy*) and between Barley and Goethe (*The Russia House*). It is partly encompassed in the term *committed doubter*, which Homberger (1986:29) ascribes to novelists and spies. It is the kind of balance which, as I suggested in chapter 3, is characteristic of the *skeptical* stance in which a character may lean more in one direction in one context and in the other direction in another. The characters who most successfully achieve such balance are Smiley (especially in *The Secret Pilgrim),* Gadi Becker (*The Little Drummer Girl*), and Leonard Burr (*The Night Manager*).

Le Carré discusses the influence on his work of the nineteenth-century German *Bildungsroman,* a novel of education in which a character undergoes a variety of experiences that results in "a changed and generally *morally reformed* figure. If that didn't happen, there was an apocalypse of some kind and he was destroyed."[52] Le Carré appears to have modified this genre by combining it with the spy novel (which he also made his own).[53] Moral growth is achieved by approaching skeptical balance. Failure to achieve such a balance frequently leads to (self-) destruction.

In several respects, Pendel resembles Charlie in *The Little Drummer Girl.* Kurtz, however, wrote a detailed script for Charlie, which she carefully rehearsed with Gadi. The Committee gave Pendel, via Luxmore through Osnard, a scenario for Pendel's own creative improvisations. Unfortunately for Pendel, Osnard is no Gadi. He is amoral and appears to lack a conscience, whereas Gadi is torn by moral dilemmas and is constantly troubled by his conscience. Osnard ends up as unscrupulous in the end of the novel as he was at the outset. Gadi undergoes moral development during the course of the story. Osnard has neither the desire nor the ability to help Pendel through his crisis of disillusionment precipitated by the shocking awareness of the consequences of his actions. Gadi devotes himself to helping Charlie recover from her similar trauma. This difference between Gadi and Osnard sheds light on the question raised in chapter 1—whether the sacrifice of conscience for the public good mitigates the consequence of actions. Smiley's and Gadi's consciences, contrasted with the moral disengagement of Osnard and many others, does make a difference—at least to their agents.

There is an important difference between characters who appear to lack a conscience by successfully ignoring it, and those who either cannot or choose not to do so. The psychological literature indicates that several mechanisms of moral disengagement or suspension of moral agency (ignoring one's conscience) operate in concert. The mechanisms that seem to contribute most to engagement in detrimental activities are "moral reconstructs of harmful conduct by linking it to worthy purposes and vilification of victims."[54] In other words, one finds an ideological rationalization to legitimate one's activity and dehumanize the victims who suffer as a consequence of this activity. In this context, goals or ends (frequently stated in ideological terms, e.g., nationalism) are the most frequently used mechanisms for justifying the nefarious means employed by states and their agents, which they buttress by presenting the enemy in less than human terms. The latter is accomplished through nihilation, such as, Israeli and Palestinian mutual nonrecognition, or mutual demonization, as characterized by East and West during the Cold War.

Because of their abuse in the exoneration of crimes committed in the name of serving them, le Carré, through Smiley, vehemently condemns ideologies. But he appears to exonerate Smiley through the unrecognized ideological guise of his own liberal humanism. What I have termed le Carré's underlying liberal temperament expresses an unacknowledged ideological position, while at the same time, attacking ideologies. I am less certain than is Stewart Crehan (1988:124; emphasis added) that "an ideological *intention* is present." Intended or not, however, the underlying ideology is there.[55] From Crehan's so-called "more democratic perspective, this self-questioning, liberal stance amounts, in effect, to little more than giving Western imperialism a human face" (103). Crehan concludes: "Liberal-humanist, imperialist fiction cannot, of course, be expected to commit suicide. Perhaps, therefore, the most one can expect of it is that it acknowledges, honestly, its silencing of the other"[56] (125). Le Carré has acknowledged his liberalism in numerous essays and interviews.

Sauerberg (1984:51) suggests, "Le Carré's answer to the dilemma is consequently not a refusal to acknowledge its necessary implication that the end justifies the means. But his special variation is to have Smiley given absolution for his employment of foul means by reminding the reader constantly that English culture has values which make such sacrifices worthwhile." He implies this is so because Smiley's doubts are of existential importance, because his quest for values goes beyond mere national interest and are redeemed through his belief in love and by his belief in the possibilities of human endeavor (53–4). In a novel interpretation, Sauerburg argues that "Karla paradoxically becomes the ultimate confirmation of Smiley's beliefs" (63). Karla (hardly a liberal humanist), too, nurses the last illusion of the love of his daughter.

Smiley is motivated to trap Karla in *self-defense* of his friends, service, country, and his concept of a reasonable balance in human affairs. The context determines the appropriateness of means when weighed against the goals. Le Carré insists that the individual is responsible for struggling with this paradox and *must* live with the consequences of his or her choice. Weber (1946:125) said, "Whoever wants to engage in politics at all, and especially in politics as a vocation, has to realize these ethical paradoxes. He must know that he is responsible for what may become of himself under the impact of these paradoxes."

Explaining Smiley's Dilemma

Here I shall address and attempt to decipher the mystery of apparently oxymoronic statements: to be inhuman in defense of our humanity; harsh in defense of compassion; and single-minded in defense of our disparity. My understanding of le Carré's message is that the key is *balance,* as I have defined it. The easiest of the three paradoxes is the question of how one can justify harshness in defense of compassion. Shakespeare gives the example of Hamlet who says to his mother, the Queen: "I must be cruel only to be kind."[57] Only by forcing her to confront the enormity of her sin (of marrying her former husband's brother and murderer) can he save her soul. More commonly, in raising children, sometimes parents must be harsh not in spite of, but because of their love for their children. In extreme cases, "tough love" is apparently one of the most effective means of helping a child who has developed serious problems such as abuse of or addiction to chemical substances. Less extreme problems require less harsh measures. Similarly, one would be justified in employing measures otherwise unthinkable, for example, the assassination of Hitler, to prevent international calamity. Wisdom is in determining in which contexts harshness is appropriate and limiting it exclusively to those—and only those—contexts.

Whereas one must be resolute (single-minded) in defending democracy against totalitarian challenges, le Carré makes clear we risk losing sight of the ends. To the extent that we do so, we tend to blur the differences and destroy the ends—the protection of democracy—through the use of means that undermine the very freedoms we sought to protect. As Gillespie (1970:51) says: "All Controls, having the same ends, use the same means and the same sources of information and sometimes even the same agents, linking as surely as if they were all working for the Internationale. Power in the service of ideas levels distinctions between the ideas or makes monsters." Only by keeping a sense of perspective can this danger be avoided. A healthy skeptical outlook, one that constantly questions assumptions and weighs ends and means, provides such a perspective.

To be inhuman in defense of humanity is most difficult for the liberal humanist, who, by definition, defines the individual human being to be of highest value. Therefore, only contexts of extremely extenuating circumstances could justify acts of inhumanity, such as the deprivation or violation of basic human rights—in the most extreme form, the killing of another human being. An example of a literature that addresses this topic is one that discusses the theory of "just war" in international relations. Jean Bethke Elshtain, in the introduction to her edited volume *Just War Theory* (1992:5), suggests that in contrast to pacifist arguments, "those indebted to just war discourse leave open the possibility that 'values must be protected and preserved by force.'" She notes that even the peace-church position, which has been nudging closer to pacifism, enjoins Christians to "resist unjust aggression." In her epilogue, Elshtain contrasts the classical formulation by Augustine with a more contemporary formulation of a vision of civic virtue that assumes (among others) "the existence of universal moral dispositions, if not convictions—hence, the possibility of a nonrelativist ethic"[58] (324). Elshtain stresses that a "*morally formed civic character* is a precondition for just-war thinking as a civic virtue" (325). Le Carré presents his readers with the challenge of determining which contexts justify extreme measures and thereby contributes to civic education and to the development of a more morally informed citizenry.

Chapter 5

The Ambiguity of Human Nature: Motives and Personality

He [Smiley] reflected for the hundredth time on the obscurity of motive in human action. (A Murder of Quality, 113)

We are what we pretend to be, so we must be careful about what we pretend to be. (Kurt Vonnegut, Mother Night)

Introduction

Le Carré consistently relates the personal to the political—for example, in the relationship between temperament and ideology. Although he repeats through Smiley and others the theme that human motivation is an unsolvable mystery, he nonetheless carefully examines the clues. He frequently discloses multiple motives without prioritizing them, as if to imply they are random. Le Carré has confidence in his readers: "The people . . . will give you the time you ask of them and the concentration you ask of them."[1] He expects them to make the effort to puzzle out meanings for themselves.[2] Ultimately, however, le Carré's view of human nature is that there is an unbridgeable gulf between the internal realities of individuals and that we can never completely identify with the feelings of our fellow human beings; we remain forever a mystery to one another.[3] In a humorous short story, he suggests that there are no objective truths about man, perhaps only about eternal nature.[4]

Le Carré's attempt to understand humanity begins with his attempt to understand himself: "I have externalized things in my own past about which I was intensely uncomfortable: forms of artificial behaviour if you like, a sense of dislocation between personal behaviour and internal reality. . . . By making the story [*The Little Drummer Girl*] function in so many different theatrical stages of the same stage I've maybe, in some quite therapeutic way, cut through personal deceptions to some sort of centre."[5]

Le Carré reveals much about himself in his introduction to a collection of photographs by Don McCullin (*Hearts of Darkness,* 1980), in which he interprets the artist's work as an externalization of his fragmented personality. All of le Carré's major characters display such fragmentation. Le Carré's observations of McCullin appear to be equally true of himself: he speaks with great fluency about himself, but, he has a lot to hide; he is "dreadfully vulnerable."[6] McCullin "hammers at the impossibility of encompassing so much of human life and staying 'one person, one anything'"[7] (11). Le Carré describes a photograph as representing a "cry of fury about his own *truncated childhood*" (12). Le Carré asks and, perhaps, projects: "Does he secretly believe he is the author of the misfortunes that obsess him?" He refers to McCullin's "unlived childhood." "he man—if there is a difference in *him,* in *me,* in *any of us* between *boy* and *man*—has been wounded" (12).

Alluding to T. E. Lawrence (of Arabia) and to *Candide,* le Carré says McCullin "does not know how innocent he is of the crimes of which he constantly accuses himself." One wonders, particularly when reading *A Perfect Spy* and *The Tailor of Panama,* about the terrible crimes of which le Carré accuses David Cornwell. He describes McCullin obsessively talking about himself, without vanity, as a phenomenon. "It's *his* life that matters, and I can understand that too. It's *his* bombarded pendulum[8] life . . . that he contemplates. . . . It's *his* life, very properly, that sets him marveling at the whole human race"(14). In his aside "I can understand that too," le Carré reveals his identification with his subject.[9] Le Carré especially identifies with victims.[10]

Le Carré also shares with McCullin (and with all serious artists and thinkers) a concern for the enigma of existence. "In a grey, confused, ever-compromising world, he has the gall to think of life and death and the purpose of existence" (18). Le Carré's novels, like McCullin's photographs, "rob us of our armoury, our blinkers, our complacency, they bring us out of our armchairs." Le Carré quotes Joseph Conrad, an author who has had considerable influence on him, who said that his aim was "to make you hear, to make you feel, it is before all to make you *see*"[11] (20). That will do as nicely for le Carré as he thinks it does for McCullin. Finally, le Carré says McCullin's sense of humor is "half way to self-parody" (21). I have already suggested that le Carré's is more than halfway there.

Interpretations of the Texts

Sometimes motive is portrayed as ideological, although le Carré only uses the term as a pejorative. For example, in chapter 16 of *Call for the Dead,* the narrator contrasts Smiley's and Dieter's motives in terms of what I call *temperament* or *ideology*. "Everything he admired or loved had been the product of intense individualism. That is why he hated Dieter now, hated what he stood for more strongly than ever before: it was the fabulous impertinence of renouncing the individual in favour of the mass. When had the mass philosophies ever brought benefit or wisdom? Dieter cared nothing for human life: dreamed only of the armies of faceless men bound by their lowest common denominators" (138). The ideological and the psychological are frequently inextricably intertwined, however, as the inclusion of temperament within a broad definition of ideology implies. Temperament is the predisposition for adhering to a given ideological doctrine. Smiley explained over dinner to his two closest allies in the case, Mendel and Guillam, Elsa Fennan's motive: "I think she dreamed of a world without conflict, ordered and preserved by the new doctrine." He recalled how she had shouted at him, "I'm the wandering Jewess . . . the no-man's land, the battlefield of your toy soldiers" (155). The new Germany rebuilt in the image of the old was too much for her. It trivialized her suffering. "I think she wanted peace" (156). Personal suffering and fear that history is repeating itself lead her to identify with the antifascist communist East.

In response to the question of Dieter's motive, Smiley replied: "God knows what Dieter wanted. Honour, I think, and a socialist world. . . . They dreamed of peace and freedom. Now they're murderers and spies" (156). This statement emphasizes a theme noted by Wallace (1985:6–7) "that admirable actions, ideals, and intentions often lead to tragic consequences." Smiley tells his friends that you had to know Dieter in the beginning to understand his evolution. "He went the full circle. I don't think he ever got over being a traitor in the war. He had to put it right. He was one of those world-builders who seem to do nothing but destroy: that's all" (156). But of course, that is not all. It never can be all. It probably only touches the surface of what made these two highly complex individuals act as they did. The possibility that a German Jew who remained as a spy in Germany throughout World War II and survived could feel guilt at having betrayed the Third Reich is impossible to explain so succinctly, if at all, even by an artist as gifted as le Carré.[12]

Another related psychological theme introduced by le Carré in this novel (and a refrain frequently repeated in others) is the cost to the agent of the repression of his feelings. The narrator tells us that during Smiley's first clandestine assignment as a "englischer Dozent" at a provincial German university, "it saddened him to witness in himself the gradual death of natural pleasure. Always withdrawn, he now found himself shrinking from the temptations of friendship and human loyalty; he guarded himself warily from spontaneous reaction. By the strength of his intellect, he forced himself to observe humanity with clinical objectivity, and because he was neither im-mortal nor infallible he hated and feared the falseness of his life" (11).

The first epigraph of this chapter, taken from *A Murder of Quality,* con-tinues: "There is no true thing on earth. There is no constant, no depend-able point, not even in the purest logic or the most obscure mysticism; least of all in the motives of men when they are moved to act violently" (113). Smiley goes even further: "I don't believe . . . that we can ever entirely know what makes anyone do anything" (130). In the final scene in which Smiley, his former colleague Ailsa Brimely, and the murderer Terence Fielding are dining, Smiley tells Fielding that "we just don't know what people are like, we can never tell; there isn't any truth about human be-ings, no formula that meets each one of us. And there are some of us— aren't there?—who are *nothing,* who are so labile that we astound ourselves; we're the *chameleons*" (148; emphasis added). Le Carré's many chameleons achieve paradigmatic representation in Magnus Pym from *A Perfect Spy.* He suggests that espionage attracts people with this type of per-sonality and that, being a spy, not to mention a double agent, cultivates this personality trait as a survival technique. They are seen by the world as "showmen, fantasists, liars, as sensualists perhaps, not for what they are: the *living dead*"(149; emphasis added). The last sentence of the novel recapitu-lates the theme. "But there was nothing to see. Only the half-lit street, and the shadows moving along it" (151). Le Carré suggests that we see only half-lit images, at best shadows of one another.

In *The Spy Who Came in from the Cold* (26) Leamas informs Control that he is game to kill Mundt, the East German agent responsible for liq-uidating his network of agents. Control replies, "Do you really feel that? . . . Yes, I really think you do. But you mustn't feel you *have* to say it. I mean in our world we pass so quickly out of the register of hate or love. . . . All that's left in the end is a kind of nausea." This is a good de-scription of the deadening of feeling in the world of espionage of which Smiley speaks so movingly. Yet Control, characteristically, is being disin-genuous. He successfully recruits Leamas to the mission by playing on his desire for revenge against Mundt. Leamas volunteers by saying "I'd like to take a swing at Mundt" (27).

Establishing a cover is an exaggeration of one's own personality and therefore may be indirectly self-revelatory. Establishing his cover, Leamas goes to seed, appears to become a drunken wreck, and is increasingly iso-lated. Although he professes to believe in nothing, his lover perceives him as a fanatic sworn to vengeance. Leamas equates love with fairy tales yet later sacrifices his life for love. When Fiedler presses him about his philos-ophy, Leamas replies, "We're nothing. Just people." Fiedler persists, asking how they can be certain they are right. Leamas, irritated, responds, "Who the hell said they were?" (143). Pressed further, he retorts, "I just think the whole lot of you are bastards. . . . I suppose they don't like Communism" (144). This vague anticommunism (an incoherent ideology), he grudgingly admitted, justified the taking of human life.[13]

The complexity of characters like Leamas cannot be reduced to labels like *cynic* or *romantic*. Peter Wolfe (1987:114) calls Leamas "very naive for a veteran hand." Two pages later he says that Leamas is "cynical, he holds no brief with friendship or religion; he reads no books and supports no political ideologies."[14] On the following page he calls him a "man of duty, faith, and courage." As paradoxical as this sounds, it is consistent with le Carré's belief that individuals with fragmented personalities can express contradictory character traits. It also accords with my interpretation of the search for balance, which entails moving back and forth between idealism and realism. Wolfe suggests that Leamas, in reaction to his career of deception and self-denial, affirms romantic love through death. The naïve cynic dies a faithful romantic.[15]

Peter Lewis (1985:71) concludes: "His last action is one of moral integrity in an amoral world, a gesture of defiance against the law that prevails on both sides of the Wall: the end justifies the means." (In *The Honourable Schoolboy*, Jerry Westerby faces an almost identical fate.) The success of the heartless double agent Mundt over the kind and decent Fiedler appears to indicate that kindness and decency are liabilities for a spy. Yet the exceptional Smiley and Gadi Becker (in *The Little Drummer Girl*) achieve a skeptical balance and survive. Leonard Burr (in *The Night Manager*) also combines these qualities and, like Smiley, ultimately loses his political battle with his fellow British rivals and their allies in the CIA, but he manages to save the life of his agent.

Liz Gold is the paradigmatic naïve victim. She is identified as Jewish (as are many of le Carré's victims[16]), and is ostensibly a communist. In chapter 19 (186), however, she compares a meeting in her Party branch to church services that she attends—which casts doubt on the depth of both her Judaism and her communism.[17] She momentarily considers the possibility that Leamas was right: "You believed in things because you needed to; what you believed in had no value of its own, no function" (187). But then she rejects this outlook: "No, it was wrong, Alec [Leamas] was wrong—it was a wicked thing to say. Peace and freedom and equality— they were facts, of course they were." In chapter 22, le Carré describes her entering the courtroom "like a half-awakened child" (213). Like his prize agent before him, the love of a woman dooms Leamas and Liz and also Fiedler.[18]

In response to a cynical justification of political expediency (quoted in chapter 4 above), Liz responds that Leamas is trying to persuade himself.

"It's far more terrible, what they are doing; to find the humanity in people, in me and whoever else they use, to turn it like a weapon in their hands, and use it to hurt and kill" (247). With the loss of illusion, but not necessarily of faith, Liz realizes how the essence of humanity—love—is used as a weapon.[19] This is dramatically illustrated in *The Looking Glass War.* Leclerc, the head of the Department, is characterized by Wolfe (1987:126–8) as a fatuous, bloodless, heartless, pompous fool whose "heart shriveled and died long ago," leaving "a moral void." Leclerc callously uses his subordinates inappropriately, without giving them proper training and support, which costs two of them their lives. He does all of this in a vain attempt to regain the lost power and glory the Department had during the war. His efforts are in vain. Wolfe notes the fact that "he's reproached by aloof, disdainful Haldane [his colleague] shows how far he has strayed from living values" (129). Since Haldane is a supreme cynic himself, this is quite a commentary.

Given these qualities, it is remarkable that Leclerc could inspire the filial love of the much younger John Avery:

> There were times when Avery felt for Leclerc a deep, protective love. Leclerc had that indefinable quality of arousing guilt, as if his companion but poorly replaced a departed friend . . . so that while at one moment Avery could hate him for his transparent manipulation, detest his prinking gestures as a child detests the affectations of a parent, at the next he ran to protect him, responsible and caring. Beyond all the vicissitudes of their relationship, he was somehow grateful that Leclerc had engendered him; and thus they created that strong love which only exists between the weak; each became the stage to which the other related his actions. (34)

Weak people tend to play off of one another's weaknesses. Weakness of character can be an inducement to spy, or at least it makes one vulnerable to recruitment. An adventurous spirit can also provide motivation. As le Carré told Hugh McIlvanney (1983:19), "Most people spy for love, love of the trip, love of the game, perhaps. For anyone who is young and naughty-minded, it's fun—because it's showbiz."[20]

Avery's skeptical wife, Sarah, chides: " 'Poor John, . . . Loyalty without faith. It's very hard for you.' She said this with total dispassion as if she had identified a social evil" (57). Yet he and his colleagues affirm a faith that "burned in some separate chapel and they called it patriotism." Avery feels his heart thrilling with love, and in his heart he thanks Leclerc for the opportunity "to become a man, shoulder to shoulder with the others, tempered in the fire of war; he thanked him for the precision of command, which made order out of the anarchy of his heart" (64). In these few lines le Carré suggests the multiplicity of factors that motivate Avery. He, like le Carré, missed World War II and envies and admires those who fought in it. The "anarchy of his heart" represents his fragmented personality pulling him in different directions and crying out for the order and discipline that Leclerc's leadership and the Department give him. Therefore, against his better judgment, he overcomes his well-founded doubts and blindly follows Leclerc.

Le Carré also makes clear that Avery (like his other spies) is running away from emotional entanglements—in this case, his wife. On returning from the fiasco of his first assignment abroad, he announces to Sarah: "I'm going to resign; I've decided" (97). But when she tells him she informed the police he was abroad on a secret assignment, he explodes with anger and tells her he can't possibly leave the office.[21] His behavior, like so many of his creator's spies, can best be described as adolescent. He has yet to mature into an adult. In another scene, he visits the house where he and Sarah lived in their first year of marriage: "Standing before it, he tried to detect in the house, in himself, some trace of sentiment, or affection, or love, or whatever it was that explained their marriage, but it was not to be found and he supposed it had never been. He sought desperately, wanting to find the motive of youth; but there was none. He was staring into an empty house. He hastened home to the place where Leiser lived." His home has become the safe house (literally as well as figuratively) where he lives during the training of his first (and only) agent, Leiser. Avery has courted Leiser and developed a more loving relationship with him than he has with his wife. When Leiser is abandoned for the sake of political expediency, Avery breaks down and pleads in the name of love to save him: "Love. Yes, love! Not yours, Haldane, mine. Smiley's right! You made me do it for you, made me love him! It wasn't in you any more! I brought him to you, I kept him in your house, made him dance to the music of your bloody war! I piped for him, but there's no breath in me now. He's Peter Pan's last victim, Haldane, the last one, the last love; the last music gone" (239).

As the adults go about their business, Avery sobs "like a child. No one heeded him" (240). The biggest cynic of the bunch, Control, has won; the cynical has-beens Leclerc and Haldane lose but accept it as part of the game. Haldane tells Smiley: "My congratulations to Control" (239). Leclerc invites Smiley to dine at his club. The disillusioned idealist Avery is sobbing, and the naïve idealist Leiser dies aiding and abetting his own deception—almost as conscious a suicide as Leamas and in exactly the same position as Westerby (in *The Honourable Schoolboy*).

What motivates a man not only to risk his life, but to undertake a suicide mission? When Haldane approaches him, his first impression was: "It was a face which at first sight recorded nothing but *loneliness*"

(108; emphasis added). He looked an innocent man, but traveled. Leiser, a Polish exile had served as an agent for the Department twenty years previously. Haldane flatters Leiser with the lie that he was remembered by everyone in the Department as one of their very best agents. He also deceives him, saying that the Department was bigger than ever. Haldane condescends to Leiser, whom he considers lower class and a foreigner. Probably because he knows the operation is doomed and doesn't want Leiser to accept, Haldane feigns anger over a remark Leiser made during dinner and walks out on him. Ironically, because Leiser looks up to upper-class Englishmen like Haldane and desperately wants to be accepted by them, Haldane's ploy had the opposite of its intended effect. Leiser calls the Department and agrees to undertake the mission, just when Haldane is telling Leclerc "he wouldn't play."

Avery asks Haldane what made Leiser change his mind. Haldane replies: "Why do agents ever do anything? Why do any of us? . . . Why do they consent or refuse, why do they lie or tell the truth? Why do any of us? . . . Perhaps he's under-employed. It's the Germans; he hates them. That's what he says. I place no value on that. Then he couldn't let us down. I assume he means himself" (120). Avery ventures his opinion, in confidence to Leclerc's secretary, that he thinks Leiser did it for the money. This is typical of le Carré. He gives his best clues indirectly, through description of Leiser's loneliness, his nostalgia for the comradeship experienced during the war, and through his unpredicted reaction to Haldane's haughtiness. Then le Carré has Haldane create a smoke screen by making a remark with a kernel of truth, about not wanting to let down the Department and himself. Finally, he has Avery, who hasn't even met Leiser yet, show off his ignorance with a nonsensical explanation. The reader has to put the right pieces of the puzzle together to get a semblance of an accurate picture.

The Department chooses Oxford as the place to train Leiser because that is where it was done in the war. Le Carré tells us how pleased Leiser was with the choice. What non-English-born citizen who aspires to be accepted as part of British society would not be enchanted by Oxford? Haldane emphasizes to Avery, "Leiser is not one of us. Never make that mistake. We touched him long ago, that's all. . . . He's an agent. He's a man to be handled, not known." When Avery persists in trying to understand Leiser's motives, Haldane replies: "I mistrust reasons. I mistrust words like loyalty. Above all . . . I mistrust *motive*. We're running an agent; the arithmetic is over. You read German, didn't you? In the beginning was the deed[22] (124). Although he had ventured a simplistic explanation previously, after meeting him Avery realizes that "no single factor wholly accounted for Leiser's recruitment" (131). He is shaken by the reality of the human being who materialized from the ideas they had courted incestuously among themselves. When Avery asks Haldane what he makes of Leiser, he is brushed off with a curt "I hardly know him," which makes clear he has no desire to do so. Haldane orders Avery to always be in Leisure's company and stresses: "He's a very *lonely* man" (133). Leiser's need to feel wanted, useful, important, and accepted is brought out by his conversations with Avery with whom he bonds as they go through his training together. Le Carré describes the training experience as: "carefree, exciting days for both of them, days of honest labour and cautious but deepening attachment as the skills of boyhood became once more the weapons of war" (141). There are interesting parallels with the relationship between Charlie and Gadi Becker in *The Little Drummer Girl.*

Le Carré frequently notes the pleasure agents derive from the direction of being run.[23] This phenonenon is especially ironic in this case, because the agent in question is being sacrificed in a futile mission that was doomed from the outset. After Leiser crosses the border to his fate, Haldane speculates on the exploitation of Leisure's love: "We never knew him, did we? . . . When we met him he was a man without love. Do you know what love is? I'll tell you: it is whatever you can still betray. We ourselves live without it in our profession. We don't force people to do things for us. We let them discover love. And, of course, Leiser did, didn't he? He married us for money, so to speak, and left us for love. . . . Love is what he gave to us" (202–3). While he is trapped in East Germany, Leiser remembers and idealizes his relationships with Haldane and Avery: "A man could go through life and never meet a set of blokes like that" (217). As he prepares to transmit to his controllers, who are no longer listening because they have closed down the operation, he checks his watch, which was synchronized with Avery's; this "gave him comfort. Like divided lovers, they were looking at the same star" (219).[24]

We first get a glimpse of the shadowy Leo Harting in the prologue of *A Small Town in Germany,* in his aborted attempt to assassinate Karfeld, a neo-Nazi leader.[25] Harting, one of the two main protagonists (although he only appears in the final scene), was the consummate outsider. "His accent was neither wholly English nor wholly German, but a privately elected no-man's-land, picked and set between the two" (6). This single sentence establishes his marginality. We later learn that he is a twenty-year "temporary" employee of the British embassy. "Unpromotable, unpostable, unpensionable. Chancery gave him living space. Not a *proper* diplomat" (46). In London, where his absence is interpreted as a defection, he is described this way: "There's a smell, that's all. A foreign smell. Refugee background, emigrated in the thirties. Farm school, Pioneer Corps, Bomb Disposal. He gravitated to Germany in forty-five. Temporary sergeant; Control commission; one of the old carpetbaggers by the

sound of it. Professional expatriate . . . some drifted into the con-
sulates . . . *No childhood,* most of them, that's the trouble" (45).

We first meet Alan Turner in the Foreign Office in London (in chapter
3). "It was known that he was a late entrant, never a good sign, and a former Fellow of Saint Anthony's College, Oxford, which takes all kinds of
people" (38). When his boss, Lumley, reads Harting's file to Turner and
mentions his lack of childhood, he apologizes to Turner and "almost
blushed," revealing Turner's lack of a childhood as well. We learn much
later he was brought up in an orphanage. Lumley, trying to understand
him, asks Turner: "What drives you? What are you looking for? Some
bloody absolute. If there is one thing I really hate it's a cynic in search of
God. Maybe a bit of failure is what you need (48).[26] Lumley tells Turner:
"Try and look as though you belong." Turner responds: "I don't though,
do I?" Lumley retorts: "All right, . . . Wear the cloth cap [symbol of the
working class]. Christ . . . I'd have thought your class was suffering from
too much recognition already" (48).

Less than fifty pages into the novel, le Carré has already established an
affinity between the two major protagonists. Both had terrible childhoods
and are outsiders in pursuit of an unknown absolute. Turner acknowledges
this affinity: "*Come on, Leo, we're of one blood, you and I: underground men, that's
us. . . . We've got the earth's dirt on us, you and I. I'll chase you, you chase me, and
each of us will chase ourselves*" (115). Others see it as well. For example, de
Lisle tells Turner: "You and Leo form a team of your own. You're the other
side of the wire. Both of you. That's your problem" (133). Both enjoy the
intellectual challenge of making order out of chaos. Like Smiley, Turner had
abandoned "the *contemplative* life of the academic in favor of the *functional*
life of the civil servant" (153). Turner recognizes the identity between Harting's fervor, his ruthless aggressive drive, and his own (161). Another character tells Turner, "you and Harting have *many* things in common" (175).

Harting and Turner both searched for moral absolutes. In recognition
of this commonality, de Lisle says to Turner, "If that's what you think about
life . . . why don't you defect yourself? God is dead. You can't have it both ways—
that would be too medieval" (182). When Turner tells him, "I'm chasing a
ghost . . . A bloody shadow," de Lisle retorts, "Your own"(198). An embassy
employee remarks, "I mean you can't pack everything up neat and tidy.
Not in life, you can't. That's for girls. That's just romantic. You get like Leo
otherwise; you can't leave a thing alone" (212). Even after he was ordered
home to London, Turner could not abandon his quest either. When
knocked unconscious, Turner "heard Leo's music whining to God in every
red timber tabernacle of his own childhood" (221).

De Lisle quips "how *like* the Foreign Office . . . to send a bull to catch
a matador" (223). He continues: "You complement one another. I look at

you and I think of Leo. You're Saxon. Big hands, big feet, big heart and that lovely reason that grapples with ideals. Leo's the other way around. He's a performer. He wears our clothes, uses our language, but he's only half tamed. . . . There's a Leo in all of us, but he's usually dead by the time we're twenty" (224).[27] De Lisle admits that he learned to live with being half finished, like most people. He tells Turner: "All right. Go and look for your untamed half" (225). De Lisle also comments on how both Turner and Harting are movers who failed to come to terms with apathy. He says of Harting, "*I have never known anyone . . . make such a meal of his disadvantages.*"

Hazel Bradfield, the last in a series of Harting's lovers, contrasts him with Turner. "He was *alive.* . . . Not like you a bit. *You're* about the deadest thing I ever met." Yet she also describes Harting as "*empty . . . just imitating life.* . . . He was caught between all those worlds: . . . You can't expect anyone to fight all those battles and stay alive. . . . He didn't live, he survived. He's always survived. Till now" (231, 233). Le Carré uses contradictory descriptions to comment on the similarities and the differences between the two characters; he also uses the contradictory attributes of a character to indicate how differently people perceive one another and to emphasize the complexity of human personality.

After discovering the Glory Hole, the basement hideout in the embassy where Harting stashed and worked on the stolen files, Turner felt as if he "was alone like Harting, contraband smuggled in, living like Harting on borrowed time; hunting, like Harting, for a missing truth . . . *That's what we're all doing, isn't it: looking for something that isn't there. . . . And whatever he found down there was the other part of coming alive*" (251). In ascribing motivation to Harting's actions, Turner includes the fact that he was half Jewish (a significant factor in his relentless pursuit of Karfeld's war crimes), his age, "sense of something left undone," a "sense of history," and of "time." "The paradoxes caught up with him, and he had to do something about it. He was also in love. . . . He'd escaped from lethargy"[28] (267). In the final scene, Turner gazes at the corpse of Harting, seeing him physically for the first and last time: "He stood on the shore, beneath the scaffold, looking at his own life, his own face, at the lover's hands grasping the cobble . . . an *innocent,* reaching beyond the square for a prize he would never find" (311; emphasis added).

In contrast to Harting and Turner, who share an uncompromising, absolute commitment to historical truth and a sense of justice, de Lisle and Bradfield represent the other extreme of complete subordination of principles to political expediency. Their form of cynicism (as I have been using the term) is expressed by Bradfield as extreme relativism: "There are no absolutes here. . . . It is all doubt. All mist" (273). "Le Carré wants us to ask whether surfaces threatening to spew out poison *should* be left undisturbed" (Wolfe, 1987:146). In this novel, le Carré's sympathies seem to lie with those who would lance the wound in order to allow the poison to spew out, rather than with those who wish to leave it undisturbed. To stay with the metaphor, he seems to imply that allowing such an infection in the body politic to fester could prove fatal. Yet Lars Ole Sauerberg (1984:58) suggests that Turner's lesson is "Absolutism cannot be fought by absolutism."

Although these characters emerge in all of their complex humanity—including Harting, who never speaks for himself and is viewed only through other's eyes—they are also prototypes who appear in other forms as well in le Carré's oeuvre. Most of le Carré's heroes are patriotic Englishmen (not simply British); there are no Scots or Welsh among them. The lone exception is Gadi Becker, an Israeli, in *The Little Drummer Girl,* whom most of the critics have strangely ignored. For example, Jim Prideaux in *Tinker, Tailor, Soldier, Spy,* is passionately English and is described as a "very patriotic bloke" (15). Connie Sacks, the colorful Sovietologist with a computerlike memory, expresses the nostalgic patriotism that pervades the novel: "It was a good time. . . . A real time. Englishmen could be proud then. Let them be proud now" (113). She calls Bill Haydon and Smiley the last of the generation who were trained to rule the empire.

During the same conversation with Peter Guillam quoted above, Smiley tells him: "The more identities a man has, the more they express the person they conceal. . . . Few men can resist expressing their appetites when they are making a fantasy about themselves" (207). Yet Smiley's interrogations of Haydon are remarkably unrevealing. Haydon expresses his deep hatred of America, and his shock at the realization that England was "out of the game." Of his preference for the East, he says, "It's an aesthetic judgement as much as anything," and then adds, almost as an afterthought, "partly a moral one, of course" (356). He began spying for the Soviets around 1950 by giving selected information that would damage the Americans without harming the English: "The Suez adventure in '56 finally persuaded him of the inanity of the British situation, and of the British capacity to spike the advance of history while not being able to offer anything by way of contribution. This sight of the Americans sabotaging the British action in Egypt was, paradoxically, and additional incentive. He would say therefore that from '56 on, he was a committed, full-time Soviet mole with no holds barred. In 1961 he formally received Soviet citizenship" (359–60).

Even an excellent interrogator like Smiley could not get the truth from Haydon. "Smiley was conscious all the while that even the little Haydon was telling him was selected with meticulous care from a greater, and perhaps somewhat different truth" (360). As Haydon spoke, "He seemed visibly to be shrinking to something quite small and mean." After hearing that Haydon had been instructed by Karla to have an affair with Ann to throw Smiley off his trail, Smiley "slipped out, not bothering to say good-by" (363).

Smiley's conclusions raise as many questions as they answer. He has the sensation of watching Haydon through the wrong end of a telescope. The more he tried to make sense of Haydon's rambling account, the more the contradictions became obvious. Smiley decides that treason is a matter of habit. He also is convinced that "Bill had loved it, too. Smiley didn't doubt that for a moment. Standing at the middle of a secret stage, playing world against world, hero and playwright in one: oh, Bill had loved that, all right." Smiley was reconciled to receiving only partial truths. "Smiley shrugged it all aside, distrustful as ever of the standard shapes of human motive. He settled instead for a picture of one of those wooden Russian dolls that open up, revealing one person inside the other, and another inside him. Of all men living, only Karla had seen the last little doll inside Bill Haydon" (367). It is more in keeping with le Carré's position, however, to assume that even Karla had not seen the last doll. In fact, it is likely that even Haydon lacked sufficient self-awareness to have seen it—following the metaphor, the last doll was empty—hollow.[29]

In his Introduction to Page, Leitch, and Knightley (1968:3), le Carré rejects "the political motive of Kim Philby."[30] He, like Cornwell, learned duplicity from his father. He loved the game for its own sake: "Deceit was Philby's life's work; deceit, as I understand it, his *nature*. . . . Philby has no home, no woman, no faith. Behind the political label, behind the inbred upper-class arrogance, the taste for adventure, lies the *self-hate* of a vain misfit for whom nothing will ever be worthy of his loyalty. In the last instance, Philby is driven by the *incurable drug of deceit itself*" (7; emphasis added). Le Carré suggests that Philby began to crack when the disparity between the dream and reality closed in on him. Indirectly, he exonerates Smiley for his unproductive interrogation of Haydon by explaining that a confession "by a man of Philby's expertise is like the peeling of an onion; even the most gifted interrogator may never reach the heart" (13).[31]

Le Carré pays particularly close attention to motive in *The Honourable Schoolboy*.[32] The role of family, the deprivation of separation from loved ones, the love between brothers, and the influence of fathers reveal the emotional wounds of major and minor characters alike. Stefan Kanfer (1987:10) observes about the central character: "The Schoolboy's odyssey is both official and personal. As colleague's perish, as the enigmatic Ko brothers become more comprehensible, as loyalties dissolve, Jerry [Westerby] finds himself questioning his own motives and, finally, his orders, the discipline of his 'tradecraft.'" Westerby's feelings about his father, Samuel, help to explain his transfer of loyalty from Smiley to Drake Ko, an opium-dealing gangster posing as a legitimate businessman and philanthropist, whom he identifies with his father.[33]

Drake Ko's devotion to his younger brother Nelson, from whom he has been separated since they were orphaned as youths, is the primary motive driving one of the key actions in the plot. Liz Worthington's possibly abusive relationship with her father and her subsequent relations with father figures ranging from her husband to her present lover, Drake Ko, helps to explain her damaged personality and consequent behavior. Even minor characters, like the opium-addicted pilot Charlie Marshall, whose unreciprocated love for his Kuomintang outlaw father make him pitiable, are dignified by insights into their personalities.

The mingling of personal and collective motives expresses le Carré's use of spying as a metaphor for universal political dilemmas. "All of the book's leading figures live apart from their closest intimates; all suffer from the rift: some risk their lives trying to heal it."[34] Drake Ko's devotion to his brother Nelson is his undoing as is Jerry Westerby's infatuation with Ko's mistress, Lizzie Worth. Lizzie's abandonment of her schoolteacher husband and their child in England for a series of affairs with assorted losers in the Far East, before she trades herself to Ko for the life of her previous lover, is partly explained by the insinuation of abuse by her father. Jerry identifies Ko with his own colorful father, toward whom he felt as ambiguous as the author feels about his. Freud would have a field day interpreting Jerry's infatuation with his surrogate father's mistress as he would with Ko's calling his mistress (who views him as a surrogate father) by his foster mother's name.

These characters are extreme expressions of what, in more moderate forms, are universal human traits:

> Others share the Ko's plight of leading an everyday existence that bypasses the interior realities ruling them. The novel collapses the distinction between external perception and inward mood, yoking consciousness and dream to the same dark source. The people in *Schoolboy* act from the unknowable impulsive, and chaotic inner life that inhabits us all and that we know so little about. . . . [Smiley reveals] the truth that rebels often act from sources deeper than reason or morality. Though these sources are hidden, their results can be predicted. . . . Several characters in the book forfeit security by following their hearts. Anyone tempted by love [in the secret world] both puts him/herself and the beloved at risk. (Wolfe, 1987:202)

The killing of Jerry, probably by the psychopath Fawn, is unjustified, even though Jerry had drawn his weapon and may have used it. (Jerry's death did not carry the same moral weight for this reader as did Harting's struggle against the cover-up of the war crimes of a dangerous German politician.) Le Carré undoubtedly loves Westerby as he does most of his characters. Nevertheless, by having Jerry, with several unsuccessful marriages under his belt, die unnecessarily for Lizzie (whom he calls "the prize of his survival" after a single encounter with her) lessens the significance and impact of his death.[35]

Far from redeeming her, Jerry's Galahad act places her in even greater danger.[36] Westerby is portrayed as a middle-aged adolescent.[37] Clearly, Jerry does not obtain balance in the way I have been interpreting le Carré. Rather, he goes from mindless obedience to Smiley's authority ("You point me and I'll march" [105]) to mindless rebellion against it ("That's the last foot in the last door for me . . . forever and a day" [522]). He simply transfers his loyalty from Smiley to the Ko brothers.[38] He acts emotionally and impulsively.[39]

The fate of a character is one indication of the author's evaluation of their relative success in coping with their life's circumstances. For example, Jerry died a "romantic" but completely unnecessary death. In addition, he gave the CIA the excuse it was looking for to intervene and take over the operation. The deaths of both Leamas and of Harting were more heroic than was the more pathetic demise of Westerby. As LynnDianne Beene (1992:103) concludes, he "dies ignominiously." Was this defeat self-inflicted? Wolfe (1987:223) suggests a death wish, "a secret love of defeat, perhaps even of annihilation pervades *Schoolboy*. This destructive impulse accounts for the death of institutions, the slaughter of people, the devastation of land, and even self-destruction." In addition to the psychological dimension driven by disturbed and even traumatic childhoods, this destructive impulse is linked to the fact that the novel takes place in the shadow of the devastating end of the war in Vietnam, which extended into Laos and Cambodia, and in the shadow of the forthcoming withdrawal of Great Britain from its last colonial holding in Hong Kong. It is a time of political uncertainty and, as Tony Barley (1986:123) points out, "a time of crisis and transition." The metaphoric "death wish" parallels the political role of the United States in Southeast Asia at the time.

In *The Little Drummer Girl*, Charlie's theatrical agent attributes her terrible childhood as a factor that sends her toward fantasy. "Dissembling. Hiding your emotions. Copying people who look happier than you are. *Or* unhappier. Stealing a bit of 'em—what acting's half about. Misery. Theft" (75). He calls Charlie a "chameleon." He claims that she, along with most actors and actresses, doesn't have opinions. "They have moods. Fads. Poses." He says they are pursued by "an absolute *horror* of unreality." Off stage, they are "hollow vessels waiting to be filled" (79). The hollowness of the chameleon is reminiscent of Bill Haydon and of Magnus Pym, among others. The fantasist in her is very similar to Harry Pendel.[40]

Charlie, characterized by McIlvanney (1983:21), quoting le Carré, as a chronically dislocated fantasist craving reality: "If I had met Charlie in the circumstances defined in the book I could have recruited her. . . . The factor of the liability of loyalty, its flexibility, was working for the Israelis when they moved in on her. And they played on her actress's nature. They offered her reality, which all actors yearn for. They offered her love and money, too. They completed her life for her." Charlie was particularly self-revealing when, under Israeli interrogation, she thinks: "They knew her through and through; they knew her fragility and her *plurality*. And they still wanted her. . . . their true allegiance, to fill the *emptiness* that had yawned and screamed inside her like a bored demon ever since she could remember" (138; emphasis added). Homberger (1986:93), who compares Charlie with Klaus Fuchs, who defined his own personality as "controlled schizophrenia," stresses the central *nothingness* of Charlie's self-identity.

Yet even the more stable Gadi Becker, in the midst of his agonized soul-searching, could identify with this aspect of Charlie's personality. "I *feel* that I am an actor, as you are, surrounding myself with versions of my identity because the original somehow went missing along the road. But in truth I feel nothing because real feeling is subversive and contrary to military discipline" (194). This death of feeling is exactly what Smiley experienced while working under cover in Germany and what he warned the young aspiring spies about in his lecture to them.

The characterization of both Charlie and Gadi, especially the development of their characters through their growing love for each other, was discussed in chapter 3. The development of Gadi's character constitutes a development in le Carré as a writer as well. In his previous novels, characters died for either their absolutist ideals (Dieter Frey, Elsa Fennan, Jens Fiedler, and Leo Harting), chameleon-like lack of character (Bill Haydon), naïve innocence (Liz Gold), or romantic love (Fred Leiser and Jerry Westerby). For the first time, le Carré leaves open the *possibility* of characters surviving traumatic disillusionment from naïve innocence and fantasist or chameleon-like character (Charlie) and the deadening suppression of self-hood (Gadi) through their mutual love and support.

In subsequent novels, people continue to die because they fail to achieve balance. The suicides are the chameleons Magnus Pym (*The Perfect Spy*), whose personality Homberger (1986:100) describes as "an absence," and Harry Palfrey (*Our Game*),[41] the fantasist Harry Pendel (*The Tailor of Panama*), and the guilt-ridden Holocaust survivor Annie Lippshitz (Lippsie) (*A Perfect Spy*), "the one person to whom Magnus Pym gives uncompromised love."[42] A chameleon in the same novel, Grant Lederer III, the CIA agent, says, "What I recognize in Pym is what I recognize in myself. . . . We're howling psychopaths, the both of us" (239). He survives but is a failure both as a human being and as a professional. Cyril Frewin (*The Secret Pilgrim),* who describes himself as a "hole" and says, "I don't exist" (312), also survives. This traitorous Foreign Office cipher clerk's fate is perhaps worse than death, however—he must live with himself, in prison. The idealistic absolutists, Goethe in *The Russia House* and Larry Pettifer (who "had the lost-boy appeal of a poet who never grew up,") in *Our Game* (1995:4), die as a consequence of behavior that is virtually suicidal. They, like Leo Harting, are much closer to the agents who die for love, because their own actions doom them.

Yet there are survivors as well who display growth or at least the potential for growth. In *A Perfect Spy,* Mary Pym although less fully drawn as a character than her husband and her father-in-law, seems to achieve a skeptical balance. Her former lover and boss, Jack Brotherhood, moves in that direction as well (although he has not progressed as far as Mary, much less Smiley or Gadi). Perhaps most surprising of all, in *The Russia House* a CIA agent, Russell Sheriton, is portrayed by le Carré for the first time as having developed in character with qualities of a skeptic. In the same novel, Barley Blair, although closer in character to Jerry Westerby than to Gadi Becker, escapes with his own life and the hope (illusion) that his Russian lover will be allowed to join him.

In *The Secret Pilgrim,* Smiley achieves a skeptical balance that speaks to the heart of his protégé, Ned, whose career as detailed in the novel shows him to be striving haltingly in that direction. But Ned fails to achieves the maturity, the balance, and the self-awareness of Smiley, Gadi, or even of his boss, Leonard Burr. During his quest he admits to having failed to come to grips with life and sees himself as a ridiculous figure. "I still looked to the world to provide me with the chance to make my contribution—and I blamed it for not knowing how to use me" (176). He defines his life as "a search, or nothing! But it was the fear that it was nothing that drove me forward"(178).

Whereas Smiley empathized with others, Ned tended to exaggeratedly overidentify at times, demonstrating an aspect of the personality trait of the chameleon. There is a difference between acting a role and assuming someone else's identity. Ned says of Hanson (a former agent): "He was assuming me, occupying me" (226). Ned even needs to be told by his boss, Burr, to leave his mistress and return to his wife and to stop being so narcissistic. On the final page of the novel, after he has retired, Ned muses: "You see your face. It's no one you remember. You wonder where you put your love, what you found, what you were after. You want to say: I slew the dragon, I left the world a safer place. You can't really, not these days. Perhaps you never could" (335).

Leonard Burr, in his cameo appearance in *The Secret Pilgrim,* is an enigma to his subordinates. Ned's first impressions of him, based on superficial appearances, fool him (261–2). Burr's capacity for intimacy, so uncharacteristic of people in his line of work—especially those in places of responsibility—completely baffles him (264). Peter Guillam, who has become head of secretariat for Burr in the aftermath of Blair's defection, explains to Ned that "Leonard was Smiley's Crown Prince for years. George rescued him from a fate worse than death at All Souls" (266). His position as head of Enforcement in *The Night Manager* gives him a very different perspective from when he was assistant director of the intelligence service. In fact, Burr is the moral center in *The Night Manager.*

Burr exceeds Ned in achieving a skeptical balance. He recognized in his agent Jonathan Pine "the kind of rebellious obedience that reminded him of himself" (61). (It also reminds the reader of Burr's mentor, George Smiley.) The narrator describes Pines reaction to Burr: "He could find no fault with Burr. Burr was from the heart, which was his saving. He might be clever. He might have mastered the grammar of intrigue, he had an eye for human strength and failing. But the heart still led, as Goodhew knew and Jonathan could feel, which was why he permitted Burr to wander in his private kingdom and why Burr's sense of mission was beginning to throb like a war drum in Jonathan's ear" (70). Pine's motives for volunteering for his dangerous assignment are discussed in the analysis of his recruitment by Burr in chapter 7. Burr manages to save Pine and his lover, whose promise of better future together mirrors that of Charlie and Gadi. Although Burr is as obsessed with his "personal Antichrist," Richard Onslow Roper, as was Smiley with Karla, ultimately his humanity prevails as he spares no effort—including seriously jeopardizing his career—to save his agent.

Our Game is, at one level, a story of the relationship between two friendly rivals: Larry Pettifer, a mercurial, radical, philandering, ex-double-agent, and sometimes professor, and Tim Cranmer, his self-loathing, uptight, unemotional, aristocratic ex-handler for twenty years. Tim, who acts as narrator, sums up Larry: "How could Larry be anything except what *we* made him; a directionless English middle-class revolutionary, a permanent dissident, a dabbler, a dreamer, a habitual rejecter, a ruthless, shiftless, philandering, wasted, semi-creative failure, too clever not to demolish an argument, too mulish to settle for a flawed one?" (24).

Larry is "a drunkard, womanizer, liar and disloyal friend, but he is a quixotic, Byronic figure with a heart of gold and a complete disregard for material comforts . . . He is also a political romantic and a lover of hopeless causes . . . who sees himself as a latter-day Lawrence of Arabia"

(Michael Scammell, 1995:13). Larry's identification with the cause of the Ingush (with whom the author also identifies) leads to his death in the Caucasus. A Joseph Conrad-like character, Larry is part mad genius turned savage (Kurtz in *Heart of Darkness*) and a romantic (Jim in *Lord Jim*). His death, like all of le Carré's absolute romantics, is futile. Larry is a more ambiguous critique of humanitarian military intervention than Conrad's Kurtz is of colonialism. That is because part of le Carré favors such efforts over inaction in the face of tragic political events, but he also sees their futility, which is why Larry dies.

In a moment of self-reflection, Timothy turns upon himself, bemoaning his inability to connect with others and what Larry called "the cavernous emptiness of . . . my dull rectangular mind." Christopher Lehmann-Haupt (1995) suggests that Timothy's quest to find his *doppel ganger*, Larry, who has disappeared, "is more a spiritual journey that lifts him out of his frozen self and into communion with Larry."

> It's clear from the start that Tim represents the post-Communist West, its head, now that the threat of sudden annihilation has passed, buried in its own backyard vineyard while the little people of the earth get trampled on. Larry may be a rash idealist, but next to the passive sensualist—next to the likes of Tim—the rash idealist is a hero and a saint. Le Carré has said as much in an op-ed piece written to accompany the novel, in which he condemns the West for ignoring the plight of the world's Ingushetias. (Menand, 1995:4)

The novel concludes: "For a moment longer I stood alone, converted to nothing, believing in nothing. I had no world to go back to and nobody left to run except myself. A Kalashnikov lay beside me. Slinging it over my shoulder, I hastened after him down the slope" (302). The conversion is not expressed through words but through actions directly contradicting the words that precede them. This merging of the personal with the political, the overt rejection of ideology while actions express an underlying liberal sentiment, is quintessential le Carré. Timothy's quest for Larry and for himself culminates in his identifying with him, assuming his commitment, and joining the battle in defense of the underdog. The personal development of his character symbolizes the author's projected hope for the West. Yet it leaves open his future as undetermined.

The Tailor of Panama, also expresses the theme that the most difficult mystery is the *human enigma.* Kurt Jensen (1996) succinctly sums up the essence of the novel: "The enigmatically human, it seems, is not something to be cracked; it can only be discerned in outline, its height and weight guessed at by impress of its fleeing footfall . . . 'The Tailor of Panama' tells us that the truth is what remains after all stories about the truth have been told." Le Carré allows one to discern whatever truths about human nature can be learned from nonverbal communication and actions rather than through verbally expressed motives.

Yehuda Gil, a real-life Harry Pendel, is a veteran field agent of the Mossad who fabricated intelligence on Syria that twice (1980 and 1996) brought Israel to the brink of war and probably contributed to the scuttling of peace negotiations in the latter instance. Gil, a Libyan-born Mossad agent since 1970, was among the veteran field agents (many from Arab countries) who felt marginalized by the Mossad's recruitment of more academically trained native Israelis and its greater reliance on technology. He reportedly suffered psychologically and wanted to prove his continued importance and that of human sources. In addition to fabricating reports that supported his hard-line nationalist ideological position (he served as secretary-general of the extreme right-wing Moledet party), he reportedly pocketed much of the $1.5 million he was supposed to have given his Syrian agents. Susser (1998:10–14) relates that his colleagues reason, "Gil felt an overwhelming need to live up to his legend. When his source dried up, he couldn't face his own impending loss of status." Such a brief characterization only hints at the complexity of the motives for such actions.

Reducing the complexity of individual characters to types distorts the richness of le Carré's portrayal and his point of view on the subject. Le Carré's characters are richly drawn, three-dimensional, complex, frequently fragmented personalities expressing conflicting attributes and impulses. Moreover, as I have shown, his characters frequently change and develop during the course of the novel. The simple topology I present below summarizes certain types of personality in le Carré's world of espionage. Each character is classified in the category closest to his or her position in their final appearance in the novel.

Conclusion

Significantly, all of le Carré's heroes have had highly problematic childhoods. David Cornwell was abandoned by his mother and by a beloved nanny, a surrogate mother, at an impressionably early age. He was haunted by the repeated betrayal of and exploitation by his father throughout most of his life. Cornwell, as the author John le Carré, projects his feelings and the consequences of his traumatic childhood onto the characters he creates.[43] In an interview with Dean Fischer (Kanfer with Fischer, 1977:51), le Carré admits that his characters, from Smiley to Westerby, "are written from an internal viewpoint: all are refractions of autobiography." He told Fischer (53), with reference to his relationship with his father, "You reach the point of emotional bankruptcy; the only thing you can do is walk away from it."

Figure 5.1 Personality Types of Selected Characters

Romantics	Absolutists	Chameleons	Skeptics	Cynics
Liz Gold	Dieter Frey	Bill Haydon	G. Smiley	Maston
Alec Leamas	Elsa Fennan	Charlie*	Gadi Becker	Control
Fred Leiser	Jens Fiedler	M. Pym	Mary Pym	Lacon
J. Prideaux*	Leo Harting	Rick Pym*	Brotherhood	Alleline
J. Westerby	A. Turner*	G. Lederer*	R. Sheriton	Enderby
Lippsie	Karla*	C. Frewin*	Ned	Leclerc
B. Blair*	Goethe	H. Palfrey	L. Burr	Haldane
Goodhew*	L. Pettifer	H. Pendel	J. Pine	Bradfield

*Exceptions in their category by having physically survived at the end of the novel. Although survivors, each suffers serious trauma and must live with a burden of guilt. All other romantics, absolutists, and chameleons die by their own hand or are killed. All skeptics and cynics survive, although the skeptics also with guilty consciences.

Developmental psychologists have established the importance of the bonds of attachment between children and parents, from infancy through adolescence, for a sense of security and emotional stability. Patterns of attachment tend to be passed on from generation to generation. But lack of support in early childhood can be compensated for in later stages. The role of parents, intimate friends, spouses, or therapists can be particularly important in breaking the link between early attachment experiences in child rearing and later behavior.[44]

Le Carré portrays children as the victims of society. "Few of the adults succeed in communicating with children" (Celia Hughes, 1981:276). His description of the domestic life of his characters is equally bleak. Marital breakdown, rather than loving and supportive relationships, is the norm for his spies. Consequently, damaged personalities are not likely to receive the emotional support necessary to heal childhood wounds. Most of le Carré's characters are emotionally damaged and incompletely mature individuals. Such types are not simply the projection of the author's personality and imagination. There are ample examples from the real world of espionage. In his review of two books on the social history of the CIA, David Fromkin (1996:169) observes of the two directors of covert operations from 1948–1961 and their two top aides: "There was a great deal of immaturity in them: a great deal of the undergraduate fraternity house."[45] The secret world seems to attract such personality types and encourages those tendencies through their subcultural norms.

Viktor Orlik (1989:30) asked le Carré why so many of his spies were "children who had not grown up or adults who have reverted to childhood."

He replied: "Such activities often attract immature, undeveloped people who have broken away from their anchor and are seeking "absolute" answers to their personal problems. . . . [They] are often narrow minded and rather helpless people who fancy that they know more than ordinary mortals and that they are better than others because they have a gun in their pockets" (30). Le Carré's spies suppress and attempt to escape from their emotions. Le Carré notes the exchange between spy and his agency: "It's willing seller, willing buyer. It's 'Join us, and you don't have to face yourself.'"[46] Monaghan (1983:580) suggests: "To seek escape from feelings guarantees that the spy will remain a perpetual child, but once he begins to exploit the feelings of others he is likely to end up completely dehumanized." The most extreme form of dehumanized individuals are described by Julian Symons (1974:61): "These agents have no characters. They are only a set of disguises, and to ask what lies behind them would be foolish, because the disguises are the people. Nothing at all goes on behind them."[47]

Rather, these pathological characters (chameleons) exhibit a hollowness, a lack of a centered personality, which they fill with the personalities others project onto them. They lack a fixed repertoire of their own. The assumption of the personality of another is an attempt to gain control over the other. It is a pathological form of manipulative personality. In le Carré's novels, if such types gain self-awareness they tend to end their own lives, unless they find a creative outlet or a loving and supportive partner or both.[48] Robert Gillespie (1970:45) says of such types: "But having no personality, only a succession of roles and disguises that creates what is not there, he is always somebody else—an infinite possibility—an infinite succession of suicides." This type in its extreme manifestation may be relatively rare, but in milder forms it is probably much more common among politicians and actors as well as spies.

Le Carré's treatment of this subject derives from David Cornwell's abandonment by his mother and his relationship with his father, also a chameleon. Charlotte Cornwell, David's half-sister, claims that their father was "criminally anarchic" and hurt David and his brother. She and her brother Rupert suffered less because they lived with their mother. She explained that even though David's mother deserted him and his brother at early ages, her mother "was a rock and she is still my best mate. She made everything bearable."[49] In the essay "Spying on My Father," which appeared the day before the release of his autobiographical *A Perfect Spy,* le Carré (1986:33) sums up his father's death: "One cremation, one funeral service, a scattering of ashes and a memorial service in London marked his passing. I attended only the first of these ceremonies, disappointing friends and family by refusing to read the lesson or deliver a eulogy."[50]

He tried writing about his father since he began writing, but his efforts were "marred by bitterness." He explains: "My earliest writings about him, dated 1959, are perfectly sickening. I was too much a part of him to see him in perspective, and I wrote, I am afraid, in the self-conscious manner of a Gosse or an Ackerley, willing the reader to believe I was a tender soul crushed by a tyrant. I was not crushed at all. I was in bitter combat for *my own identity*, of which my father seemed to me to be the unlawful keeper."[51] Each time he finished a novel, he unsuccessfully returned to the manuscript about his father, only to abandon it and take "refuge in proxy father-figures such as George Smiley—who was significantly parentless— and I weighed them down with my unfocused broodings about love and loyalty."[52] He attempts to deal with Ronnie in a "watered-down" version as the father of his hero in *The Naive and Sentimental Lover*, in Jerry Westerby's father in *The Honourable Schoolboy*, and through Charlie's fantasies about her father in *Little Drummer Girl*. His failure to mention a much earlier short story is particularly revealing.

In "Dare I Weep, Dare I Mourn" (1967), le Carré's main character is tricked by his father into crossing the border from West to East Germany to fulfill his last wish to be buried in the West. When he arrives, he discovers his father is alive. The father devised this scheme to force his son to smuggle him to the West in a coffin. Because he fears the repercussions if the East German guards open the coffin to inspect it and the social embarrassment his working-class father might cause him in his new but insecure social status in the West, the son allows his father to suffocate to death by not opening the coffin for fresh air. His character thinks: "A man must overcome his past. . . . A man must shake off his heritage, overcome his past" (60). When the guards open the coffin to reveal the dead father, the son sheds tears and thinks: "A man feels for his father" (60).[53] The author's extreme ambivalence toward his own father is expressed in the following statement: "Had I loved him or hated him? It no longer mattered: the distinctions had disappeared."[54]

Susan Laity contends that writing *A Perfect Spy* was a kind of alternative suicide for le Carré through which he asserts control over the circumstances of his life. Laity (1987:164) concludes: "For, in the fragmentation of himself into his double, the text, and into his doubles in the text, le Carré throws down pieces to shore up his defense against, and revenge upon, time." The same point applies to his treatment of Harry Pendel in *The Tailor of Panama*. In a lengthy interview with Andrew Ross (1996; emphasis added), le Carré reveals "when you've seen the world shape up as I have, there are only two things you can do: laugh or kill yourself. I think my leading character [Harry Pendel] effectively does both." Le

Carré claims, "It's a very *personal* book. *I was exploring the relationship between myself and my own fabricator.*"

He admits to having a "sense of *guilt*" about using "all of life" as material for his "*fabulations.*" "So I found some kind of buzz running between me and the main character, which I had not had since 'A Perfect Spy.'" Le Carré suggests:

> What Harry did is, in a sense, merely an exaggeration of what we all do to coexist. . . . But *people who've had very unhappy childhoods are pretty good at inventing themselves.* If nobody invents you for yourself, nothing is left but to invent yourself for others. . . . By the age of nine or 10, I knew, like Harry Pendel, that I had to cut my own cloth and make my own way. . . . *He really believes he's responsible for the whole world because it is he who doesn't fit in with it. . . . as Pendel does, I am still making order out of chaos by reinvention.*
> (Ross, 1996; emphasis added)

As Kurt Vonnegut tells us (in the second epigraph to this chapter), we are what we pretend to be. Le Carré concludes this fascinating interview with the following revealing remarks: "I think the ones [novels] I want to be buried with are *A Perfect Spy* and this one [*The Tailor of Panama*]. I have the most affection for the characters in those stories, and somehow, *they come closest to the bone. By closest to the bone I mean as near to my own center, the most intimate and personal to myself*" (Ross, 1996; emphasis added). When I asked Cornwell why Pym and Pendel, his two characters with whom he most closely identified kill themselves, he replied, "That's too big a question, really." But he added: "For both, the game was up: for Pym the spy and inheritor, and for Pendel the artist whose fabulations were taken for real."[55] I think this is a candid, but partial, explanation.[56] He told George Plimpton (1997:61), "If you see the world as gloomily as I see it, the only thing to do is laugh or shoot yourself. My guy does both." He concluded both novels with a "forfeit" (72).

Le Carré's genius is in his ability to transpose his attempts to deal with his own fragmented personality into a more universal exploration of human nature. He fulfills his "hope to provide a metaphor for the average reader's daily life." As he says, "What gives my works whatever universality they have is that they use the metaphysical secret world to describe some realities of the overt world." Leroy L. Panek (1987:47) characterizes le Carré as follows: "We cannot really know other people who are forever locked in themselves. All we can know is the external history. . . . The world of espionage, for him, intensifies the human condition and highlights questions of identity and existence." As le Carré (1996:5) himself puts it: "The longing we have to communicate cleanly and directly with people is always obstructed by qualifications and often with concern about how our messages are received—whether we will lose face because those messages will be received untruthfully." Le Carré effectively explores the use of language in deception.[57] Human communication is at its most problematic when filtered through the maze of bureaucratic politics and spying.

Chapter 6

Bureaucratic Politics: Domestic and International

> *Power is the means, and the end of espionage is the control of others. The ideal end is world domination, making the world safe for one's political system, one's way of life. (Robert Gillespie, 1970:50–51)*

> *Behind the treachery of the spies and the agents and the double agents . . . lies the duplicity of our political life. (John Atkins, 1984:175)*

Introduction

Espionage, by its very nature, is political. Intelligence is frequently used in the formation of policy or to justify policies already made. Like war, espionage is also an extension of politics. Because intelligence agencies are bureaucratic institutions, a great deal of politics also takes place within and between them. In his novels le Carré treats bureaucratic politics at both the domestic and international levels. The domestic bureaucratic politics involve the internal politics of the Circus and interagency competition between the Circus and other British agencies and departments. At the international level, it concerns the rivalry between British and American intelligence, alliances between factions in the CIA and in British intelligence, and competition with alliances between U.S. and British Arms and Drug Enforcement agencies. There is a complex relationship among domestic factional relations and cooperation and competition with the agencies of another nation.

The Politics of the Circus: Background

David Monaghan notes how le Carré plunges into his imagined world—having readers experience it immediately without first giving them potted summaries as background. To compensate for the confusion that some readers experience from "the satisfaction of living in, rather than merely learning about the world of the Circus," Monaghan (1986:8) recreates le Carré's imaginative blueprint of the organizational structure, the building, the staff, their jargon, the history of major operations, and a who's who of the occupants of this "miniature but three-dimensional and completely functioning world."[1] As Eric Homberger (1986:43–4) observes, through seemingly inconsequential dialogue, such as informal conversations over tea, le Carré portrays the "collective memory" of the Circus and how it becomes "a large government bureaucracy, much given to intrigue and territorial disputes."

Although the first historical reference to it is 1918, the Circus only takes form around 1928, when Steed-Aspery and a group of Oxford and Cambridge scholars operating as the Overseas Committee for Academic Research recruit George Smiley, Bill Haydon, and Jim Prideaux, among other bright students, before the Second World War. With the war, the size and activities of the Circus expand greatly. After the war, with the onset of the Cold War, radical changes transform the Circus. The headquarters is moved from the terraced house in Knightsbridge to a building in Cambridge Circus (London) from which it derives the nickname.[2] The old guard of Oxbridge academic amateurs who ran the Circus until then and many of their former students whom they recruited as agents are retired after the war.

As major attention focuses on the communist threat, a new generation of agents are recruited, including Percy Alleline and Peter Guillam (whose father and mother both worked for the Circus during the war). Le Carré graphically portrays the transformation of the Circus in *Call for the Dead:*

> The NATO alliance, and the desperate measures contemplated by the Americans, altered the whole nature of Smiley's Service. Gone for ever were the days of Steed-Asprey, when as like as not you took your orders over a glass of port in his rooms at Magdalen; the *inspired amateurism* of a handful of highly qualified, under-paid men had given way to the efficiency, *bureaucracy,* and *intrigue* of a large Government department—effectively at the mercy of Maston, . . . a man who could reduce any colour to grey, who knew his masters and could walk among them. And he did it so well. (12–13)

Maston, a wartime transferee from the Civil Service, becomes the Minister's Adviser on Intelligence (described as the "Head Eunuch")[3], effectively dominating from 1945 until the end of the Fennan Case in 1961 the increasingly complex bureaucratic institution the Circus has become. In *Call for the Dead,* Smiley describes Maston as "off the peg," like his clothes, wearing a monocle, and looking like "a barmaid's dream of a real gentleman" (19). Resisting Maston's pressure on him to collude in the cover-up of Fennan's death, Smiley considers him a contemptible, posturing sycophant. Patrick Dobel (1988:201) points out that Maston's insincerity, ruthlessness, and mastery of bureaucratic intrigue exemplifies a type who are "more concerned with their own promotion, power, and status than the actual results of the craft or the welfare of their agents." Smiley walks out on Maston and resigns so that he can continue his investigation and declines Maston's offer of a promotion as an inducement to return to the Circus. Smiley is repelled by the way in which the bureaucratic priority of preserving appearances ends up distorting the mission of intelligence, which is to discover and tell the truth (see chapter 8)[4].

Competition Among British Intelligence Agencies

The Looking Glass War, like the social histories of the CIA discussed by Fromkin (1996:166; emphasis added), brings "the reader into a world in which nations and peoples, national interests and political causes are relegated into the background, and conflicts concern not politics and morality but *turf and personality,* organizational charts and chains of command."[5] It is a study of the dire consequences for Military Intelligence (in the novel, "the Department") of its rivalry with the Circus. (This rivalry mirrors the feud between the CIA and G2, the U.S. Army's intelligence staff, in the early years of the CIA, and the rivalry between the Israeli Mossad and Aman or military intelligence.)[6] The Circus is now headed by Control, who took over in 1961 and runs it until his forced retirement in 1972.[7] When Avery suggests to his boss that the operational job he is proposing should be carried out by the better-qualified Circus, Leclerc is adamant: "Their charter is political, exclusively political" (26). Later, Haldane, who is more senior than Avery, also unsuccessfully urges Leclerc to give the job to the Circus (59).

The Foreign Office refuses to issue the Department false passports since military intelligence lost their covert agents after the war (27). Instead, they are issued an invalid passport[8] (82). The Department is known in Whitehall as "the Grace and Favour boys" (60). Their courier service has been disbanded, and the Foreign Office denied them use of its bag service. Leclerc violates a basic principle of intelligence and uses untrained personnel from the overt side for a clandestine operational assignment (42–3). In short, the Department is a shadow of its former self and lacks the resources and support to successfully carry out a covert operation. But, because covert operations carry greater prestige in the world of intelligence than does analysis (which was the Department's only strength), Leclerc was driven to gain power and status by restoring an operational capability to the Department.

Leclerc, expressing his jealousy of the Circus' greater resources calls them "cheats": "Lying's second nature to them. Half of them don't know any longer when they're telling the truth." He goes on to lie, himself, by claiming that their rivalry during the war is "all over now" (29). Contradicting this statement, he warns Avery not to tell Smiley *"anything"* about the operation during his briefing with him (29). Leclerc anticipates both internal opposition within the Department as well as from the Circus to Operation Mayfly, which is what he calls the penetration of Leiser into East Germany. Through his pathetic attempt to deceive Control and the Circus about the true nature of his operation, which he pretends is merely an exercise, Leclerc gives Control the excuse to give him inadequate support, forged documents, and an inferior and easily traceable radio sender that belonged in a museum, all of which essentially sabotaged the operation.

The pathetic attempt by Leclerc to revive his Department's wartime status reflects the attempt by Great Britain to assert autonomy beyond American influence in world affairs. Envy and fear of America replace faith in a decaying empire.[9] Leclerc says: "Politically, this would be a bad moment to go hiding our faces in the American skirts. After all, as the Minister puts it, we still *have* one or two teeth of our own. Haldane said sarcastically, 'That is a charming notion'" (50). Le Carré vividly portrays a bureaucracy without a purpose. Only Haldane's research was of any value. "The rest would draft projects which were never submitted, bicker gently among themselves about leave, duty rosters, and the quality of their furniture, give excessive attention to the problems of their section staff" (77). Leclerc bargains with the undersecretary by claiming he could do the job for half the price the Circus would charge. As an indication of the low status of Leclerc's Department, the "Minister did not look up as they came in" (73). On gaining approval to run the operation, he obtains a desperately sought status symbol in the form of a car on loan from the ministry pool (78).

Having obtained a car from the ministry pool, Control cynically puns about the Department, located in an inelegant section of London on Blackfriars Road: "Isn't it fun? So the black friars have won the pool" (159). In another exchange with Smiley, Control jokes about the completely outdated World War II vintage radio sender: "They wouldn't get far with *that,* would they?" (179). Later Smiley speculates aloud to Control: "We handed it to them. The passport that was canceled . . . a clapped-out wireless set . . . who told Berlin to listen for him? Who told them what frequencies? We even gave Leclerc the crystals, didn't we? Was that just Christian charity too? Plain, idiot Christian charity?" (226). Control cynically replies in pretended shock: "What *are* you suggesting? How *very* distasteful. Who ever would do a thing like that?" (227).

Robert Gillespie (1970:53) observes that: "conflict originates in the area of responsibility, and insofar as different concepts of agency responsibility dominate, they mirror the larger war between differing political ideas and powers. The mirror shows that the political concept of morality is bureaucratic; that bureaucracy is invisible; that morality therefore can not exist." Such amoral bureaucratic politics is demonstrated in a powerful scene in the penultimate chapter, when Smiley is sent by the minister to close down the operation immediately because Leiser has murdered a border guard and is transmitting so slowly, his capture is imminent. The agent is cynically sacrificed to *raison d'état:* "There was nothing in Smiley's face but compassion, nothing in his voice but that dreadful patience with which we speak to the insane" (236). By this point, Leclerc appears to have lost his tenuous hold on reality, and Smiley is justified in treating him like a mental patient.[10] Smiley promises him a joint conference to discuss the target of the operation, and Leclerc willingly abandons his agent, rationalizing his action as "the war rules" (238).

Steven Marcus (1965:20) points out that the Department is "like the Empire it served and the class system it embodied—it has all gone to pot; it is irrelevant to the contemporary world. . . . His characters, like the England he describes, are tired seedy, and middle-aged." He sums up le Carré's position on the nostalgia for an earlier age: "Indeed it is precisely their yearning to reinstate that past which prevents them from dealing with the present. Their blundering nostalgia for World War II and its values leads to the ruination of their plot. Yet, Carre [sic] is saying, it is also true that their blindness and foolishness contain a note of truth, that the War was, by comparison with the present, a time of meaning and of heroic possibilities. Nevertheless, it is courting disaster to live by such assumptions today. . . . in this novel he has read the Cold War in light of World War II." Much of the nostalgia for World War II reflects the desire for the clarity of issues at stake in that war. If during the Cold War the issues were vaguer than in the confrontation with fascism, in the immediate post–Cold War era they appear to have disappeared altogether into a fog.

The Circus and Relations with the CIA

The struggle for control of the Circus frames the action in *Tinker, Tailor, Soldier, Spy.* Haydon (the Soviet mole) and Karla (his Russian boss) devise a scheme to get rid of Control, who constitutes a threat, and to replace him with the stooge Percy Alleline. They provide a fictitious high-level Russian source code-named Merlin, whose "product" (intelligence reports) is called Witchcraft. Control searches for the mole he suspects has penetrated the Circus at a high level. He sends Prideaux to Czechoslovakia to make contact with a defector who knows the identity of the Soviet mole in the Circus. Haydon's sabotaging of Prideaux's mission finally brings Control down. The seriously ill Control dies shortly after his replacement by the pliable Alleline as head of the Circus in 1972.[11]

Smiley was pushed out because of his close association with Control. By maneuvering Alleline into the top position Haydon radically restructures the Circus in such a manner that he actually dominates it through a small elite known as London Station.[12] Le Carré perceptively shows the importance of personal networks, patron-client relationships, and factions in bureaucratic politics. Monaghan observes that when Control is forced out, intelligent and "loyal officers are either dismissed, like Smiley, Collins, Connie Sachs and Westerby, or removed to fringe positions, like Guillam"(19). Similarly, once Smiley exposes Haydon and is brought in to replace the discredited Alleline, most of Haydon's loyal clients are fired, among them, Roy Bland, a former client of Smiley's who had pledged allegiance to Alleline. The exception was Toby Esterhase, who strategically switched support back to Smiley from Alleline during the investigation. Those who previously had been fired because they were loyal to Smiley are reinstated, and those who had been demoted (like Guillam, who loyally aided Smiley's investigation) are promoted.[13]

Throughout all of the infighting within the Circus, Oliver Lacon, a high official in the Cabinet Office who functioned as a senior adviser to the Circus, remained the real power. When Smiley first approached him with his suspicions of a highly placed mole in the Circus, he had been ordered by Lacon to abandon his inquiries. But a year later, Lacon called on Smiley to conduct the investigation of the Circus. The minister responsible for the Circus at the time, Miles Sercombe, is a cousin of both Ann (Sercombe) Smiley and Bill Haydon. The latter connection may have had something to do with his initial reluctance to sanction Smiley's investigation and the former with his later insistence that Smiley, rather than the internal security service, which Lacon refers to as "the competition," conduct the investigation.[14]

Smiley's perusal of the files and his memory reveals the history of the development of factions within the Circus based on personal antagonisms and conflicting attitudes toward the Americans. For example, according to Haydon, Control and Alleline learned to hate each other at Cambridge. Control had been Alleline's don when he was an undergraduate. "Alleline was Control's pupil and a bad one, and Control taunted him" (129). Alleline was recruited to the Circus by Maston. There had been a scandal and row with Control after Alleline had been transferred to Cairo. "Alleline had involved himself in a silly American plot to replace a local potentate with one of their own. Alleline had always had a fatal reverence for the Americans. . . . Whereas Control, like most of the Circus, despised them and all their works, which he frequently sought to undermine" (131). We thus are introduced to the relationship between internal factions within the Circus and alliances with and antagonism toward the American "Cousins." This is an important theme explored in greater depth later in this chapter.[15]

In *The Honourable Schoolboy,* Smiley assumes the directorship of the morally, politically, financially, and physically depleted (staff having been reduced by three quarters) Circus in November 1973. A graphic metaphor was the tearing apart of the Circus headquarters, at Smiley's orders, to locate the large number of electronic listening devices hidden when Haydon had alterations made to the building. Operation Dolphin takes place in 1974–75, during Smiley's brief tenure as chief. This period is demarcated in Circus legend by having been given the Biblical label "after the fall," with its connotation of a loss of innocence and a fall from grace. It is also a period characterized by increasing dependence on American support in the field of intelligence.[16]

Smiley, as the new head of a devastated agency, has to deal with Lacon (whose title is now senior adviser on intelligence in the Cabinet Office) from a weak position. Although Lacon refuses to authorize it in writing, he tacitly approves Smiley's putting an agent in the field in Hong Kong. "Once you make a formal approach, I shall wash my hands of you entirely. It is the Intelligence Steering Group, not myself, who determine your scope of action" (90). Lacon advises Smiley that if he brings in the Americans he is sure to gain the committee's support, but Smiley insists, "I would prefer to stay my judgement on that, if you don't mind" (90). Lacon warns him that without the Americans, he won't get the support of Defense or the Home Office. Assessing the vagaries of interdepartmental politics, Lacon predicts the "Treasury's a toss-up and the Foreign Office—depends who they send to the meeting and what they had for breakfast" (90–91). Smiley also declines Lacon's offer to send an advocate on his behalf, saying, "Oh, I think I can manage, thank you!" (91). And manage he does.

Smiley reveals his tactic to Peter Guillam. "If we cut them [the Cousins] in, they'll swamp us. If we don't, we've no resources. It's simply a matter of *balance*"[17] (91; emphasis added). While recognizing his dependence on American support, Smiley attempts (unsuccessfully) to maintain control of the operation. The meeting, described in chapter 8 under the title "The

Barons Confer," takes place in the Foreign Office conference house. Saul Enderby, who plays a pivotal role in the story, leads the Foreign Office contingent and acts as chair. Le Carré's descriptions are graphic: "The Foreign Office sat one end, the Colonial Office at the other. The separation was visceral rather than legal" (167). He notes that no one took their six-year union in the short-lived diplomatic service seriously. Smiley and Guillam sat at the center. "The rest of the committee sat across from Smiley and Guillam and had the air of seconds in a duel they disapproved of" (167). They included representatives of the Internal Security Service, the Treasury, and Oliver Lacon, who sat alone, "apart from everyone, for all the world the person least engaged" (167).

Each received a copy of Smiley's eighteen-page submission labeled "Top Secret Withhold" (which meant keep it away from the Cousins). Le Carré's description of the meeting is a masterpiece—from Lacon's pretense of ignorance of the proposed operation to Smiley's devastating demolition of his arguments. Treasury quibbles about improper use of funds, and the Colonial Office jealously guards its territory and riles against the Americans. Minor players are allowed "irrelevant questions in order to get themselves a mention in the minutes" (175). Smiley tactically "availed himself of the after-luncheon torpor to raise what Lacon had called the panic factor" (177). His ploy works. He ingeniously finesses the question of liaison with the Americans and, by deliberately asking for more than he needs, gets exactly what he wants.

After the meeting ended, Enderby applauding Smiley's victory says (and jibes): "Nice little meeting. Lot achieved. Nothing given away. Nicely played hand. Land this one and you can just about build an extension, I should think. And the Cousins will play ball, will they? . . . You've tested the water there? They'll carry your bags for you and not hog the match? Bit of a cliff-hanger that one, I'd have thought, but I suppose you're up to it" (187). This brief passage portends meaning that only becomes clear to the reader much later. In reaction to Enderby's comment, Guillam thinks, "Nice little conspiracy too." This refers to his sudden realization that Smiley must have reached an understanding with the CIA before he went in to the meeting. Later, however, it will relate to the conspiracy led by Enderby, in alliance with the CIA, which results in his replacing Smiley as the head of the Circus.

Le Carré shows how Smiley gets caught in cross-fire between the Colonial Office which brands him as "anti-Colonial and pro-American, and Enderby's men from the Foreign Office, who accuse him of ultraconservatism in the handling of the special relationship" (392). This is the classic position of the liberal—to be caught between more extreme positions—and reflects yet another sense of the term *balance,* which is the essence of Smiley's (and le Carré's) liberal temperament: "Much more serious however was Smiley's impression that some hint of the row had reached Martello [CIA] by other routes, and that he would be able to exploit it. For example, Molly Meakin's sources spoke of a burgeoning relationship between Enderby and Martello at the personal level" (392). Enderby and Martello's children studied in the same school. The men spent weekends together fishing in Scotland. "Enderby's third and newest wife was American and rich" (392).

Chapter 22, ironically titled "Born Again," begins with Smiley's top experts on the Soviet Union and China, Connie Sacks and Doc Di Salis, waiting in vain to interrogate Nelson Ko. After hearing that he had been flown to the United States, they learn they are not to participate in the interrogation. The Americans insist on using a Harvard professor (who has based much of his research on Connie's reports), and Di Salas is replaced by a client of Enderby's from the Foreign Office. They were the first to be "retired" with Smiley. Connie perceptively observes: "The old order's hoofing it. . . . That twerp Enderby is oiling through the back door. It's a pogrom" (527).

Lacon, Enderby, and Martello (London CIA station chief) call on Smiley at his home to inform him that "American enthusiasm for Enderby's appointment [to replace Smiley] had been overwhelming." Sam Collins, who had conspired with Enderby against Smiley becomes head of operations. The narrator wonders whether there was "a conspiracy against Smiley, of the scale that Guillam supposed?" (532). There was clearly a secret understanding between Enderby and Martello. The Cousins get Nelson Ko in return for their support for Enderby as Smiley's replacement. The narrator verifies that Lacon and Collins were party to the plot. Westerby gave them the excuse they were looking for. Among other things, this episode reveals how extra-national networks can influence internal agency politics and even the appointment of the head of a major intelligence agency.

Guillam's suspicion that Smiley knew of the conspiracy and possibly even welcomed it was mentioned in chapter 1, in which Smiley's observation in a letter to Ann that his being stabbed in the back was the judgment of his peers was cited. Dobel (1988:203) suggests that when Lacon removed Smiley from command at the end of *The Honourable Schoolboy* (1977), "He did both Smiley and the service a favor. Smiley hated the bureaucratic politics, even as he excelled at them, while Enderby, not at all incompetent, could better defend the service in the new world." That may be, but in abdicating without a fight, Smiley let down his allies. Sacks and Di Salis might have crowned their careers with success and honor rather than being humiliated by being fired. It also seriously set back the career of the loyal Peter Guillam, who was demoted and kept away from important positions for years thereafter.

An important subtheme in this novel involves the tensions and rivalries between the American drug enforcement agency and the CIA on one hand, and the Circus and the faction in the Foreign Office led by Enderby, who successfully plots to take over the Circus, on the other. Smiley makes a deal with for cooperation but retains control of the operation and reserves the right to first interrogate Nelson Ko. The CIA, in violation of their agreement, discloses the operation to the drug enforcement agency before Smiley informs the Coordinating Committee of the collaboration. Smiley says, "Do you realize that not even my masters know we are in collaboration with you? God in heaven." Martello replies: "Ah, come on now, George. *We have politics, same as you.* We have promises to keep. Mouths to buy. Enforcement's out for our blood . . . That's showbiz, George" (270; emphasis added). Both sides withhold information from each other, from their respective counterparts, and from those to whom they are ultimately responsible. This scenario is even more elaborately drawn in *The Night Manager.*[18] It illustrates the limitations of rational-actor models of bureaucratic decision making, which assume adequate flows of accurate information.

In chapter 4 of *Smiley's People,* Smiley has yet again been called to meet with Lacon. In an indirect manner ("In Lacon's world, direct questions were the height of bad taste but direct answers were worse"), Lacon tells Smiley he is needed to "damp down potential scandal" (45) of the murder in London of Smiley's former agent, Vladimir. We eventually learn that a new Labor government (formed three years previously) had restructured and significantly curtailed the intelligence agencies. A mixed interministerial steering committee, composed of representatives from Westminster and from Whitehall, is known as the Wise Men. This committee brought together Cabinet and major Whitehall customers, who were "placed *between* the intelligence fraternity and the Cabinet. As a channel, as a filter, as a brake" (50).

The members of the new government treat their intelligence services with suspicion and mistrust, "as if British intelligence were a sort of wholly owned subsidiary of the Conservative party" (51). Lacon incredulously tells Smiley: "Do you know, they're even reviving all that talk about a British Freedom of Information Act on the American pattern? From *within* the Cabinet?" (51). The Wise men reviewed the Circus' resources and significantly cut them. Just as seriously, they composed a codex of forbidden practices, including the use of double agents and the use of East European exile groups. Therefore, Lacon needs someone who is no longer connected with the Circus to handle matters because the murdered agent was connected with an exile group.

Lacon makes his case for considering the murder to be unconnected with the service. He indicates that he can get his minister's backing for a cover-up as long as things don't come "unstuck" (65). He uses the disastrous consequences that the Circus would suffer in the present political climate if there were to be a public scandal to induce Smiley to cooperate. He plays on Smiley's loyalty to the Circus and, with an oblique reference to Haydon's treason, the collective guilt his generation bears for its vulnerable condition. Lacon itemizes the terms he sets for Smiley's mission: "One, that you are a private citizen. Vladimir's executor, not ours. Two, that you are of the past, not the present, and conduct yourself accordingly. The *sanitized* past. That you will pour oil on the waters, not muddy them. That you will suppress your old professional interest in him, naturally, for that means ours" (68). Smiley's earlier observations sum up Lacon rather well: "But sophistry was Lacon's element. He was born to it, he breathed it, he could fly and swim with it, nobody in Whitehall was better at it"[19] (65). And this: "Against stupidity, the gods themselves fight in vain, thought Smiley; but Schiller had forgotten the bureaucrats" (67). Smiley, however, ignores Lacon's terms. "In his mind already, Smiley was accountable to nobody but himself"[20] (272).

Enderby desperately wants Karla to defect so that he can have the Cousins at his mercy. Yet he is seriously concerned about the political constraints imposed by the Cabinet. He asks Smiley if it was always like that. Smiley replies: "Yes. I suppose it was. I suppose that in one form or another it always *was* like that. . . . as if the answer mattered to him deeply" (273). Enderby gives Smiley his "totally deniable blessing," adding, "Sorry you've become an instrument of the imperial hypocrisy but there's rather a lot of it about"[21] (276).

British Intelligence and the CIA

A Perfect Spy offers a few observations pertinent to the subject of this chapter and, in particular, to relations between British and American intelligence. Edward Behr (1986:46) considers that this novel "comes closer to depicting the true state of Britain's secret world than any of the author's previous works." Mary Pym recalls her husband's reference to his boss, Nigel, as "one of the idiots who are supposed to be introducing a breath of Whitehall realism. If ever I heard a contradiction in terms, that's it, Magnus had said" (112). We learn "everything he disliked about the way the Firm [MI6] was going: its retreat into bureaucracy and semi-diplomacy, its pandering to American methods and example" (161). When Jack Brotherhood pleads with his superior to save their blown networks, they refuse for fear of alerting the Americans. Brotherhood says, "So the Joes [agents] will die for the Special Relationship. I like that. So will the Joes. They'll understand" (180).

CIA headquarters in London is described by Grant Lederer, a Pym-like CIA agent in a manner that stresses the artificiality of the agency's perspective and its remoteness from the real world outside its walls. "In the false walls, false windows looked on to plastic flowers. From places like this . . . America lost her wars against the little brown men in black pajamas. From places like this . . . from smoked-glass rooms, cut off from human-kind—America will lose all her wars except the last" (231). In chapter 9, the meeting between CIA and British Intelligence is a tense one as the Americans present conclusive evidence linking Czech radio transmissions wherever Pym happens to be stationed and the British pretend that it is a Czech frame-up. "There is hostility in the air, and it is forming on national lines"(237).

After the meeting, Lederer has an unauthorized conversation with Brotherhood from which he correctly guesses that Pym is on the run. When he reports this to his boss, however, he is chastised for exceeding his competence. His boss adds a note to Lederer's file to cover his own back "while at the same time knifing an unpleasing interloper. Never bad" (249). Meanwhile, Brotherhood's boss refuses to admit that Pym is a double agent because of the political implications. "There is still no justification for me to raise a public hue and cry. To go to my Minister and say 'We've found another one.' Least of all to the Americans. Bang go the barter treaties. Bang goes the intelligence pooling and the private line to Langley that often means so much more than normal diplomatic links. Do you want me to risk all that until we *know?*" (317). It is pervasive bureaucratic politics as usual both within British and U.S. intelligence and between them.

Le Carré, having dropped the use of the term Circus in the previous novel, in *The Russia House* the "Service" has a grand new headquarters in a high-rise block on the Embankment. The physical structure embodies the political and bureaucratic changes. Changing the name from the Circus also indicates that spying is no longer fun.[22] A brick outstation in Victoria known as the Russia House is headed by Ned. Because Ned, the main character in le Carré's next novel, *The Secret Pilgrim,* is identified as a protégé of Smiley's and a member of the Circus, we can assume that this is the same Service. But the political infighting within the Service, as well as rivalry with other British services and bureaucratic departments and with the CIA, continue unabated.

In chapter 2 a secret interministerial committee of enquiry is appointed by Whitehall to investigate the events that constitute the plot of the novel. The narrator of the novel was the committee chair and drafted the report.

He divulges:"What conclusions our committee reached, if any, remains the loftiest secret of them all, particularly from those of us who sat on it. For the functions of such committees, as we all well knew, is to talk earnestly until the dust has settled, and then ourselves return to dust. Which, like a disgruntled Cheshire cat, our committee duly did, leaving nothing behind us but our frightfully secret frown, a meaningless interim working paper, and a bunch of secret annexes in the Treasury archives"[23] (23). Such committees engage in ritual suppression of issues while their ostensible raison d'etre is to investigate and to resolve them. Were they to conduct proper investigations, too many powerful people would have to take responsibility for their errors of judgement. Horatio Benedict dePalfrey (a.k.a. Harry or old Palfrey), legal adviser to the Service, narrates the story and drafts "our official whitewash of the operation we called the Bluebird and of its protagonist, Bartholomew, alias Barley, Scott Blair" (30).

Le Carré illustrates the incompetence of British bureaucracy by having the salesman who has been entrusted with top-secret documents in Russia unsuccessfully try to pass on the documents to four separate Whitehall ministries because he wasn't taken seriously. Finally, at the Foreign Office, he manages to dash past the guard and encounter a clerk, to whom he gives the documents. The clerk keeps them for two nights, reading them before passing them on to intelligence. "He was a *diplomat,* not a *Friend,* as the spies were called. . . . Indeed it was his outspoken *resentment* that the orthodox Foreign Office to which he belonged resembled more and more a cover organization for the Friend's disgraceful activities" (28; emphasis added). Disregarding standing orders, he consults a senior colleague in the research department, who calls Ned on a special telephone. In an all-night meeting at the Russia House, the Bluebird team is assembled. Ironically, the infraction of the rules has the unintended consequence of getting the material to the proper agency. In espionage and in politics, unintended consequences play important roles.

In contrasting two intelligence officers, le Carré vividly portrays what Max Weber called "ideal types." Clive, deputy director of the Service, is a suburban espiocrat of the modern school who believed only in facts. "If he liked anything at all in life apart from his own advancement and his silver Mercedes car . . . it was hardware and powerful Americans, in that order." In contrast, Ned, his subordinate who heads the outstation, "was by temperament and training an agent runner and captain of men. Live sources were his element and, so far as he knew the word, his passion. He despised the in-fighting of intelligence politics and left all that happily to Clive, just as he left the analysis to Walter." Ned is the determined primitive whose forte is human nature, which, to Clive is "one unsavoury quagmire"(89). Le Carré associates bureaucracy and emphasis on technology with America and pro-American Brits. His humane and passionate agent runners are Englishmen.[24]

Once again, the British coordinate their operation with the CIA. Barley is interviewed by Bob, one of the few CIA agents le Carré treats sympathetically. (He was "nearer to the Service's way of doing things than Langley's"[25]). The narrator says: "Langley's power struggles were a mystery to those who were involved in them, and certainly—however much we pretended otherwise—to our barons of the twelfth floor" (96). This is particularly significant, given the influence of the Americans on British policy and intelligence. Ned expresses grave concern that Bluebird's "product" is being distributed too widely among the Americans, which put their agent's security in jeopardy. Clive is a pure political opportunist.[26] British dependence on the Americans in strategic matters is absolute. The narrator (Palfrey) speculates about Clive's having spent the entire day at the U.S. embassy: "What had he given away to whom for what?" Palfrey asks Clive, "What are you brewing with the Americans?" (153). Clive declines to reply. The Americans are involved both because of the general government policy of cooperation and the specific alliances made between individuals and factions in the respective intelligence agencies.

When (in chapter 9) new Americans appear during a critical phase of the operation, Ned calls them "bloody carpetbaggers" (175). "They wore navy blazers and short hair, and they had a Mormon cleanliness that I found slightly revolting" (176). All of the British, except Clive, and even some of the Americans seem discomfited by their presence. Clive is described as being "closeted with his Mormons" (178). Clive takes Walter (the research analyst) off the operation and transfers him to the training section, because his blatant homosexuality "raised too many eyebrows on the other side . . . of the Atlantic"[27] (189). Bob had the decency to feel ashamed.[28]

Palfrey describes the prevailing atmosphere of the week's interrogation of Barley Blair as one of underlying terror. Le Carré describes symbolically how Clive "had managed to paint himself out of the picture. He sat among Sheriton's young men and had pushed his chair back till they *hid* him" (233; emphasis added). Russell Sheriton, former CIA station chief in London, has become the agency's head of Soviet operations and directs the interrogation. In an allusion to the Cambridge moles who had betrayed American as well as British secrets to the Russians, Sheraton says to Barley: "No English reticence, no old-school persiflage. We've fallen for that horse manure before and we will never, *never* fall for it again" (234). Clive has no objection to the CIA administering a lie-detector test to Barley.

Much to everyone's surprise, Sheraton announces that he believes Barley's claim that Goethe is a genuine source. "I believe in Mr. Brown [alias Barley], I believe in Goethe, I believe in the material. And I'm scared shitless" (237). He confides over dinner that the American politicians don't like Bluebird's story.

> You know what's the worst thing for our democratically elected Neanderthals? The total worst? It's the implications against *us*. Moribund on the Sov side means moribund *our* side. The mullahs [politicians] hate that. So do the manufacturers . . . That means our intelligence estimates are ludicrously exaggerated? [245] . . . How do you peddle the arms race when the only asshole you have to race against is yourself? Bluebird is life-threatening intelligence. A lot of highly paid favourite sons are in serious danger of having their rice-bowls broken, all on account of Bluebird. You want the truth that's it. (246)

When Palfrey asks why, under the circumstances, he is sticking his neck out, Sheriton takes a long time to answer. He finally replies, "I am a glasnostic, Harry. . . . Quote me and enjoy me."[29]

Typically, le Carré provides a variety of points of view regarding the evaluation of *glasnost, perestroika,* and their meaning for East-West relations. A diversity of ideological perspectives can be found in every agency. When Barley suggests the Cold War is over, Ned responds "Oh my dear Lord" in alarm. The hawk Walter exclaims: "Cheap political theatricals and feigned friendships! . . . it is a reason for spying the living daylights out of them twenty-five hours a day and kicking them in the balls every time they try to get off the floor. God *knows* who they won't think they are ten years from now!" Walter also comments on the political importance of crisis. "Our leaders *adore* crisis. Our leaders *feast* on crisis. Our leaders spend their lives quartering the globe in search of crisis to revive their flagging libidos! . . . We may even con ourselves into believing the threat has gone away. It never will. Never, never, never" (99, 107). In both essays and in interviews, le Carré reveals that he is much closer to Barley's evaluation than to Walter's. For example, in an interview with John Blades (1989:2), he calls the viewpoint expressed by Walter "understandable but shortsighted." He continues: "Even the most elementary lessons of history would tell us that we desperately need the Soviet Union as partners in a great alliance against new enemies which are very clear to forward thinking people on both sides of the crumbling Iron Curtain."[30] For the first time, le Carré feels, in the changing global political context the frozen frames of reference of Cold War politicians and rigid-minded bureaucrats and espiocrats can be countered by popularly supported fresh ideas.

Domestic Institutional Rivalry and Cross-National Alliance

In *The Secret Pilgrim,* Leonard Burr has replaced Clive, who, in the aftermath of Barley Blair's defection, is exiled to head of station in Guyana.[31]

Ned observes: "There is nowhere quite like the Service—except possibly Moscow—for becoming an unperson overnight" (261). Because in a bureaucracy authority is largely a matter of position, once an individual loses his position of authority, he generally loses his influence as well. Ned recounts how he finally overcame his naïveté regarding politics in the Circus. "I realised that the Circus was much the same as any other British institution, except that it was more so, since it played its games in the safety of sealed rooms, with other people's lives for counters" (103). This realization leads him to take responsibility for his actions and to follow his own instincts more often. On one occasion, when he reports his discovery that a couple of his agents have been conning the Service, he is ignored, accused of being tired, and told to stop telling what was clearly the truth, because the faked intelligence enables the Circus to enlist the support of the Foreign Office and the Americans. Ned it promoted to head of Office Registry to keep him from exposing the charade.

Like his mentor, Smiley (in le Carré's first novel), Ned is ordered to investigate a cipher clerk named Cyril Arthur Frewin in the Foreign Office for a security check that would more appropriately have been handled by internal security. Burr's reasons for insisting Ned handle it are not restricted to rivalry among the services. He explains that they have different priorities. The following statement is particularly ironic because in *The Night Manager,* Burr heads the enforcement agency and reflects a markedly different institutional perspective: "All that those churchy buggers across the Park can think of is a judgeproof prosecution and a bunch of medals to hand around. I collect intelligence for the marketplace. If Frewin's bad, maybe we can keep him going and turn him around. He might even get us alongside Brother Modrian back in Moscow. Who knows? The security artists don't, that's for sure" (262). Burr makes clear to Ned that he has chosen him for the job because he has "broken as many rules as you've stuck to"—that is, he likes his independence. "You've got heart too, which is more than I can say for some of the capons in this outfit" (264). Interestingly, le Carré admires what Americans consider the typically American traits of independence and individualism but does not associate them with American intelligence services.[32] After carrying out the mission with skill, Ned is promoted by Burr to head of Secretariat. These two examples show that it is possible to gain promotion for reasons that subvert the purpose of the agency (in the first case) and for exemplary performance of one's duties (the second case).

The Night Manager is a virtual handbook of bureaucratic politics.[33] In chapter 4, where Leonard Burr recruits Jonathan Pine, permission to do so came "after weeks of Whitehall infighting, despite the mounting clamor from Washington and Whitehall's perpetual urge to earn merit in the fickle corridors of Capitol Hill" (47). The man most responsible for the success in negotiating this political obstacle course is Rex Goodhew, "a mandarin," or high-ranking civil servant in Whitehall:[34] "the Sunday papers had once described Rex Goodhew as Whitehall's Talleyrand without the limp. But as usual they had it wrong, for Goodhew was nothing that he seemed. If there was a separateness about him, it came of virtue, not intrigue. His mangy smile, flat cap and bicycle concealed nothing more sinister than a high-minded Anglican of reforming zeal. And if you were lucky enough to penetrate his private life, you found, instead of mystery, a pretty wife and clever children who adored him" (47).[35]

Burr gets an early warning from Goodhew about the unreliability of his minister, to whom he refers as "my master." "My master is a bit *chary,* frankly, Leonard. . . . Yesterday it was all about the cost, today he's not keen on aggravating an uneasy situation in a former colony" (47). Goodhew's minister is described as "a silky politician not yet turned forty," a statement that conveys his slickness and lack of experience. When Goodhew asks Burr when he intends to advise "our friends across the river," meaning "Burr's former service and present rival, which traded in Pure Intelligence from a grim tower block on the South Bank," Burr retorts belligerently, "Never." Goodhew advises him: "My master regards your old colleagues as realists. Far too easy, in a small, very new, and dare he say it, *idealistic* new agency such as yours, not to see beyond one's fence. He'd feel more comfortable if you had the River boys aboard" (48).

Burr objects to involving his former colleagues of Intelligence in his operation, explaining that his years of experience working with them has convinced him of their corruption and the wickedness of their chief, Geoffrey Darker. Despite his anger over pressure to do so, Burr realizes that "Goodhew is the best and only champion he had," so he complies (49). The narrator remarks, "Burr had a tendency to see conspiracy everywhere" (50). His elaborate efforts to disguise the existence and the identity of his agent elicits from his colleague Rooke the question: "Paranoia?" (51). If paranoid, he proves the adage that even paranoids can have real enemies. The Joint Steering Committee gives exclusive planning and execution of the operation (code-named Limpet) to Enforcement (Burr), clearly stating that the River House (Intelligence led by Darker) is "to provide support in aid, theirs is not to reason why," like their counterpart, the CIA (53).

Goodhew establishes the principle of "like to like." British Enforcement and the U.S. Enforcement Agency collaborate, while British intelligence and the CIA provide support on a need-to-know basis. Unfortunately for Goodhew, Burr, and the success of the operation, the same principle is used to reverse roles when the CIA, in collusion with Darker and Goodhew's "master," succeeds in taking control of the operation through exactly the kind of conspiracy that the "paranoid" Burr sought to avoid. Although Burr, his American counterpart Joseph Strelski, and Pat Flynn from U.S. Customs accomplish a model collaborative relationship, they are no match for the guile of the espiocrats from Pure Intelligence and the CIA.[36]

Le Carré also vividly portrays bureaucrats at play: "WHITEHALL IS A JUNGLE, but like other jungles, it has a few watering holes where creatures who at any other hour of the day would rip each other to pieces may assemble at sunset and drink their fill in precarious companionship. Such a place was the Fiddler's Club" (57). In the banter around the bar Goodhew is accused of being in the pay of a foreign power that is "deliberately eroding the citadel from within" (58). He replies, "My master is merely concerned to drag the intelligence services into the new era and help them to set down their old burdens" (58). "But Geoffrey Darker just listened with his eyes and smiled his mirthless smile" (59). His smile reflected his confidence that he would succeed in aborting Goodhew's crusade to reform British Intelligence.

On another occasion, Goodhew is reported to be in "fighting fettle. He had spent the first half of the morning successfully urging Burr's cause to his master, and the second half addressing a Whitehall seminar on the misuses of secrecy" (86). He encounters a colleague from the Home Office who expresses concern about aspects of the operation. Goodhew explicitly warns him not to communicate anything about the operation to the River boys (87).

Chapter 8 opens with an exceptional meeting of covert action teams involved in Operation Limpet with representatives of their respective intelligence agencies and with selected politicians. The British and American enforcement agencies are attempting, through disinformation, to hide the existence of Pine from their respective intelligence agencies. Le Carré satirically supplies the local color, the informal banter, as well as the more serious dialogue.[37] Strelsky (head of the U.S. Enforcement) deliberately tries to put everyone to sleep. "In his word-heavy monotone, the most sensational intelligence is turned to ash. . . . With a superbly tedious sentence, read from a prepared text, unpunctuated and full of false emphases, he hastens his audience on its way to sleep" (109). One of Strelski's assistants has been put up to asking about human intelligence so that he can say they are working on it, as if the joint British and U.S. enforcement team didn't have an agent to penetrate Roper's operation. After the briefing, Strelski tells Burr: "Thirty-three grown people in that room. . . . Nine different agencies, seven pols [politicians]. Must be a couple of 'em telling the cartels Joe Strelski and Leonard Burr don't have a humint [human intelligence] source worth shit" (112).

Although he said nothing, Burr was concerned that the intelligence agencies had asked few questions. Sure enough, Palfrey (the double agent between Darker and Goodhew) reports to Goodhew: "Darling Katie [Darker's station chief in Washington] is as mad as a wet hen. . . . Katie says the Cousins are waking up to what they've got. They've decided that Strelski lulled them into imbecility in Miami and you and Burr aided and abetted him" (156). A cold shudder passes over Goodhew, "raising the hair down his spine and causing him to sneeze several times in succession." In response to the question "What do they *want,* Harry?" Palfry replies, "Limpet" (158). Goodhew is beginning to understand that Burr's "paranoic" concerns are well founded and that he had seriously underestimated Darker.

Chapter 15 is devoted entirely to the unfolding conspiracy. Goodhew and his "minister had received a summons to the U.S. Embassy" (202). Though twenty years younger than Goodhew, what his master "lacked in vision he made up for in ambition" (203). In a meeting with the CIA station chief in London and representatives from Darker's agency, Goodhew and his minister are pressured to turn the operation over to Intelligence. Goodhew finally realizes the accuracy of Palfrey's warning: "*Darker is launching a putsch to recover his lost territories. . . . He's proposing to go in behind the American flag.*" The CIA chief argues the implications of the operation for "*geopolitics*" and demands that Intelligence take it over. Goodhew's minister replies: "'Well, *obviously,* Rex,' he said, striking that nasal whinny peculiar to the Conservative front benches, 'if the Cousins *are* going to take over the Limpet case on *their* side of the pond, willy-nilly we here on *this* side are going to have to take a cool position about whether to follow suit. Aren't we? I say *if,* because these are informal discussions. Nothing's come through on the formal net so far. Has it?'" (204, 205–6).

Because his minister chairs and Goodhew is the secretary of the Joint Steering Committee, the minister and Darker's assistant attempt to pressure Goodhew into convening a rump meeting then and there to reassign authority to Intelligence for the operation. Darker's assistant urges Goodhew: "In a choice between a graceful shimmy and a head-on collision, I go for the shimmy every time. Don't want to see you hoisted on your own petard, or anything" (206). Goodhew holds his ground. A week later, Goodhew is nearly crushed between several trucks that box him as he bikes to work. He takes the warning sufficiently seriously to rewrite his will (280).

Darker forms a new committee code-named Flagship, the members of which (called Mariners) include members of the River House, bankers, civil servants, members of parliament, arms manufacturers, and unbeknown to Goodhew, his minister.[38] A week after he is nearly crushed to death cycling to his office, "Rex Goodhew goes to war. Quietly. In the autumn of his career. In the mature certainty of his cause. Without drama or trumpets or large statements. A quiet outing of his fighting self. A personal but also an altruistic war against what he has come inevitably to refer to as the Forces of Darker. A war to death. . . . My head or theirs. A Whitehall knife fight, let's stay close. . . . He is sending clear signals to his hidden enemies in Pure Intelligence. . . . *Goodhew plays with open cards.* More or less" (279; emphasis added). Although probably not determinative of the outcome, Goodhew's chivalrous playing by rules to which his opponents did not adhere put him and Burr at a serious disadvantage. Goodhew sequesters twelve musty attic rooms on the top floor of his office building, insisting on taking the dingiest one for himself—in sharp contrast to le Carré's other bureaucrats, who tend to boost their egos with elaborate offices. He has the offices electronically swept and removes telephone lines that can be tapped. "He becomes a bureaucratic Robin Hood, fiddling the government's accounts in order to ensnare its wayward servants"(280). He announces: "I intend to sink their Operation Flagship with all hands. . . . Darker won't have a Mariner left when I've done with him" (281).

Burr is skeptical. "Burr's concern is that, even now, Goodhew is unaware of the scale of the octopus" (281). Burr has been denied access to documents three times in the past week that are directly connected to the operation of which he is supposed to be in charge. He discovers an ominous sign when the target of the operation, Roper, switched a major arms purchase from the Czechs to the Americans. "But while Burr grimly noted this development, Goodhew appeared unable to grasp its implications," (283) demonstrating the difference between the professional's sophistication and the nonprofessional's naïveté. On the other side of the Atlantic, Strelski is getting the same runaround and is denied access to vital information. Burr accurately concludes that "Flagship is nothing but a fence to keep us out" (284).

The analyzed revelations of Pine's reports were shocking even to the professionals. "It was not so much the tentacles of the octopus as its ability to enter the most hallowed shrines that left them aghast. It was the involvement of institutions that even Burr had till now presumed inviolate, of names above reproach. For Goodhew, it was the very pageantry of England was dying before his eyes" (284–5). He decides to convene the Joint Steering Committee. When Goodhew expresses confidence that he can get the support of Merridew in the Foreign Office, Burr warns him that Merridew's brother is a top officer in a firm that had invested two and a half million pounds sterling in bearer bonds in Roper's company only the previous week.

After the discovery that Palfry had betrayed the name of one of their agents in Roper's organization to Darker, Burr debates whether to pull out

Pine before he, too, can be betrayed. Goodhew incredulously says, "But good heavens, Leonard, Pure Intelligence is on our side. We have our differences, but they wouldn't endanger *our* sources merely because of a turf war between" Burr interrupts him. "Oh yes they would, Rex, . . . That's who they are, you see. That's what they do" (290). Burr is right. Yet his failure to withdraw Pine from the operation nearly gets him killed. Goodhew's reading of his ability to swing a majority of the Steering Committee is no more accurate than was his reading of Darker's reluctance to betray the agent of another British agency. He makes an extremely costly blunder by showing the list of Roper's backers to his minister. Because Pine had photographed the list after sneaking into Roper's private study, knowledge of the fact that the list was in British hands would be Pine's death warrant. Roper soon learns that the names had been passed on to the British authorities.

Goodhew articulates his conflicting loyalties. He pleads to Burr: "Leonard, I had no alternative. I am a servant of the Crown. I serve a minister of the Crown. It is my duty to inform my master of the progress of your case. . . . I have my loyalties, Leonard. To my principles as well as to him and to you" (318). Burr immediately tells his assistant to stop giving Goodhew "unrefined" reports, but it was too late. The murder of the agent of American Enforcement after Palfrey revealed it to Darker put an enormous strain on the relationship between Strelski and Burr and the collaboration between their agencies.

In a telephone conversation with Goodhew, Burr learns that Goodhew has been pushed aside. Although Goodhew reports it as good news, he is to head a new Whitehall watch committee, which will report directly to the Cabinet secretary. He is to make an in-depth study of all aspects of the secret world. He is to start at once and to give up his present work.[39] Burr was left without his most important (and probably his only) champion at the higher levels of Whitehall. Having lost both his political support and control of the biggest operation of his career, which would have resulted in the capture of his nemesis, Roper, the only constructive thing he could do was to save the life of his agent. He accomplishes this through a brilliant bluff. He promises to bury the case for release of Pine and his "girl."[40]

Although Roper's observation that governments are worse than the arms dealers may be a rationalization to excuse his own moral turpitude, le Carré appears to agree with him (336). In this story, at least one member of the British Cabinet and other respected politicians and public figures collude with corrupt officials of British intelligence, the CIA, and an illegal arms and drug dealer to frustrate the enforcement agencies of the United Kingdom and the United States.

Conclusion: A Metaphor for Our Time

Le Carré's summary interpretation of *The Tailor of Panama* as it relates to this subject is particularly illuminating:

> In the story we have somebody working for an entirely corrupt British institution who is soliciting intelligence which is fabricated. . . . as far as he's concerned, it plays upstairs, they like it in the board room, so he lets it ride. In the board room they're already re-writing it because they want to serve it up to the politicos and their customers and to the people who finance the secret service. So we've got at every level, cost effectiveness, price consciousness and privatization—all these extolled virtues that Mrs. Thatcher so admired in Reaganomics and imported into Britain. In my story, we've got them running wild, which seems to me to be a metaphor for our time. (Ross, 1997:27)

Le Carré considers that the American invasion of Panama "was probably necessary." Paraphrasing the American novelist Richard Koster, who lives in Panama, he says, "The United States performed a brilliant piece of surgery for lung cancer on a patient to whom it had been providing cigarettes for the last 30 years." He reports the unsubstantiated rumor that the CIA had turned a blind eye to Noriega's drug trafficking (including to the United States) in return for arms to the Contras, implying that he believes it to be accurate: "taking sides, arming groups, and so on—you really are operating on a pretty dangerous basis. Everything has its consequences in this business. Nothing goes away. The deals and the promises that you make today really do come home to roost. The more secrets, sometimes, the more violent the response" (Ross, 1997:28).

Le Carré (1986:42) warns of the danger of the expansion of power of the secret services. He is highly critical of "the artificial protection accorded the secret services in cabinet, parliament, the Civil Service, but most of all by the media, that for three post-war decades perceived them in their complacency and self-delusion." Because the bureaucratic politics in and among intelligence agencies takes place in secret, it is imperative they be checked to ensure they act according to government policy and the national interest. Le Carré sees his role as holding up a mirror to the secret world, showing it the monster it could become. Particularly given the centralized system in Great Britain and the unusually strict limitations, for a democracy, of the Official Secrets Act, he has played an extremely important role (see chapter 8).

With the end of the Cold War, the ends of Western policy have become more ambiguous than at any time in living memory. In such circumstances, it becomes increasingly difficult to make intellectually and morally persuasive arguments to justify the excesses of Western intelligence services. Particularly in the absence of clear policy goals, the imperatives of bureaucratic politics are likely to play an even greater role in driving competing intelligence agencies as they search for new priorities to justify their power and resources. Yet, as Walter Laqueur (1998:310) observes, "intelligence is, or should be, the very antithesis of bureaucratic thought and practice." The drive for power within agencies and among them becomes played out in complicated ways as nations compete to maintain and spread their influence and markets abroad.

Chapter 7 ▰▰▰

The Culture and Craft of Espionage

Together, le Carré's novels of the second half of the decade explore the nature of closed communities and their ability to persist in the face of challenge and social change; they offer a powerful and pessimistic image—not only of the bureaucratized world of diplomats and security services but also of the paralysis of the British official class itself. (Eric Homberger, 1986:57)

THE CURSE IS THE PATRIMONY OF AN ELITE SECRET SOCIETY that degenerated into an elitist bureaucracy, an inbred tribal culture. . . . They were different. Rules and laws were not for them. (Tim Weiner, 1995:66)

Introduction: Credibility
Rather than Authenticity

David Cornwell's experience in the secret world gives John le Carré's novels much of their verisimilitude.[1] Le Carré stresses in a number of interviews, most recently with Andrew Ross (1996:7–8), that he "would rather be credible than authentic. Authentic is non-fiction, the reality. . . . In the authentic world, almost no espionage case is ever resolved."[2] Le Carré's secret world is unquestionably credible, and according to many accounts, it is authentic as well.[3]

In my analysis of the particular subculture of intelligence vividly portrayed by le Carré, be it authentic, metaphorical or even mythical,[4] I examine some of the most important espionage activities. Agents must be recruited, trained, and handled. The attributes of a good case officer are essential to the successful conduct of all of these activities. The craft of interviewing and interrogation is essential to that part of intelligence gathering that involves human intelligence as well as a vital part of the protection of a nation's secrets known as counterintelligence. Although this covers only a small part of tradecraft (the techniques of espionage), they constitute the core of the craft.

Agent Recruitment

Elite Recruitment of Nationals: Smiley Gets the Call

In the first chapter of *Call for the Dead,* George Smiley is scouted by his Oxford tutor, Jebedee, who prods the reluctant spy and aspiring academic to meet with the interviewing board of the Overseas Committee for Academic Research. Although they did not introduce themselves, Smiley recognized among them several leading scholars from Cambridge, the School of Oriental Languages, and Oxford. Smiley remembered the meeting as "a fan dance; a calculated progression of disclosures, each revealing different parts of a mysterious entity" (10). Most of the recruits to the Circus of Smiley's generation were similarly scouted by one of their professors at Oxford or Cambridge. This informal "old-boy" network appears to have been the primary means through which the Circus recruited intelligence officers until after World War II.[5] Even Steed-Asprey's secretary, the aristocratic Ann Sercombe (Smiley's sometimes spouse), had family connections in politics and intelligence. Her cousin Miles served as the minister responsible for the Circus in the early to mid-1970s.

Non-elite Recruitment: Leiser

The recruitment of field agents during the war involved foreign nationals as well; but they were generally not of the same educational and social background as their English controllers. In chapter 10 of the *Looking Glass War,* Fred Leiser, a Polish émigré who had served as their agent during the war, is recruited back to the Department for a final mission. He is flattered as they lie about how he is remembered after twenty years as one of their best agents. Haldane plays on his admiration for the English gentleman, and his condescending behavior appears to have solidified Leiser's resolve to undertake the mission. Under instruction, Avery courts him assiduously so that ultimately Leiser acts out of love for him, much as Charlie acts for love of Gadi in *The Little Drummer Girl.* One of the most damning criticisms le Carré levels at the world of intelligence is their deliberate exploitation of their agents' and others' humanity expressed, in its highest manifestation, through love.[6]

Recruitment of Foreign Nationals:
The Israelis Recruit Charlie and Dr. Alexis

The recruitment of Charlie is a case study worthy of a textbook. It is the most complete portrayal of the recruitment of an agent in le Carré's body of work. From the figurative seduction of Charlie by Gadi on a beach on the Greek island of Mykonos through Kurtz's masterful psychological manipulation of her during a three-day interrogation vividly portrayed in chapters 6 and 7, the insight into character and how a certain type of impressionable personality can be mastered by someone with great skill and will is a genuine tour de force. It is one of the most effective portrayals of the systematic invasion of a personality ever portrayed in fiction. Le Carré told Hugh McIlvanney (1983:21) that Charlie's "erratically middle-class upbringing left her chronically dislocated, a fantasist craving reality, conventionally desperate for love. . . . whose powerful spirit is a playground for half-formed political ideals, a confusion of unfocussed strengths."

Previously, le Carré's conviction that he could have recruited her under the circumstances was cited. "They offered her reality, which all actors yearn for. They offered her love and money, too. They completed her life for her" (McIlvanney, 1983:21). Le Carré told Melvyn Bragg (1988:134), "What the Israelis offer her is all the things which I believe actresses, or for that matter women of that age, would fall for: a direction, a purpose, a mission, the family attachment; the mind control, if you like, which tells her what to think and who to be." Pym and a host of others demonstrate that susceptibility to manipulation is not restricted to young women. Particularly gullible adolescents and young adults seem to be easy targets. The control's manipulation of the agent is very similar to the author's manipulation of his characters and, through them, his readers.[7]

Gadi draws Charlie away from her acting family and brings her to her new Israeli family. Kurtz plays the role of "the father Charlie never had," flattering "the virtuous daughter in her" (Homberger, 1986:94). The Israelis offer her a home and a homeland. She is introduced to the plight of the Palestinians through Gadi, one of le Carré's most complex and paradoxical characters, acting the role of her Palestinian lover. Le Carré makes the point that "to the uninitiated, the secret world is of itself attractive" (109). Kurtz offers her the choice between the excitement of the role of a lifetime or to "go home to a safer, duller life" (110). By turning her interrogation into an audition, Charlie is made to feel center stage, which is exactly what she needs. "In her whole life, it seemed to Charlie, no group of people had been so attentive, so appreciative of her performance. They understand, she thought" (113).

After having undergone what could be characterized as a kind of psychoanalysis before an audience, Charlie is then grilled about her politics. She exposes her "uncertain faith" and the insecurity and inconsistency of her political convictions, which Kurtz sums up as "the extreme centre" (129). She is no match for the more sophisticated interrogator. She confesses her desire for acceptance and is offered the Israeli team's friendship. She thinks: "They wanted her. . . . She lay back and let them carry her, *assume her, have her.* Thank God, she thought: a homeland at last" (138; emphasis added). Her psychological submission has a sexual aura to it, which reflects her underlying motive—her love for Gadi. Afterward, Kurtz compliments Gadi on his role in the seduction: "Masterful, high-minded, incisive . . . All that a girl adrift could wish for in her saviour" (140).

An entirely different kind of recruitment by Kurtz of a contact in German internal security, Dr. Alexis, takes place in chapter 11. Le Carré indicates that Alexis had recently fallen out of favor and been demoted. The information that Kurtz had about Alexis shocked him—from the knowledge that his new wife was pregnant before Alexis had informed any of his colleagues, to the exact nature of his duties in a dead-end job. Casually discussing the terrorist bombing in Bad Godesberg (a suburb of Bonn) with which the novel opens, Kurtz lets Alexis know the Israelis have valuable information that the Germans lack. Kurtz tells Alexis that Jerusalem is not happy with his successor and that they are willing to help rehabilitate Alexis by "unofficially" providing him with valuable intelligence in return for his full cooperation with the Israelis. Although they met at ten o'clock at night, "It was well after dawn before the two men walked out and shook hands on their bargain. But Kurtz was careful not to thank his latest recruit too lavishly, for Alexis, as Kurtz well knew, was of a type to be alienated by too much gratitude" (203).

The "re-born Alexis" makes his report and is rewarded with a promotion, and certain powers and facilities, including "a non-accountable operational fund to be opened in Switzerland and dispensed at his sole discretion" to pay the fictional Arab agent who is supposedly supplying the information he receives from Kurtz. Kurtz reports back that "Alexis has bitten, . . . but he's going to need one hell of a lot of shepherding" (204). Later, when Alexis balks at cooperating with the operation at a certain stage, Kurtz threatens to inform his superiors about the true nature of his Swiss bank account. Naturally, Alexis cooperates.

Quasi Self-Recruitment: Jonathan Pine

The last example of agent recruitment I discuss illustrates a case where an agent practically recruits himself. Such volunteers are seen with suspicion.

They are thoroughly investigated. In *The Night Manager,* Jonathan Pine, a combat veteran of a special military unit that operated in Northern Ireland, receives information about an illegal arms deal from Sophie, the mistress of an Egyptian gangster, with whom he is infatuated. Pine passes the information to a contact in British intelligence attached to the embassy in Cairo, with whom he sails. This information is leaked to the arms dealer, resulting in Sophie's brutal murder. Later, while working in a hotel in Switzerland, at his own initiative Pine obtains further information involving the same international arms dealer responsible for Sophie's death, which he again passes on to the British authorities. It is only after having twice supplied them with valuable information on the primary target of an investigation being conducted by the newly created British Enforcement agency that he is recruited by the head of this agency. Chapter 4 begins: "THE RECRUITMENT of Jonathan Pine, former undercover soldier, by Leonard Burr, former intelligence officer, was conceived by Burr immediately after Jonathan presented himself to Wing Commander Quayle" (47).

Burr tells his agent in Switzerland whom Pine contacted; "I'll not flirt with him till I know I can have him. I've been that road before" (51). The use of the term *flirt* in the recruitment of an agent conveys the seductive nature of the enterprise.[8] Burr, like Smiley, was an experienced case officer before rising to his executive position. He thoroughly investigated not only Pine's background in minute detail but also that of his father, who was a combat sergeant who had fought in several of the former colonies and had an impressive record. Burr had studied the son's progress through army foster homes after the death of his mother, civilian orphanages after the death of his father, and military school. Burr reads inconsistent reports on Jonathan, who is characterized as "back and forth like a pendulum," and becomes indignant with the accusation that Jonathan was *"unreconciled."* "Who the hell ever decreed . . . that a sixteen-year-old boy of no fixed abode, who's never had a chance to know parental love, should be *reconciled?"* (52). This thorough prior research and sensitive understanding of personality traits contribute to the successful recruitment.

The actual recruitment takes place in chapter 5. Burr has traveled to Zurich. He introduces himself to Pine: "My name's Leonard. . . . I do crooks" (61). Burr, immediately "going for the point of most resistance," mentions Sophie's death in Cairo. Burr identifies with Pine's "rebellious obedience." He plays on his own "common"Yorkshire roots to put Pine at ease and to establish rapport with him. Burr contrasts his humble roots with the aristocratic background of the arms dealer who is the target of the operation. Burr takes Pine to a restaurant. "As always for an operational encounter, Burr's field manners have been meticulous" (62). He has carefully chosen the restaurant, tipped the headwaiter to reserve the table he wants in advance, and provides Pine with a cover story to explain who Burr is in the unlikely event he sees someone he knows.

Burr questions Pine about his background but knows the answers to the questions he is asking. They discuss Roper, the target of the operation. Burr has cast Pine as the agent to penetrate Roper's closed circle (a role similar to that of Charlie). "Jonathan was surprised to rediscover excitement: the feeling of edging toward the secret center, the pull of action after too long away" (67). Burr confesses his personal hatred of Roper and expects Pine to feel the same because he was responsible for the death of Sophie. Pine admits only to feeling anger but unconvincingly claims not to hate him. "Nevertheless, the idea of hate, dignified by Sophie's murder—of hate turned perhaps to revenge—began to appeal to Jonathan. It was like the promise of a distant great love, and Burr had appointed himself it procurer" (68).

Burr also plays upon Pine's deep patriotism. He reveals to Jonathan that Pine's father had been an undercover agent. Burr explains: "They had to put him back into uniform after he was shot." After playing this important card, he plays his ace. His ace in the hole is Operation Night Owl. Pine, as a member of a close observation platoon, reluctantly admits to having killed three suspected IRA terrorists (whose faces he had seen explode through his telescopic gun sight), an act that has so weighed on his conscience that he has been living in self-imposed exile from England ever since. Burr, appealing to his patriotism, offers Pine another opportunity to serve his country. He appeals to his idealism by offering him a chance to work for the common good, a "five-star unimpeachable cause, guaranteed to improve the lot of mankind or your money back in full. Bye-bye to the old Jonathan, enter the new blue improved product. Resettlement afterwards, a new identity, money, the usual." In addition to this new start in life, he offers him a great challenge and adventure: "You'll be feeding the rat three meals a day, hanging on by your fingernails in force twelve gales, there's not a scrap of you won't be used, not for an hour you won't be frightened stiff. And you'll be doing it for your country, same as your dad . . . And you'll be doing it for Sophie, too" (78).

In addition to the aforementioned inducements, "Burr was talking about *justice*" (78; emphasis added). He claims that when he gets to run the world, "I'm going to hold the Nuremberg Trials Part Two. . . . Then I'd napalm the lot of them [the arms traders and their accomplices]. Fizz" (79). Burr's sincere and, to Jonathan, alarming anger rises as he discusses Roper, and Burr thinks about the complicity of Geoffrey Darker, his former intelligence boss and his corrupt former colleagues. Speaking of Roper (and possibly still thinking about Darker) Burr tells Pine: "He's a villain, and you'd better believe it. *Evil exists*" (81; emphasis added). Burr presses him:

"Do we sign you up or write you off, Jonathan? I was never one for long courtships." Jonathan sees in his mind's eye the exploding face of one of the boys that he shot, the smashed face of Sophie who had been brutally beaten before she was killed, the dead face of his mother, and "Roper's face, coming too close as it leaned into Jonathan's private space" on the occasion when he met him (83).

Burr tells Pine, "I want to rewrite your life from day one and make you love yourself at the end of it." Having gotten Pine to confess his guilt, (reflected in his vision of the faces), he now offers him salvation. Tossing an air ticket onto his bed, Burr tells him, "You don't need time to think about it. You've had nothing but time since you jacked in the army and your country" (85). Pine thinks: "There's no such thing as a decision." He again thinks of the sources of his sense of guilt, and of Roper's mistress, with whom he is fascinated, if not infatuated, and of living up to his father's heroism. "And a sweaty Yorkshire Pied Piper whispering in my ear to come and do it all again" (86). Without recording a formal reply, Jonathan appears in the following chapter in the field at the outset of the operation.

These examples demonstrate that successful recruitment depends to a large extent on careful research in selecting appropriate candidates and in analyzing their backgrounds and personalities so that an appropriate appeal can be made. Clearly, social, cultural, and political circumstances play a role as well. The closed world of class made elite recruitment through personal relations in the two major universities in England the norm until the Second World War. The end of the war provided special conditions for recruitment, including a broadening of the social base, as did the myths prevailing during the Cold War, which made ideological appeals more effective. (Problems of recruiting and maintaining agents in the post–Cold War era are discussed in chapter 8.)

Agent Training

Fred Leiser's Brief and Inadequate Retraining

The depth of psychological insight required to recruit an agent is similarly required to train and handle one. The previously discussed abbreviated retraining of the long-retired agent, Fred Leiser, in *The Looking Glass War* takes four weeks (with a brief break in the middle) and is presented in chapters 12 and 14. The choice of Oxford (where they had trained agents during the war) appealed to Leiser's fervent desire to be English. The illusion that nothing had changed in the Department was assiduously fostered (133). Leiser is not allowed to be alone. Avery accompanies him in training and whenever he leaves the safe house. They practice shooting (although, much to his dismay, Leiser is not allowed to take a gun when he goes to East Germany). He practices observation and memory exercises by using audiotapes made from old gramophone records and visual memory through viewing films. They also practice unarmed combat and the use of a knife. Too little time is devoted to ciphers, Morse code, crystals, and radio transmission on a vintage sender. Leiser is so slow at transmitting and the equipment is so dated that it virtually ensures that his mission is suicidal.

Much attention is paid to developing the agent's dependence on his handlers Haldane and Avery. The narrator notes that Leiser "loved to *confide*. He was their creature; . . . he took *pleasure in their command*" (148; emphasis added). Le Carré repeatedly stresses the pleasure agents take in being well run. But they also need to be individuals who can operate independently in hostile environments. Avery (under instruction) develops a close friendship with Leiser, which hints at latent homosexuality. Although there are similarities between the relationship of Leiser and Avery and that between Charlie and Gadi, the amateurish and inadequate training of Leiser contrasts dramatically with the very professional training (in the form of rehearsals) Charlie underwent for her mission.

Training from Infancy: Magnus Pym

The training of Magnus Pym (*A Perfect Spy*) in the clandestine life began early. By the time he is in boarding school, he conducts his first clandestine operation (71). He covers for his father, who is taken away by the police (79). Pym learned how to look honest while lying, and to destroy incriminating evidence to protect those he loved (96, 97). He embarks on his first clandestine encounter on his father's behalf as a teenager (154). Hence, by the time he is formally recruited into the secret world, Pym has already acquired vast training and experience in duplicity. Little attention is paid by the author to his formal training.

Agent Handling

The East Germans: Elsa Fennan and Dieter Frey

In *Call for the Dead,* Guillam explains to Mendel and Smiley that they only knew a few cases of the East Germans' handling of agents. "My impression is that they run their agents direct from Germany with no contact between controller and agent in the operational zone. . . . They prefer to run foreign nationals . . . In exceptional cases where they have an agent resident in the target country, they work on a courier system, which corresponds with the Soviet pattern" (74). He describes "G.D.R. technique" as "never waiting at a rendezvous, never meeting at the stated time but twenty minutes before; recognition signals—all the usual conjuring tricks that give a gloss to low grade information. They muck about with names, too. A courier may have to contact three or four agents—a controller may run as many as fifteen. They never invent cover names for themselves. . . . They get the agent to do it for them" (75). This information enables Mendel to provide a valuable clue in solving the case. Similarly, once Smiley learns that his former student and agent, Dieter, is running the East German operation in London, he is able to use his familiarity with Dieter's personal tradecraft to trap him.

Leamas: The Agent Deceived

A delicate balance of trust and distrust is one of the prevailing characteristics of the relationship between the handler and the agent. The relationship would be impossible without minimal trust. Yet there is an inherent degree of distrust in a world whose main modus of operations is through deception. While waiting for his agent to cross from East Germany in the first chapter of *The Spy Who Came in from the Cold,* Leamas muses about how the agent had lied to him by omission about his mistress. "You teach them to cheat, to cover their tracks, and they cheat you as well" (13). "Leamas swore, not for the first time, never to trust an agent again" (14). Yet Leamas deliberately withholds information from his superiors in London for fear they would take over his network and wouldn't need him any more (90). As I have already noted, Leamas was tricked and betrayed by Control, who used him as a pawn (or, perhaps, a rook) to checkmate Fiedler and protect the British mole Mundt. This distrust contributes to the enormous psychological strain suffered by the agent in the field.[9] Such severe strain inevitably influences the agents' ability to function in their jobs as well as their personal lives.[10]

Leiser, Haldane, and Avery

Given the loneliness and insecurity of the life of the agent, it is little wonder that, despite the aforementioned constant suspicion, he or she develops great psychological dependence on their handler. In *The Looking Glass War,* "Leiser looked to Haldane as an ailing man looks to his doctor; a sinner to his priest" (147). As was mentioned in earlier chapters, the religious analogy is especially rich in this novel. But religious metaphors are also used in many others; for example, in *Smiley's People,* Smiley is called the last vicar of the Riga Group, of which his agent, General Vladimir, was the leader. Le Carré plays on the analogy between closed and mysterious worlds, which require a unique dedication, or "calling," in which renunciation of self and submission to higher authority are required. Religion and espionage also offer a kind of certainty and direction that certain people crave and on which they thrive.

Jerry Westerby: An Agent Rebels

Fear is universally felt by all agents. Jerry Westerby in *The Honourable Schoolboy* experiences "a wave of dismay hit . . . and he knew it was fear. He was hungry. He was tired. Why had George left him alone like this?" (119). The extremes of boredom and excitement are the lot of the spy: "Bloody inertia interspersed with bouts of bloody frenzy" (135). In *The Russia House,* espionage is characterized as "normality taken to extremes. Spying is waiting" (151). This last sentence is a frequent refrain that emphasizes the drudgery of much of the agent's work. It is "out of sheer boredom" that Westerby exceeds his brief and launches his own private investigation. Jerry doesn't consider his act disobedient, "for there is not a fieldman born who does not at one time or another stray across the borders of his brief" (144). But Jerry's investigation leads him to identify Drake Ko with his father, which, along with his infatuation with Ko's mistress, causes his rebellion and death. "There is a kind of *fatigue,* sometimes, which only fieldmen know: a *temptation to gentleness* that can be the kiss of death" (164; emphasis added). He is portrayed having "the standard post–operational manifestations of a fieldman. A sense of *guilt,* coupled with foreboding, and involuntary movement of affiliation toward the target person" (300; emphasis added).

Craw and Phoebe

A cameo portrayal of agent/handler relations in *The Honourable Schoolboy* is that between Craw, a Circus agent working under cover as a journalist, and one of his informants, Phoebe Wayfarer. Craw loves his "secret whisperers" (189). He brings her orchids. "His manner was gentle and solicitous." He calms her fears yet encourages her to maintain her vigilance. Despite receiving a copious amount of useless intelligence, he is sure that "one day, she was going to be right" (192). The narrator tells us that Craw had "the *golden gift of listening,* which at Sarratt [the Circus spy school] they prize higher than communication" (206; emphasis added). Having patiently listened to her gossip for ten years, she finally provided information that was crucial in the success of Operation Dolphin. Had Craw not been attentive, he might have easily missed the diamond of true intelligence among the reams of useless material.

Craw's informants, like Phoebe, "were his family, and he lavished on them all the fondness for which the overt world had somehow never given him an outlet. He raised and trained them with love that would have done credit to a father" (194). "A little money, a little patronage, a little love, a little patience," is how he does it (195). Craw, in a lecture to the students of Sarratt, said that Phoebe was the bastard daughter of a Chinese mother and an English father. She identified Craw and the Circus with her father.[11]

Gadi and Charlie

In *The Little Drummer Girl,* Gadi Becker's ideological questioning of his government's policies and his falling in love with his agent Charlie, both the result of long-term processes (the former longer than the latter), bring about his moral development. He is not simply infatuated after a brief, superficial acquaintanceship, as are many of le Carré's characters, nor is his critique of his government unreflective, as is Jerry Westerby's. Remaining loyal to his service and his country through the completion of his mission, Gadi dedicates himself to salvaging their love by trying to help rehabilitate Charlie and, through her, himself. He therefore hints at possibilities previously absent in le Carré's heroes, including George Smiley.

Pym and Poppy

If Magnus Pym was a perfect spy, he had the perfect handler in Poppie, a.k.a. Axel. In a perhaps unintended dig at his British handler, Jack Brotherhood, Pym writes: "I wish I could adequately describe to you, Jack, the pleasure of being really well run. . . . But however frayed Pym's nerves when he arrived at the rendezvous, Axel reclaimed him every time they met. . . . Oh, how he studied Pym! How delicately he coaxed and gentled him! How meticulous he was, always to put on the clothes Pym needed him to wear—now the mantle of the wise and steady *father Pym had never had,* . . . now the soutane of Pym's one *confessor,* his Murgo absolute. He had to learn Pym's codes and evasions. He had to read Pym faster than he could read himself. He had to scold and forgive him like the parents who would never slam the door in his face, laugh where Pym was melancholy and keep the flame of Pym's faiths alive when he was down and saying, I can't, I'm *lonely* and *afraid* (426–7; emphasis added). Axel uses every trick he knows to manipulate, coax, cajole, and exert his will over Pym. He made their mutual survival and success dependent upon their relationship. "Pym and Axel drew still closer together, each laying the irrational burdens of his country at the other's feet" (427). Axel personifies the accomplished and successful agent handler.

Ned and Barley

Among the British case officers, Ned, in his appearance in *The Russia House,* receives high marks. Even though his agent essentially defects, blowing the operation, Ned is not at fault. Ned is described as capable and commanding, with the "voice of a good officer" (31). Ned is also described as a "born listener," which is an essential quality in handling agents, interviewing, and interrogation. Ned "was by temperament and training an agent-runner and captain of men. Live sources were his element and, so far as he knew the word, his passion" (89). Just as Kurtz had created a family atmosphere to appeal to Charlie, Ned successfully develops a family atmosphere as well. "Most of all he took to the family atmosphere which Ned, with his instinct for the unanchored joe [agent], assiduously tended—the chatty suppers, the sharing and being the star of the family, the games of chess with old Palfrey" (102).

"It was Ned's show. Ned's joe" (103). Ned selected a pretty Edwardian cottage in Kinghtsbridge, a section of London where Barley was not known for his training. Although expensive, since the Americans were paying for it, his boss could say nothing. Ned tells Barley, "This is your home from home for the duration" (103). During one of his late-night chess games with Palfry, Barley gets Palfrey angry by asking too many personal questions about his private life. Palfrey (who is the narrator) thinks: "Definitions of happiness and love were none of his damned business. He was a joe. It was my right to come close to him, not the other way around" (104). This gives a clear indication of the unbalanced nature of such relationships. Although Barely is very much a free spirit, "as the day of reckoning drew nearer, his submissiveness became total" (105). Although it may have been at the time, it did not remain so.

Smiley: The Model Case Officer

George Smiley, Ned's mentor, was his and many others' role model as a case officer. In *The Secret Pilgrim,* his skill is summarized by Ned, who narrates the novel:

> An intelligence officer is nothing if he has lost the will to listen, and George Smiley, plump, troubled, cuckolded, unassuming, indefatigable George, forever polishing his spectacles on the lining of his tie, puffing himself and sighing in his perennial distraction, was *the best listener of us all.*
>
> Smiley could listen with his hooded, sleepy eyes; he could listen by the very inclination of his tubby body, by his stillness and his understanding smile. He could listen because with one exception, which was Ann, his wife, he expected nothing in his fellow souls, criticized nothing, condoned the

worst of you long before you had revealed it. He could listen better than a microphone because his mind lit at once upon essentials; he seemed able to spot them before he knew where they were leading. (249; emphasis added)

Clearly, Smiley's tradecraft is paradigmatic.

Interviewing/Interrogation

Smiley as Interviewee and Interviewer

The art of interviewing and being interviewed (or interrogated) is an important one for an intelligence officer or agent, because the eliciting of information is the essence of the profession. In *Call for the Dead,* Smiley explains his chameleon-armadillo system for beating the interviewer by adapting himself to the image of the interviewer: "The technique is based on the theory that the interviewer, loving no one so well as himself, will be attracted by his own image. You therefore assume the exact social, temperamental, political and intellectual colour of your inquisitor. . . . Sometimes this method founders against the idiocy or ill-disposition of the inquisitor. If so, become an armadillo. . . . place him in a position so incongruous that you are superior to him" (45). He explains that when he was being prepared for confirmation by a retired bishop, he imagined the bishop's face covered in fur in order to maintain his ascendancy over him. Even the master interviewer and interviewee could lose his detachment, however; for example, through fatigue, as he did during his "interrogation" of Karla in a Delhi jail, or through excessive empathy, as in dealing with Elsa Fennan.

Smiley's interview of Elsa Fennan in chapter 12 reveals this sensitivity:" "You must have been terribly lonely. . . . No one can stand it for ever. It takes courage, too, and it's so hard to be brave alone. They never understand that, do they? They never know what it costs—the sordid tricks of lying and deceiving, the isolation from ordinary people. . . . You've got to hate, and it needs strength to hate all the time. And what you most love is so remote, so vague when you're not part of it" (99–100). Although Smiley was clearly trying to gain her confidence so that he could break her will and extract a confession, he could empathize with her; he related to her through his own experience. When she began to cry, he felt both triumph and shame. "He felt an obscene course bully" (104). Yet he had not really broken her. She concocts a convincing story that she was merely covering for her husband, Samuel, who she claimed was the spy. She gives a moving speech, playing on her painful experiences of persecution, which temporarily throws the sensitive Smiley off the scent

(107). Le Carré implies that although sensitivity is a most valuable asset, carried to excess it can also be a liability.

In *A Murder of Quality*, Smiley interviews Stanley Rode, the husband of the murder victim and the prime murder suspect. Rode is surprised by Smiley's ability to identify with his loneliness. Smiley doesn't overidentify with him, however. On the contrary, Smiley is "continually irritated by Rode's social assumptions, and his constant struggle to conceal his origin. You could tell all the time, from every word and gesture, what he was; from the angle of his elbow as he drank his coffee, from the swift, expert pluck at the knee of his trouser leg as he sat down" (75).[12] The narrator explains why Smiley could identify with the lonely, obscure Rode. "Smiley himself was one of those solitaries who seem to have come into the world fully educated at the age of eighteen. Obscurity was his nature as well as his profession" (77). But being put off by his social pretensions provided a sufficient emotional buffer for Smiley to view Rode with objectivity.

Smiley's final interview of Rode in chapter 19 elicits a revealingly accurate picture of Rode's wife that puts the case in a new perspective and enables Smiley to solve the mystery. Smiley's impassive but sympathetic appearance seems to draw Rode out. Smiley realizes that "the most important thing about Rode was that he had no friends. . . . He felt a movement of sudden *compassion* towards Rode, such as children feel for the poor and parents feel for their children" (140; emphasis added). Smiley takes him to his home for dinner, where Rode pours his heart out: "I had to tell somebody. . . . I thought you'd be a good person." Smiley's ability to empathize and yet maintain his objectivity, along with his compassion and ability to listen, elicits the vital information that finally allows him to crack the case. Smiley's final interview with the murderer, Terence Fielding, in the concluding chapter, illustrates Smiley's consummate professionalism and moral concern.

Leamas Interrogated by Peters, Fiedler, and Mundt

In *The Spy Who Came in from the Cold*, Leamas is interrogated in stages by the East Germans, to whom he is pretending to defect. He is contacted in England and taken to Holland for his first interrogation by Peters. Leamas tells him that because they are both professionals, Peters need not pretend to have fallen in love with him. He is asked about his war service, who ran the Circus, his colleagues, his agents, and how agents are described in the Banking section, where he worked after his return from Berlin. "Peters watched him coolly, appraising him like a professional gambler across the table. What was Leamas worth? What would break him, what attract or frighten him? What did he hate; above all, what did he know?" (86).

Even though he was only pretending to defect, Leamas has to deal with the stigma of treachery because he must give his interrogator valuable information in order to be credible. Peters is also caught in a polarity: he "must give Leamas comfort and destroy his pride" (87). Peters had to nail the inevitable lies he expected from Leamas—taking into account his appearance as an alcoholic wreck. "Leamas even seemed to respond to the dispassionate *professionalism* of his interrogator—it was something they had in common" (88; emphasis added). Peters is most anxious to find out whether Leamas' prize agent had help from someone in an even higher position. Peters refused to believe that his agent could have obtained such highly classified information on his own. During the second day of interrogation, Leamas reveals the story he was planted to tell. On the third day, Peters informs Leamas that he was wanted in Britain for an offense under the Official Secrets Act. This was not part of his agreement with Control, and Leamas realizes that Control has made it impossible for him to back out. He is flown to Berlin for the last stages of interrogation.

Fiedler conducts a more philosophical interrogation of Leamas and develops a close rapport with him. The extremely friendly interrogation of Leamas by Fiedler, in which Leamas reveals that there had been no full-scale search for Mundt in England during the Fennan case (*Call for the Dead,* chapters 13, 14, and 18), even after he had murdered two people, is sharply contrasted with his hostile interrogation by Mundt in chapter 17. After killing a guard, Leamas had been knocked unconscious. Mundt's interrogation is direct and blunt. "Mundt despised technique: he was a man of fact and action. Leamas preferred that" (176). Mundt presses him about Smiley's role in the operation while Leamas can barely maintain consciousness because of his head wound. Fiedler later visits him in a hospital to which Leamas has been taken. Fiedler, too, had been arrested and beaten by the sadistic anti-Semite Mundt, who whispered "Jew" as he tortured Fiedler. (Ironically, Mundt is defended in the secret tribunal by Karden, a former inmate of Buchenwald.) Fiedler continues pressing Leamas about the relationship between ends and means and concludes: "We're all the same, you know, that's the joke" (184). The refrain repeated by Liz to Leamas, "It makes you the same, . . . the same as Mundt and all the rest" (247), is the main motif of the novel.

Interviews in *The Honourable Schoolboy*

Schoolboy illustrates a variety of interview techniques. In chapter 4, Smiley interviews Sam Collins to obtain critical information about the transfer of funds from the Soviet Union to Hong Kong, the record of which had been destroyed by Bill Haydon (the Russian mole). Smiley patiently makes Sam go over his story in minute detail, pretending that there is a discrepancy in the records of the case that need to be clarified. "Smiley . . . fought only to keep his mind opened to the devious options of a fieldman's life" (64). To read Sam's moves, Smiley speculates on the various reasons why he might be hiding something from him. So Smiley "wanders" with Sam through the details. He is acutely aware that fieldmen are congenitally secretive about their sources. Smiley discovers, among other things, that Sam had moonlighted for the local narcotics bureau. This seemingly irrelevant fact becomes important later.

Smiley's sensitivity as a listener is revealed by the narrator: "Smiley's ears were so sharp at that moment that he could have heard a leaf fall; but what he heard, metaphorically, was the *sound of barriers being erected,* and he knew at once, from the cadence, from the tightening of the voice, from the tiny facial and physical things which make up an exaggerated show of throw-away, that he was *closing on the heart of Sam's defences*" (68). Biding his time, Smiley conducts this interview as if it were a chess match. He closes his eyes and appears to doze but heard precisely "Sam Collins trod very lightly round a certain personality" (71). Smiley reminds him that he had previously mentioned a "dumb blonde." Smiley's remark that Sam is a ladies' man makes the latter nervous. Again, Smiley's sensitivity and skill yields another valuable clue in the person of Elizabeth Worthington.

Having intuitively felt the girl was a potential lever, Smiley (who "at heart" was still a "case man") interviews her abandoned husband. The narrator says, "Honourable men recognise each other instinctively" (209). Peter Worthington and Smiley establish rapport instantly. "Smiley was acting himself, but more so, as they say at Sarratt" (210). This is le Carré's standard description of "cover," or an assumed identity of an agent. Among the attributes they shared is that they are both cuckolds.[13] Smiley "found himself staring directly into Peter Worthington's honest, abject eyes; and for a moment the two masks slipped simultaneously. Was Smiley observing? Or was he being observed? Perhaps it was only his embattled imagination—or did he sense, in himself and in this weak boy across the room, the stirring of an embarrassed kinship? . . . You never knew your Elizabeth, Smiley thought, still staring at Peter Worthington; and I never knew my Ann" (217).

Using another assumed name and pretending to be an investigator for security company assigned to get character references on their daughter, who is supposed to have applied for a job, Smiley interviews Elizabeth's parents, the Pellings. Mr. Pelling suspects Smiley of working for the Secret Service and that his daughter does so as well. Smiley handles the aggressive Pelling entirely differently than he did the cordial Worthington (Pelling's son-in-law). There were long silences in their conversation, which Smiley was at no great pains to end. The narrator describes Smiley's "bedside manner" in handling him. Pelling, a retired Post Office employee, is finally responsive to the bureaucratic forms Smiley produces, "for in Mr. Pelling's world . . . forms were the legitimisation of everything. . . . So the men worked together like two friends solving a crossword" (224).

Smiley displays gentle forbearance as Pelling reveals important information amid a great deal of nonsensical ranting. Smiley memorizes a letter from Pelling's daughter revealing she had worked for the Circus agent Sam Collins under his alias, Mellon. Smiley obtains even more information from Mrs. Pelling during a brief conversation in her bedroom. She then tells him he had better go, because "I can't do with trustworthy faces round me. Sorry, darling, know what I mean?" (231).

A very different style of interviewing is displayed by Connie Sacks and Doc di Salis in their interrogation of Mr. Hibbert, an eighty-one-year-old retired Baptist missionary, who, with his late wife, were unofficial foster parents to the Ko brothers in China. Connie and di Salis were research analysts and area experts, not trained operatives. Connie's interview skills were far superior to those of her colleague. She and di Salis pretended to be interviewing Hibbert about Drake Ko because he had been nominated for a knighthood. Connie requested permission to take notes. "For it is Circus folklore that when the sound is being stolen [surreptitious recordings], notes should be taken, both as a fall-back and for cover" (235).

Connie is careful to "match the old man's pace" (235). As Hibbert rambled, she shut up di Salis, who was about to intervene, with a look that said: "*Let him run. . . . Force him and we'll lose the whole match.*" She deftly pulls him back to the subject whenever he strays too far. Whereas di Salis makes counterproductive interjections, like "you *must* . . . You must tell us *everything*. It's your duty" (239, 246). When Hibbert makes a derogatory comment about spies, "Connie beamed her agreement" while "di Salis gave a squeaky, offended wheeze" (247). "Di Salis in his excitement was growing positively avid. His ugly face had sprung patches of colour and he was fidgeting desperately on his chair" (249).

Di Salis fires a battery of questions at Hibbert. "Go on, please. *Please* go on" (249). Initially, Hibbert is amused by his enthusiasm. But, Connie can't restrain di Salis, who presses "tactlessly, stridently, . . . He cared for nothing now except the answers" (249). Hibbert's voice and zeal die, and "it was suddenly clear that Mr. Hibbert didn't trust di Salis any more, and indeed that he didn't like him" (250). When Connie attempts to end the interview, di Salis presses on. Mr. Hibbert refuses to answer more questions, but his daughter, Doris, supplies more information. Di Salis, demanding specific dates, snaps: "'Be precise, *woman*,' and he was making Connie seriously anxious. But when she tried to restrain him, he again ignored her. . . .

Connie had actually risen to go. She knew the limits, she had the eye, and she was scared of the way di Salis was hammering on. But di Salis on the scent knew no limits at all" (251). He accuses the Hibberts of withholding information. The narrator describes di Salis as "yapping information down at the old man's head. . . . He grabs a fistful of [the old man's] shawl in his feverish little hand. . . . His squeaky words flew about the firelit room like ugly spirits" (252). Whereas Connie had been trying to make a graceful exit, di Salis' conduct prompts Mr. Hibbert to order them to leave. While putting on her coat, Connie intuitively asks Doris if the name Liese means anything to her. Doris replies that it is her mother's name.[14]

On the way home, Toby Esterhase (who acted as their driver), Connie, and di Salis squabbled about the latter's lack of restraint. Nonetheless, they all triumphantly report their discovery to Smiley.[15] What is noteworthy about this interview is that in spite of di Salis' outrageous conduct, they succeeded beyond their hopes in obtaining key information. Just as Haldane's rude behavior had the unintended consequence of prompting Leiser to volunteer for the operation in *The Looking Glass War*, although di Salis eventually alienates Mr. Hibbert, he does succeed in extracting valuable additional intelligence from Doris. It is the more tactful and intuitive Connie, however, who keeps the interview from ending in disaster and elicits the most important information.

Smiley Again

In *Smiley's People*, both Smiley and Toby Esterhase have been pushed out of the Circus as a result of Saul Enderby's successful coup. Smiley has been called in to cover up the murder of General Vladimir. He desperately needs information from his former colleague who, at the time, under the name Benati, is a proprietor of a less than respectable art gallery. Toby is discomfited by Smiley's questions: "I don't like these questions. A friend, an old boss, my own house—it upsets me, okay?" (160). Smiley needs to know why Vladimir had demanded to speak to him directly and not his "postman" Esterhase. "Against all protocol, against all training, and against all precedent. Never done it before" (161).

Smiley lets Toby know that he has a witness to the fact that Vladimir, who used to think highly of him, had become very bitter about him. In a not-so-veiled threat Smiley says, "I'd like to keep it away from the police if I could, you see. For all our sakes." But this only awakened the fieldman in Toby who knew that "interrogations, like battles, are never won but only lost" (162). Smiley intuits that Toby had refused a request from Vladimir and finally gets him to reveal the details. Toby had refused to act as a courier for Vladimir to pick up something for him in Hamburg. After Smiley deliberately provokes Toby's temper, Esterhase reveals he refused to do it because the contact was an unreliable informant who fabricated intelligence: "Holder many times of our Creep of the Year award" (166).

Toby admits, "George, I owe you. . . . you pulled me from out the gutter once in Vienna when I was a stinking kid. I was a . . . bum. So you got me my job with the Circus. So we had a lot of times together, stole some horses." He reminds Smiley of his own advice about retirement: "When it's over. Pull down the shutters, go home!" (168). He urges Smiley not to pursue the case. But "in the end, as a reluctant gift of friendship, Toby told it as Smiley asked, straight out, with a frankness that was like defeat" (169). Even then, however, he did not tell Smiley all he knew. Smiley knew his customer: "Smiley looked at Toby, and remembered him, and remembered also that in all the years they had known each other and worked together, Toby had never once volunteered the truth, that information was money to him; even when he counted it valueless, he never threw it away" (174). Therefore, Smiley had to pry the most vital information he needed to solve the case from Toby, who was holding it back. The narrator characterizes Smiley "by a succession of cautious movements [that] grew into his own strength of body and mind, probing the motives of his adversary as he probed his own" (176).

Introspection, sensitivity, an acute ear for what is not said as well as what is said, and the ability to empathize with his subject contribute to Smiley's success. Stephen Schiff (1989:64) observes that "Cornwell is a wonderful, avid listener." Le Carré (1979:114) compares the performance by Alec Guinness with his own intention for Smiley: "His Smiley, like mine, is frequently an abstraction which is only defined by the collisions of each encounter. Seeing to the heart of his adversary, Smiley-Guinness *becomes* the heart; his interrogations ennoble as well as reveal." This quality sets Smiley apart from all other le Carré characters' mastery of interrogation. Smiley has more than mastered technique. His critical empathy makes the interviewee feel ennobled.

Extreme Interrogation: Kurtz and Yanuka

Chapter 9 of *The Little Drummer Girl* contains a detailed summary of the preparation of a team of experts for the interrogation of Yanuka, brother of the leader of the Palestinian terrorist cell who is the target of the Israeli operation. Kurtz warned his two interrogators that they had a maximum of six days in which to complete their interrogation. Kurtz himself took up the reins on the fourth day. "It was a job after Kurtz's heart" (164). Every phase of planning and implementation are described in detail—both long term and "last-minute improvisation that Kurtz and all of them loved" (166). Although the love of improvisation is a stereotypical characteristic, it accurately captures a typical Israeli cultural trait. In this case, it involved a hasty hunt to find an interrogator experienced in the successful use of hallucinatory and disintegrating drugs.

The psychological breaking of Yanuka and manipulation of his personality by fragmenting it, building on his fear and dependence, and on his fear of the imminence of the dreaded Israeli interrogation still to come, parallels the much more subtle manipulation of Charlie. Delusion, deception, and the superimposition of a fictional reality was accomplished through psychological manipulation (including the use of mind-altering drugs) without resort to physical violence. Kurtz believed that if you had to resort to violence, "Always be sure to use it against the mind, not the body" (177). We see through these various portrayals increasingly coercive types of manipulation playing upon the active collusion of the victim through his or her willingness to engage in self-delusion. Le Carré equates these more extreme forms of psychological manipulation with the more subtle common forms. He abhors them even as he uses the latter to manipulate his readers.

Tough Love: The CIA and Barley

The week-long interrogation of Barley Blair by the CIA in chapter 12 of *The Russia House* represents an altogether more genteel type of mental violence. British intelligence and their American Cousins are allies closely cooperating in Operation Bluebird. The Americans need to establish the credibility of the Russian source, Goethe, and the reliability of the unorthodox British "agent," Barley. The interrogation takes place in a mansion on an island off the coast of Maine. Barely, treated like an honored guest and prisoner, is given the bridal suite. The first day of interrogation, which takes place in the billiards room, is led by Russell Sheriton, CIA head of Soviet operations. The narrator (Harry Palfrey) defines as "underlying terror" the atmosphere of the week.

Sheriton compares Goethe's intelligence to a Picasso and Barley as the one who is trying to sell it to them, for he is the only one among them who has met Goethe. He calls Barley the "linchpin," "*the man*" (234). Sheriton alludes to their having been fooled by Bill Haydon and emphatically declared they will "*never*" fall for British deception again. Sheriton deliberately riles Barley with barbed and provocative questions, relating, for example, to his father's left-wing politics. Sheriton challenges Barley about his notorious drinking and the friends in the jazz world with whom he associates. In a startling revelation, Sheriton declares his belief in Goethe and makes clear he is putting his career on the line so that he deserves Barely's candor, which he demands. Barley agrees to further and more intense interrogation.

The second day is led by Larry Quinn, a West Point graduate who, it is said, "talks to Defense, he talks to the corporations, he talks to God" (238). Quinn, not convincingly pretending to only play the devil's advocate, suggests Goethe's intelligence is "*Smoke,*" or deception. Ned tells us "Quinn's shadowed eyes continued glowering at Barley" as he questions him about his drinking, his memory, and his Soviet friends. Harry and Ned are worried because Barley supplies three excuses where one would have been enough, thereby making him appear suspicious to the experienced interrogator. Ned's boss, Clive, agrees to let the American administer a lie detector test on Barley.

Todd takes over the questioning. Palfrey describes him as one of those "men who make a crusade of their charmlessness and learn to use their verbal clumsiness as a bludgeon" (242). Barley is more than a match for Todd. His final retort to Todd's insinuation of a homosexual relationship and a faulty memory is: "I remember what's important to me, old boy. If I haven't got a dirty enough mind to match yours, that's your bloody business" (244). As dull as Todd is, Barely's next inquisitor, Brady, is described as "bright as boot-buttons." An elderly American occasional professor who spoke with a southern lilt, Brady (who claimed that was his real name) began by thanking Barley. After exchanging jazz gossip about mutual friends with Barley, Brady steers the "conversation" to British politics and elicits Barley's criticism of Mrs. T (Thatcher). Barley calls her "a bloody Red" because she favors the corporation over the individual.

Thus, having put Barley at ease, Brady has him go through his account of his meeting with Goethe again. Whereas none of the others detected it, Brady perceived a gap of approximately fifty minutes in his account. Brady skillfully extracts from Barley the information he had been hiding. Barley had bought Katya a fur hat and had telephoned her to make sure she was all right. He told her to destroy the copies of Jane Austen he had given her because they had questions for Goethe printed into the text. Afterward, Brady advised Clive (Ned's boss and the highest-ranking representative of British Intelligence present) to "drop him [Barley] down a hole. . . . He's flakey, he's a liability and he thinks too damn much" (254). Brady's insightful assessment of Barley proved prophetic. Palfrey dates "Barley's journey away from us" from this interrogation (256).

The successful interrogation, having penetrated Barley's defenses, left him with a sense of having been violated. Ironically, the lie detector test that convinced the CIA to take over the operation was the straw that broke the camel's back—precipitating Barley's defection.[16] "Something happened to his pride" (262). In this type of case a "successful" interrogation is ironically counterproductive. It contributed to producing ends that it had sought to prevent. This is another dramatic illustration of the role played by unintended consequences.

Conclusions

The case officer or agent handler plays a variety of roles with different agents and even with the same agent. He or she can become a literal lover, as Gadi becomes with Charlie. More usually, the handler is a figurative lover, as is Avery for Leiser. Very often, he is a surrogate father (Kurtz/Charlie, Craw/Phoebe, Smiley/Westerby, both Brotherhood and Poppie/Pym, and Burr/Pine). He may be like an older brother (Tim/Larry in Our Game). Given the damaged childhoods and immaturity of le Carré's agents, the need for surrogate parents—particularly the authority of a loving father, is a deep psychological need, which the case officer fills. Frequently, like another kind of father, he acts as a confessor, hearing confessions and granting absolutions. He is often called upon to judge his agent as well and grant clemency for offenses.

By the nature of the relationship, he must be a sensitive psychologist, exemplified by his being a good listener, given the personality types attracted to spying and because of the severe psychological strain demanded of an agent. Loneliness, distrust, insecurity, fear, guilt, fatigue, and the extremes of waiting and boredom countered by the adrenaline rush of high excitement are occupational hazards of all agents. The case officer, both in his capacity of agent handler and as interviewer and interrogator, must be a good judge of human nature. She or he must have the bedside manner of that extinct species known as the old-fashioned family doctor. Compassion and empathy are the qualities of the most successful ones, and are epitomized by Smiley. But empathy must be balanced by skepticism, lest the interrogator lose his objectivity and be deceived. These are also the rarest of qualities along with personal and professional integrity.

As with so many other human relationships, the relationship between agent and handler, as the names imply, is one of subordination and domination. It is by definition not a balanced, completely reciprocal relationship. Rather than being based on mutual respect, trust, and consideration, it is more typically characterized by distrust and manipulation. It tends to be a relationship based on power rather than authority.[17]

Le Carré's depiction of the closed world of British intelligence, the inbred culture of an arrogant elite, portrays the paralysis of a class and the end of an era dominated by it. There are important parallels to be drawn between this fictional world and the real world—and they have special relevance to the current crisis in U.S. intelligence.

Chapter 8

Fiction and the Real World of Espionage

If you're going to be involved with espionage you've got to be motivated. It's not fun and games. It's dirty and dangerous. There's always a chance you're going to be burned. In World War II, in the O.S.S., we knew what our motivation was: to beat the goddamn Nazis. In the cold war, we knew what our motivation was: to beat the goddamn Russians. Suddenly the cold war is over, and what is the motivation? What would compel someone to spend their lives doing this sort of thing? (Richard Helms[1])

Intelligence runs against the grain of American political culture. (Walter Laqueur, 1998:301)

Introduction: Life Imitates Fiction

Life, it is said, imitates fiction.[2] In addition to the enjoyment derived from reading fiction, one reads novels for insights that can be gained about the world. This chapter focuses on the insights about espionage to be gained from le Carré's fictional portrayals of it. Occasionally, literature may even influence policy. For example, James Burridge (1992:18) bemoans the influence in Washington of le Carré's bias against SIGINT (signals or electronic intelligence) and in favor of HUMINT (human intelligence): "But it is galling to know that his books and public comments make marginally more difficult the task of ensuring that resources are allocated within the Intelligence Community on the basis of real contributions instead of on the basis of myth and mystique. It is also ironic that the CIA would benefit from all this in even a small way, since le Carré has made his distaste for that organization so obvious."[3]

Sometimes it is difficult to tell when fiction imitates life. For example, Markus Wolf, who retired as head of East German foreign intelligence in 1986 after thirty-three years in office, has been reported to have been the model for Karla and even more probably for the Jewish intellectual East German intelligence officer Fiedler, in *The Spy Who Came in from the Cold.* Le Carré explicitly denies this as "sheer nonsense."[4] Wolf, however, told Timothy Garton Ash (1997:12) "that he had read le Carré's novel soon after it came out in 1963, and was amazed at the uncanny way in which the novelist had echoed, in the Fiedler-Mundt conflict, the tensions of his own relationship with his superior, Erich Mielke, the Minister for State Security. Was British intelligence that good, he wondered." But when Wolf was asked by J. M. Bik (1997) what he thought of being considered le Carré's model for Fiedler, "He mumbled something like 'ridiculous, but useful in the work I had.'"[5] Both spy novelist (le Carré) and intelligence officer (Wolf) have been quoted contradicting themselves. Both are masters of deception. Ash (1997:12) asks: "So can one, even now, really disentangle fact and fiction, author and spy, Wolf and 'Wolf'?"

There is a connection between the political and ethical concerns in le Carré's work about the role of espionage and contemporary problems and dilemmas: le Carré does not comprehensively address all such problems, but he does highlight key ethical dilemmas that thinking citizens of democracies need to contemplate and confront.[6]

Post-World War II United Kingdom and the Post-Cold War United States

Le Carré's depiction of Britain's loss of mission after World War II parallels the experience of the United States at the end of the Cold War. Tim Weiner (1995:67) quotes Milt Bearden, the last chief of the CIA Soviet division, who claims the agency once had such a mission: "And the mission was a crusade. Then you took the Soviet Union away from us and there wasn't anything else. We don't have a history. We don't have a hero. Even our medals are secret. And now the mission is over. *Fini.*"[7] He also quotes the chief of the directorate for intelligence, John Gannon, who reveals that his analysts feel adrift.[8] Robert B. Bathurst (1993) shows how the Cold War contributed to "mirror-imaging" when United States and Soviet intelligence analysts each interpreted the other's motives and behavior through their own cultural lenses.[9]

This sense of loss of direction is the most important of a number of parallels between post–World War II Britain and the post–Cold War United States. In contrast with Ian Fleming, Lars Ole Sauerberg (1984:170) notes le Carré's "interest is in the analysis of the premises which prevented England from immediate recognition of the changes in international relations and from adapting herself to them." Le Carré indicts the Establishment for its inflexibility and explains the Philby affair as a manifestation of the subculture of the English Establishment as it dominated both the government and the secret world. Sauerberg (171) perceptively interprets le Carré's novels of the sixties as "an effort to place responsibility for the national decline" and reflecting a "need for re-orientation."

Reading these novels as allegories of Britain's loss of a sense of direction, unwillingness to face new realities, and failure to adapt to them, one finds in the Britain bewildered by the changing international environment an echo of the present condition of the United States. The obvious difference is that the United States remains the dominant military and economic power in the world. Therefore, its loss of direction has particularly serious implications. Just as le Carré's Circus helps one to understand contemporary England, the CIA may be an apt metaphor for contemporary America.[10] For example, the lack of resolve in U.S. foreign policy in the Middle East has facilitated the current deadlock which, if not broken, is destined to lead to further bloodshed and instability in the region.

In *Small Town in Germany,* the twin threats are represented by fascism and Americanism.[11] The cynic De Lisle decries American optimism: "That's the trouble with Americans, isn't it really?[12] All that emphasis on the future. So dangerous. It makes them destructive of the present. Much kinder to look *back,* I always think"[13] (117). Symbolic of this disregard for the past, the CIA destroyed or "lost" nearly all documents relating to its involvement in the overthrowing of the government of Iran in 1953.[14] Le Carré's character's commentary on Americans' carelessness with their past contrasts with his belief in the past's redemptive power. But he also warns against the danger of an unhealthy obsession with the past in *A Murder of Quality* and *The Looking Glass War.*[15] The Soviet Union, in contrast, was generally oriented toward the future and operated on crisis time in which life was lived in the shadow of impending catastrophes. "Present time [in the Soviet Union], being always transitional, lacks a compelling reality."[16] A balanced perspective situates present policy within the context of past experiences and future goals.

Le Carré's analysis of the symptoms and his prescription for a remedy to Britain's ills of the past three decades are equally applicable to the present plight of the United States as it struggles to overcome the loss of confidence suffered from the Vietnam War and the disorientation of political leaders and policy makers in the aftermath of the Cold War.[17] The United States and its intelligence agencies have lost their sense of mission. A sense of mission is generally beneficial for any organization. But if it takes the form of a *crusade,* it can lead to excess and increase the danger of the intervention of intelligence agencies in politics. This danger was most conspicuous in the Bay of Pigs operation, when Director of Operations Richard Bissel lied to the director of the CIA, the Joint Chiefs of Staff, and the president.[18] The politicization of intelligence became the norm during the reign of William Casey, the activist director of the CIA who was appointed by President Ronald Reagan.

The Politicization of Intelligence:
Deceiving Three Presidents

Under Casey's leadership, the Directorate of Intelligence was reorganized in 1982 (an action reminiscent of the reorganization of the Circus by Bill Haydon). As a consequence, "The boundaries between intelligence and policy making—especially at the highest CIA echelon—were practically removed," according to Uri Bar-Joseph (1995:31). Bar-Joseph concludes that Casey was the most political director in the agency's history: "Never before in the history of the CIA was the intelligence process so systematically corrupted and the professional integrity of the organization so severely undermined as in the period when the 'activist' policy triumphed over the 'traditional' approach" (33). This process culminated in the notorious Iran-Contra scandals.

The CIA knowingly gave the president and the Department of Defense reports from agents it knew were under control by the Russians. This was a violation of its obligation to speak truth to power. As Weiner (1995:104; emphasis added) observes: "Passing along information without revealing that its source works for the other side is putting poison in the well. The officers in question thought *they knew best.*" It as if they stepped out of The Tailor of Panama: "IT IS THE BUSINESS OF INTELLIGENCE TO REPLACE ignorance and fear with knowledge and confidence. The CIA has been imprisoned by its own lies, living in fear, unsure of its history, uncertain of its future. . . . The agency had suffered yet another self-inflicted wound, this time to its *soul*" (ibid.). They concealed from three presidents, whose policies were influenced by the tainted intelligence, information that the sources were double agents, thanks to the treason of Aldrich Ames. Weiner (December 9, 1995:5) perceptively argues: "This self-deception was crucial to the success of the scheme." The symbiotic relationship between deception and self-deception is central to my analysis of le Carré's work.

John Deutch, who served as deputy secretary of defense prior to becoming director of Central Intelligence, said that the disinformation forwarded by the turned agents had the capacity "to influence U.S. military research and development and procurement programs costing billions of dollars."[19] These American agents, like the German agents in World War II who had been turned by Sir John Masterman in the double-cross system, were kept in play to report back fake information. The main difference was that the Germans did not know their agents had been turned, and the CIA had very good reasons to suspect that theirs had been.

Edward Jay Epstein (1994:42) observes: "The best kept secret of intelligence services is the inherent weakness of the espionage business. The ultimate danger of this enterprise is not that spies will be captured and killed. . . . Rather, it is that they will be captured and spared, for the far more important business of misleading their government." Epstein argues that thanks to the treachery of Ames, the Soviet Union was in even a better position to mislead the Americans in the 1980s than were the British to trick the Germans in World War II. He claims that this partly accounts for the CIA's egregiously overestimated Soviet economic and military strength (as in *The Russia House*) and the underestimation of Soviet nuclear weapons.

John Deutch, appointed by President Clinton as director of Central Intelligence, with a mandate to reform the agency in the aftermath of the debacle created by Ames (during Clinton's first administration), addressed the deceiving of the president and others by these CIA officials. "This deception reflected *supreme arrogance,* Deutch says, 'an arrogance that let them ignore the fundamentals of their profession'" (Weiner, 1995:104; emphasis added). He quotes Ames's explanation for his treason: "Call it arrogance, if you will, but I'd say: "I know what's damaging, and I know what's not damaging, and I know what the Soviet Union is really all about, and I know what's best for foreign policy and national security. . . . I do." This attitude precisely reflects the mentality expressed in the memo of George Young when he was vice-chief of the British SIS in 1955 (see the conclusion to chapter 3). It is also the same moral arrogance used by George Blake to justify his treason as a Soviet mole (see chapter 4).

In his sentencing statement, Ames justified his treason by rationalizing that in peacetime the espionage business had become "a self-serving sham, carried out by careerist bureaucrats who have managed to deceive several generations of American policy makers and the public about both the necessity and the value of their work" Epstein (1994:43) interprets this as meaning "in peacetime the means of espionage—recruiting sources—had completely replaced the end, which is getting useful intelligence." Even if his evaluation of the current American intelligence establishment is accurate, it in no way justifies any form of treason, much less the magnitude of Ames' betrayals. Ames certainly belongs in the same category with George Blake, Kim Philby, and the fictional Bill Haydon.

Evaluation of Additional Weaknesses
of the CIA and Needed Reform

In his review of Thomas Powers' *The Man Who Kept Secrets,* a biography of Richard Helms, the former director of the CIA, le Carré (1979:48) lists three fatal ills that undermined the CIA: mismanaged covert operations; lack of sufficient political control of its operations; and "the American political romanticism that one moment espouses openness at any price, and the next revels in the high alchemy of secret panaceas and swift, unconventional, totally illegal solutions." Many intelligence experts have discussed these themes as well. One subject that receives much attention, perhaps because its failures have been most dramatic, is covert operations.

Covert Operations: Evaluation and Congressional Oversight

Covert operations (among other activities) were provided with legal "cover" by Larry Houston, who as legal adviser for the CIA from 1947 to 1973 filled a position similar to that of the fictional Harry Palfrey. Richard Helms, CIA director from 1966 to 1973, gave the eulogy at the funeral of Houston. "He praised Houston as a man who always told the clandestine service what it *could* do, not what it could *not*. 'And that,' he said dryly, 'was essential at the CIA in those days'" (Tim Weiner, 1995:66; emphasis added).

Covert operations have been a ubiquitous part of U.S. foreign policy since the founding of the republic. Arthur S. Hulnick (1996) questions whether the United States should continue to use covert actions as a tool of foreign and security policy.[20] Hulnick, a former CIA analyst, discusses how such activity should be managed and who should control it. Tracing the origins of U.S. covert actions from the revolution against the British and the administration of George Washington, Hulnick claims that every American president has asserted "executive privilege" against congressional attempts to exercise oversight over intelligence activities. After the hearings of the Church Committee (1975), both houses of Congress established oversight committees to review the activities of the intelligence agencies.

American intelligence oversight has varied in intensity over the years. Loch K. Johnson (1989:8–9) traces the development from benign neglect in its earliest stage, the "Era of Trust" (1947–74),[21] through an "Era of Skepticism" (1974–76), to an "Era of Uneasy Partnership" (1976–1986), characterized by congressional assertiveness in the post-Watergate, post-Vietnam War period. Johnson asserts that in this decade, intelligence policy was more accountable and democratic. But these checks failed to alert Congress or stop the Iran–Contra operation, which dealt a serious blow to the attempt to balance accountability with security and initiated a new "Era of Distrust" in 1986.

Other experts, like Amos Yoder (1996), in his review of CIA covert actions, are even more critical of covert activities.[22] He agrees with former CIA director Stansfield Turner's evaluation that covert action has done more harm than good to the CIA and seriously detracts it from its primary role of collecting and evaluating intelligence. Yoder cites the conclusion of the Senate Committee on Intelligence (1973; emphasis added) in his own conclusion: "The United States must not adopt the tactics of the enemy. *Means are as important as ends.* Crisis makes it tempting to ignore the wise restraints that make men free. But each time we do so, each time the means we use are wrong, our inner strength, the strength which makes us free, is lessened.[23]

President Lyndon Johnson put it less elegantly but forthrightly when he ordered an end to political assassinations: "You don't get into a pissing contest with a skunk."

Nevertheless, even the critical investigations of covert action by the Church Committee, the Rockefeller Commission, and the joint investigation of the Iran-Contra affair concluded that, although they needed to be much more carefully controlled, such activities were vital to national security. The Brown Commission, appointed in the aftermath of the Ames affair, also recognized the need for a covert action capability in compelling circumstances, although (at least in the public version) it failed to delineate what the parameters of such circumstances should be. Nor did it determine more rigorous measures of oversight to guarantee accountability. Ironically, given the crisis that precipitated its appointment, the commission completely ignored counterintelligence. Loch Johnson, the sole academic member of the commission (who has recommended serious reforms of covert action and counterintelligence), called it a "symbolic reassurance commission."[24] The ritual function implied in Johnson's statement is reminiscent of the "secret committee of enquiry" described in chapter 2 of *The Russia House* to which I have alluded in chapters 3 and 6.

Walter Laqueur (1998:305–6) warns that even though covert action is not an option to be chosen lightly, "in the absence of such an option a global power may be doomed to impotence." Given the consensus regarding the need for a covert capability for the U.S. president, the question remains one of establishing the appropriate management and control of such activities (which some consider a mission impossible) and the determination of appropriate criteria in selecting targets. In terms of management, Harry Howe Ransom (1970) argues in favor of organizationally separating intelligence gathering and analysis from covert actions. Hulnick favors maintaining institutional integration and argues for even greater communication between field agents and analysts. This issue sharply divides intelligence experts (and cannot be adequately treated here).

Most experts tend to debate various proposals for structural, that is, institutional, reforms. Laqueur (308–9) emphatically states: "In the perspective of three decades it has at least become clear which approaches do not work. This goes above all for attempts at organizational reform." Few deal with the needed changes in the *culture* of the espionage community, which is at least as important, if not more so, than organizational reforms. Mark M. Lowenthal (1992:167), who analyzes the different "mind-sets" (subcultures) of intelligence consumers (policy makers) and producers (analysts) comes close when he concludes, "The production and use or disuse of intelligence as part of the policy process is the net result of several types of mind-sets and behavior within and between two groups that are more disparate than most observers realize."[25]

Evaluating the success of covert action is extremely difficult. Hulnick cites the long-term disastrous consequences of CIA operations in Guatemala and Iran as examples of operations initially judged successful but which, in the long run, now appear to have been failures. He stresses how unintended consequences, like the efforts to overthrow Castro, have a way of backfiring and achieving the opposite of desired results. Sometimes, as in Nicaragua, desired results are achieved in spite of rather than because of covert action. Probably more often, the results are so ambiguous it is impossible to determine success, as in Afghanistan, which has descended into chaos. Consequences also need to be evaluated in the context of alternatives that would have been the likely outcome had this option not been employed.

For example, the Mossad's bungled attempt to assassinate the Hamas leader Khaled Mashal in Amman, Jordan, on September 28, 1997, was profoundly ill advised for many reasons. But it would have been even more damaging to Israel's relations with Jordan and the United States had it succeeded. Whereas le Carré accepts the necessity for intelligence, he rejects "intervention, destabalization, assassination, all that junk" (Plimpton, 1997:63). He warns that the consequences of intervention are unpredictable and almost always embarrassing.

The Need to Redirect Intelligence Targeting

The end of the Cold War has presented the challenge of redirecting the focus of much of Western intelligence efforts. Laqueur (1998:310) suggests: "The central effort of U.S. intelligence has been misdirected for a long time: there has been an overemphasis on strategic-military intelligence." Regarding intelligence targeting, Hulnick quotes former director of the CIA James Woolsey, who identifies the threat posed by the development of weapons of mass destruction by hostile nations like Iran, Iraq, and North Korea, and the threats posed by terrorism, narcotics, and foreign organized crime to the security of the United States[26] Obviously, these constitute threats beyond the security of the United States, and it is not coincidental that two of the three have been the subject of le Carré's post–Cold War novels. For example, *The Little Drummer Girl* explores more deeply than any other novel a covert counterterrorist operation. Le Carré considers counterrorism to be a top priority. He says, "You cannot make a case for not spying on terrorist organizations. You've got to spy the hell out of them" (Plimpton, 1997:64). It also effectively captures the essence of the Israeli-Palestinian conflict, which tragically continues to capture the headlines. Unfortunately, terror has become a common currency in contemporary politics and has reverberated in the United States from the World Trade Center in New York City to Oklahoma City.[27] There is scarcely a nation or would-be nation on the planet that has not been the victim or, in some cases, the perpetrator of one form of terrorism or another.

The Night Manager examines a covert operation launched against organized crime that combined the traffic in drugs and illegal arms—another pressing problem highlighted by Woolsey. Although such illegal activities played a role in earlier novels, like *The Honourable Schoolboy*, in this work they take center stage. Le Carré stresses that one of the greatest threats these activities pose to society is the corruption of officials in the very agencies charged with combating them as well as in the higher levels of government. In *The Night Manager*, the enforcement agencies managed to maintain their integrity but they were defeated by corrupt officials in the British and American intelligence agencies. One suspects that le Carré has only exposed the tip of a much larger iceberg of public corruption caused by organized crime. The cost of the plague of drugs, however, extends well beyond such public corruption.

One real-world problem outlined by Woolsey that le Carré has not yet touched is the threat posed by rogue nations, although he lists the danger of "maverick weapons" as a priority target of intelligence.[28] Perhaps he has refrained from tackling this subject, because it has been done so poorly by other writers with skills inferior to his own. Iraq is the type of target for covert action that would make a good plot for a novel. Prior to the Gulf War, the former Soviet Union had approximately fifteen thousand military advisers in Iraq (among whom undoubtedly were a number of GRU and KGB agents). At that time, the disintegrating Soviet Union (and later its constituent parts) were desperate to attain "most favored nation" trade status with the United States. It was in the interests of the United States and the rest of the West (not to mention the vast majority of the Iraqi people) to be rid of Saddam Hussein, especially after his invasion of Kuwait. An argument could be made that it would have been more humane (in terms of loss of life), not to mention more cost effective, to assassinate the Iraqi dictator than to have launched Operation Desert Storm.

Cooperation between the Russians and Americans in such an operation might have been an auspicious start to their new post–Cold War relationship in a twist worthy of le Carré. Of course, political assassination of foreign officials is strictly prohibited by U.S. law. The political and ethical issues raised by such an operation would entail the kind of moral dilemmas le Carré's novels encapsulate. Having missed the opportunity to get rid of Saddam Hussein when it might have been possible to do so, the CIA has spent about $110 million over the past six years unsuccessfully trying to overthrow him. In the process, it may have been the victim of an elaborate confidence trick perpetrated by Saddam Hussein that would have also been worthy of le Carré's imagination.[29]

A major area of activity of espionage in the post–Cold War era is economic. Ian Traynor (1997:2) reports one Western intelligence insider's estimate that "about 25 per cent of our work is finance-oriented these days." Traynor estimates there are 300 spies (140 Russian and 100 American) presently operating in Germany, with approximately 1,000 "on the loose in the edgy job market." (Markus Wolf estimates that in the 1950s, "there were as many as eighty secret service organizations operating in Berlin" alone[30]). The economic turn in espionage, particularly against political allies, has led to unprecedented tensions. For the first time since the American occupation of Germany in 1945, an American agent was ordered out of the country for attempting to recruit a government official in order to obtain inside information on German economic policy toward Iran. The U. S. National Security Agency runs a giant eavesdropping station in Bavaria, with approximately one thousand employees monitoring European telecommunications traffic. *Der Spiegel* claimed that this facility "was instrumental in winning the US $6 billion in aerospace contracts from Saudi Arabia against European competition" (Traynor, 1997:2–3).

The French, who are among the most active in economic espionage against their allies, expelled four CIA agents after unveiling a spy ring aimed at obtaining French trade policy secrets. The CIA identified France, Israel, China, Russia, Iran, and Cuba as the countries most extensively engaged in economic espionage. One would not expect the CIA to include the United States on this list, but it would not be surprising if it is on the list of the Germans, French, Israelis, and Japanese (among others). Economic espionage is unattractive, however, to many intelligence operatives and partly accounts for the large number of resignations from the CIA. Traynor (1997:3; emphasis added) quotes an American spy in Germany nostalgic for the Cold War: "These days it's all backstabbing and competition between and within agencies. They're cutting back and dropping agents. Now technology is the key. Everything's economic, about who's got the best and cheapest product, about the best way to produce it and keep jobs. So we either have to wait for another war or change our outlook. *Spying's not so much fun anymore.*"

Spies and Counterspies

The end of the Cold War in no way diminished the activity of intelligence and counterintelligence agencies—on the contrary. Traynor (1997:3) reports that the FBI is investigating approximately two hundred espionage cases and is spending more resources on counterintelligence than it did before the collapse of the Soviet Union. In addition to the two high-ranking CIA agents, Aldrich Ames and Harold Nicholson, the FBI arrested one of its own agents, Earl Pitts, on suspicion of selling secrets to the Russians. Earl Edwin Pitts is only the second FBI agent ever to be charged with espionage.[31] Brian Knowlton (1996:1) reports FBI director Louis Freeh as saying that Pitts's treason constituted "a significant threat to our national security." Knowlton quotes U.S. attorney Helen Fahey, who said that Pitts had access to "a wide range of sensitive and highly classified operations," which included national defense secrets and "personal, medical and family information on fellow FBI agents who might be vulnerable to recruitment" by the Russians. Pitts was a supervisor in the bureau and actively spied for Moscow from 1987 to 1992. After a dormant period, he was trapped in 1995 in an FBI sting operation.[32]

Harold Nicholson, who rose from trainee to station chief (ambassadorial rank) in a decade, was caught largely due to his poor tradecraft.[33] Weiner (1996:10), quoting an informant, says that "had he not been caught his career path would have taken him to the highest ranks of the agency's clandestine service." Shades of Bill Haydon. A *Washington Post* (1996) editorial about the affair noted: "The CIA and the FBI have found a silver lining in the arrest of Harold Nicholson, the highest-ranking CIA official to be accused of spying for Moscow. Between them the agencies say that a new alertness to bad apples at CIA and their own improved cooperation,[34] plus counter intelligence reforms put in place after the capture of nine-year super-mole Aldrich Ames in 1994, made it possible to sniff trouble when the new suspect had allegedly spied for only a year and a half, and to bring charges "relatively rapidly" only a year after that. Heavy damage was done, the agencies conclude, but it could have been worse . . . His haul apparently included the identities and assignments of Americans training to be secret agents overseas—in Moscow, too.[35]

Crisis at the CIA

Walter Pincus (1996:7) quotes CIA spokesman Mark Mansfield as admitting to "a disproportionate number of resignations" over the past few years in one of the clandestine service's divisions. Other sources revealed to him that almost a dozen younger clandestine officers resigned in recent years in the Far East division alone. The morale problem prompted the CIA to launch an internal investigation, headed by the CIA inspector general, into why large numbers of younger clandestine operatives and intelligence analysts are leaving the service. Intelligence experts agree that the end of the Cold War and the new emphasis on less traditional targets, like combating illegal drugs, is part of the explanation. Perhaps this is why, in June 1997, MI5 resorted to recruiting through newspaper advertisements.

Pincus reports the comments of retired senior CIA operations officer Vincent Cannistero: "There is a crisis in morale out there. . . . a vacuum of leadership, mission and objectives. Now it is not as psychologically rewarding, and it is hard to keep people motivated with the new targets." Another intelligence source blames anger over the leadership of former CIA directors John Deutch and R. James Woolsey, whose affirmative action policies of hiring more women and minorities changed the "old boy' network" that has traditionally run the clandestine service. This network is the functional equivalent of the dominance of the Establishment, or what Ann Smiley termed the "Set" in le Carré's England. In addition, well-educated and talented university graduates—particularly among minorities—can earn much better salaries in the private sector.

An additional possible reason for some young CIA agents to leave the agency might be behavior of the agency that suggests that it is beyond the law. In support of John Deutch, then newly appointed director of the CIA, the *New York Times* urged Jeffrey Smith, general counsel of the CIA, to set appropriate guidelines in dealing with nefarious characters.[36] The editorial noted that Smith "starts with the premise that some misconduct, even extreme misconduct like torture and murder, may be acceptable if the intelligence is important enough to the country." While recognizing that this may be required under extreme extenuating circumstances, it declared: "The United States must live by a higher code, with a foreign policy firmly grounded in American principles, but it cannot be defenseless against rogue states or groups." This is the classic dilemma posed by le Carré. The editorial concluded: "The checks and balances imposed by the Constitution have not worked badly over the last 220 years. It is time the CIA tried them."

Whistle Blowing Doesn't Pay

Sometimes, for the checks and balances to work, courageous individuals need to report violations. The example of a State Department official with a conscience is a lesson for other potential whistle-blowers. It also ominously illustrates the lack of accountability of the CIA and the inability of Congress to maintain meaningful oversight of its activities. The *New York Times* (December 1996) condemned John Deutch for stripping Richard Nuccio, a State Department official, of his high-security clearance: "Mr. Nuccio's mistake was believing in 1995 that Congress ought to know what the CIA knew about two killings in Guatemala earlier in the decade. One victim was a U.S. citizen, the other a Guatemalan guerilla married to an American."[37] The CIA had failed to inform the appropriate congressional committees that a Guatemalan military officer on its payroll was linked to both cases.

Nuccio informed Senator Robert Torricelli (in his former capacity as a member of the House Intelligence Committee), who publicly condemned the CIA for withholding the information. Investigations "confirmed serious lapses by the CIA, and Mr. Deutch punished several agency officials for misconduct." Nuccio, however, was also punished for being the whistle-blower. The editorial concludes: "Mr. Nuccio acted in the public interest. If his government cannot understand that, President Bill Clinton ought to educate his colleagues and restore Mr. Nuccio's security clearance and good name." The President allowed the career of a dedicated State Department official to be jeopardized because he acted with integrity. This case might be a strong disincentive to others to follow Nuccio's moral example. Nuccio eventually resigned from the State Department and joined the staff of Congressman and later Senator Torricelli.

William Pfaff (1996:9) claims that President Clinton's deputy national security adviser, Sandy Berger, "discussed the matter with Mr. Nuccio but appears to have been indifferent to the fundamental issue, which is whether the United States has an intelligence agency that obeys the law." The CIA claims to be acting to assert its control over national secrets. Pfaff retorts, "The secret it was protecting in this case was the secret of its own illegal behavior, and the body from which it was keeping this secret was the Congress." Pfaff concludes: "Either the CIA tells the truth to the appropriate committees of Congress, or it is a rogue agency and needs to be suppressed." The tone of such criticisms of the excesses of the CIA are remarkably like the tone of le Carré's critiques in his novels. For this reason, among others, his novels speak so compellingly to important issues and dilemmas of our time.

Further Scandals: The National Reconnaissance Office

The CIA is really only the tip of the enormous iceberg of U.S. intelligence agencies.[38] The even more secretive National Reconnaissance Office, a Pentagon agency that operates spy satellites and reportedly receives approximately 80 percent of the intelligence budget, managed to lose and then find *$4 billion* in 1996. A lead editorial in the *New York Times* (May 16, 1996:14 E) blamed "incompetent bookkeeping and obsessive secrecy." The editorial points out that whereas the director of Central Intelligence "helps set spending goals for all the spy agencies, he directly controls only about $3 billion of the $26 billion annual intelligence budget, and employs only a fraction of the work force." The deputy secretary of defense has real power over the Pentagon spy agencies. The editorial supported the proposal of the chairman and vice chairman of the Senate Intelligence Committee to give the director of Central Intelligence an enhanced role in selecting the chiefs of the intelligence services within the Pentagon and greater authority in managing their budgets and operations. But more than structural tinkering is required.

John Nelson, a top financial manager of the reconnaissance agency who was appointed to solve its problems, called it a "fundamental financial meltdown."[39] Weiner (1996) summarizes: "One of the nation's biggest intelligence agencies misinformed Congress, the Director of Central Intelligence and the Secretary of Defense about how much money it had on hand, Mr. Nelson said." As mentioned in the introduction, this is the same agency that built itself a secret headquarters outside Washington for more than $300 million without disclosing its true cost and size to the appropriate congressional committees. The agency's financial managers treated the construction project like a covert operation. They fragmented and hid the costs. This reveals an even deeper cultural pattern that won't be changed simply by introducing better management techniques.[40]

Conclusion: Ethics and Intelligence

To capture the essence of the problem in his scholarly study *The Intelligence Establishment,* Ransom (1970:236) resorts to the same literary allusion used by le Carré in *The Looking Glass War:* "One enters, therefore, the realm of Alice in Wonderland, where confusion is compounded by definitional and conceptual caprice." The main problem posed by intelligence systems identified by Ransom (237) is that because they defy controlled observation and understanding, "they may also defy the policy controls implicit in a democratic system." Such control is essential to the maintenance of democracy.[41] For example, he discusses how the trauma caused by CIA secret subsidies to university research centers, private foundations, publishers, the National Students Association, and labor and cultural organizations poisoned the academic wells.

Given the power of intelligence to shape the perceptions of political reality of top decision makers, it is imperative that they give as objective a report of conditions as is humanly possible. This is particularly crucial in a changing world in which previously held assumptions about the nature of international relations are no longer relevant. Ransom's conclusions are as pertinent today as when they were written: "The threat of a gargantuan intelligence establishment can best be contained by an alert press, and by vigilance on the part of Congress, the public, and the scholar about what will certainly be a continuing problem. And the promise of an intelligence system is intimately related to an acknowledgment of its dangers and closer attention than previously given to its proper policy, organization, and control" (254).

In reply to a question by Robert McNeill, who asked if spying is an honorable profession, le Carré responded that he thought that it could be.[42] This book has investigated his exploration of different aspects of this theme. E. Drexel Godfrey, Jr. (1978:625; emphasis added) observes: "To some the mere juxtaposition of ethics and intelligence may appear to be a contradiction in terms. But at heart intelligence is rooted in the severest of ethical principles: *truth telling* . . . the end purpose of . . . the intelligence community . . . is to provide the policy maker with as close to a truthful depiction of a given situation as is humanly possible. Anything less is not intelligence." As a rapidly changing world makes the context in which politicians must make their decisions more ambiguous, the importance of accurate intelligence becomes even more imperative. Godfrey (627) argues: "Intelligence must promote international security, or the ethical compromises necessary to accommodate the requisite collection methods cannot and should not be stomached." Godfrey's analysis of the amorality and constructive use of illegality in American intelligence leads him to conclude, echoing Smiley's lecture to the graduates of the spy academy, that "the biggest loser may be the clandestine officer" (631).

Godfrey (633; emphasis added) recommends that: "each management level of the clandestine services, . . . should have an officer who plays the role of '*nay-sayer.*' His task would be to review operational plans for their ethical consequences and occasionally to remind the imaginative subordinate that daring and innovativeness must sometimes bow to prudence." In other words, he suggests having a George Smiley around to question assumptions and set ethically acceptable limits. Lowenthal (1992:166; emphasis added) points to a similar solution to problems created by the jaded pose assumed by analysts, whose fear of appearing naïve before their peers prevents them from acknowledging new situations: "It largely depends on production managers who continually ask *skeptical* questions, forcing their analysts to rethink. It is not easy, but it is achievable."

It is well beyond the scope of this work to evaluate the specific proposals made by experts on intelligence to reform the intelligence systems of the United States or other countries to make them more responsive to democratic, legal, and ethical constraints.[43] A good starting point, however, would be Pat M. Holt's (1995:18) suggested two informal rules of thumb for the president and key decision makers to ask themselves. The first is, "If the people knew about this, would they support it?" The second: "If a proposed action gives you the kind of feeling you got when you were a little boy and were thinking about doing something you did not want your mother to know about, you had better not involve the U.S. government in it now that you are grown up."[44] Johnson (1989) urges that more attention should be paid to the qualities of openness, flexibility, and skepticism discussed in this book, in selecting individuals for key intelligence and policy posts.[45]

Chapter 9

Learning to Live with Ambiguity: Balancing Ethical and Political Imperatives

We are left with the question whether it is possible to be a secret agent and a fully human being—or rather, since the agent in this formula is merely an exemplar, whether personal integrity can ever be preserved in the corrupting world of action. The true le Carré hero, Smiley, is the test case. (Andrew Rutherford, 1978:146)[1]

Le Carré's ethical and political concerns are expressed through his characters' struggles to achieve a balance between the need to act in this world, and the need to protect one's humanity and integrity. The spy represents, in an extreme form, the obligations of citizenship. My political interpretation of le Carré's espionage novels emphasizes the tensions produced when his characters confront ethical dilemmas and are forced to choose among competing moral imperatives, and especially between conflicting personal and political loyalties. Although such dilemmas have confronted human beings at least since the beginning of ancient civilization, their literary representation in fiction is a relatively modern phenomenon.[2]

The wrenching moral conflicts posed by le Carré in the rapidly changing context of the decades following the end of World War II fully justifies this critical approach to his work. As Irving Howe (1992:254–5) points out: "Novelists committed to political themes do not have to arrive at political solutions: it is usually better that they not try to. But there is, I think, a strong psychological and even moral need among both writers and readers of novels . . . to feel that the rendered situation may not be utterly intractable; that sooner or later, there may be a slight motion of change."

Le Carré does not offer political solutions, but his more recent novels suggest slightly more optimistic possibilities than did his earlier ones. It is ironic that *The Little Drummer Girl,* in dealing with the intractable conflict between Israeli and Palestinian nationalism—a resolution to which le Carré offers no solution—represents a turning point in this regard.[3] Through the character of Gadi Becker, le Carré portrays an Israeli patriot who comes to recognize the humanity of the Palestinians and can convincingly articulate their legitimate aspiration for national rights. In Gadi, le Carré anticipated the necessary change in the perception of the Other, which made possible the Oslo accords (mutual recognition between Israel and the PLO) and the interim agreement between Israel and the Palestinian Authority. Whereas the vicissitudes of Middle East politics are such that the ultimate outcome of the peace process is unpredictable, le Carré does not foreclose the possibility of reconciliation. Although Charlie is not a Palestinian, because she undergoes a "conversion" while among them, she may be seen to indirectly represent the Palestinian "Siamese twin" of the Israelis.[4] The open-ended conclusion of the novel (which I discussed in chapter 3) allows for the possible reconciliation and accommodation of the national rights of both peoples.

The tone of *The Russia House,* following le Carré's personally liberating experience of having grappled with his ambivalent feelings toward his father in *A Perfect Spy,* is even more optimistic. Le Carré told Charles Truehart (1989: D1): "At least in my lifetime, political issues have never been so clear as they are now. It's a time when the man in the street can see as clearly as any politician what the choices are for us. . . . It's no longer possible to say it's all a game, it's all a conspiracy to delude us." He acknowledged to Truehart "the unashamedly idealistic nature of the story" (D2). He says the book is "the beginning of what for me would be an exciting rejuvenation—personally in my writing. . . . I feel very excited about the future." Le Carré's enthusiastic support of *perestroika* and *glasnost* makes him much more hopeful for the chance of cooperation between East and West than he is for rapprochement between Israel and the Palestinians. Undoubtedly, his heart is on the side of those in the West who back the reforms and cooperation. He even gives Russell Sheriton, the CIA head of Soviet operations, the qualities of skepticism associated with George Smiley and Gadi Becker. Once more, although the ending is open-ended (Barley is waiting in Lisbon for Katya), the possibility of East and West being joined in a harmonious future remains viable. In contrasting the present with the "impossible circumstances" faced by Smiley, le Carré says, "The circumstances are slightly less impossible" (Truehart, 1989: D2).[5]

Although the conclusion of *The Night Manager* is less optimistic about the outcome of the war against the illegal traffic in drugs and arms, it shows not one, but two characters successfully balancing ethical and political imperatives. Leonard Burr and Jonathan Pine demonstrate that Smiley, Gadi Becker, Mary Pym, and Russell Sheriton are not isolated exceptions that prove the rule. The balancing act, as difficult as it is, is not completely impossible. In addition, through Rex Goodhew, le Carré portrays the first high-level espiocrat who is an idealistic reformer. But the realistic side of le Carré has Goodhew defeated by the political cynics. Goodhew's idealism was not balanced by the healthier skepticism of his ally, Burr. Yet Burr's skepticism failed to compensate for his political weakness (due largely to Goodhew's political naïveté). In politics, one must have power or the support of those in power to achieve one's goals.

Although the outcome of *Our Game* is even more ambiguous, it ends with Tim Cranmer, whose last expressed thought is "believing in nothing," picking up a Kalashnikov and running down a mountain slope to join the defense of a persecuted minority people fighting for autonomy from the Russians. Because Tim represents the indecisive West, whose inaction in such calamities as the Bosnian "civil" war le Carré condemns, his committing himself to action can be interpreted as an optimistic note from le Carré's point of view. This is an excellent demonstration of how le Carré expresses politics through actions rather than through articulating an ideology.[6] James Boyd White (1994:276) observes: "In my view the most important differences in our positions are marked not so much by the generalities we propound as by the particular enactments we perform." In other contexts, however, le Carré has been critical of American activism. For example, he told Truehart (1989: D1) that "the American national character requires that when you know something, you do something about it." He criticizes the tendency for knowledge among the Americans to almost automatically lead to action. Once again, le Carré's preferred option is finding an appropriate *balance*—in this context, between restraint and action.

Le Carré's ambiguity is rooted in his fragmented personality, reflects his liberal temperament, and is an effective literary device for his unique form of moralizing. This playful self-parody is a type of ambiguous moralism. The ambiguity blurs the distinction between fiction and reality and softens the radical moral critique. The self-parody identifies the author/moralist with the target of his criticism. He especially loves the characters whom he most severely ridicules. Like Jan Steen, he undermines his moral message with subversive wit. Le Carré most closely identifies with Magnus Pym and Harry Pendel, who end up taking their own lives. Such deliberate ambiguity does not make him as radical a relativist, particularly in terms of values, as some have suggested. Nor is he a preacher of doctrinaire ethics. Le Carré's balanced skepticism is firmly based in his deeply internalized liberal sentiments.

George Smiley is the moral center who embodies and expresses the ethical dilemmas that constitute the core political themes in le Carré's novels in which he appears. Smiley surrogates perform the same function in le Carré's other novels. Most critics disagree with le Carré's claim that Smiley is a developing character. This is accurate only to the extent that Smiley fails to resolve the unresolvable liberal dilemma. This does not mean, however, that Smiley fails to grow as a character. Comparing Smiley's last appearance in *The Secret Pilgrim* with his earlier appearances, one can trace not only the continuity of his liberal temperament and humanism but also a clear tilt in his skeptical outlook toward what he describes as a more "radical" critique of the state. His critique of ideologies eloquently expresses his liberal humanism more clearly and comprehensively than in the previous novels. In a sense, Smiley's growth as a character reflects his creator's maturation as a writer.

Le Carré has entered a more self-confident, optimistic, and slightly more "radical" stage of his life at a time in which he is able to see greater political possibilities in the aftermath of the Cold War. This may help explain why characters like Gadi Becker, Jonathan Pine, and maybe even Barley Blair have the possibility of a more fulfilling love life than does poor old Smiley. George even enjoys Ann's occasional visits to his cottage in North Cornwall. Le Carré has not substantially revised his world view. He remains a liberal humanist in the best English-Scottish tradition.[7] Nonetheless, his liberal sentiments gain clearer ideological expression in more recent essays and fiction. He also employs exactly the same ambiguous moralism to still greater effect in his most recent novel, *The Tailor of Panama,* than in *A Perfect Spy.* Although the more recent novel has a lighter touch and is more playful than the earlier one, nevertheless the hero also destroys himself. Le Carré is more optimistic than in the past, but he has not become a Pollyanna.

Le Carré rejects E. M. Forster's simplistic choice of loyalty to friends over nation, which is essentially a false choice. No truly thoughtful person could fail to understand that by betraying one's country in time of war (particularly a war of such unambiguous nature as World War II), he or she betrays many more friends than the one to whom loyalty is professed. Interpretations of le Carré that suggest his support of such a simplistic and unsophisticated position are completely implausible.

The main moral point in *A Perfect Spy* and *The Tailor of Panama* is that the greatest victims of deception and betrayal are the two central characters, both of whom are extreme fantasists. Each deceives and betrays himself as he deceives and betrays others. It is the realization of the consequences of their actions when reality penetrates their fantasies that drives them to destroy themselves. Le Carré implies that espiocrats and politicians are especially prone to self-deception and warns of the dangerous consequences that can result if such tendencies are not checked by healthy skepticism.[8] Richard K. Betts (1978:88; emphasis added) concludes his analysis of the inevitability of intelligence failures with the claim that: "two general values . . . remain to guide the choice of marginal reforms: anything that facilitates *dissent* and access to authorities by intelligence producers, and anything that facilitates *skepticism* and *scrutiny* by the consumers. The values are synergistically linked; one will not improve the use of intelligence without the other."

Le Carré's world of espionage is a perfect metaphor for the wider world of politics. The disproportion between the socially constructed appearances and the underlying realities are probably more exaggerated in the make-believe culture of the intelligence community, dominated as it is by an aura of perpetual crisis, secrecy, and conspiracy. But the difference from the world of politics is only one of degree. Smiley, in *The Secret Pilgrim* (1990:154, quoted in chapter 3), says that spies rarely meet the reality with which they play and that the rare encounter with it can be humbling. Le Carré's fully drawn characters manifest a wide range in their ability to cope with reality. Those who appear most "successful" professionally in terms of their bureaucratic and political careers are the "realists" or cynics. All but one of le Carré's top civil servants and espiocrats are cynics. They have neither ideals nor illusions. Though professionally successful, they are failures as human beings. The only happily married family man is the idealistic Rex Goodhew, who is deceived and betrayed by his own minister as well as by his enemies in Pure Intelligence, who are in alliance with the CIA.

As I have shown, those on the other extreme end of the continuum, the fantasists, end up taking their own lives. The one exception is Charlie (in *The Little Drummer Girl),* who might not have survived her traumatic encounter with reality without professional psychiatric help from the Israelis and the emotional support of Gadi. The more inclusive category of chameleons tend to fare no better. Their emptiness is filled by assuming the personas projected on them by others. This passive–aggressive means of coping is highly manipulative. It generally leads to self-destruction. Those who survive appear to have ephemeral connections with reality. Their form of coping can become pathological. Le Carré suggests that such types are especially attracted to the secret world and that their symptoms are intensified by their experiences in it. Greater attention should be paid to such personality characteristics when vetting recruits to security services.

The romantics don't fare much better. The majority kill themselves or are killed. (Alec Leamas and Jerry Westerby are killed by their virtually suicidal acts.) Le Carré may admire their romantic affirmation of love, but he clearly shows they are ill equipped to live in the real world. Even Pym's beloved Lippsie commits suicide (just as Cornwell's real nanny returned to

Europe and disappeared in Hitler's inferno). Those with absolutist commitments fare no better. All but two are killed, and the "survival" of these exceptions is only physical. For example, Smiley realizes that Karla might be better off dead when he wishes, for Karla's sake, that he would be shot while crossing the border.

Idealism (one's dreams) must be balanced with realism if one is to survive the vicissitudes of contemporary life. This requires considerable flexibility. The quest for balance, which le Carré's heroes represent, is the struggle to achieve a skeptical perspective. Although extremely difficult to achieve, the exceptional hero succeeds in coming close to achieving it. Using the metaphor of the tightrope walker, one may say that Smiley may have lost his balance at the conclusion of *Smiley's People* but had found it again by *The Secret Pilgrim*. Smiley, Gadi Becker, and Leonard Burr prove that even under the least congenial circumstances, one can act resolutely while struggling to maintain one's integrity.

Raison d'état, the political imperative of the state, forces the citizen to confront dilemmas that challenge his or her conscience and integrity. Espionage is a dramatic exemplar because it claims that its mandate, or ends, justify the nefarious means it employs. These means would be universally condemned if used in a personal capacity for other than the good of the nation. The West claims, as the foundation of its democratic system, to honor the rights of the individual (which it repeatedly violates), along with many other hallowed principles like open and accountable government, in the name of protecting those very rights and principles. Le Carré dramatically shows the costs to individuals, institutions, and the wider society of the repeated sacrifice of such principles through the employment of immoral means. Le Carré, whose personal horror of manipulation screams out in his portrayal of the exploitation of love in the name of reason of state, avoids reducing this paradox to simplistic solutions like Forster's.

Le Carré's analysis of the mind of the double agent, whose arrogance presumes to always know what is best, may reflect in a more extreme form a more common, mild version which is nonetheless a dangerous general tendency among those engaged in the secret world. It is uncanny how close are the words and attitudes expressed by the high-ranking British espionage officer George Young to those expressed by the Russian moles George Blake and Aldrich Ames cited previously. Blake's proud assertion that he possesses the ability to separate the personal from the official (see chapter 4) is an excellent example of moral disengagement of conscience, required to a certain extent by all agents and by the intelligence community in general. More broadly, in politics (as well as with individuals), conscience and moral restraints are most commonly disengaged by using ideological rationalization and the dehumanization of one's opponents. For this reason, le Carré condemns ideologies and institutions that diminish the humanity of individuals and groups to justify their goals.

Le Carré's use of paradoxical, apparently oxymoronic, statements (White's "countersaying" in Shakespeare) is a form of *civic education*. He forces his readers to confront moral dilemmas and to evaluate the contexts in which certain kinds of activities may be justified. Just as "tough love" might be justified in treating an addicted child but not under other circumstances, measures that might justifiably be used to prevent a political assassination of a head of state or a major act of terrorism would be inappropriate in preventing a misdemeanor. A skeptical attitude maintains a proper perspective in making such judgments. The literature on "just wars" is an example of an attempt to evaluate when war can be justified. Defensive espionage (which is broader than counterespionage) can be justified in a manner similar to defensive war. Jean Bethke Elshtain (1992:325, cited in chapter 4) stresses the importance of *"morally formed civic character"* in making such evaluations. Le Carré contributes to making his serious readers better informed about moral issues.

Despite le Carré's repeated professions (through his fiction, nonfiction, and interviews) of his belief that no person can completely know and understand another, he persistently explores the complexity of human nature in everything he writes. One frequently gets more understanding of David Cornwell when le Carré writes about others than when he writes or talks about himself. For example, in his revealing introduction to the book of Don McCullin's photography (see chapter 5), he is particularly self-revealing of his obsession with himself as means of understanding the whole human race and the enigma of existence.

Le Carré is convinced that people act for a variety of reasons, psychological, sociological, and political (ideological). Some act out of an absolute commitment to principle or ideology, whereas others are motivated by intense emotional commitments. As I have previously mentioned, when individuals are unbalanced by any kind of absolutist commitment on one hand, or by a cynical, single-minded service to a career, an institution, or a state on the other, they lead emotionally impoverished lives and may come to unhappy ends. The saddest characters are the empty ones, the living dead. Le Carré's portrayal of the fragmented self in fictional characters is remarkably like what Klaus Fuchs described as his "controlled schizophrenia," which Richard Trahair analyzes as the compartmentalized selves of Fuchs and the Soviet mole George Blake. What le Carré presents in pathological extremes is a more widespread phenomenon in milder forms, as he observes in his comments on the fantasist Harry Pendel in his interview with Andrew Ross (see chapter 5).

Le Carré was speaking of himself, as well as Pendel, when he told Ross (1996), "He really believes he's responsible for the whole world because it is he who doesn't fit in with it. . . . as Pendel does, I am still making order out of chaos by reinvention." Le Carré universalizes his personal experience. He told Alan Watson (1969:55, 57), "What I try to do as a writer is to illustrate in my books the tensions which I feel myself. . . . I've never felt I belong anywhere. . . . I've led a lot of lives in an odd way. I don't feel that I belong to any of them." The world of espionage symbolically represents the human condition under dramatic or intense conditions. Human communication, problematic under the best of circumstances, becomes virtually impossible in the world of deception and political intrigue inhabited by le Carré's characters.

I examined the nature of bureaucratic politics in order to reveal the inherently political nature of espionage. Espionage is conducted for the benefit of politicians in their roles as decision makers.[9] As actors in bureaucratic institutions, espiocrats of different agencies within one country and among allied nations compete with each other as much as they compete with their rivals in hostile countries. By tracing the evolution of the Circus from a small, informal organization run by a clique of academicians to a complex bureaucratic organization run by professional managers, le Carré vividly illustrates major transformations in British society and the declining role of Great Britain in world affairs.

As in so many other respects, Smiley and the other Smiley-like heroes personify the attempt to successfully play the political game while maintaining a semblance of personal integrity. We see Smiley win and lose several political battles. His most important victory in one sense (albeit at considerable cost to his conscience), the entrapment of Karla, is accomplished while operating independently of the official espionage agencies. In a way, he recreated the comradeship based on personal loyalty that was characteristic of an earlier era. Le Carré suggests that the growth in size and budgets of intelligence agencies correlates negatively with their successes; a point that has also been made by academic experts on intelligence.[10] Le Carré is particularly critical of the triumph of bureaucracy over the art and craft of intelligence gathering and analysis.

His portrayal of all of the top espiocrats but one is negative. Yet these mostly opportunistic masters of political intrigue who lack ideals and conscience invariably defeat their adversaries who possess these attributes. The contest between the thoroughly evil and cynical Geoffrey Darker and the idealistic reformer Rex Goodhew in *The Night Manager,* which ends with a victory for the forces of Darker, is paradigmatic. Although individuals like Clive in *The Russia House* may get what they deserve (exile to Guyana in *The Secret Pilgrim*), the world of politics, represented by Whitehall, is a jungle, and the law of the jungle prevails. Goodhew plays with open cards and is defeated by those who cheat. As Max Weber (1946:123) says, "It is *not* true that good can follow only from good and evil only from evil, but that often the opposite is true. Anyone who fails to see this is, indeed, a political infant." Le Carré suggests that even though a healthy skepticism is perhaps the best personal defense against the cynic, it is no guarantee against the expanding power and excesses of the secret services.

My discussion of le Carré's treatment of the culture and craft of espionage argues for its credibility, if not its authenticity. His portrayal of the recruitment of espionage officers and various kinds of agents, and their training and handling, provides a feel for this world that cannot be obtained through more academic studies. Le Carré is especially effective in portraying the psychological strain that results from the loneliness, insecurity, fear, distrust, deception, duplicity, fatigue, and guilt that are endemic to this world. It is little wonder that the agent becomes dependent on his handler who frequently performs the role of father, confessor, friend, and even lover, among others.

Le Carré stresses the importance of being a good listener and of having empathy and compassion in handling agents and as an interviewer. Again, Smiley is the model of the consummate professional in these as well as other traits and skills. Other professionals, such as Kurtz in *The Little Drummer Girl* and the various CIA interrogators of Barley Blair in *The Russia House,* demonstrate a wide range of techniques and styles. To be effective, the agent handler and the interrogator must be an astute judge of character in order to motivate others to act or to divulge information. This almost invariably involves manipulation of the agent or the informant. Le Carré demonstrates the difficulty and the rarity of maintaining personal and professional integrity under such circumstances.

In the previous chapter, I illustrated how le Carré's novels mirror trends in the real world of espionage. It is sometimes difficult to determine when fiction is imitating life and vice versa. The loss of trust, honor, values, and a sense of mission in le Carré's fictional British secret service is remarkably similar to what is presently taking place in the CIA. The end of the Cold War has left the agency rudderless and drifting aimlessly. The ship also appears to lack a compass while a succession of captains attempt to plot a new course. Le Carré suggests that a nation's secret service is an appropriate metaphor for the society it serves. As a result of the rapidly changing international conditions, contemporary America is undergoing some of the disorientation that Great Britain experienced after World War II.

In le Carré's novels, English preoccupation with the past tends to obscure future policies, whereas American preoccupation with the future tends to be destructive of the present. A balanced perspective that neither privileges the past nor the future, and is also not exclusively situated in the present seems to be the best vantage point for both intelligence analysis and the making of policy. Whereas national cultures condition temporal perspectives, education and training stressing a disciplined analytical perspective can help counter such cultural biases. More important, however, than the general culture is the influence of the subculture of the intelligence community. The cloud of secrecy that surrounds this world, the romanticization of the covert side that, politically and professionally, privileges operatives over analysts, and the endemic lack of appropriate oversight over their activities fosters the kind of supreme arrogance that leads to the worst abuses by intelligence agents and agencies.

It is much more difficult to orchestrate cultural change than it is to institute organizational change. Perhaps that is the main reason most proposals for the reform of intelligence agencies focus almost exclusively on institutions rather than culture. But if my reading of le Carré is correct—assuming that he has accurately depicted the reality of the world of espionage—much more serious attention needs to be paid to changing the norms prevailing within the intelligence community. Although the ethics of espionage may appear to be an oxymoron, if democratic societies seriously desire to protect themselves from the dangers presented by their own secret services, they must set ethical standards in which the business of espionage is to be conducted and devise effective means for ensuring that these standards are followed. When these standards are violated, the violations must be uncovered, and the appropriate officials (and not just some low-level sacrificial lambs) need to be judged and the guilty appropriately punished.

Although few, if any, nations in the world have sufficient oversight and checks on their intelligence communities, several appear to be moving in the right direction. For example, the newly elected Labor government in Great Britain has promised to amend the Official Secrecy Act to liberalize the draconian controls limiting public discussion of the secret world that have long been in place in the United Kingdom.[11] Israeli intelligence has gradually become more law abiding and more immune from parochial political interests than in the past. Unfortunately, this has not prevented serious blunders, ranging from the failure of the internal security (Shin Bet) to prevent the assassination of Prime Minister Rabin in 1995 to the Mossad's failed attempt to assassinate a top Hamas leader in Jordan in 1997, and their inability to detect the fabrication of intelligence by one of their own agents until it almost led to two wars and contributed to the deadlock in peace talks with Syria.[12] Throughout the former Soviet Union and its Eastern bloc, attempts are being made to reform the intelligence agencies and to make them more responsive to the generally more democratic governments elected in recent years. In chapter 8, I alluded to trends and proposals for various reforms in the United States. Although some of these trends are encouraging, they most certainly do not constitute a basis for complacency.

Conclusions: Learning to Live with Ambiguity

My reading of le Carré's political ethics focused on the importance of learning to live with ambiguity rather than insisting on certainty. There is no better example of the importance of this expression of the liberal temperament than the disorientation experienced by those who lack such a temperament and whose perceptions of global political realities were entirely shaped by the Cold War in the aftermath of the collapse of the Soviet Union. Because all culture is sustained by belief in myth, relative skepticism is optimal, whereas cynicism is self and socially destructive. Those who skeptically question illusory mythical constructions of reality are less prone to such disorientation when the disparity between myth and reality is no longer sustainable. Just as a reasonable degree of illusion is essential to sustain the human spirit, so a reasonable degree of shared cultural illusion is essential to sustain social order and a stable polity. Balance between idealism and realism can be achieved through a skeptical stance.

Echoing Rabbi Hillel, le Carré calls for balance between obligations and loyalties to self, to significant others, to institutions, and to the state. Either extreme of egoism or selflessness can have pernicious psychological and political consequences. Individuals in their private lives as well as policy makers as state actors must achieve a proper balance between restraint and action. Ends must be constantly evaluated and weighed against means. Obligations to the past, present, and future must also be carefully balanced. Le Carré gives no hard and fast rules or formulas. Each individual, in changing contexts, must evaluate priorities based on personal moral and political temperaments and ideologies. One of the reasons le Carré is so adverse to ideologies is because he fears that rigid doctrines (his notion of ideology) constrain individual choice.

This judgment is shaped by le Carré's own liberal temperament which, in turn, has been influenced by the wider humanistic and more specific Anglo-Scottish liberal tradition in which he was educated. Wilson Carey McWilliams (1995:212; emphasis added) addressing the American political tradition in which liberals and conservatives share the moral language of individualism, calls for a return to the first grammar of American life—Biblical language that speaks of virtues and righteousness—as a "first step toward rearticulating the inner dialogue—the ambiguity and irony—that is the soul of the liberal republic." This also reflects the spirit of le Carré's writing as well: given his family background, he was likely exposed to the Bible from an early age.[13]

Ambiguity and irony are the soul of a liberal republic because they facilitate dialogue, which is the life-blood of democratic life. Dialogue is encouraged because ambiguity allows people with different interests and ideologies to imagine that they share common myths.[14] Le Carré's use of ironically ambiguous moralism simultaneously provides an ethical critique and a political education for his serious reader. His work can be interpreted at different levels and from various points of view. My reading has focused on the relationship between his ethical critique and his political pedagogy. *Flexibility and balance* are the keys. One needs to develop a *skeptical* stance from which to judge each situation in its *context* and to *balance* competing obligations to self and others, competing loyalties to persons and institutions, the optimal position between idealism and realism, the most appropriate means to accomplish one's ends, and to balance the lessons of the past against future goals to give meaning to the present. Le Carré emphatically rejects predetermined doctrines that offer noncontextualized set formulas for solving such perennial dilemmas.

Although le Carré leans in the direction of Max Weber's ethic of responsibility, he recognizes the need to combine it with an ethic of ultimate ends. His heroes follow the model suggested by Weber (1946:127):

> "It is immensely moving when a *mature* man—no matter whether old or young in years—is aware of a responsibility for the consequences of his conduct and really feels such responsibility with heart and soul. He then acts by following an ethic of responsibility and somewhere he reaches the point where he says: 'Here I stand; I can do no other.' That is something genuinely human and moving. And every one of us who is not spiritually dead must realize the possibility of finding himself at some time in that position. In so far as this is true, an ethic of ultimate ends and an ethic of responsibility are not absolute contrasts but rather supplements, which only in unison constitute a genuine man who *can* have the 'calling for politics.'"

Le Carré demonstrates through the struggles of his heroes like Smiley that the age-old attempt by individuals to honor their responsibilities as citizens while maintaining their personal integrity is similar to Sisyphus rolling the boulder up the hill, only to have it roll down the other side.[15] Yet the value and meaning is in the struggle, for even the most worthy heroes can only approximately achieve the formidable task. But rather than discourage his readers, le Carré's self-parody reveals an aspect of himself to be among the most pitiable and unheroic of his creations—those who fail most miserably at achieving balance and go off the deep edge into the abyss.

Fortunately, le Carré's vicarious fictional suicides are not only apparently therapeutic for the author, they provide dramatic negative examples for his readers. Le Carré does not wish his readers to emulate Magnus Pym or Harry Pendel. On the contrary, although one may sympathize with these characters because they have been so lovingly created by their author, one is repelled by their lack of balance and by the consequences of their actions. Just as David Cornwell used his father as a negative role model, he offers his fictionalized surrogate selves (influenced respectively by a father and by an uncle who were similar to Cornwell's father) as negative role models for his readers. They teach through negative example, just as Smiley and his surrogates teach through positive example, how to balance personal integrity and public responsibility. Harry Pendel is the mirror image of George Smiley and represents John le Carré at his best as ambiguous moralist and political skeptic.

Throughout this book, it has been suggested that le Carré's secret world represents the wider world of politics. His heroes speak to the question of leadership addressed by Weber (1946:128; emphasis added):

> Politics is a strong and slow boring of hard boards. It takes both *passion* and *perspective*. Certainly all historical experience confirms the truth—that man would not have attained the possible unless time and again he had reached for the impossible. But to do that a man must be a leader, and not only a leader but a hero as well, in a very sober sense of the word. And even those who are neither leaders nor heroes must arm themselves with that *steadfastness of heart* which can brave even the crumbling of all hopes . . . Only he has the calling for politics who is sure that he shall not crumble when the world from his point of view is too stupid or too base for what he wants to offer. Only he who in the face of all this can say "In spite of all!" has the calling for politics.

Le Carré does not write just for the prospective politician. His message, artistically wrapped in wonderful entertainment, offers lessons in citizenship for everyone. He dramatically demonstrates that all actions have consequences—frequently unintended ones—for which individuals and societies must take responsibility. He offers lessons in coping with disillusionment and developing an ability to question conventional assumptions. He portrays examples of how to deal with conflicting personal and institutional loyalties. He warns of the price paid for making too-great sacrifices for *raison d'état*. He gives insight into the infinite complexity of human nature and the extreme difficulty of mutual communication and understanding.

Le Carré graphically portrays the political infighting that anyone who has ever worked in a bureaucracy will immediately recognize. But he also shows connections among factions in agencies across nations that few of us have contemplated, much less experienced. He conveys insights into and an understanding of the culture and craft of espionage through fiction that has immediate relevance to major issues in the post–Cold War era. I fully agree with Le Carré's (perhaps counterintuitive) prediction that the role of espionage will likely grow in importance in the uncertain future ahead. While acknowledging the inevitability of the pervasiveness of the secret world, he time and again warns of the pernicious consequences of allowing it to escape democratic scrutiny. Le Carré has thereby significantly contributed to the education of a wide public on these and related issues. This discussion of his work has, I hope, helped to clarify the importance of his political ethics.

Appendix

Dramatis Personae[1]

Abraxas, Mickie (*The Tailor of Panama*). As the best friend of Harry Pendel, Mickie helped Harry find a doctor for Marta after she was badly beaten by Noriega's police for having participated in a protest demonstration. As a result, Mickie was imprisoned, tortured, and raped repeatedly. After this traumatic experience, he became a broken drunk. Pendel makes him the courageous leader of a fictitious democratic Silent Opposition to the regime. Consequently, Mickie is again hounded by the police and ends up committing suicide. Harry feels enormous remorse yet uses Mickie's death to make a martyr of him—just the excuse the Americans need to launch their invasion of Panama.

Alleline, Percy (*Tinker, Tailor, Soldier, Spy*). The Scottish son of a Presbyterian minister, Percy has had a problematic relationship with Control since Percy was his student at Cambridge. Hired by the Circus and mentored by Maston, he cultivates political support in the Conservative party. Alleline becomes head of the Circus after Control's resignation in 1972. Smiley's exposure of Bill Haydon, for whom Alleline has been an unwitting tool, ends his career.

Alexis, Dr. (*The Little Drummer Girl*). Investigator for the German Ministry of Interior, Alexis is the son of a father who resisted Hitler. He is considered erratic and philosemitic by his colleagues. On the losing end of a power struggle in his department, Alexis is recruited by Israeli intelligence, who provide him with invaluable information about the terrorist bombings he is in charge of investigating. This intelligence enables him to reverse his fortunes and advance his career. When he balks during one phase of their collaboration, Kurtz (head of the Israeli operation) threatens to reveal to his boss that Alexis has pocketed the funds he was supposed to be giving to his fictitious Palestinian informant (to account for the information he received from the Israelis). Alexis immediately cooperates.

Avery, John (*The Looking Glass War*). After graduating from Oxford, where he majored in German, he briefly works in publishing before joining the Department (military intelligence). Within four years he becomes aide to the director, Leclerc. Father of a son in a loveless marriage to Sarah, who despises him, Avery develops a close relationship with his agent, Fred Leiser. In the last scene of the novel, Avery sobs when Leiser is abandoned to certain death in East Germany. His disillusionment with the secret world is traumatic.

Becker, Gadi (a.k.a. Joseph) (*The Little Drummer Girl*). A complex and paradoxical character, Gadi shares with George Smiley important character traits as a moral agent. Officer in an elite Israeli military unit, Gadi bears physical and psychological scars from three wars. During his service in the Mossad (Israeli intelligence), he operates in Arab countries. After resigning, he is called back by Kurtz for a special antiterrorist assignment. Gadi successfully recruits and trains Charlie to penetrate a Palestinian terrorist cell and lead the Israeli team to their leader. As he falls in love with Charlie, Gadi engages in anguished soul searching. His troubled conscience and his increasing political consciousness contribute to his moral and ideological development. Gadi's recognition of the humanity and legitimate claims of the Palestinians and final commitment to his psychologically damaged agent/lover show a character who has evolved more in a novel than any other created by le Carré.

Blair, Bartholomew (Barley) Scott (*The Russia House*). The son of an aristocratic press baron, Barley read history at Trinity College, Cambridge. He is a saxophone-playing jazz buff who drinks to excess and runs the family publishing house. Described as "a many-sided soul" (51), he is said to "hear a whole self-accusing chorus" (68) inside him that drove him crazy. After gaining the confidence of Goethe, a dissident Russian physicist, he becomes embroiled in efforts to have Goethe's exposé of the flaws in the telemetry of Soviet ballistic missiles published in the West. Caught between warring factions in British intelligence who recruit him and the CIA who take over the operation (leading to the death of Goethe), Barley trades the list of questions the CIA has given him to ask Goethe for the lives and promised freedom of Barley's Russian lover and her family.

Bland, Roy (*Tinker, Tailor, Soldier, Spy* and *The Honourable Schoolboy*). A docker's son, Bland becomes a don at St. Anthony's College before being recruited to the Circus by Smiley. Bland serves nine years in Eastern Europe. Upon returning in the early 1970s, he allies himself with the Alleline-Haydon faction, which fires his mentor, Smiley, for having loyally supported Control and because he constitutes a threat to Haydon. Bland is dismissed after Smiley exposes Haydon.

Bradfield, Rawley (*A Small Town in Germany*). Head of Chancery (political section) of the British embassy in Bonn, Bradfield's wife Hazel has had an affair with Leo Harting. Bradfield elevates hypocrisy to a uniquely English form of salvation. He serves the "appearance" of things. He serves the weak and corrupt English without expectations. He prefers futile power plays to the impotence of neutrality. Along with his assistant, de Lisle, he articulates the despair of the upper class and the bankruptcy of British policy.

Bradshaw, Sir Anthony Joyston (*The Secret Pilgrim, The Night Manager*). Recruited by Alleline, Bradshaw is an unscrupulous freelance arms salesman who makes a fortune supplying arms to the highest bidders in the Balkans and Central Africa. Ned's last assignment before retiring is to try to persuade the cynical Bradshaw to stop blackmailing Her Majesty's Government. Ned is unsuccessful in doing so. In the second novel, Bradshaw is described as an "occasional satrap of

Darker's so-called Procurement Studies Group" (50). In other words, he acts as an unofficial (deniable) arms agent for British intelligence which, in turn, frequently acts on behalf of the CIA. He is an associate of Roper (the main villain in *The Night Manager*).

Brotherhood, Jack (*A Perfect Spy*). Brotherhood is a British intelligence officer in the Firm, who recruits Magnus Pym, mentors him, and acts as his controller and surrogate father. He is of country stock, whose "forebears were gypsies and clergymen, gamekeepers and poachers and pirates" (160). Jack is godfather to the Pym's son and is very close to him. Although the discovery of Pym's treachery makes a mockery of his career in intelligence, Brotherhood seems more hurt and concerned by his personal betrayal than by Pym's treason against his country. There are indications that his disillusionment may lead to greater self-awareness. However, Jack's incipient skepticism is not as well developed as that of Mary Pym, with whom he had an affair before she marries Pym (with Brotherhood's blessing).

Burr, Leonard (*The Secret Pilgrim, The Night Manager*). Described as "Smiley's Crown Prince," Burr replaced Clive as deputy director of the Service in *The Secret Pilgrim* (266). As the head of a new drug and arms enforcement agency, with his Fabian conscience he is the moral center of *The Night Manager.* Fighting the combined forces of his corrupt former boss in intelligence and his counterpart in the CIA, Burr recruits and successfully penetrates an agent (Pine) in the heart of the circle of his nemesis Roper, a major dealer in illegal arms and drugs. Although the operation is taken over by British and American intelligence, which leads to its failure, Burr manages to save Pine's life. Burr, a Yorkshire man, artist, and rebel, displays many of the qualities of character (skeptical balance) associated with his mentor, Smiley.

Cavendish, Geoffrey (Boom-boom) (*The Tailor of Panama*). A large, tweedy, outdoors Englishman, Cavendish had the voice of an upper-class cricket commentator. Freelance arms and oil dealer with an office in Saudi Arabia, he chairs the Planning and Application Committee, which oversees the British covert operation in Panama. He is the creature of Ben Hatry, who is the real leader of the committee. Cavendish is an influence peddler, defense lobbyist, and self-styled statesman's friend. He struck the deal with Luxmore to launch the operation in Panama, encouraged him, bolstered his budget and his ego, and lobbied parliamentarians and bankers. Using Hatry's influence in the media, he drummed up support for Hatry's trans-Atlantic interventionist politics.

Charmian (Charlie) (*The Little Drummer Girl*). Charlie is le Carré's first female title character and the one (of three central characters) around whom the novel turns. She is a twenty-six-year-old English actress recruited by Israeli intelligence (Mossad) to penetrate a cell of Palestinian terrorists operating against Israelis and Jews in Europe. Charlie, the privately educated daughter of a stockbroker, is a fantasist with a chameleon-like personality. She falls in love with Gadi Becker, whom she nicknames Joseph when she sees him on a beach before she meets him, and finds in the Mossad team a substitute family and a cause. She is also "converted" to the Palestinian cause by Gadi (playing the role of her fictive Palestinian lover) and by the Palestinians she meets in the refugee camps in Lebanon. Although severely emotionally damaged by her starring role in the "theatre of the real," in the final scene she walks off to an uncertain future with Gadi. Le Carré's deliberately ambiguous ending is highly significant.

Clive (*The Russia House,* mentioned in *The Night Manager*). Deputy director of the Service and Ned's boss, "Clive knew nothing of unfairness because he knew nothing of its opposite. As to passion, it was what you used when you needed to persuade people" (45). His face seemed to have been embalmed when he was a boy, and he had hard eyes with nothing behind them. In one allusion, a subordinate describes him as a "spineless, arse-kissing toady" (189). Allied with the CIA, Clive contributes to the conditions that lead to the death of Goethe and the defection of Barley. He is one of the few espiocrats in le Carré's novels who is actually demoted. As a result of Barley's defection, we learn in *The Night Manager* that Ned has been assigned as head of station in Guyana.

Collins, Sam (*Karla Trilogy*). Rumored to have cheated in order to take an unexpected first at Cambridge, he is recruited to the Circus by Haydon in 1953. Collins spends his entire field career in Southeast Asia. After returning to London in 1972, he is used by Control in his search for the mole in the Circus. Fired in the aftermath of Control's failed operation in Czechoslovakia, he returns in 1975 to the Circus. Collins conspires with Enderby, who replaces Smiley as head of the Circus. Collins becomes operational director as a reward for his role in the plot. "The betrayal of Smiley is the first step on a path which terminates in 1978 in the transformation of a once carefree buccaneer into a groveling sycophant willing to go to any lengths to protect his pension" (Monaghan, 1986:66).

Control (*The Spy Who Came in from the Cold; The Looking Glass War; Tinker, Tailor, Soldier, Spy; The Honourable Schoolboy*). Control recruits Connie Sachs in 1938, was briefly a don at Cambridge in the early 1940s, and is Smiley's supervisor in the 1950s. He succeeds Maston as head of the Circus in 1960. During 1971–72, he is obsessed with discovering the identity of the Soviet mole who penetrated the top level of the Circus. The failure of his last operation launched to achieve this goal leads to Control's forced resignation in November 1973. He dies of a heart attack the following month. Smiley is the only one who attends his cremation.

Cranmer, Tim (*Our Game*). A former British intelligence officer, Tim retires to his stately Somerset manor, where he tends his vineyard. When his lifelong friend, who for twenty years was his double agent (Larry Pettifer), disappears (as does Tim's young mistress), he goes on a quest for Larry that becomes a search for himself and for meaning in his life. Said by Larry to epitomize the morally torpid West because he remains aloof from the turmoil in the world, Tim feels differently. After tracing Larry and discovering his death in the Ingush revolt against the Russians, although he thinks he believes in nothing, Tim takes up a Kalashnikov assault rifle and joins the struggle.

Craw, Bill (*The Honourable Schoolboy*). An Australian journalist and Circus agent, Craw is modeled on Richard Hughes, a legendary Australian *Sunday Times* correspondent in Hong Kong. Le Carré (1984), in a loving obituary to Hughes, reveals that his friend had given him permission "to libel him to the hilt" in his characterization of Craw. Titular head of the Shanghai Junior Baptist Conservative Bowling Club, a group of cronies with whom he drinks and smokes opium, Craws speech is "punctuated with Vatican-style courtesies favoured by Australian journalists in the 1930s" (Monaghan, 1986:70). He is a colorful and richly drawn character.

Darker, Geoffrey *(The Night Manager)*. Head of British Pure Intelligence (also known as the River House), whose Procurement Studies Group is a multimillion-pound racket involving "*bent bankers, brokers and middlemen and corrupt intelligence officers on both sides of the Atlantic*"(209), Darker conspires with his allies in the CIA to take over the operation initiated by Leonard Burr's enforcement agency against the illegal arms and drug dealers Roper and Bradshaw, with whom both intelligence agencies have had longstanding relationships. A cynical and accomplished political infighter, Darker (and his American allies) get the necessary political support to take over and essentially abort the sting operation designed to trap Roper. Burr's main political ally, Goodhew, is no match for Darker.

D'Arcy, Felix *(A Murder of Quality)*. Senior tutor and French master at Carne School, he is a snob and a stickler for protocol. He essentially blackmails Terence Fielding to teach without tenure because of a homosexual affair in which Fielding had engaged. D'Arcy knew that Stella Rode had been blackmailing Fielding who, he deduced was her likely murderer. He withheld this information from the police and from Smiley to protect the reputation of Carne.

de Lisle, Peter *(A Small Town in Germany)*. Assistant to Bradfield, the Head of Chancery (political section) of the British embassy in Bonn, de Lisle is an aristocrat. He expresses in an extreme form the nihilism and despair which some men of his class in public service felt after the decline of the role of Great Britain in world affairs. He claims not to know what he is defending since his country lacks a coherent foreign policy. He would gladly lie for his country but cannot, as the truth he would need to conceal is unknown even to England.

de Palfrey, Horatio (Harry) Benedict (a.k.a. old Palfrey) *(The Russia House, The Night Manager)*. Legal adviser to the British secret service and narrator of *The Russia House*, he is described as "another one of those Englishmen with hope in their faces and none in their hearts" (22). Disappointed in love, disillusioned professionally, and disenchanted with life in general, Palfrey chose "the safe bastion of infinite distrust in preference to the dangerous path of love" (352). Acting as a double agent who spies on his boss (Darker) in intelligence for the top espiocrat in charge of intelligence (Goodhew) and vice versa, information he divulges to the former causes the death of an agent in *The Night Manager*. Having become a drunken cynic, this last incident is a fateful one, leading to old Palfrey deliberately stepping in front of a London bus.

di Salis, Doc *(The Honourable Schoolboy)*. Nicknamed the Mad Jesuit, he is a scholarly Orientalist and the head China expert of the Circus. He was recruited while a Jesuit serving in China during the war. A complete antisocial misfit, he supplies Smiley with crucial information that helps him discover and understand the Ko brothers. However, he almost ruins a crucial interview of a key informant through his unorthodox techniques.

Enderby, Sir Saul (*The Honourable Schoolboy, Smiley's People*). Foreign Office expert on Southeast Asia, he acts as the link between the Foreign Office and the Circus (and behind Smiley's back with the CIA). Enderby's surreptitious collusion with the London station chief of the CIA leads to his replacement of Smiley as head of the Circus. He gives his deniable authorization of Smiley's "private" operation to achieve Karla's defection, which is successful (no thanks to Enderby).

Esterhase, Toby (*Karla Trilogy, The Secret Pilgrim*). Recruited while a starving Hungarian student in Vienna by Smiley, Toby eventually becomes head of the "lamplighters"—the Circus department providing support services—watching (visual surveillance), listening (electronic surveillance), transportation, and safe houses for major operations. Toby becomes third in command of London Station under Alleline and Haydon but because he helps Smiley uncover the mole, he survives the ensuing purge. During the tenure of the Labor Government, the lamplighter's activities are severely restricted, and Toby is forced into retirement. He is recalled by Smiley to organize the entrapment of Gregoriev. Although an opportunist, he displays genuine affection for and loyalty to Smiley. In *The Secret Pilgrim,* he has become head of Vienna Station.

Fawn (*Tinker, Tailor, Soldier, Spy* and *The Honourable Schoolboy*). A bodyguard and assassin assigned to the "scalphunters," a section of the Circus that handles special operations (including kidnapping and murder), which are too dangerous for resident agents. He becomes obsessively protective of Smiley while serving as his factotum in Operation Dolphin. He appears to crack, engaging in random acts of violence, and is the probable murderer of Jerry Westerby. He disappears after this and is never heard of again.

Fennan, Elsa (*Call For the Dead*). A Dresden Jew born in 1917, Elsa Freimann survived a Nazi concentration camp in which she suffered from 1938 to 1945. She marries Samuel Fennan in 1952 and three years later is recruited by Dieter Frey to the East German Intelligence Service. Shaped by her wartime experiences and her fear of the resurgence of fascism in the new Germany, she betrays both her husband and her adopted country.

Fennan, Samuel (*A Call For the Dead*). Born in Germany, he flees to England well before the war. Although he joins the Communist Party while a student at Oxford in the 1930s, Fennan leaves the party after joining the Foreign Office. Suspecting that his wife is passing on confidential information on which he works at home, he writes an anonymous letter denouncing himself in order to make contact with counterintelligence. Fennan is murdered by an agent of East German intelligence (named Mundt) because his meeting with Smiley is observed by Dieter Frey (who heads their operations in England). Smiley is ordered to cover up Fennan's death but ends up killing Frey and uncovering the East German operations in the United Kingdom.

Fiedler, Jens *(The Spy Who Came in From the Cold)*. Fiedler is deputy head of security and head of counterintelligence for the East German Abteilung. His Jewish parents fled with him to Canada with Hitler's rise to power but returned after the war. Trained in law, Fiedler is an able career intelligence officer. Fiedler suspects that his boss, Mundt, is a British double agent. A dedicated communist, he is curious to understand the ideology of his Western counterparts. Fiedler establishes a personal relationship with Leamas and sympathizes with his Jewish communist lover, Liz. He is the primary target and victim (Leamas and Liz being accidental victims) of the Circus operation to protect Mundt.

Fielding, Terence *(A Murder of Quality)*. Senior housemaster at Carne School and brother of Adrian, a former colleague of Smiley in the Circus. Because of a homosexual relationship with an airman during the war, Fielding never received tenure and will retire without a pension. Fielding, a melodramatic chameleon, murders Stella Rode because she has threatened to expose him and murders his favorite student because he can provide incriminating evidence.

Flynn, Pat *(The Night Manager)*. Legendary special agent of U.S. Customs, Flynn invented a pinhole lens pole camera for surreptitious observation. He is also an accomplished case officer who ran the most important agent connected with Roper's operation before the recruitment of Jonathan Pine. Partnered with the American enforcement official Strelski, both bonded closely with Burr during the operation to trap Roper. Flynn is able to obtain key information through contacts in American intelligence who are sympathetic to his cause.

Fran *(The Tailor of Panama)*. The only woman member of the Buchaneers (the group within the British embassy in Panama privy to the conspiracy to depose the government), Fran has been Osnard's secret lover. She objectively observes that the excited men in their secret conclave give off a sexual heat in their altered state. Fran's excitement makes her more skeptical and detached. She is humiliated with self-disgust by having been taken in by Osnard. Fran wrestled with the knowledge that "she was sharing her life with an amoralist whose lack of shame or scruple had at first attracted and now repelled her" (342). On the rebound, she responds to the devotion of her infatuated ambassador.

Frey, Dieter *(Call From the Dead)*. Smiley's former student and Circus agent in Germany during World War II. A Jew, Frey survives the war and joins the Abteilung after the partition of Germany. He is station chief of East German intelligence operating in Britain when the story takes place. Coincidentally having seen Samuel Fennan talking to Smiley in a park, he has his agent (Mundt) murder Fennan and make it look like a suicide. Smiley's investigation leads to his confrontation with Dieter, during which Dieter refrains from shooting Smiley and drowns in the Thames as a result of his struggle with him. Although depicted as a fanatically ideological communist, Dieter spared Smiley's life out of loyalty to their friendship.

Goethe (Yakov Yefremovich Savelyev) *(The Russia House)*. A Russian physicist modeled on Andrei Sakharov (whose guilt about his key role in developing the Russian hydrogen bomb le Carré sensed), Goethe exerts moral influence by his eloquent silence. His mother was a painter whose work was never allowed to be exhibited, and his father was a martyr, having been shot after an uprising. Although fifty, he considers himself nearer to death than life. His work murders the humanity in himself, for he is tormented by the fact that it can destroy mankind. He desperately wants to do penance by publishing evidence in the West that Soviet ballistic missiles cannot be aimed accurately. Expanded knowledge of his identity in British and American intelligence lead to his exposure and execution.

Gold, Liz *(The Spy Who Came in from the Cold)*. A young English Jew, Liz becomes the lover of Leamas after they meet while working together. Although ostensibly a communist, she is a naïve romantic rather than an ideologue. She unwittingly is manipulated to give evidence that exonerates Mundt and incriminates Fiedler. Her childlike innocence contributes to her victimization. She dramatically articulates le Carré's abhorrence of the manipulation of love for ulterior purposes.

Goodhew, Rex *(The Night Manager)*. Mistakenly described in the press as Whitehall's Talleyrand, Goodhew is a virtuous, high-minded, and dedicated civil servant. He is secretary of the Joint Intelligence Steering Committee, which his minister chairs. Rarely for a le Carré character (especially for an espiocrat), he is happily married, with adoring children. Rex is the only idealistic top-level bureaucrat created by le Carré. In his attempt to reform British intelligence he has created a new agency to enforce the law governing the arms trade and appointed Burr as its head. Owing to his loyalty to his minister (who does not reciprocate Goodhew's loyalty) and his naïveté, Goodhew inadvertently leaks information that contributes to the take-over of the operation by the alliance between British intelligence (led by Darker) and the CIA. Goodhew, who narrowly escapes an attempt on his life, loses his battle against Darker and ends up with a "promotion" to an innocuous and powerless position as head of a new Whitehall watch committee. He becomes the Comptroller of Intelligence.

Guillam, Peter *(Call for the Dead; The Spy Who Came in from the Cold; Karla Trilogy)*. The son of parents who both worked for the Circus, he began his Circus career during World War II. A protégé of Smiley, he becomes an expert on Eastern Europe. Aiding in the capture of Mundt, he helps turn him into a double agent. After becoming head scalphunter (dirty tricks) in 1972, he aids Smiley's investigation that uncovers the Soviet mole in the Circus. Peter is devastated by the discovery that the mole is Haydon, whom he idolized. As Smiley's devoted associate, his career waxes and wanes with that of Smiley. As a middle-aged adolescent, after a string of affairs, he finally marries a young French woman in 1978.

Haldane, Adrian *(The Looking Glass War)*. A graduate of Oxford, Haldane is the cynical head of Registry (research) for the Department (military intelligence). The reluctant director of Operation Mayfly, the snobbish Haldane is condescending toward his agent, Leiser, about whose fate he appears to be indifferent. Although conscious of the collective self-deception that characterizes the operation (and the Department in general), he lacks the integrity to oppose it.

Harting, Leo *(A Small Town in Germany)*. A German, half-Jewish survivor of the Holocaust, Harting is a twenty-year temporary employee of the British embassy in Bonn. He disappears with forty-three files including one which Harting hopes to use to expose a Nazi war criminal named Karfeld. Karfeld is a rising neo-fascist leader of a popular political movement with whom the British have formed a secret alliance in return for support for joining the European Economic Community. Harting is a romantic idealist who believes in the Western liberal values which the British used to represent, but have abandoned for the sake of political expediency. In the end, to protect their political interests, the British sacrifice Harting, who, in desperation, was at the point of attempting to assassinate Karfeld.

Hatry, Ben *(The Tailor of Panama)*. A media baron, Hatry is the dominant member of the Planning and Application Committee. He is called the greatest opinion-maker in the world. Foul-mouthed Hatry bullies everyone. Hatry authored *If Not Now When?,* which argues that the Anglo-American alliance must exploit the United States' hegemony while it can by taking full economic and political advantage of the situation. Although he claims to hate the "American Loony Right" with whom he allies, his views are very compatible with theirs.

Haydon, Bill *(Tinker, Tailor, Soldier, Spy; posthumously, The Honourable Schoolboy)*. Recruited by both the Circus and Moscow Centre while at Christ Church, Oxford, he is the son of an aristocratic high-court judge. Haydon, the prototype for le Carré's more fully developed chameleon-like characters, is a master of deception who thrives on his treasonous duplicity. He does enormous damage to British (and American) security. After Smiley succeeds in revealing his treachery, he is killed by Jim Prideaux (whom he betrayed both as a colleague and a lover) while waiting to be traded to the Soviets for British spies held captive in Russia. Among his many personal betrayals is his affair with Smiley's wife (his cousin), Ann, in order to undermine Smiley's investigation.

Hibbert, Doris *(The Honourable Schoolboy)*. Daughter of Reverend Hibbert, Doris is middle-aged, unmarried, and bitterly dutiful in caring for her aged father. Born in Shanghai and incarcerated by the Japanese during the war, she shared the life of a missionary with her parents in China until the communists took power. Having turned down an invitation to be the mistress of her childhood companion (and foster brother) Drake Ko, she provides Connie Sacks and Doc di Salis with an important clue that helps Smiley trap the Ko brothers.

Hibbert, Reverend *(The Honourable Schoolboy)*. He is a retired aged former missionary in China who took in and educated street children in Shanghai. Hibbert and his wife, Liese (who is killed during the Japanese invasion), became surrogate parents to the orphaned Ko brothers. Reverend Hibbert provides important information in the case. His religious faith, which he translates into a lifetime dedicated to others, his belief in the good in others, and his tolerance of religious, political, and cultural differences make him an admirable and memorable character.

Jebedee (*Call for the Dead, A Murder of Quality*). While Smiley's tutor at Oxford, Jebedee recruits him to the Circus in 1928. Jebedee is himself a leader of the Circus but disappears in France in 1941. He is one of several intellectual amateur spies who are legendary heroes with whom le Carré disparagingly (and invidiously) compares the later espiocrats who replace them.

Karla (*The Karla Trilogy*). Smiley's nemesis, Karla, heads Moscow Centre (Soviet intelligence). Little is known about him. He remains mysteriously mute during the few scenes in which he appears. There are rumors that his father was a member of first the czarist and later the Soviet secret police. Karla operated in Spain in 1936, during which he visits England and recruits Bill Haydon. He rejects Smiley's offer to defect and reverses a plot against him during purges in 1955. Karla becomes head of the Thirteenth Directorate, an elite group in Soviet intelligence responsible to the Central Committee of the Communist Party in 1955 and serves in this position until his defection in 1978. Portrayed as a relentless ideological absolutist, Karla is blackmailed by Smiley into defecting because his love for his insane daughter had led him to embezzle funds to have her treated in Switzerland.

Khalil (*The Little Drummer Girl*). Khalil is the mastermind and bomb maker of the Palestinian terrorist cell operating against Jewish and Israeli targets in Europe. He is the older brother of Yanuka (a.k.a. Michel and Salim), who is captured, interrogated, and killed by the Israeli counter terrorist team. A committed Palestinian nationalist, Khalil claims he kills for love and justice. A refugee from the 1967 war, he claims not to profess anti-Semitism which, he insists, is a Christian invention. Yet he considers the Israeli professor he plans to kill—a disciple of Martin Buber who argues for recognizing the legitimate rights of the Palestinians—to be "worse than Hitler" (391). Khalil compares terror to theater and claims that the guerrilla is the greatest actor in the world. Khalil is killed by Gadi Becker just as he discovers that Charlie is working for the Israelis.

Kirby, Tug (*The Tailor of Panama*). Known in Westminster as the "minister with the very long portfolio" for his sexual prowess and the long list of defense companies with which he is associated, Kirby is the third British member of the Planning and Application Committee, which meets with two American counterparts. He is powerful and menacing, with the "mean stupid eyes of a bull" (304). He even eats with clinched fists at the ready. He asserts the right of the British to control the fictional democratic opposition in Panama. He also insists on a presidential visit to London to give political support for the prime minister. After they leave, Kirby calls the Americans "shits."

Ko, Drake (*The Honourable Schoolboy*). The orphaned son of Chiu Chow boat people, Drake and his brother, Nelson, are taken in by the Reverend and Liese Hibbert. After having been drafted and having served in the Chinese nationalist army, he returns to Shanghai, where he works on the docks in order to educate his brother. He later flees to Hong Kong where, through prostitution and smuggling, he makes a fortune. After gaining respectability he is awarded an OBE and reads law at Gray's Inn. Owner of racehorses and yachts, he has extensive business interests (legal and illegal) throughout Southeast Asia. His only son dies at age ten. He calls his mistress, Lizzie Worthington, "Liese" (the name of his surrogate mother). He risks everything to help his brother escape from China.

Ko, Nelson (*The Honourable Schoolboy*). Like his brother, Drake, he is raised by the Hibberts. During the war he is evacuated to Chunking and becomes a believing communist. Nelson joins the illegal communist movement and works for them while he studies engineering. After receiving advanced training in Leningrad, where he is recruited as a Soviet spy, he returns to China. Ko's career advances, apart from a setback during the Cultural Revolution, and the increasingly important positions he holds are invaluable to Moscow. An escape attempt is aborted in 1973, but Nelson succeeds in escaping by boat in 1975 to Hong Kong, only to be captured by the CIA and taken to the United States for interrogation.

Kurtz (*The Little Drummer Girl*). Kurtz is the leader of the Mossad (Israeli intelligence) antiterrorist team operating in Europe. He is described as a Jewish Caesar, more European than Hebrew, an impresario, a general, and as "too paradoxical, too complicated, made up of too many souls and colours" (27). A Holocaust survivor, Kurtz joined the Haganah (Jewish underground prior to independence) upon reaching Palestine. He hoped to prevent Israeli military action in Lebanon against the PLO by destroying the Palestinian terrorist cell operating against Israeli and Jewish targets in Europe. Le Carré has succeeded in creating such a complex character in Kurtz that the critics are deeply divided in their interpretations of him.

Lacon, Oliver (*Karla Trilogy*). Lacon is senior adviser to the Circus in the Cabinet Office, which is a substantial part of his power base. Son of a dignitary in the Presbyterian church and an aristocratic mother, Lacon was educated at Cambridge. Although he initially rebuffed Smiley's suggestion that there was a Soviet mole in the Circus, he later supports Smiley's efforts in 1973 to expose Haydon and helps Smiley rebuild the Circus after the devastation Haydon caused it. After his wife leaves him for their daughters' riding instructor in 1978, Lacon reveals a more human side as he loses some of his arrogant, protective shield.

Leamas, Alec (*The Spy Who Came in from the Cold*). The divorced father of teenage children, Leamas is the burned-out agent who is the dupe of a complex plot to protect a British agent (Mundt) in East German intelligence. Raised in Holland for nine years, he is a linguist. Educated at Oxford and recruited there by Fielding and Steed-Asprey, he operates in the Netherlands and Norway during World War II. After the war he is briefly stationed in London before serving the rest of his career in Berlin, where he became station chief in 1957. After losing all of his agents (a price paid by London to advance Mundt's career), he returns to London in 1961 and is sent on his last mission, unbeknown to him, to protect Mundt. Although seemingly cynical, Leamas dies a romantic.

Leclerc (*The Looking Glass War*). Director of the Department (military intelligence), Leclerc launches the disastrous Operation Mayfly, which costs the lives of two of his agents and signals the demise of his agency. Leclerc's desperate attempts to regain the status and power his agency had during World War II is symbolic of

Britain's status in the postwar era. His illusions become increasingly remote from reality, signifying his drift toward madness and Britain's nearly pathological obsession with its past glory.

Lederer, Grant III (*A Perfect Spy*). A CIA agent, Lederer is in charge of investigating his "old friend from Washington," Magnus Pym. A law graduate from South Bend, Indiana, he is the son of a morally dubious lawyer for whom honesty is not a strong suit. Lederer recognizes himself in Pym: "We're howling psychopaths, the both of us" (239). He sees through Pym's cool English veneer to his controlled instability. He proves how much like Pym he is through his own behavior.

Leiser, Fred (*The Looking Glass War*). A Pole from Danzig, Leiser operated behind German lines for the Department during World War II. Having immigrated to England, he was operating a garage in London when recruited by the Department for Operation Mayfly. Playing on his loneliness, worship of the English gentleman, and pathetic desire for acceptance, Leiser is courted by Avery in such a way that he is also motivated by love for him. But the mission for which the middle-aged Leiser was poorly retrained and equipped, is doomed from the outset to failure. He combines the qualities of romantic naïveté common among le Carré characters who engage in virtually suicidal acts (like Leamas and Westerby, among others).

Lippschitz, Annie (a.k.a. Lippsie) (*A Perfect Spy*). A German-Jewish refugee, Lippsie is a nanny and surrogate mother (his best and most attentive one) for Magnus Pym. She plays a key role in his life and is constantly mentioned by him. She takes a job at the boarding school where Pym studies, teaching painting, drama, and remedial studies and doing administrative work as well. After being pressured by Rick Pym to send him blank checks from the school, she commits suicide. She is overcome by guilt at having survived the Holocaust, having had an adulterous relationship with Rick, and having stolen the checks. She represents the second mother who abandoned Pym. Le Carré modeled Lippsie on his real nanny during the war. The real Lippsie is possibly one of the reasons why le Carré generally treats his Jewish characters so sympathetically.

Luxmore (*The Tailor of Panama*). A bearded Scot who was in charge of Iberia and South America for the British secret service. After having been disastrously associated with the Falklands, his career was going nowhere until the Planning and Application Committee selected him to head the operation in Panama. Prodded from above, he encourages Osnard to disregard evidence that Pendel was making up his reports and to push him further to produce a pretext for the Americans to intervene in Panama. A blatant anti-Semite, Luxmore doesn't believe Pendel's reports but passes them on to the committee as if they were legitimate.

Maltby, Ambassador (*The Tailor of Panama*). The American-detesting British ambassador to Panama is in his late forties and undergoes a midlife crisis. Bored and looking for sexual and political adventure, Maltby pressures Stormont (who hates the ground he walks on) to support the British plot based on Pendel's fictitious reports so that he can embezzle funds and run off with Fran, an employee with whom he is infatuated.

Marta (*The Tailor of Panama*). Marta is the assistant and unconsummated lover of Harry Pendel. Her parents, sister, brother-in-law, and baby niece were killed in the American invasion, when their poor dwelling takes a direct hit. A young idealist, she was badly mutilated by a beating with a baseball bat administered by members of Noriega's Dignity Battalions for wearing a white shirt, the symbol of democratic protest against his regime. She immediately sees the evil in Osnard and unsuccessfully warns Pendel against him. In spite of her disapproval of Osnard, out of loyalty to Pendel she helps him invent reports for the English.

Martello, Marty (*The Honorouable Schoolboy*). London CIA station chief, Martello assists Enderby's plot to replace Smiley as head of the Circus. He is a Yale graduate, as are many of le Carré's CIA officers. His children attend school with those of Enderby, with whom he fishes in Scotland. He reveals a cruel streak in calling Westerby a "rogue elephant," implying that he should be eliminated (which he was). Martello's callowness and callousness are characteristic of many of le Carré's CIA agents, causing many critics to accuse him of being anti-American.

Martindale, Roddy (*Tinker, Tailor, Soldier, Spy* and *The Honourable Schoolboy*). Roddy is a type even more devastatingly satirized than are the American "Cousins." An effete old Etonian, Roddy represents the Foreign Office on the Intelligence Steering Committee (popularly known as the Wise Men). He is an incorrigible gossip. Conspicuously gay, when Enderby takes over the Circus he becomes persona nongrata because of the puritanical American influence.

Maston (*Call for the Dead*). As Minister's Adviser on Intelligence, Maston is effectively head of the Circus from 1945 until the end of the Fennan case (1959 or 1960). His refusal to support Smiley results in Smiley's resignation. Although he has a knighthood, Smiley considers him a barmaid's idea of a gentleman. Maston is a cynical, hypocritical, and ambitious sycophant. He is one of le Carré's few characters who is not given a single redeeming virtue.

Mendel, Inspector (*Call for the Dead; A Murder of Quality; Tinker, Tailor, Soldier, Spy; Smiley's People*). A retired member of the Special (Police) Branch, Mendel helps Smiley investigate several cases and becomes his loyal friend over the course of four novels. Mendel's father was Jewish. He is a former boxer, keeps bees, and cares for his house in Surrey. A no-nonsense policeman, "Mendel is a straightforward man who believes in humility, common sense, thoroughness and precision and is suspicious of emotional weakness" (Barley, 1986:130). Mendel's Achilles's heel is a strong anti-German bias.

Mikhel (*Smiley's People*). A double agent who betrays General Vladimir, Mikhel is a former officer in the Estonian Cavalry and an active member of the Riga Group in Paris. At the time of the action (1978), he runs the Free Baltic Library. Mikhel's jealousy of Vladimir derives from Vladimir's affair with Mikhel's wife and his having always been in the shadow of the more charismatic general.

Mundt, Hans-Dieter (*Call for the Dead, The Spy Who Came in from the Cold*). A former member of the Hitler Youth, he remains a blatant anti-Semite throughout his career in the Abteilung, including after he is "turned" by the British and becomes their undercover agent. Mundt murdered Samuel Fennan and another character and nearly kills Smiley before his capture by Peter Guillam. With the help of the British, who betray their own agents in East Germany Mundt is promoted to second in command and head of operations of East German intelligence. Control's operation succeeds in saving Mundt from the suspicions of Jens Fiedler.

Ned (*The Russia House, The Secret Pilgrim*). Head of the Russia House, the branch of the Firm that targets the Soviet Union, Ned is described as "in appearance the very archetype of quiet British self-command and balance" (56). A protégé of Smiley, Ned is capable, a leader, resourceful, a doer, a planner, and a linguist. He is foremost a case officer who specializes in human intelligence or agent running. Ned believes in his agent, Barley Blair, and is protective of him in dealing with his superior as well as with the CIA. Ned is the main character in *The Secret Pilgrim*, which is essentially a collection of short stories tracing his career and personal as well as professional development. As he listens to his old mentor's lecture at the spy school that Ned directs, Smiley speaks to Ned's heretical heart—to the secret questioner within him. Ned reviews his life and career in his journey toward maturity and a developing skeptical outlook.

Osnard, Andrew Julian (*The Tailor of Panama*). A large-bodied twenty-seven-year-old man, Osnard had the eyes of a fox and a voice that had acquired a serrated edge. He is composed and impervious to embarrassment. The son of self-impoverished aristocrats, he was expelled from Eton for sexual misconduct and possibly for not paying his fees. He understood and exploited England's decadence. Having played with the idea of going into journalism, the Anglican Church, and the BBC, he found that the post–Cold War secret service was amenable to his larcenous nature. The Service had plenty of money and nowhere to spend it. A thoroughly amoral cynic, Osnard is a willing accomplice of his boss Luxmore and of the Planning and Application Committee, by his refining Pendel's reports to fit what Luxmore and the committee want to hear. Blinded by greed, he embezzles a large part of the funds he was supposed to pay Pendel and his fictitious network. Marta (Pendel's associate) instinctively recognizes that he is evil.

Palfrey, Harry (see de Palfrey)

Pendel, Harry (*The Tailor of Panama*). The title character, Harry, is the orphaned son of a Jewish father (from whom he inherited his chutzpah) and an Irish mother (from whom he got his blarney). He was partly raised by a larcenous uncle, for whom he served time in juvenile prison. An impetuous and unrepentant innocent until Andrew Osnard appears, Harry is a born impersonator and fantasist who lacks a center and a will. He is the proprietor of an exclusive tailor shop in Panama City. Blackmailed by the threat to expose to his wife that he has squandered her inheritance in a speculative investment that left him heavily in debt to a corrupt banker, and lured through the promise of adventure, wealth, and service to his native England, Pendel is induced by Osnard to become an agent of British intelligence. With the implicit encouragement of Osnard, Pendel invents a fictional plot to overthrow the Panamanian government, of which he makes his best friend the leader, and his wife and his assistant, Marta, active accomplices. When his fabulations get out of hand, resulting in the death of his friend and another bloody American invasion, Pendel feels that he has lost his soul. He takes his own life by walking into the inferno of battle. In so doing, he acts on a maxim told to him by a friend: "A man's got to pay for his own dreams" (115). Although a loving husband and father, he abandons his family to their fate. Le Carré has acknowledged that he put much of himself into Pendel.

Pettifer, Dr. Lawrence (Larry) (*Our Game*). A prematurely retired British penetration agent in Soviet intelligence and reluctant don at Bath University, Larry has disappeared. He is depicted as a bored, chaotic, "directionless English middle-class revolutionary, a permanent dissident, a dabbler, a dreamer, a habitual rejecter; a ruthless, shiftless, philandering, wasted, semicreative failure" (24). Larry, a parson's son, attended the same public school and Oxford University with his older friendly rival, Tim Cranmer. With his former KGB handler, Larry embezzled 37 million pounds from the Russians to buy arms for the Ingush independence movement against Russia, a cause for which he ends up dying.

Pine, Jonathan (*The Night Manager*). Pine is the "orphaned only son of a cancer-ridden German beauty and a British sergeant of infantry killed in one of his country's many postcolonial wars, graduate of a rainy archipelago of orphanages, foster homes, half-mothers, cadet units and training camps, sometime military wolf-child with a special unit in even rainier Northern Ireland, caterer, chef, itinerant hotelier, perpetual escapee from emotional entanglements, volunteer, collector of other people's languages, self-exiled creature of the night and sailor without a destination" (33). Recruited by Leonard Burr, he penetrates the closed circle of the illegal arms dealer Richard Roper. After successfully supplying Burr with highly incriminating evidence against Roper, Pine is exposed and tortured. A brilliant bluff by Burr saves Pine's life and that of Roper's lover, who has collaborated with Pine.

Poppy (a.k.a. Axel) (*A Perfect Spy*). A Carlsbad-born Czech intelligence officer, Axel befriends Magnus Pym when he is a seventeen-year-old student in Berne, Switzerland. Poppy later recruits Pym in Gratz when he is doing his national service in military intelligence. He becomes Pym's best friend, controller, and surrogate father. Poppy, posing as a German journalist, makes nine trips to the United States during 1981–82 while Pym is serving there. He fails to convince Pym that the time has come for him to defect before he is caught. He defines himself and Pym as licensed crooks who serve the state. Poppy is an accomplished intelligence officer and demonstrates deep understanding of Pym's character (or lack of one) in order to manipulate him. However, he is also genuinely fond of Pym and sincerely tries to save him from his fate (as do Mary Pym and Jack Brotherhood).

Prideaux, Jim (*Tinker, Tailor, Soldier, Spy*). The son of a lesser aristocratic family, Jim is educated in Paris, Prague, and Strasbourg prior to studying at Oxford. He excels as an athlete and establishes a close friendship with Bill Haydon (with the implication that they were also lovers) at Oxford. Prideaux, a passionate patriot, joined the Circus at the outbreak of World War II and rises to head of the scalphunters in 1972. Betrayed by Haydon while on a mission to Czechoslovakia, Prideaux is seriously wounded. He is released from the Circus shortly after he is returned through an exchange. Jim makes a living as a substitute teacher in boarding schools. Jim breaks Haydon's neck at the end of the novel. Although Smiley suspects him, he says nothing about the incident to the police and Prideaux returns to his teaching at Thursgood's school.

Pym, Dorothy Godchild Watermaster (*A Perfect Spy*). The mother of Magnus, Dorothy is institutionalized for insanity when he is a small boy. Pym calls her an abstraction: "An unreal, empty woman permanently in flight" (30). A very disturbed child, Dorothy is pushed over the edge of sanity by her husband's psychological abuse. Among other things, his blatant infidelity may have included a *menage à trois* with Lippsie. Pym feels abandoned by her when she is taken away to the asylum, and she remains a major absence in his life.

Pym, Magnus Richard (*A Perfect Spy*). Pym is le Carré's surrogate self in his most autobiographical novel. Son of a confidence man and a mother who goes insane when he is very young, Pym is the consummate chameleon. In his desperate attempt to please everyone, he fills his empty self with the personalities projected onto him by others. Freed by the death of his father, Rick, Pym writes an autobiographical apologia to explain his life of betrayal and deception inherited from his father and in order to break the chain of this line of inheritance. He is pursued by his wife, by his British and Czechoslovak handlers (both of whom are surrogate fathers), and by the CIA. Upon completing his confession, Pym kills himself. Through self-parody, le Carré successfully deals with his extremely ambivalent feelings for his own father and engages in ambiguous moral commentary.

Pym, Mary (*A Perfect Spy*). The second wife of Magnus Pym, whom he marries because both his British and his Czechoslovak handlers advised him to do so to advance his career. Mary, who comes from a distinguished aristocratic family long associated with the military and British intelligence, worked for Jack Brotherhood (Pym's controller), with whom she had an affair before marrying Pym. Although many of le Carré's female characters are skeptical, Mary is the first one to be written with a more fully drawn character exhibiting the skeptical outlook identified with George Smiley.

Pym, Richard (Rick) Thomas (*A Perfect Spy*). A parody of le Carré's real father, Rick is the father of Magnus. He is an extraordinary confidence man who serves time in prison. Described as pagan and amoral, he marries Pym's mother after getting her pregnant to prevent her brother from prosecuting Rick for embezzling funds from his church. He teaches his son deceit and betrayal by example and encouragement. The long list of "lovelies" who share his bed do not set a good example for Pym's future relations with women. Rick is "bent" in le Carré's terms and bends (or twists) his son for life.

Roach, Bill (Jumbo) (*Tinker, Tailor, Soldier, Spy*). Roach is a fat, nearsighted, asthmatic student at Thursgood's school. Distressed and feeling guilty about his parents' divorce, he is a loner and an observer. He is befriended by Jim Prideaux, who helps him develop self-confidence. Their friendship is the only redeeming relationship in a novel replete with multiple betrayals. Le Carré has remarked that he was a lot like Roach at that age and, on another occasion, that Roach was like a young George Smiley.

Rode, Stanley (*A Murder of Quality*). A science teacher at Carne School, Stanely is the obvious suspect in the murder of his wife. He takes pains to hide his social background and conform to the snobbish standards at Carne. For example, although raised in Chapel, he attends the High Anglican services at Carne. "Smiley also comes to realize that by cutting himself off from his roots Rode has become completely isolated and is therefore a object of pity rather than scorn" (Monaghan, 1986:153).

Rode, Stella (*A Murder of Quality*). The daughter of an important nonconformist family, Stella is murdered by Terence Fielding at Carne School in 1960. Smiley learns that there is a dramatic contradiction between her appearance as an unpretencious, honest and charitable person and of the reality of a vicious woman who mistreats animals and humans alike. She is a complete hypocrite who her own father judges to be evil and malicious. She is murdered by Fielding because she has been humiliating and blackmailing him.

Roper, Richard (Dicky) Onslow (*The Night Manager*). An aristocratic dealer in arms and drugs, Roper is repeatedly referred to as the worst man in the world. "Tall, slender and at first glance noble. Fair hair stirred with gray, swept back and flicked into little horns above the ears. A face to play cards against and lose. The stance that arrogant Englishmen do best, one knee cocked, one hand backed against the colonial arse. . . . *Roper is so English*"(19). Always traveling with a large entourage, Roper is incredibly rich and powerful. His cynicism is sharply contrasted with Burr's (and, to a lesser extent, Pine's) balanced skepticism.

Sachs, Connie (*Karla Trilogy*). Former Oxford don (and daughter and sister of Oxford dons), Connie is the brilliant Circus expert on the Soviet Union and its intelligence establishment. Recruited by Control as a young woman, she accumulates an encyclopedic knowledge of Moscow Centre until purged by Haydon in 1972. She continues to help Smiley, who brings her back when he becomes head of the Circus in 1974 and is a major assistance in supplying him (through her legendary memory) with intelligence destroyed by Haydon in the successful Operation Dolphin and in the entrapment of Karla. She is retired after Operation Dolphin and is living with a former Circus employee (in an implied lesbian relationship) in the outskirts of Oxford. Connie is a physical wreck from illness and possibly alcoholism. She is one of le Carré's most successfully drawn and memorable minor characters.

Sawley, Viscount (*Call for the Dead* and *Murder of Quality*). Cousin of Lady Ann Sercombe Smiley, Sawley expresses his snobbishness and lack of sensitivity by the cruel remarks he makes about Smiley at the latter's wedding. Sawley even makes a special trip to his club to entertain his friends with satirical barbs about what he considers to be an obvious mismatch. He is amused when the marriage proves a failure.

Sercombe, Miles (*Tinker, Tailor, Soldier, Spy*). Eton-educated cousin of Lady Ann Sercombe Smiley, he is minister with responsibility for the Circus at the time of Smiley's investigation of Bill Haydon, who is also the minister's cousin. Neither Ann nor Smiley respect him. He is self-absorbed, status conscious, and rude. He courts the media and is more concerned about his political career than the substance of issues for which he is responsible.

Sheriton, Russell (*The Russia House*). Head of Soviet operations in the CIA, Sheraton is a fifty-year-old self-described "glasnostic." After a twenty-five-year career as a Cold Warrior, Sheriton believes Barley and Goethe when many of his colleagues don't. He also believes in the possibility of change in the Soviet Union. He is one of the few CIA agents whom le Carré treats sympathetically, and the only one who manifests a skeptical balance.

Smiley, Lady Ann Sercombe (*Call for the Dead; A Murder of Quality; Karla Trilogy*). One of le Carré's most mysterious characters because she is seen almost entirely through others' (primarily Smiley's) eyes. She rarely speaks directly for herself. A member of an old aristocratic and political family, her childhood is spent in Cornwall and at her cousin's Sawley Castle in Dorset. She meets Smiley while working as a secretary for his boss, Steed-Aspery, in the Circus. They marry soon after his return from Germany in 1943. The Smileys move to Oxford after the war, but after two years she runs off with a Cuban racing driver. They reconcile and move to 9, Baywater Street in Chelsea. She has a series of affairs throughout their marriage, until Smiley leaves her for good in 1974. However, she still visits him in Cornwall, where he moves after his final retirement from the Circus. The symbolic significance of Ann and Smiley's relationship is discussed in the text.

Smiley, George (*Call for the Dead; A Murder of Quality; The Spy Who Came in from the Cold; The Looking Glass War; Karla Trilogy; The Secret Pilgrim*). Le Carré's most important and enduring character (see chapter 1). Le Carré says he lacked a childhood. He attends an unimpressive school and unimpressive college at Oxford, where he specializes in baroque German literature. (The date he begins studies at Oxford is adjusted by le Carré from 1925 to 1934, to give Smiley greater longevity.) He gives up the promise of an academic career to join the Circus in 1928. After serving in Germany and Sweden during the war, Smiley marries Ann Sercombe in 1943. After the war, they move to Oxford. George returns to the Circus in 1947. He transfers to Counterintelligence in 1951 and returns to Maston's section ten years later. He resigns to conduct an unhampered investigation of the Fennan case and the murder at Carne school (both in 1960). He is still in retirement when Control launches his operation to protect Mundt, in which Alec Leamas and Liz Gold die. Smiley returns to the Circus after this (in 1962 or 1963) and reluctantly follows Control's orders in schemes of which he does not approve. By

1971, Smiley is among the top officers of the Circus but is forced to resign after Control's forced resignation and death. Smiley is called back in 1973 and exposes Haydon as the mole. Smiley becomes head of the devastated Circus. He launches the operation that leads to the capture of Karla's mole in China, but a successful conspiracy between Saul Enderby and the CIA station chief in London lead to his replacement by Enderby. In 1978, Smiley is again recalled to cover up the murder of his former agent, which leads to his blackmailing Karla into defecting. Even after his final retirement, Smiley is asked to chair the Fishing Rights Committee, formed to identify intelligence targets of mutual interest to the Circus and Moscow Centre after the thaw in the Cold War. His speech to a graduating class of intelligence officers is the clearest statement of le Carré's political views ever expressed in his fiction.

Steed-Aspery (*Call for the Dead; Murder of Quality; Tinker, Tailor, Soldier, Spy; The Honourable Schoolboy*). A don at Magdalen College, Oxford, he is a member of the committee that recruits Smiley to the Circus. He recalls Smiley from overseas in 1943 because his cover has been blown. Steed-Aspery personifies the gentleman amateur but is an accomplished professional whose tradecraft influences Smiley. He founds his own club (of which Smiley is a member), which has no rules except that it will cease upon the death of its original forty members. His sensitivity and thoughtfulness are symbolized by the Dresden china group he gives Ann and Smiley for a wedding present.

Strelski, Joseph (*The Night Manager*). A U.S. drug enforcement official, Strelski closely collaborates with Burr in the sting operation to trap Roper. Stationed in Miami, he is as obsessed with the drug cartels as Burr is with Roper. Described as a "tight-jawed American-born Slav in training shoes and a leather jacket," he appears to be permanently angry (55). Strelski is a maverick, which endeared him to Burr, a kindred spirit. His monotone debriefing of Allied intelligence agencies, which is designed to create a smokescreen and lull them into a false sense of security, almost works. After his agent is brutally murdered (due to a leak from intelligence) Strelski is accused of exceeding his brief and being too cooperative with the British. His career suffers a major blow if it is not ended.

Stormont, Nigel (*The Tailor of Panama*) Nigel is Head of Chancery (political section) in the British embassy in Panama. He had an affair with a colleague's wife in Madrid, whom he eventually married. The scandal resulted in his posting to Panama. His wife is seriously ill and in need of expensive medical treatment that he can't afford because he is paying alimony to his former wife and subsidizing their children's university education. Therefore, he is persuaded by Ambassador Maltby (whom he hates) to collaborate in the embezzlement of gold and cash earmarked for the fictitious Panamanian opposition. He makes enough to retire and have his wife treated in an expensive Swiss clinic.

Strickland, Lauder (*Tinker, Tailor, Soldier, Spy* and *Smiley's People*). A singularly unpleasant Scot, Strickland is a sycophant, a snob, and a bully. Le Carré depicts him as "either bullying or fawning, depending on rank and clout" (*Smiley's People*, 4:42).

His career in the Circus is unimpressive, ranging from the financial aspects in the Banking Section to acting as a factotum for Saul Enderby after he replaces Smiley in a palace coup.

Tatiana (*Smiley's People*). Karla's schizophrenic daughter by a mistress later executed for her dissident politics. Tatiana is imprisoned and undergoes treatment for mental disease in Russia. Karla illegally arranges for her treatment in a clinic in Berne. This proves to be his Achilles's heel, which enables Smiley to blackmail him into defecting. An intelligent but pathetic figure with a deeply dichotomized identity, she might be interpreted as a symbol of Russia under the Soviets.

Turner, Alan (*A Small Town in Germany*). A special investigator for the British Foreign Office, Turner is sent to find Leo Harting and, more importantly, the files that are missing from the British embassy in Bonn. Turner, who is from working class background, was raised in an orphanage. He was a fellow of Saint Anthony's College, Oxford before joining the Foreign Office. Turner is unforgiving of his unfaithful wife. As he investigates Harting, he discovers how much they have in common. Both had terrible childhoods, are underground men, outsiders, principled, and uncompromising. His boss calls Turner a cynic in search of God. Turner also shares may characteristics with George Smiley in the first novel by le Carré in which Smiley does not appear.

Vladimir, General (*Smiley's People*). Born in Estonia, he fought for the Bolshevik Revolution and Russia in World War II. Vladimir spies for the Circus before defecting. The general founds and leads the Riga Group, which fragments into rival factions. He is expelled from France in 1975 because of his political activities. The general's renewal of his pursuit of a Russian agent in Paris leads to his murder by one of Karla's hitmen. Smiley's investigation of the circumstances of his murder leads him eventually to Tatiana and to Karla's defection. The General was an honest and courageous agent but did not refrain from having an affair with the wife of a long-time colleague and friend, who returned the favor by betraying him to Karla.

Walter (*The Russia House*). Walter is an analyst in the Russia House who assists Ned. He is taken off the Bluebird case by Clive (deputy director of the Service) out of deference to the puritanical sensitivities of his CIA counterparts, who are offended by Walter's blatant homosexuality. Walter is described as "a teased out Falstaff of the richer common rooms" (59). He is round, wispy, and fragile. He looked "as if he were in danger of falling off the edge of the world each time he left his chair" (106). Walter is a military hawk who had seriously considered taking holy orders. Clive is the brunt of his caustic wit.

Wayfarer, Phoebe (*The Honourable Schoolboy*). Daughter of an English father and a Chinese mother, Phoebe is a freelance journalist and Circus agent in Hong Kong who makes seven trips to mainland China. Although most of her information is useless, she provides her controller, Craw, with valuable information about Lizzie Worthington. The paternal-daughter relationship between Craw and Phoebe is discussed in chapter 7, under the section on agent handling.

Westerby, the Hon. Clive Gerald (Jerry) (*Tinker, Tailor, Soldier, Spy* and *The Honourable Schoolboy*). Eton and Oxford educated, he is the second son of an aristocratic press baron. Jerry serves as an officer in the war and is recruited as a part-time agent. His main career is in journalism, but he serves as a Circus "occasional." Jerry is a good example of a character who makes a cameo appearance in one novel and gets the lead in another. He plays a small but important role in helping Smiley uncover Haydon. Because he was so unimportant, he was one of the few agents whose identities Haydon did not reveal to the Russians. Because of this and his experience in the Far East, Smiley calls him back for Operation Dolphin. Jerry's disillusionment with the operation and the Circus, identification of Drake Ko with his father, and infatuation with Lizzie Worth lead to his final, fatal actions.

Worthington, Elizabeth (Lizzie) (a.k.a. Liese Worth) (*The Honourable Schoolboy*). An unstable fantasist, Lizzie had a very unconventional childhood and education. There are hints that she may have been abused by her father. She marries Peter Worthington, with whom she has one son, and she deserts both her husband and her child after an adulterous affair. She makes her way to the Far East, where Sam Collins employs her as a part-time agent. Lizzie becomes the mistress of a drug dealer who betrays Drake Ko. She saves her lover's life by becoming the mistress of Ko, who calls her Liese (after his surrogate mother) Worth. Collins blackmails her into betraying Ko. Westerby dies for her, and she is imprisoned for drug smuggling. Monaghan (1986:192) says that, "Lizzie is essentially the prisoner of other people's dreams. . . . As a result Lizzie has no firm centre or self and can escape other people's definitions only through her own fantasies and/or flight."

Worthington, Peter (*The Honourable Schoolboy*). The cuckolded husband of Lizzie. An idealistic teacher in a state-run school, Smiley establishes instant rapport with him. Although decent, he is essentially weak and unable to acknowledge the true nature of his circumstances and his wife's betrayal of him and their marriage.

Yanuka (a.k.a. Salim, Michel) (*The Little Drummer Girl*). Younger brother of Khalil, the leader of a cell of Palestinian terrorists operating in Europe, he is a minor member of the cell. A handsome playboy, he is captured by a Mossad team using an attractive agent as a decoy. Yanuka is broken by the Israelis, who use hallucinatory drugs to wear him down. Through Gadi, who plays the part of Yanuka while rehearsing Charlie for her role, he most clearly articulates the plight of the Palestinians. By loving Gadi as well as Michel (her name for Yanuka), Charlie identifies with the Palestinian cause. Yanuka is blown up in a car carrying explosives he was supposed to be transporting in a desperate attempt by Kurtz to pacify militants in the Israeli government and prevent them from attacking the PLO in Lebanon.

Notes

Introduction

1. Quoted in Tim Weiner (1994: 4E).
2. See Philip Knightly (1986).
3. Bar-Joseph (1995:7–8) has an interesting interpretation of this case.
4. This is not a conventional work of literary criticism, for I am neither a literary critic nor a professor of literature. My mentor, Max Gluckman (1964), warned scholars who cross the boundaries of their academic disciplines to be wary of the limits of their professional naïveté. Many would say that such a notion no longer holds in an age when the distinction between genres such as the humanities and the social sciences, have become blurred, as Clifford Geertz (1980) observed. Nevertheless, in my opinion, Gluckman had a point.
5. He made an almost identical statement to Robert McNeill (1989): "I think this is more a metaphor and I tried to use the secret world to describe the overt world, if you will." Pearl K. Bell (1974:15) opposes this approach: "To distort his admittedly unconventional view of British Intelligence, seeing in it a symbolic representation of Larger Issues; to draw high-toned moral profundity from the exhausted seediness of Alec Leamas, the spy who came in from the cold, is to misrepresent and distort le Carré's extraordinary achievements as an original and mesmerising writer working within the strict boundaries of a difficult genre."
6. Lars Ole Sauerberg (1984: 65) suggests that "Le Carré's work may be read as a gradual approach to moral allegory: the removal of the political issues from a concrete to a spiritual dimension in which Smiley and his adversaries represent fundamental forces in the human mind."
7. Unless otherwise indicated, emphasis in quoted material appears in the original throughout this book.
8. Postmodern deconstruction, new historicism, "queer theory," and feminist readings of texts (not to mention various Marxist and neo-Marxist approaches) tend to focus on power and politics. These days, anthropologists and even a few political scientists analyze the "poetry of politics" (McWilliams, 1995). Many of the younger generation of anthropologists writing in this mode tend to take their inspiration from poststructuralism, which made its first major inroads in the American academy through the

analysis of literature. Most political scientists who study literature are political theorists (i.e., political philosophers). I am an anthropologist but neither a postmodernist nor poststructuralist. I am also a political scientist but not a political theorist. I share with these scholars, however, a rejection of the excesses of a rigid scientism that insists on conformity to the standards set by the physical sciences. I especially share with the theorists a concern for the "moral dimension of politics." See Catherine Zuckert (1995:189–90).

9. For example, John G. Cawelti and Bruce A. Rosenberg expertly trace the development of *The Spy Story* (1987) from James Fenimore Cooper's *The Spy* (1821) to our times. They convincingly argue that "John le Carré, more than any other practitioner, has transformed the secret agent adventure story created by earlier writers . . . into a distinctive genre of its own." They, and others whose work I cite, are concerned with such issues as the evolution of the genre, the structure of the spy novel, and the literary influences on le Carré. In my study, however, such issues are of peripheral interest. Style is important to my analysis only when it expresses underlying political sentiments and ideas.

10. See, for example, Geertz (1973:193–233), Ricoeur (1986), and Aronoff (1989: xiii–xxviii) for more inclusive treatments of ideology.

11. I use the term myth in the neutral, anthropological—and not the pejorative, everyday—sense of the term. For an interesting and unconventional analysis of the role of myth, particularly the Cold War and the new world order, and of le Carré's contributions to our understanding of these phenomena, see John S. Nelson (1994). Nelson is particularly interested in the contributions that spy stories can make to theories of international politics.

12. The only spy novel Howe mentions in his major work is Joseph Conrad's *The Secret Agent* (1907), which Howe (1992:94) says "is a work of enormous possibilities, far from fully realized but realized just enough to enable us to see how Conrad thwarts and denies his own gifts." Perhaps this is the reason Howe also ignored the work of Graham Greene.

13. Tom Maddox (1986:159) asserts that "like Dickens, he [le Carré] has transformed a popular form into high art." Eric Homberger (1986:103–4) suggests that le Carré's use of the spy formula is a pretext "for profound and fully serious investigations of the central issues of our time." Homberger (1986:104) concludes that le Carré's novels constitute "an ethics of the way we live now." Cawelti and Rosenberg (1987:179) assert: "The spy story is as le Carré sees it, a statement about the inescapable dilemma of the mid-twentieth century."

14. Ty Burr (1998: AR9) quotes Orwell ("Why I Write") who says he spent his career trying "to make political writing an art."

15. In fact, le Carré (1968) had explored this theme in an earlier short story, "What Ritual Is Being Observed Tonight?," a Daumier-like satirical caricature of academics (among other things).

16. Tony Barley (1986), Eric Homberger (1986), and LynnDianne Beene (1992) are exceptions upon whose insights on this subject I build. Neither ideology nor politics appear in the indexes of the others' works—including that of John L. Cobbs (1998), which was not available until after this work was completed and in production for publication.

17. W. Carey McWilliams (in a personal communication) points out the similarity with Thucydides. See Clifford Orwin (1994).

18. I realize this interpretation conflicts with others. Not being an expert on Plato, I merely point out the appropriateness of this reading of Plato's literary technique for an understanding of le Carré's.

19. Wilson Carey McWilliams (1995:175–212). Tracing liberal ideology from Hobbes, Locke, and Kant, he suggests liberalism's lodestar is liberty, and the other two pillars on which it rests are secularism and free exchange. Both temperaments and doctrines fall within my broader definition of ideology, although it is useful to make the analytical distinction between the two, particularly when discussing the tension between them.

20. Although Homberger (1986:79) mentions Smiley's political temperament, he neither defines nor develops the notion. Because he is a literary critic, one would not have expected him to do so. Homberger (1986:80) states: "It is Smiley, the moral centre of gravity of le Carré's imagination, who humanizes the vast machinery of plot."

21. In chapter 1 I elaborate this point. Homberger (1986:77) says: "I don't think he [le Carré] is really interested in political ideas, at least not in the fashion of Koestler for whom the human (let us say the Forsterian) dimension was weaker than the ideological contention." That le Carré attacks rigid ideological doctrines and more ambiguously expresses his politics through actions rather than words does not mean that he is disinterested in political ideas.

22. This is what Barley (1986:1) calls the "many John le Carrés" or the "many faces and voices" that compete with one another in his fiction.

23. Cawelti and Rosenberg (1987:185) point out that "le Carré is too good an artist to state explicit philosophic principles without qualifying ironies."

24. "It is the absence on the author's part of a clear, coherent political position, complete with its implied programme, recommendations and solutions, which induces him to adopt a method of political presentation that dramatizes ambivalence as problematic. Le Carré's political method acts not to transmit authoritative opinion but to play out as sharply as possible the conflict between antagonistic positions."

25. Green (1988:26).

26. Personal communication from David Cornwell, November 11, 1996. My evaluations of le Carré's empathetic treatment of his Jewish characters were written before the publication of a review of *The Tailor of Panama* in the *New York Times* by Norman Rush (1996:11). Rush claimed that the main character, Pendel, is "yet another literary avatar of Judas." Le Carré's (1996:4.22) reply to this charge makes clear how

much he identifies personally with Pendel. Garson (1987:79) also notes the author's "great sympathy for the Jews." In an interview with Douglas Davis (1997:19), le Carré discusses in depth his feelings toward Jews and Israel.

27. Pym feels responsible for Lippsie's suicide and for his mother's mental illness (see chapter 16 of the novel, 423). One of Pym's women says, "He never loved a woman in his life. We were enemy, all of us" (7:181). Pym's thoughts are: "You women want nothing but to drag us down" (11:298); the narrator comments, "Women are abhorrent to him" (11:299).

28. See, for example, his essay "Spying on My Father" (1986). He explains why he could get closer to the truth of his relationship with his father through fiction rather than through autobiography.

29. Lelyveld (1986:91).

30. Various reports have identified his involvement in espionage. Alexis Gelber and Edward Behr (1983:43) cite a retired British intelligence source who claims that he was recruited as early as age 17, when he spent a year at the University of Berne. They quote Cornwell's cryptic remark, "I have nosed around in the secret world. But it was a long, long while ago." Hugh McIlvanney (1983:18) also dates his "apprenticeship in intelligence work" to his year at the University of Berne, claiming that le Carré "said as much" during his interview. In his essay "Don't Be Beastly to Your Secret Service" (1986:41–42), le Carré says: "Of my nearly 50 years' relationship with British Intelligence more than 40 have been vicarious." Le Carré told Walter Isaacson and James Kelly (1993:33) that during his years in the Foreign Service, he was working for the secret intelligence service: "I was recruited almost when I was still in diapers into that world. My really formative years . . . were all taken over by the secret world . . . I entered it in the spirit of John Buchan and left it in the spirit of Kafka." McIlvanney (1983:18) confirms, "It was when he joined the Foreign Service . . . that the heavy connection with espionage was established." James Burridge (1992:15), in a journal published by the CIA, states "He was a case officer in the 1950s and 1960s."

31. Vivian Green (1988:37), his senior tutor at Oxford, rather elliptically seems to confirm his involvement in internal security while at Oxford and, after graduation, his consideration for security clearance abroad.

32. Anthony Masters (1987:229) confirms that "David Cornwell joined MI5, in the late fifties." Masters (1987:237) corroborates Cornwell's recruitment by Maxwell Knight, the veteran head of MI5's countersubversion department. Cornwell had illustrated Knight's book, *Talking Birds,* which was published in 1961. Masters (1987:240) also confirms that "in 1960, David Cornwell left MI5 for MI6. A front cover was established for him, first as a second secretary at the British embassy in Bonn, and later consul in Hamburg. Before leaving for Germany, former intelligence sources relate, Cornwell was put through an intensive course at an Intelligence training camp in England."

33. Access to Cornwell's records, which I requested under the Freedom of Information Act, was denied under exemptions (b)(1), "applies to material which is properly classified pursuant to an Executive order in the *interest of national defense or foreign policy*"; and (b)(3), "applies to the Director's statutory obligations to protect from disclosure intelligence sources and methods, as well as the organization, functions, names, official titles, salaries or numbers of *personnel employed by the agency.*" Letter dated April 28, 1997, from Lee S. Strickland, information and privacy coordinator of the CIA (emphasis added). Although my appeal for reconsideration was granted, the denial of access was upheld. In the political notes section of the *International Herald Tribune,* May 15, 1997, 3, it was reported that "the government—except the CIA—spent $5.23 billion on classification last year." When Representative David Skaggs (D-Colo.) asked the head of administrative services at the CIA how much the agency spent on classification, he was told the information is classified.

34. Cawelti and Rosenberg (1987:183).

35. Barley (1986:25).

36. Thomas Powers (1995) reviews four books on the Ames case. David Wise (1995) receives the most favorable review. The other books mentioned in this essay are Tim Weiner, David Johnston, and Neil A. Lewis (1995), Peter Maas (1995), and James Adams (1995).

37. I am grateful to my colleague Carey McWilliams, who raised this point in a personal communication.

38. My general theoretical orientation is phenomenological. I view the nature of cultural perceptions of reality and of social and political institutions as an ongoing dialectical process of social construction, deconstruction, and reconstruction. My formulation of this approach builds upon the work of Peter Berger and Thomas Luckmann in *The Social Construction of Reality* (1966). My primary analytic approach is hermeneutic, based on the interpretation of the humanly created collective cultural meanings that, however tenuously, explain and give meaning to the social world. (See Geertz, 1973, 1983, and 1995). I define these meanings as ideological when they provide legitimacy for the allocation of scarce resources (particularly status and power) in the polity. In this context I use a broad notion of ideology in contrast with the narrower one more commonly employed.

39. Lewis (1985:24) observed, "The moral problem of how far you can go to preserve a society without destroying the very values you are trying to defend pervades le Carré's fiction."

40. A $347 million, million-square-foot new headquarters (one fifth the size of the Pentagon) for the top-secret U.S. National Reconnaissance Office was kept secret from congressional oversight committees by being buried in the agency's secret annual budget (reputed to be approximately $6 billion).

41. Cawelti and Rosenberg (1987:224–28) give a valuable list of bibliographies, research guides, histories of espionage, scholarly studies of espionage

organizations and practices, and works dealing with major spies and episodes of espionage.

42. For example, events in Israel over the past few years have eroded the cloud of secrecy surrounding Israel's intelligence services and have also led to more critical questions regarding their activities. See Dan Raviv and Yossi Melman (1990), and Ian Black and Benny Morris (1991). The most recent annotated bibliography is Frank A. Clements (1995). For an interesting comparative analysis, see Uri Bar-Joseph (1995).

Chapter 1

1. Because le Carré's works have been published in so many different editions by different publishers, I refer to the year of first publication. Quotations are accompanied by reference in brackets to the chapter and page from the edition I cite. Complete references are given in the bibliography.

2. In *The Perfect Spy* (see chapter 2) le Carré reveals in fictional form much about his turbulent relations with and ambivalent feelings for his father, a convicted con man. For a revealing interview with le Carré based on this book, see Joseph Lelyveld (1986). In *The Secret Pilgrim* (1990:11) le Carré, speaking through Ned, says: "There were times when I thought of him as some kind of father to replace the one I never knew." Many, if not most, of le Carré's central characters express similar sentiments.

3. Michael Adams (1989:1046) notes the ironies in his name. "His name is doubly ironic since Smiley wears an emotionless mask, and George is the name of England's dragon-slaying patron saint and of the kings who were heads of state during the two world wars."

4. I briefly discuss each in this chapter, including very briefly *A Murder of Quality* (1962), which is really more of a murder mystery than a spy novel, as is *A Call From the Dead* (1961). Glenn W. Most (1987) gives a fascinating analysis of le Carré's work in terms of the mystery genre and his radical innovations, which he suggests, may herald the demise of the genre.

5. LynnDianne Beene (1992:24) concludes that Smiley "epitomizes British decency and the ineffectual efforts of an existential humanist beset by the psychological and moral dilemmas his profession symbolizes." Abraham Rothberg (1987:53) notes "Smiley's role as the voice of reason, common sense, and decency" and as "the defender of an independent and competent intelligence service." Peter Wolfe (1987:67) maintains that Smiley "isn't trying to salvage innocence, which vanished long ago, if it ever existed, but a modicum of integrity. Amid tawdriness, he stands for honor, duty, and decency." Laurence Stern (1977:E1) describes him as "an English bull of tenacity and loyalty to agency and *patria*." For Lars Ole Sauerberg (1984:35), "Smiley and the other le Carré heroes are constantly endeavoring to restore the world according to their sense of human decency." Eric Homberger (1986:86) comments that: "Smiley accepts the logic of the service; however, he tries to temper it with compassion and humanity."

George Grella (1976:25) observes that Smiley provides a "moral center" in those novels in which he appears. Richard Bradbury (1990:131) says, "Smiley becomes the personification of moral and political pragmatism and . . . the 'living centre' of the novels; the character with whom the reader is 'required' to identify."

6. There is considerable discussion in the literature attempting to identify the real person(s) and literary characters who served as the model for Smiley. For example, see Carter S. Wiseman (1975:26) and Beene (1992:148). Charles A. Brady (1985:282) and S. S. Prawer (1980:132) suggest that Father Brown, Chesterton's fictional clerical hero, may have been an additional literary model for Smiley. Homberger (1986:34) claims, "It was to [Maugham's] Ashenden that we owe Smiley." Among other qualities, he points out the "healthy scepticism" they both shared. I develop the importance of skepticism in chapter 4. See also Paul Vaughan's (1979:339) interview with le Carré. In an earlier essay, in honor of the ninetieth birthday of P. G. Wodehouse, le Carré (1971:25) mentions a man with whom he worked in the embassy in Bonn, "a prince" who shared Cornwell's fondness for Wodehouse and Wodehouse's (and Smiley's) nostalgia for "an England before the Fall."

7. In response to a direct question by Robert McNeill, who paraphrased a lengthy speech by Smiley, le Carré replied: "Yes, it is me talking and this was me talking really before the perestroika began and it was me being terribly tired of the stalemate in the cold war" (McNeill-Lehrer Report, 1989). Although many contemporary literary critics believe that it is either impossible or irrelevant to determine the author's point of view, I think that it is both possible and important to do so.

8. That same year, he was assigned as second secretary to the British embassy in Bonn. "At the time, so the consensus of rumour goes, le Carré served in M15 under Maxwell Knight." (Bold, 1988:13).

9. Helen S. Garson (1987:73–4), playing on the metaphor, says: "Smiley is a prince forever imprisoned inside the frog." Leroy L. Panek (1987:36–7) alludes to the couple as "Beauty and the Beast," "Princess and the Toad," and compares Smiley to Mr. Toad from *Wind in the Willows,* who becomes "more frog-like than ever." Perhaps part of Smiley's appeal to me is that since my youth, when I caught tadpoles in a local pond and watched with fascination as they became frogs, I have had a special fondness for them.

10. His portliness is also conveyed through descriptions of his fleshy, bespectacled face and his chubby wet hands. Bill Roach, a schoolboy in *Tinker, Tailor, Soldier, Spy,* is a friendless, fat asthmatic from a broken home and a natural "watcher." In an interview, le Carré volunteered that at school, he was much like Roach. Le Carré describes Smiley as "the final form for which Bill Roach was the prototype" (*Tinker, Tailor, Soldier, Spy,* 18).

11. *The Honourable Schoolboy:* 41, 489.

12. Sauerberg (1984:114) points out the "pariah" nature of le Carré's heroes. Although Smiley is a "social misfit" and all le Carré's heroes have "outsider status," the term pariah is too strong.

13. When referring to his biography, I use David Cornwell's real name, and when referring to him in his capacity as author, I use his pen name.

14. The mystery of human motivation is explored in Chapter 5.

15. Having run off with a Cuban racing driver, "she announced enigmatically that if she hadn't left him then, she never could have done" (1:7). "With grudging admiration she admitted to herself that if there were an only man in her life, Smiley would be he" (1:8).

16. Garson (1987:74–5) considers his love for Ann "Smiley's greatest vulnerability." Panek (1987:37) defines Smiley's quest for her love as "Sisyphean." Charles A. Brady (1985:283) calls Smiley "a figure of pathos." Wolfe (1987:70) contrasts his "core of steel" with "his softer side, which makes him a victim of the past, of his dreams, and of his spiritual unrest."

17. Wolfe (1987, in a chapter titled after the first chapter in *Call for the Dead*, "A Brief History of George Smiley") notes his frailness, remoteness, gentleness, kindness, tenderness, compassion, magnanimity, caring, and rich humanity.

18. John Halperin (1980:20) mistakenly says that Smiley is labeled "the Head Eunuch."

19. In *The Spy Who Came in from the Cold* (8:85), Alec Leamas reveals Smiley's transfer to his interrogator. Andy East (1983:172) notes his return a decade later in his profile of Smiley.

20. Wolfe (1987:70). I discuss these changes and the topic of bureaucratic politics in chapter 6.

21. Alvin P. Sanoff (1989).

22. In Henry Zieger (1965:123). Cited in Andy East (1983:170).

23. Owen Dudley Edwards (1988:44–7), in a persuasive line-by-line comparison of le Carré's account with Sir Arthur Conan Doyle's *The Sign of Four*, concludes "that the entire passage seems not merely a debt to Conan Doyle, but an act of homage to him," and that by comparing Dieter with Stapleton, "we can see more clearly Dieter's redemption at his moment of death." Edwards discusses many other important literary influences on le Carré as well.

24. "Who was then a gentleman" was the call of Wat Tyler's peasant revolt in fourteenth century England. It was taken from the phrase "When Adam delved and Eve span, who was then a gentleman?" from the revolutionary sermon at Blackheath of John Ball, an excommunicated priest, who fomented Tyler's insurrection. Ball (and Tyler) advocated the claims of bondsmen to be put on terms of equality with the gentry. Their project was to set up a new order founded on social equality. This was the only instance of such a radical social theory appearing in the Middle Ages. Le Carré associates the radical Dieter with the first social radicals in English history. I have been told that this inscription is carved on the misericord (a support

against which choir members can lean while standing) in Worcester Chapel in Worcester, England. I am grateful to Michael Zuckert for drawing my attention to this. See *Oxford Dictionary of Quotations* (1977:11) and Sir Leslie Stephen and Sir Sidney Lee, eds., *The Dictionary of National Biography* (1968:1:995).

25. He had just murdered one of his agents in cold blood to prevent her from being taken prisoner by the British. He had previously had her husband, an innocent third party, murdered in an effort to prevent him from exposing his wife (Dieter's agent). He had attempted to kill a friend of Smiley's who was assisting him on the case. His agent killed a garage owner and tried to kill Smiley whom he seriously wounded. At the time, Dieter directed East German espionage against the United Kingdom.

26. Sauerburg (1984:51) suggests that Smiley's survival "assures the reader that the missions are worth the sacrifices." In chapter 4, I demonstrate that le Carré is not as unambiguous as Sauerburg implies.

27. The novel is essentially about the closed world of the British "public" (private, in American usage) school and is a devastating critique of the class system. Le Carré writes about his own experiences as a "prisoner" of the public schools in "England Made Me" (1977: 25).

28. I discuss this novel, which vividly illustrates the theme that what appears to be reality is an illusion of human construction, in more detail in chapter 3. The same year as the publication of le Carré's best-seller, Kim Philby was exposed as the third man in the infamous Cambridge spy ring for the Soviet Union.

29. Smiley mysteriously follows Leamas (8:79), pays the rent that Leamas owed after he has "defected" (11:115), and offers assistance to Liz (11:117–20), even giving her his calling card with his real name, address, and telephone number on it. This last clue positively confirms that he was not operational, because Smiley's tradecraft was much too good to have done that if he had been with the Circus. Lewis (1985:71; emphasis added), whose chapter 2 is entitled "A Far from Saintly George," suggests that "Smiley, . . . has helped to *engineer* her [Liz's] fate and must carry some of the responsibility for what happens to her." This would mean that Smiley was in on the operation all along. But, this would be completely out of character for Smiley and contrary to my understanding of le Carré's intent which I elucidate in note 30.

30. "A second theme is that admirable actions, ideals, and intentions often lead to tragic consequences" (Douglas Wallace, 1985:6). Smiley, therefore, bears only indirect responsibility for their deaths.

31. John le Carré, "To Russia, with Greetings" (1966:5). See also chapter 5.

32. Most (1987:94) suggests that Control planted the false report that set the operation in motion. Bureaucratic politics, dramatically illustrated in this work as well as others, is another significant topic in le Carré's work discussed in chapter 6.

33. In this novel, le Carré is particularly effective in portraying how all of the various characters participate in the creation of a delusional sense of

reality that seals their fates. He also explores the need for belonging and approval that motivates each to participate in self-delusion and collective delusion (see chapter 3).

34. The theme of the relationship between loyalty and betrayal is discussed in more depth in chapter 2.

35. Brady (1985:276) suggests that Karla is modeled after Yuri Andropov, former head of the KGB. Others suggest that he is modeled after Markus Wolf, former head of East German external intelligence from 1952 (when he was 29) until 1983. Wolf retired in 1986.

36. "As it was, the next thing I knew I was talking about Ann. . . . Oh, not about *my* Ann. I assumed he had one" (207). "I could have sworn I was getting through to him, that I had found the chink in his armour; when of course all I was doing . . . was showing him the chink in mine" (209).

37. He tries the line of kinship: "Don't you think it's time to recognise that there is as little worth on your side as there is on mine?" (211). "Did he not believe, for example, that the political generality was meaningless?" (212). But in the end, "He would rather die than disown the political system to which he was committed" (212).

38. This point is explored more fully in chapter 3.

39. Scholars interpret this passage differently. Sauerberg (1984:60) says that through Westerby's perspective, Smiley appears as "a pompous man given to superficial and routine reflections on the justification of their common work." Lewis (1985:149) gives a fairly literal reading but emphasizes the need for commitment rather than the anticommunism theme. Homberger (1986:84–5) suggests that Smiley pitches his speech to appeal to his less sophisticated agent. Pointing out the contradiction between the Cold War tone of this speech and an earlier expression of Smiley's attitude toward anticommunism, Homberger suggests that this expresses the moral ambiguity demanded by his profession rather than a shift in Smiley's ideology.

40. Sauerberg (1984:125) notes that Smiley simultaneously plays the double roles of questing hero and superior. I disagree with his equating Jerry's reaction to Smiley's speech with Leamas' reaction to Control's speech in *The Spy Who Came in from the Cold*. Westerby was *much* more tolerant of Smiley, whom he affectionately considered a father figure. Leamas displays no such feelings for Control.

41. An explanation of this dilemma is elaborated in the conclusion of chapter 4.

42. I tend toward the latter interpretation. By "heroic," I mean more than the fact that he is the central character. To qualify as a hero, the person should be admirable for some significant quality, like moral courage. By quixotic (from Cervantes' romance *Don Quixote*), I mean that the character combines attributes that are ridiculous and those that are admirable.

43. But she paradoxically suggests, "It is only Smiley's increasing struggles and ultimate disenchantment that define him as a success" (Beene, 1992:26).

44. Monaghan (1986:165) supports Peter Guillam's theory, expressed in the novel, that Smiley was aware of the plot against him and accepted it. Mon-

aghan adds that Smiley felt it was just retribution for his having probably authorized the murder of his renegade agent Jerry Westerby. Other critics have ventured the opinion that Smiley ordered Westerby's death. There is no question that he bears at least indirect responsibility (he was in charge of the operation), but le Carré is vague on this point. It is more likely that the assassin, a psychopath who bore a strong personal grudge against Westerby, acted on his own initiative. He could have operationally justified his action, because Westerby had drawn his weapon. Given Smiley's acceptance of responsibility and his strong conscience, Monaghan's explanation would hold even if Smiley had not given the order to shoot. Dobel (1988:207) suggests that Smiley's hatred of "the interbureaucratic battles necessary to win money and turf for his policy" may have been an additional reason why "Smiley may actually have welcomed his replacement by Enderby" (see chapter 6).

45. "Smiley's pure, patriotic zeal is simplified, and distorted, by his thirst for revenge" (Kanfer, 1987:9).

46. Shakespeare's line when the queen says, "The lady protests too much, methinks" comes to mind (Hamlet, Act III, scene 2, line 219).

47. This anguished soul-searching makes Beene's (1992:106) characterization of Smiley as an "absolutist" "impassively" watching Karla cross over difficult to comprehend.

48. Edwards (1988:51) suggests: "Holmes acquired much momentum from Conan Doyle's enjoyment in writing chivalric romances of the fourteenth century, *The White Company* and *Sir Nigel,* and it is the science of chivalric symbolism that a knight may carry and fight to reclaim the token of his faithless lady, only quietly to discard it when the relevant quest is over."

49. When Enderby tells Smiley he would find it grating to have Karla keep a lighter given to him by his wife, Smiley replies: "It was just an ordinary Ronson. . . . Still, they're *made to last,* aren't they?" (277; emphasis added). The Ronson slogan also refers indirectly to marriage vows.

50. Rothberg (1987:62) gives an additional political interpretation of the scene: "If Smiley and Ann remain childless and thereby signal the end of their line, symbolically and literally the end of Britain's might, the last of the glories of the past, then Karla's daughter is a schizophrenic madwoman who proclaims what the Soviet state promises for the future." This evaluation is more pessimistic, however, than the more optimistic tone and open-ended conclusion of *The Russia House.*

51. Whereas this points to the common humanity of Smiley and Karla, McWilliams (1980:31) points out that it also highlights the difference between the political systems of the East and the West. "The Russians can be blackmailed because human weaknesses are not tolerated by the regime." It should be noted, however, that Westerners are not impervious to blackmail—especially for their sexual conduct (or misconduct).

52. By the phrase "combining Smiley's halves," I take it that she means the balancing of thought and action (15). By "his termination," I surmise that she

is referring to Smiley's "spiritual death," when he adopts Karla's absolutism (see, e.g., 5, 12). Beene (1992:115) also argues that "Smiley's redemption arises from his relativism and perpetual doubt." She ignores the significance of Smiley's appearance (spiritual resurrection) in *The Secret Pilgrim*.

53. He continues, "Smiley's humanity corresponds to le Carré 's own."

54. Citing an interview with Byron Rogers (1982:90), he quotes le Carré: "This was to be Smiley's confrontation with Karla that would destroy them both, Smiley by an act of professional absolutism, Karla by a lapse into humanity. It was to be a moral Reichenbach Falls with no happy moment when Smiley returns to bee-keeping."

55. Alec Guinness' brilliant portrayal of Smiley in the BBC production of the television movie *Tinker, Tailor, Soldier, Spy* and *Smiley's People* was said by le Carré to have so inhabited the role as to have stolen Smiley from him. Alec Guinness "took the character away from me. . . . In a sense his screen success blew it for me" (Melvyn Bragg, 1983:22). He told Thom Schwartz (1987:20) that "Smiley became confined by Guinness. He became the property of Guinness. . . . Until then he's in everybody's imagination, and they find what they like. So I thought it was a good time to move on." Le Carré (1979:111), in "At Last, It's Smiley," said "I found myself writing Guinness, not Smiley." For this and other reasons, Smiley does not appear in le Carré's next three novels. Le Carré dedicated this book to "Alec Guinness with affection and thanks."

56. David Cornwell also has a home in Cornwall.

57. In a personal communication to me, November 27,1996.

58. Masters (1987:252), who does not quote le Carré's revelation in his interview with Miriam Gross, comes to the same conclusion through convincing arguments and suggestive clues. Le Carré confirms this in his interview with Plimpton (1997:56).

59. In another interview le Carré said, "With time, I found him a damn nuisance. . . . I didn't enjoy looking at life through the eyes of such an old and disenchanted person. I found the limitations of his sex life irritating" (Tom Mathews, 1989:57). In an interview with David Leitch (1987:50), le Carré says, "Smiley's too old, not sexy enough, too inhibited, too predictable. There's no danger any more." Indeed, the scenes depicting sex in the Smiley novels are conspicuous by their absence (especially for the spy genre). Even his post-Smiley novels are very sedate by the standards of the genre.

60. In anticipation of criticism for comparing a "popular" writer like le Carré with an "icon of high art" like Shakespeare, I call upon the authority of Marjorie Garber who is William R. Kenan Jr. Professor of English at Harvard University. Garber reminds us that Shakespeare began publishing his plays in quartos, which were the "instant books" of their day. "It was only in the 18th century that the myth of 'Shakespeare,' and the Shakespeare text, began to be invented." See her Bookend essay, "Back to Whose Basics?" (1995:55).

61. My colleague Irving Louis Horowitz calls le Carré "both a sophisticate and a naïve" in a personal communication to me dated July 7, 1993. As his comment implies, one must resort to paradox in attempting to come to terms with le Carré. Le Carré teaches us that we must resort to paradox to understand ourselves and our world as well.

62. Alan Bold, in the Introduction to his edited volume *The Quest for le Carré* (1988:16), notes that the exchange of places between the two main characters (one of whom is modeled on the author) in *The Naive and Sentimental Lover* "implies that opposites not only attract: they interact." He notes that "Smiley and Karla, are two sides of the same coin even though one is burnished, the other tarnished." With le Carré, characters frequently have fragmented personalities, and they also merge as well as exchange roles.

63. John le Carré "Why I Came in from the Cold," 1989.

64. This apparently paradoxical statement written in nonfictional form is, I think, intended by le Carré to be taken literally. It means exactly what it says. In the present world political context, he feels that the kind of idealism he recommends is a most realistic stance. As I indicate below, his other oxymoronic statements may also be given a more literal reading; context determines how apparent opposites can be reconciled.

65. Le Carré "Tinpots, Saviors, Lawyers, Spies" (1993; emphasis added).

66. "Le Carré subverts the nationalistic, even jingoistic, assumptions underlying normal spy fiction to cast a questioning eye on the ethics of the Cold War and on the West's overconfident beliefs that right must always be on its side and that its democratic hands are clean" (Lewis: 68).

67. From the perspective of Crechan (1988:106), this constitutes "ideological closure," a "reformist" approach, calling for "revitalizing" that takes for granted the need for spies. Although le Carré is extremely critical of them, Crechan is correct in his assessment that he never radically questions the continued existence of M16 or the CIA. This is because of his realism in recognizing that they are a necessary evil.

68. Barley (1986:94) suggests that Smiley reveals himself to be both "a principled liberal and humanist" and a "guilty liberal," which seems redundant. A liberal disposition inherently entails a certain degree of guilt.

69. He continues: "My books can be defined first by what I do not believe in; constancy, group values, obligations. I see in what I write a constant progress toward individual values and an anger that is growing more intense toward injustice."

70. Elie Wiesel (1976:24) observes, "All human dialogue is ambiguous. If Good always had the appearance of good and Evil could always be recognized, life would be simpler indeed. But it isn't simple. Not even in paradise."

71. Barley (1986:25) suggests that "only being fully won over to espousing an alternative position can foreclose the issue, and that necessarily entails the complete rejection of liberalism and individualism."

72. "From his first appearance Smiley possesses a well-developed and comprehensive world view which commits him to the task of holding in balance forces that are essentially unreconcilable. Consequently, unless he completely alters his approach to experience, Smiley can never progress because he can never reach what he is striving towards. Rather than tracing development, then, Smiley's various fictional appearances record a series of heroic but inevitably unsuccessful attempts to weld the differing circumstances with which he is faced into a harmonious whole."

73. For example, Andy East (1983:173) suggests that "le Carré slowly fused Smiley's maturation process with the crises he faced in the Service." In fact, he calls the Smiley books a "psychological cycle."

74. "The only way for Smiley to reconcile ends with means is to distort the reality of the situation in which he is placed. And this he refuses to do, accepting instead the need to struggle painfully, knowing there is no hope of resolution, to come to terms with the moral implications of his acts. Smiley's only reward for living so completely is that he remains intensely human" (David Monaghan, 1986:169).

75. For example, Gadi Becker in *The Little Drummer Girl* and Leonard Burr in *The Night Manager* (1993), manifest similar skeptical qualities and are the moral center of the novels in which they appear.

Chapter 2

1. Sophie, who is Jonathan Pine's "Secret Sharer" in *The Night Manager* (1993:414).

2. Anthony Quinton (1984:30–32), in his review of Judith N. Shklar's *Ordinary Vices* (1984), points out that betrayal "is not a quality of character; it is a species of action." He suggests that she should have followed Montaigne and written of "disloyalty." While I use both terms, I use betrayal more frequently because I am primarily dealing with the actions of characters and because conventional usage of the term conveys greater gravity than does disloyalty.

3. Judith Shklar (1984:158; emphasis added) observes of Montesquieu, that he appears to be "both particularly poignant and self-divided; hence he was instructive on this very point."

4. Lewis Anthony Dexter (1993:64).

5. Cited by Andrew Rutherford (1978:152). See George Eliot (1886:88).

6. Shklar (1984:156–7) criticizes Forster's declaration for trivializing the complexity of the dilemma, for its mindless dogmatism and self-righteousness, and for ignoring both the problem of the conflicts of loyalty and the political nature of treason. She cites the great discussion of the tension between public and private obligations in Plato's *Crito,* in which Socrates refuses Crito's plea to escape from his unjust death sentence by fleeing Athens. In the Introduction, I comment on the similarity between White's interpretation of the relationship between Plato's literary technique and his

philosophical stance in *Crito* to suggest a similar relationship in le Carré's work. I discuss below a theme that was at the heart of this classic.

7. Both Eric Homberger (1986:44) and, more explicitly, Peter Wolfe (1987:79, 92) mistakenly, in my opinion, suggest that Samuel Fennan was a spy as well. From my reading of the text, it is clear that Smiley correctly deduced that Elsa Fennan alone was the spy (see chapter 17, 151–2).

8. Wolfe (1987:92) points out the association between the location of the scheduled meeting between Samuel Fennan and Smiley in Marlowe and the murder of his wife by Dieter in London's Sheridan Theatre while they watched a play by Christopher Marlowe. He neglects to point out that Marlowe (who appears to have been involved in espionage) was also murdered, thereby providing perfect symmetry with the murder of the Fennans. See Charles Nicholl, *The Reckoning* (1992), for a fascinating analysis of the murder of Marlowe.

9. Obviously, this is much too simple an explanation. People act for more than one reason. In chapter 5, I explain le Carré's characterization of the mystery of motive.

10. Rothberg (1987:54) emphasizes Dieter's culpability: "It is Dieter who caused Mrs. Fennan to betray not only the country which had offered her sanctuary after her persecutions at the hands of the Nazis, but also the husband she loves—ultimately to his death at the hands of the new East German authoritarians. Is such betrayal not personal enough? not political enough? And is it not far worse than the sexual betrayals of Smiley's Lady Ann?" He claims, "Le Carré does not consider or resolve that dilemma, or even face it squarely as, say Sophocles had done more than two thousand years earlier in the *Antigone.*" Although I disagree that le Carré does not face the dilemma, I agree he that does not resolve it because, as I argue below, it is irresolvable.

11. She related this story during an appearance on "Villa Felderhof," presented by Rik Felderhof on NCRV, which appeared on Netherlands television's Channel 1 on October 21, 1996. My summary is a paraphrase from notes I took from the broadcast and not from an official transcript. Significantly, her memoirs of her experience in the underground do not refer to this incident. (Menger, 1982).

12. I discuss the psychological mechanisms through which the conscience is disengaged in chapter 4.

13. This is paradigmatic. The man is incapable of articulating his feelings of love to the woman who needs these verbal assurances. He is only capable of demonstrating his love through his action, which, unfortunately, comes too late for her to appreciate it.

14. One of the only references to such a family in his work occurs when Magnus Pym, the central character of *A Perfect Spy,* stays in the home of Herr Ollinger in Switzerland: "Once in our lives it is given us to know a truly happy family" (194). Rex Goodhew (*The Night Manager*) is exceptional. He is happily married and has children who adore him (47).

15. "'Prideaux and Haydon were really very close indeed, you know,' Lacon confessed, 'I hadn't realized'" (224). See also the letter written by Bill Haydon to his tutor Fanshawe nominating Prideaux for recruitment to the Circus (261–3). Smiley thinks: "This man was my friend and Ann's lover, Jim's friend and—for all I know—Jim's lover, too" (345).

16. Dobel (1988:213) suggests that Jim "goes slightly mad from the pain and isolation." He also reminds us that this wrecked Smiley's plans to trade Haydon for Western spies betrayed by Haydon who were being held in the Soviet Union.

17. In *Smiley's Circus,* Monaghan provides a history of the Circus and its major operations and a "who's who," with biographies of the characters. It is essential and fun reading for dedicated le Carré fans.

18. Reg Gadney (1974:75) says that Haydon "isn't *actually* Philby; he just seems quite incredibly like him." Homberger (1986:76) suggests that he is an amalgam of Philby and Blunt. Robert D. King (1998:331) suggests, "Le Carré merged the personae of Guy Burgess and Kim Philby—with a dash of Anthony Blunt—to create Bill Haydon."

19. Halperin (1980:33), after detailing the many similarities between them, concludes unambiguously that "Haydon is Philby in these books, and Smiley is Dick White, with a little of Sir Maurice Oldfield thrown in." Margaret Scanlon (1990:98) points out differences between Haydon and Philby. There is a voluminous literature on the Cambridge spies. See, for example, Andrew Boyle (1979); Elinor Philby (1967); Bruce Page, David Leitch and Philip Knightley (1968); Chapman Pincher (1984, especially chapter 19); Nigel West (1984); and Peter Wright (1987). Undoubtedly, the wide public interest and publicity surrounding the exposure of these sensational real-world Soviet double agents contributed to the success of le Carré's novels.

20. Like Philby, he acted as a liaison between British and U.S. intelligence for several years.

21. See chapter 8.

22. See chapter 5.

23. Dennis Kucherawy (1989:55), in suggesting that "the theme of redemption through love" characterizes this novel, also seems to imply a more simple explanation than the text warrants.

24. Sauerberg (1984:202) suggests that Smiley's battle with Karla is "an allegorical battle about the human situation. Smiley and Karla represent alternative existential possibilities."

25. I discuss this in more detail in chapter 3.

26. Trahair (1994) reports that in Klaus Fuchs' confession he described how he compartmentalized his thoughts in order to separate his work in Los Alamos from his betrayal of these secrets to the Russians. George Blake (discussed below and in later chapters) was also able to make this kind of separation. Trahair (1996) identifies four selves in Blake in an unpublished manuscript and a personal communication, December 3, 1996.

27. He said: "It left me feeling free and in some ways much stronger and potentially much better as a writer." In "Spying on My Father" (1986), le Carré said: "The truth, it seemed to me, was more likely to emerge through fiction than through the specious arrangement of documentary information. Moreover Ronnie [his father] himself was never certain which of the two categories he belonged to. Was he art, was he life? Like a novelist, his fictions were his reality." Masters (1987:245; emphasis added) points out: "David Cornwell tried to write about Ronnie many times, but always with unsatisfactory and painful results. He was *too much a part of his father* to see him with any perspective. . . . Ronnie's death did not mean the passing of his influence on his son."

28. Personally, I find *The Tailor of Panama* (1996) even more successful as a tragicomedy.

29. He calls it "his safe house away from all other safe houses" (1:22).

30. This tractate of the Mishnah, a part of the Talmud, is a classic in Jewish literature. I use the Sephardi transliteration of the Hebrew word for *fathers* (standard form in modern Israel), some editions use the Ashkenazi (European) transliteration (*avos*). Various English editions translate the English title and subtitle differently. Obviously, there are also slight variations in the translation of the text as well. Like the Bible, there is a standardized method of citation which, for this passage, is I.14. Le Carré is known to do prodigious research for his novels. This is a perfectly fitting reference. It strengthens my intuition that he has an unusual empathy with Jews. R. Travers Herford (1962:1), who edited, translated, and wrote commentary for an English edition of this work, wrote in his Introduction that if he failed to faithfully render the meaning in his commentaries, "It will be due to the fact that the present writer is not himself a Jew, and may perhaps be deaf to melodies which sing divinely in a Jewish ear." Neither le Carré nor Herford are deaf to such melodies. Although I found Herford's hearing a little faulty in his commentary on this particular passage, le Carré's placing of it indicates that he has perfect pitch.

31. Shklar equates this with the primeval fear of the failure to distinguish kin and stranger exemplified in acts of treason, which become perceived in terms of sacrilege.

32. Le Carré has expressed understanding of the Soviet mole Kim Philby: "I always knew what made Kim run. . . . A part of me could have gone that way—we were unequal clones of the same syndrome" (Tom Mathews, 1989:52).

33. "At Last, It's Smiley," 1979:114.

34. In expressing his ambivalent feelings to Brotherhood about having to track Pym down for the CIA, Lederer says: "'I feel really bad, Jack,'. . . . 'Nobody seems to understand what it's been like for me to have to do this to a friend'" (9:245). But, he turns around and reports to his boss that this had been a ruse in order to elicit Pym's whereabouts from Brotherhood. The passage illustrates how much Lederer is really like Pym.

35. Pym seems oblivious to the consequences of this reversal for the widow with whom he had identified so sympathetically. As in his larger betrayals as a double agent, he betrays both sides by attempting to be "loyal" to both. Pym first betrays his father to the widow, then betrays the widow to his father. He ends up adoring his father, who turns the situation around through lies and deceit—publicly humiliating the widow whom Rick had already indirectly widowed and directly impoverished. Laity (1968:4) sheds light on the subject: "Duplicity for Kim Philby was something of a family tradition. However, Philby reacted to his eminently distasteful father, whether he wished to destroy or outshine him, or merely to follow in his footsteps, he could hardly fail, in the outposts where they lived, to inherit many of his characteristics."

36. If the reader finds this reaction of exultation hard to believe, compare it with the autobiographical account of the real double agent George Blake (1990:19), who describes his "exhilarated feeling," which he compared with his first parachute jump, after passing his fist highly classified information to his KGB handler. He also expressed "great relief" and that he now "had a purpose" when he was accepted by the KGB as their mole (146).

37. An even more elaborate and convoluted case of collusion in the manufacture and dispersal of bogus intelligence forms the basis of the plot of *The Tailor of Panama* (see chapters 3 and 4).

38. Similarly, Blake (1990) repeatedly expresses his love for Britain and the British people. See, for example, the Introduction by Phillip Knightley (ix); there are many such indications throughout the book. With (perhaps unintended) irony, he says he would have trouble explaining to the Soviets who the people were who helped him escape from prison and why they helped him. "It seemed to me that *only in England could people like this be found*" (243; emphasis added).

39. Cornwell has three siblings (a brother, a half-brother, and a half-sister), but he made Pym an only child with only one son.

40. Bloom (1987:1), citing Poppy's critique of Pym's lack of authenticity and originality, being put together from bits of others, asks: "Is this le Carré's own anxiety, despite his vast audience and growing critical acclaim?" Bloom suggests that his voice "sometimes can be mistaken for that of Conrad or Greene." Bloom's critique derives from his theory of poetry expounded in *The Anxiety of Influence (1973)*. On a more prosaic level, le Carré's allusions to his predecessors are like academic acknowledgments of intellectual debts to peers. This acknowledgment of literary influences bespeaks integrity. Le Carré's authentic literary voice is clearly recognizable. Following the clues of literary allusion simply provides an additional pleasure, a kind of bonus, for those who recognize them. He says, "They're part of literary memory; they're what's in the pot" (Ross, 1987:26).

41. "The son has finally killed the father, in the hope of giving life to another son" (Laity, 1987:161). Masters (1987:246) notes Cassidy's plots to kill his father in *The Naive and Sentimental Lover.*

42. Homberger (1986:54) observes that "Le Carré is often very careful to undercut the professed beliefs of his characters."

43. "I think it's the unconscious, irreconcilable fact inside one's own self, feeling a very flawed person and really making a search through the possibilities of one's own character" Le Carré quoted by Plimpton (1997:70).

44. "I don't mean to preach, but I do know I do, and I'm a very flawed person. It's quite ridiculous" Le Carré quoted by Plimpton (1997:70).

45. Forster, like the Cambridge spies Burgess and Blunt, was a member of the secret Cambridge Conversazione Society (known as the Apostles). Forster's statement reflects views popular among some young British intelligentsia in the 1930's.

46. I agree with Green that spiritual affinity is a more important an aspect of love than physical attraction for le Carré. This is one of the reasons why sexual scenes play such a minor role in his work.

Chapter 3

1. Leigh Crutchley (1966:549) interview with le Carré.

2. This approach is well suited to explaining competing realities—the subject of fiction and of much contemporary political anthropology.

3. As he told Robert McNeill in an interview in May 1989.

4. David Monaghan (1985, especially in chapter 2) effectively analyzes the role of metaphor in le Carré's work. See also his chapter in Bold (1987:117–35).

5. In his autobiographical statement in Wakeman (1975:841), le Carré says: "I find it hard to write about women; although I can understand intellectually why they act as they do, I find it difficult to imagine myself acting in that way." For analyses of the role of women in le Carré's novels, see Margaret Moan Rowe (1988:69–86), and Brenda R. Silver (1987:14–40). Barley (1986:17–20), Homberger (1986:91–3), and Lewis (1985:182–3) briefly discuss the subject as well.

6. "'You're safe with that,' Leclerc said. 'The Minister signed it. He used red ink, you know. It's tradition'" (102).

7. Le Carré, in his introduction to Page, Leitch, and Knightley (1968:4), states, "Similarly, the posturing chauvinism of his [Philby's] superiors would long have passed for idiotic in the outside world; in the secret world it passed for real."

8. An internal CIA inquest blamed the "agency's own institutional arrogance, ignorance, and incompetence" (Weiner, 1998:6).

9. John le Carré, quoted by David Streitfeld (1992:15). In the same interview, le Carré says that he often wished that there would have been women present as such times to talk sense and to say, " 'You guys are going nuts.' Nobody said that, so we went nuts together." Masters (1987:240) notes that le Carré was serving in Germany under diplomatic

cover during crises involving the Berlin Wall, the Bay of Pigs incident, and the fall of the Adenauer government (see chapter 8).

10. Homberger (1986:66) reads it as a "thriller of ideas—about beliefs, national decline, class consciousness, and Englishness."

11. Peter Wolfe (1987:144) mistakenly identifies Karfeld as the West German chancellor.

12. In a rare slip, Homberger (1986:65–6) identifies de Lisle as the ambassador. However, le Carré places his office in the Chancery (19), where he works directly under Bradfield. The ambassador would hardly pick up a lowly foreign office investigator at the airport, as does de Lisle (50).

13. In fact, Homberger (1986:69) suggests that he is no less a tragic victim than is Harting.

14. E. H. Carr (1947) also warns against the dangers of extreme realism and idealism in world affairs.

15. Emphasis has been added to the original. Philip O'Neill (1988:169) and Beene (1992:100) point out this contradiction.

16. O'Neill (1988:171) points out the parallel le Carré draws "between the public school, the Secret Service, and the outside world."

17. Ian Buruma (1991:9) notes le Carré's own position in what George Orwell defined as the "lower upper class," whose attitude to the upper class is complicated and ambivalent; "in some cases a mixture of fawning snobbery . . . and the wish to kick it in the shins."

18. "Fairy-tale and legend are common to schoolboy and agent. Both appropriate the world too easily in terms of right and wrong, good and bad. At the end of *Tinker Tailor* the reader is made to see that this is all a dream" (O'Neill, 1988:185).

19. Shakespeare (1988) expressed by Jaques in *As You Like It*, scene 2, act 7, line 139.

20. In an interview with Melvyn Bragg (1988: 130 and 136), le Carré relates that Charlie is partly based, as a point of departure, on his half-sister Charlotte, who is an actress with the Royal Shakespeare Company. Sauerberg (1984:107) identifies Charlie, Becker, and Kurtz as the heroes.

21. "Charlie had been a passionate opponent of apartheid . . . a militant pacifist, a Sufist, a nuclear marcher, an anti-vivisectionist, and, until she went back to smoking again, a champion of campaigns to eliminate tobacco from theatres and on the public underground" (79).

22. I expand the discussion of these and other Smiley-like qualities below in this chapter.

23. Techniques of interrogation are analyzed in chapter 7.

24. The notion of "time out," or the bracketing of social interaction, has been developed most extensively by Erving Goffman in several works. See, for example, (1982).

25. Rowe (1988:80) notes that for the first time in his espionage fiction, "le Carré gives substance to present sexual energy."

26. A dramatic example of the effect of similar politically targeted terrorism by Palestinian opponents of the peace process with Israel was the profound impact that the spate of suicide bombings in Israel, shortly before the 1996 election, had on the outcome. The heightened sense of insecurity among Israelis caused by these bombings is largely responsible for the precipitous loss of support by Shimon Peres (Labor), whose vision made possible the Oslo Accords with the PLO. This gave the extremely narrow margin of victory (less than 1 percent) to Benjamin Netanyahu (Likud), who had strongly opposed them. See Myron J. Aronoff and Yael S. Aronoff (1996).

27. In an interview with Andrew Ross (1997:17), le Carré says, "I received such awful letters from organized Jewish groups that I never felt on safe ground after that. My great sin was in suggesting that the state of Israel—that Palestine—was in fact a twice-promised land."

28. This is not a surprising conclusion for a dovish Israeli intellectual, because le Carré's point of view on the issue is remarkably similar to that of the Israeli peace camp and to that of the reviewer. Sauerberg (1984:63) also suggests that "le Carré's sympathy seems to be on the Israeli side . . . the doves only."

29. Melvyn Bragg (1988:138) quotes le Carré: "The linch-pin is her relationship with her agent runner, her controller . . . a kind of Pygmalion relationship. He's the link man." He also tells Bragg that he found Gadi the most difficult character to write; because "we had to experience him in the first instance through her, I could not cut away into Joseph's [Gadi's] own mind because to do so would destroy the mystery of who he was, which was kindled in Charlie."

30. This statement is qualified by adding "the special circumstances in which she is placed and the closeness of her approach to the precipice of disaster lessen the impact of the novel's emphatically romantic ending" (Monaghan, 1985:201). See also his comments on pages 195 and 200.

31. Laity (1987:147) also finds the ending problematic: "The fulfillment offered in that ending remains problematical, however, for Charlie and Joseph arguably have been destroyed by their experiences."

32. Homberger (1986:98), however, finds that the ending reveals le Carré's true romanticism. William F. Buckley, Jr. (1987:114), concludes: "The emotional tension of the postlude elevates it into a full fourth act. A wonderful achievement."

33. Monaghan (1985:187) portrays Kurtz as being "free of all burdens of self-doubt, egotism, or moral uncertainty." He contrasts Kurtz with Smiley, who has consciousness which, he claims, Kurtz lacks.

34. Monaghan obviously meant Kurtz's lack of humanity. However, through his exaggerated (in this author's opinion) portrayal and interpretation of his character, it is Monaghan who actually "dehumanizes" Kurtz—which was certainly not le Carré's intent. As evidence, I cite below several examples to illustrate Kurtz's respect and affection for Becker.

35. Citations of references to Kurtz as a tyrant, a man completely lacking in moderation, and a fanatic are misleading, because Monaghan fails to identify who makes the statement and in what context. For example, he is called a fanatic by a character who, le Carré has made clear, is a blatant anti-Semite by having him say, "I know you Izzies" (301).

36. Sauerberg (1984:108) makes a passing reference to "a certain similarity between Becker and Smiley" but fails to develop the significance of the observation, having argued the greater similarity between Kurtz and Smiley. Sauerberg (1984:115), in claiming, "In contrast to Becker, Charlie's situation undergoes development," implies that Becker's character does not. I show why I believe his character does dramatically develop in the novel.

37. Bloom (1987:4) fails to justify this evaluation, with which I strongly disagree. He considers the book the best le Carré had produced at the time his essay was written. He claims the Israelis "scarcely have le Carré's sympathy, which is essentially with the Palestinians." I disagree with this assessment. Bloom contrasts a passage in which le Carré describes the Israeli bombing of a Palestinian quarter in Beirut with the bombing by Palestinians of a synagogue in Istanbul the week before he wrote his essay. Bloom's emotional reaction to this event may have influenced his interpretation of le Carré's position. In the same volume, edited by Bloom, William F. Buckley, Jr. (1987:114) calls Gadi "the most mysterious character to have appeared in recent fiction. . . . His persona on the one hand is central, on the other hand continuingly elusive. And when finally he exists for Charlie, after the entrapment, after Khalil is gone, the magnetism is enormous."

38. This is an interesting example of how le Carré composes characters as composites of real people and draws dialogue from real life. In an essay, "Memories of a Vanished Land" (1982:9–10), le Carré reports meeting an Israeli journalist who had lost a son in the war of 1973 at a funeral of another Israeli soldier killed in the war in Lebanon. The man, who he describes as being "in a state of almost manic grief," told him, "In '73, we fought for the peace that was round the corner. . . . What do we fight for now?"

39. The interpretations of all readers, including so-called experts, are shaped by personal experiences and professional and ideological orientations. That I have dual U.S. and Israeli citizenship, lived in Israel for more than ten years, served in the Israeli army, and identify strongly with the Israeli peace camp undoubtedly shapes my perceptions and, in particular, my interpretations of this novel.

40. When Bragg (1988:136; emphasis added) asked what was his "point of view" for this novel, le Carré replied: "I settled for the *irreconcilability* of the problem."

41. See Aronoff and Atlas (1998).

42. In reply to Schwarz (1987:21), who asked him if he intended to bring Gadi back, le Carré replied: "No, I'm finished with him."

43. Silver adds: "But for this ending to be convincing, for it to unsettle or rewrite the traditional conclusion of woman's story, le Carré must also convince us that he can envision a role for woman that transcends dichotomy of wife or agent." She suggests he may have done so in this novel but, like le Carré, leaves her conclusion open ended.

44. Since the 1996 election of the Israeli government led by Prime Minister Benjamin Netanyahu and dominated by nationalist parties and the renewal of Palestinian terrorist attacks, the chances for progress in the peace process are as uncertain as the prognosis of Charlie and Gadi's future together.

45. Bloom (1987:3) succinctly concludes: "Pym . . . is a nihilist, and dies a nihilist's death." Beene (1992:123) agrees and suggests that he never faces "his true demon, his own intellectual and spiritual abyss."

46. According to John Blades (1989:2), who interviewed and quotes le Carré, Andrei Sakharov, the Nobel prize-winning nuclear physicist and human rights activist, was the "intellectual model" for the fictional Goethe. When le Carré met Sakharov in Russia he sensed his guilt over his crucial role in the development of the Russian hydrogen bomb.

47. Robert J. Kohler, a vice president of TRW (which manufactures spy satellites) and former chief of the CIA's development and engineering office, said: "There's a culture shock from being involved in something that was at the forefront of defending the country, to something that some people now question why you're doing it at all" (Eric Schmitt, 1992:A16).

48. The thoughts of Goethe (alias Bluebird) paraphrased by Katya in a conversation with Barley in *The Russia House* (1989:170; emphasis added).

49. This latter image was the title motif for the credits of the BBC production of *Tinker, Tailor, Soldier, Spy.*

50. In the same interview, le Carré stresses Barley's nobility and the fact that he is a "free man."

51. This book appeared after the publication of the previously cited scholarly studies of le Carré's work (except Beene's).

52. Beene (1992:15) seems to exaggerate le Carré's relativism. The absence of "absolute standards" certainly implies a degree of relativism but not necessarily absolute relativism. Although she does not say explicitly that his relativism is absolute, her conclusions imply it.

53. David Remnick (1993:23), sarcastically suggests: "This time le Carré has crafted a solid 100-minute Hollywood feature, a *Goldfinger* for grown-ups." Whereas the protagonists of this novel tend to be somewhat more exaggeratedly good and bad than in his other novels, Remnick's critique is much exaggerated in my opinion and misses what, I argue in chapter 4, are much more important points.

54. Pine also shares some Smiley-like qualities, including the fact that he was unreconciled (52). Clearly, he differs from Smiley in many other important respects. In age and military experience, for example, he is closer to Gadi Becker.

55. A copy of the manuscript of this novel came into my hands well before publication. It confirmed for me le Carré's uncanny political instincts for anticipating important international developments.

56. From the front inner flap of the dust jacket of the Alfred A. Knopf edition.

57. Christopher Lehmann-Haupt (1995).

58. Le Carré concludes his Acknowledgments, "Without Graham Greene this book would never have come about. After Greene's *Our Man in Havana,* the notion of an intelligence fabricator would not leave me alone" (410). In another literary reference, Pendel is code-named Buchan an allusion to John Buchan-a British spy novelist of an earlier generation who is best known as the author of *The Thirty-Nine Steps* (1915, 1974).

59. Pendel suggests "pendulum." Le Carré describes the school evaluations of the young Jonathan Pine in *The Night Manager* as being inconsistent, "back and forth like a pendulum" (52). The term fluence may derive from the cons he performed for his father: "He was using me. . . . I was his *fluent* boy, his charming clown" (Alexis Gelber with Edward Behr, 1983:45, emphasis added).

60. Broadcast November 2, 1996.

61. David Streitfeld (1996:24).

62. While standing on his balcony watching the fires ignited by the American bombardment, Pendel (whose father was Jewish, although he had an Irish Catholic mother) silently intones a parody of the prayer recited on the solemn Jewish Day of Atonement (Yom Kippur): "We have harmed, corrupted and ruined, we have made mistakes and deceived" (401).

63. Lockard and Paulhus (1988).

64. "To le Carré political absolutism and expediency are temptations to be overcome, because they appeal too easily to man's longing for order and system" (Sauerberg, 1984:208).

65. I follow Carey McWilliam's definition quoted earlier. In describing the difference between the "liberal" and the "flexible" mind, Eviatar Zerubavel (1991) suggestively (but not altogether persuasively) contends that the former attempts to achieve a balance between "rigidity" and "fuzziness," while the latter moves back and forth between them in terms of dealing with the making and breaking of categorical distinctions. The reason I am unconvinced by Zerubavel's distinction is that I understand the liberal mind to operate in the manner which he describes for the flexible mind.

66. Sauerberg (1984:135) mentions Smiley's "thin ethical tightrope." He also says, "Smiley prefers the English way of life because of its respect for the individual and for its traditional skepticism" (190). Bradbury (1990:133) also mentions Smiley's (and his creator's) skepticism.

67. *Concise Oxford Dictionary,* 9th ed. (1995). The English spelling is "sceptical."

68. The quotation is from George Blake (1990:168). Richard C. S. Trahair (unpublished manuscript) also cites Tom Bower (1995):181 for the same passage.

69. Exactly such arrogance led ranking officials in the CIA to withhold from the White House and the Pentagon the fact that information on the So-

viet Union was provided by agents whom they knew or strongly suspected were controlled by Moscow (discussed in chapter 8). Fromkin (1996:166; emphasis added) explains why they felt entitled to withhold such vital knowledge from their leaders: "A plausible theory is that it was only one aspect of an *arrogance* that dates back to the years in which the agency was created, the special dispensation from the rules of law and morality that CIA agents were granted, and the sort of men who stepped into that environment and set the tone for the agency."

Chapter 4

1. "To Russia, with Greetings: An Open Letter to the Moscow *Literary Gazette*" (1966:5).
2. From "Politics as a Vocation," in H. H. Gerth and C. Wright Mills (1946:121); hereafter cited as Weber (1946).
3. Bartoszewski (1989:29) observes that one of several attributes shared by myth and the world of espionage is that in their internal logic, "The end justifies the means." This and other similarities between the two are discussed in chapter 7.
4. Anne Karalekas (1985:66). Cited by Arthur S. Hulnick (1996).
5. My thanks to Rita Aronoff for the translation of this passage.
6. David Remnick (1993:20–22).
7. From his review of Thomas Powers, *The Man Who Kept Secrets* (1979). In his review of this biography of Richard Helms, former director of the CIA, le Carré offers an explanation of the failure of American espionage which is discussed in chapter 8.
8. Cited by Myron J. Smith (1976:v). Pat M. Holt (1995:19) quotes this passage from Charles W. Brown (1989:61).
9. Clifford Orwin (1994:195–6).
10. More than 1.3 million pages of German intercepts handed over by the British were recently declassified by the United States National Security Agency.
11. General Eisenhower described the Ultra intelligence "as a decisive factor in the Allied victory, and as having saved thousands of British and American lives" (John Slessor, in his Foreword to F. W. Winterbotham [1974:11]).
12. "As late as September 1944, a British diplomat argued against publicizing the atrocity stories on the grounds that it would compel officials to 'waste a disproportionate amount of their time dealing with wailing Jews'" (Michael Dobbs (1996:1, 12). John Keegan (1996:9) verifies that similar information is recorded in the second volume of Britain's official history of intelligence operations, edited by F. H. Hinsley, that was published in 1981. He argues that the need to keep Ultra secret justified the suppression of this intelligence. In fact, he even goes further: "Cipher superiority became a vital weapon of the Cold War, and keeping Ultra secret from the Soviets was deemed vital." Churchill biographer Martin Gilbert's claim that news

of the mass murder of Jews only reached London in June 1944 is contradicted by this evidence. Gilbert's *Churchill: A Life* was published in 1991, ten years after the publication of the official history of British intelligence operations. Zara Steiner (1998:10) notes that David Stafford's *Churchill and Secret Service* (1998) "has little new to say about Churchill's relative inaction after reading the 1941 decrypts on the mass killing of the Jews."

13. Richard Trahair, personal communication, July 19, 1995. I am grateful for his suggestion of appropriate examples from le Carré to illustrate the point.

14. John le Carré, interviewed by Robert McNeill on PBS, August 16, 1980. Louis Menand (1995:4) suggests that the meaning of the refrain that both are alike is "that the defense of liberal democracy requires, in the end, the same duplicity, the same willingness to exploit the exploitable, the same blind gamble that your side is History's side, as the defense of the 'workers' state.'" He argues that the Berlin Wall is the symbol of the incommensurableness of ultimate ends and that le Carré and his heroes prefer a decadent democracy to a ruthless authoritarian state.

15. Homberger (1986:66).

16. Most (1987:101) notes: "If modern society is directed solely to the future rather than to the past, if the necessary and sufficient goal of national policy is survival, if the appearances must be preserved because there is nothing else besides them, what place can remain for the detective who seeks to decipher the enigma of the past, whatever the cost for the present? . . . In the murder of Harting is figured the death of the traditional mystery novel. . . . The insight to which le Carré has given voice in *A Small Town in Germany* may well anticipate the end of the genre. Future generations may no longer understand why the past century has been so obsessed with the discovery of the truth and the punishment of crime. For them, the mystery novel may become as mysterious in a way we would prefer not to envision."

17. Le Carré has remarked in numerous interviews that his was the last generation trained in the British imperial tradition. Many of this generation felt betrayed by the loss of empire and the decline of British influence in world affairs. One such interview was the aforementioned one on August 16, 1980, with Robert McNeill, in which he calls himself an "empire baby."

18. Sauerberg (1984:178) suggests that: "both Westerby and Smiley are defeated, personally, but their salvation is in their involvement. They care." I question whether caring and involvement are sufficient.

19. Le Carré remarked that "the Brits know that the law is just a nice little veneer over what we really do." David Streitfeld (1992:15). I discuss a real-world character like Palfrey in chapter 8.

20. He told Robert McNeill (May 1989), in response to a question about the individual decisions of the main characters in *The Russia House,* that there comes a point when institutional commitment and even patriotism "actually outlives its purpose and imposes on me and on my conscience individual strains which I cannot support."

21. "Percherin showed there was nothing disloyal in betrayal provided you betrayed what you hated and fought for what you loved" (87).

22. Colonel Pyotr Popov, a mole for the CIA, refused to defect, saying: "I'm a Russian and it's my country, my land. I'll die a Russian in Russia. I don't give a damn what they do to me." He was executed. (see Pincher [1987:2]). This is why Count Claus Schenck von Stauffenberg and those who plotted to assassinate Hitler refused to collaborate with the Allies—because they saw themselves as patriots, and collaboration with the Allies would have made them, in their own eyes, traitors. See Christopher Lehmann-Haupt's (1986:9) review of Joachim Fest, *Plotting Hitler's Death: The Story of the German Resistance.*

23. As Tom Mathews (1989:57) observes, "The thought puts reverse English on an old crack of [Kim] Philby's."

24. Broadcast on CNN (August 1993). Although he did not comment on the unambiguous happy ending given to the movie, in response to a question by Larry King, le Carré expressed a preference for the British television production of his earlier work.

25. Le Carré claims to have been asked this question by a member of the audience at the Library of Foreign Literature in Moscow, when he spoke there while researching *The Russia House* (Mathews, 1989:55). If so, the questioner was merely rephrasing a question that le Carré had asked himself previously. For example, in the McNeill interview, he said: "One has to ask oneself in terms of methods how long it is possible to defend democracy by these methods of subversion, endless threats of massive destruction and remain a society worth defending." Note that the epigraph introducing this chapter was published in 1966: this is perhaps the most central question that le Carré repeatedly asks himself and his readers throughout his career.

26. "Did I understand you were appealing to my *conscience?* . . . *I don't give a fart.* The difference between me and other charlies is, I admit it. If a horde of niggers—yes, I said *niggers,* I meant *niggers*—if these *niggers* shot each other dead with my toys tomorrow and I made a bob out of it, great news by me. Because if I don't sell 'em the goods, some *other* charlie will. Government used to understand that. If they've gone soft, tough titty on 'em" (333).

27. For these reasons and because he feels the author's treatment of women in this novel is cartoonish (citing some admittedly convincing examples), Remnick (1993:20) suggests that this novel "seems at moments like these to be a James Bond novel as written by a superior Ian Fleming."

28. Remnick (1993:23) calls it "the novel of his post-cold war disorientation." In his review of *Our Game,* Louis Menand (1995:4) says: "The end of the cold war therefore (let me be the hundredth reviewer to say it) made a problem for le Carré." Le Carré admits that he "stumbled a couple of times" in the transition, but that the end of the cold war was liberating for him as a writer (Plimpton, 1997:63).

29. I have never been able to force myself to read a James Bond novel, and hence I may be wrong. My impression, however, is that Bond always triumphs over the forces of evil. See Gerth and Mills (1946:123) for the quotation from Weber.

30. Palfrey, legal adviser to British intelligence, explains to the innocent Goodhew, "The going rate for introductions is five percent of the action, payable to the Procurement Studies Widows and Orphans Fund at the Bank of Crooks and Cousins Incorporated, Liechtenstein" (211).

31. When he concludes his deal of all deals, Roper "was in a state of grace" (315).

32. "For tea. Opium for tea. Barter. Came home to England, captains of industry. Knighthoods, honors, whole shebang. Hell's the difference? Go for it! That's all that matters. Americans know that. Why don't we?" (310).

33. Pointing out the Conradian undertone of the novel, he suggests that "Tim, responsible and overcautious, makes a plausible enough Marlow, and the suspense in the story comes initially from the uncertainty whether the man he is searching for is Kurtz [*Heart of Darkness*] or Jim [*Lord Jim*]—whether Larry is a mad genius turned savage or the West's last genuine romantic." Whereas Menand concludes he is the latter, it is more likely that le Carré intends us to view him as both.

34. Scammell (1995:13).

35. President Clinton can be seen as a Larry-like figure torn between conflicting impulses, with the added political problems of having to deal with conflicting advice and the constraints of the American checks and balances that include, in his case, a Republican-dominated Congress.

36. Hatry claims to hate the American "loony right" and their British blood brothers, but as a "realist" he was prepared to make alliances with them (301). But his opinions make it seem as if these alliances are not as uncomfortable a stretch for him as he claims.

37. "The spies of the post–Cold War era, he had observed, were enjoying the best of times and the worst of times. The Service had money to burn but where on earth was the fire?" (210).

38. Luxmore is literally ordering Osnard to find or create evidence of a conspiracy.

39. "Inventing and joining. Organizing, repairing. Perfecting. Enlarging out of recognition. Distorting. Making order out of confusion. So much to tell. So little time. Japs in every cupboard. The mainland Chinese abetting them. Pendel flying" (285).

40. It is clear that the committee has no real confidence in Luxmore, who Hatry calls "the arsehole who screwed up the Falklands operation for us single-handed" (302). When Hatry asks Cavendish if Luxmore's report is true, he replies, "True *enough*, Chief. . . . True in *parts*. Not sure about its shelf-life" (302). Hatry tosses the report back to Cavendish and says of the Americans: "Well at least they'll know the fucking way this time" (302).

41. "Sounded discreet alarm bells in the City and the oil companies, cuddled up to the imbecile Conservative right . . . conjured visions of an eleventh-hour crusade before the election . . . made the same pitch in a different language to the Opposition. . . . made us *aware* . . . turned rumour into received certainty by the ingenious use of arm's length columnists . . . not only on the Hatry-owned channels but on rival channels too—since nothing is more predictable than the media's parroting of its own fictions and the terror of each competitor that it will be scooped by the others, whether or not the story is true" (300).

42. "Our man, meaning our leader. Our puppet. Our mascot" (310).

43. "From a silted diplomatic backwater we shall become the hottest post in the ratings. Promotion, medals, notice of the most flattering kind will overnight be ours" (320).

44. Maltby concludes: "A golden future stretches ahead of us. The crime in such cases is to waver" (328).

45. Maltby, in the midst of a midlife crisis, needs money for a divorce settlement and to make a play for a young colleague he lusts after. Stormont's wife is seriously ill and needs expensive treatment.

46. Although all are driven primarily by greed (with Stormont's altruistically inspired), the men construct a romantic aura that is ironically expressed by the code name they had given themselves—the Buchaneers.

47. By the time Pendel informs Osnard of Mickie's "professional shooting," Osnard has already had his suspicions that Pendel was conning him confirmed by Pendel's wife (who had just learned the nature of his activities herself). But he continues to play along with the con by reporting to Luxmore that Mickie had been killed in a "professional wet job" (372). His last words are, "Chaps back home are getting out the war drums" (373).

48. Norman Rush (1996:11) suggests that the narrative has a two-tiered moral structure: at the top are "the Machiavels, the conscious servants of immoral power," which he contrasts with the pawns at the bottom, who collaborate in the evil done, "but they do so under coercion or out of misplaced love or loyalty to particular friends or lovers." This reflects a popular misunderstanding of Machiavelli, who advised the Prince that only during the founding of a regime do the ends justify the means. My thanks to Joe Romano for calling my attention to this point.

49. Similarly, the legendary American football coach, Vincent Lombardi, is reputed to have said, "Show me a good loser and I'll show you a loser" (Robert Lekachman, 1984:32).

50. John le Carré, interviewed by Scott Simon (1996). As indicated in the Introduction and chapters 2 and 3, which were written before the publication of the Rush review, I am convinced that le Carré has exceptional empathy for his Jewish (and in the case of Pendel, partly Jewish) characters. I firmly believe Rush's accusation to be baseless and a case of overzealous symbolic interpretation, a malady common to both anthropologists and literary critics. Subsequent correspondence with Cornwell

on the subject reaffirms and gives further personal evidence to support my conclusion. I find his explanation to Plimpton (1997:69) very convincing. He concludes: "It is the one issue in my life on which I may say I have a clean record."

51. John le Carré, interviewed by Robert McNeill (1980). This appears to contradict Beene's (1992:15) assertion that characters who "balance thought and action," like Smiley, "destroy their spirits."

52. Barber (1977:44; emphasis added).

53. I am grateful to Eric Aronoff for pointing this out. As mentioned in the Introduction, I leave the discussion of genre to the experts.

54. Albert Bandura, Claudio Barbaranelli, Gian Vittorio Caprara, and Concertta Pastorelli (1996). See also Albert Bandura (1990).

55. The question of consciousness is one that only le Carré can answer and he's not telling.

56. Literary critics such as Crehan are no more forthcoming in acknowledging their ideological biases than are novelists.

57. William Shakespeare, *Hamlet, Prince of Denmark,* act III, scene IV.

58. Michael Waltzer (1992) also postulates universal moral principles, for example, that civilians should never be targeted. My thanks to Yael Aronoff for the reference.

Chapter 5

1. John le Carré interviewed by Mark Phillips (1996:25).

2. This holds even more for those who interpret his work to others. Cornwell very kindly but firmly refused my requests for an interview and to comment on my analysis of his work. He claims that he has never read any of the analyses of his work: "I will provide the stories, and others can provide the interpretations. For me to attempt both functions would ultimately do us both out of a job" (personal communication June 23, 1996). This position is elaborated in le Carré's "What Every Writer Wants" (1965).

3. Wallace (1985:6).

4. "Confront me with a busload of bank clerks and I will spin you any tale: . . . I will regale you with anything but the truth. But a horse worries me; he threatens me with truths that are eternal, incorruptible and objective; a horse unlike man, is Nature, and Nature, in my book, is to be taken very slowly, a little at a time" (le Carré, 1968:4).

5. In an interview with Melvyn Bragg (1988:143). On another occasion, le Carré (1965:145) states that a "writer makes order out of the anarchy of his heart."

6. McCullin "reminded me of my own feelings about being interviewed: how, long ago, I had set up my defenses which today only the stray shot penetrates. How I developed my stock responses to recurring bloody silly questions from even sillier people, a whole handful of bland and seemingly

confessive phrases to fill their notebooks. *For my own protection*" (17; emphasis added).

7. These are almost the exact words used to describe both Smiley and Gadi Becker.

8. Le Carré is attracted to the metaphor of a pendulum to describe the personality swings of the artist and the spy. In *The Russia House* (102), he mentions that Barley Blair is a pendulum. He names the main character of *The Tailor of Panama,* Harry Pendel. As Kurt Jensen (1996) observes, "His name just one, hesitant '-um' from a full trio of swinging syllables."

9. There are many other commonalties. "He's careful about whatever reward he gets, he conserves gratefully, and with a sort of wonder. Nobody is ever going to put him back where he came from. As a matter of fact, the same goes for me, yet again" (14).

10. George Plimpton (1997:73).

11. Le Carré humorously describes himself on horseback, "while he strung together thoughts that would make the world, if not hold its breath, then at least chew more thoughtfully on its olive" ("A Writer and a Gentleman," 1968:4).

12. I vividly remember visiting a friend in Amsterdam whose parents, German Jews—the sole survivors, in their entire family, of the Holocaust—proudly displayed on their mantel the picture of the father in his World War I German army uniform, with decorations for bravery conspicuously showing on his chest.

13. Fiedler and Leamas develop a liking for each other. Eventually, Leamas tries to protect Fiedler as well as Liz but in so doing dooms them both, which, in turn, seals his fate as well.

14. Lewis (1985:76) also considers Leamas cynical: "It may be necessary in a hopelessly fallen world to employ what is foul to prevent something even worse: the Cold War is preferable to a third world war." Depending on one's position, this might also be considered a skeptical rather than a cynical position.

15. Frank N. Magill (1984:1613) makes a similar argument: "Leamas has a sharp-edged cynicism, but when he meets Liz, a devoted but naïve Communist, . . . he feels for her, believing that she can give him 'faith in ordinary life.' She is his tender spot; she also becomes his Achilles heel."

16. Neither all of his Jewish characters are victims, nor are all of his victims Jews. As I mentioned earlier, Le Carré (1966:5) states that he uses Jewish characters to "engage our protective instincts." Homberger (1986:42) notes le Carré's "considerable insight and sympathy" in his portrayal of Jews.

17. What is a nice Jewish communist doing attending church? The two most logical explanations are either that le Carré goofed, which I seriously doubt, or that this is a literary device to indicate that her attachments are more emotional than intellectual. A third possibility is that she simply enjoyed the ritual of the services. Liz appears to be a prototype for Charlie, in *The Little Drummer Girl.* Charlie, however, is much more fully developed in the novel and, unlike Liz, survives her disillusionment.

18. In an extremely rare slip, le Carré has Fiedler (a Jew) smile at Liz "as if in recognition of her race" (226). No Jew, especially not a German Jew, would think of Judaism in racial terms—especially after the Holocaust.

19. Magill (1984:1613) reminds us that both Leamas and Liz "are betrayed by the men and institutions in whom they have faith and hope, and to whom they have given their loyalty."

20. Chapman Pincher (1987) also notes the vulnerability of the young. See chapters 15 and 16 for his analysis of personality traits and defects of character (respectively) of traitors.

21. In chapter 3 I discussed the "second vow" in which Avery (and others) overcame skepticism by affirming their faith in the Department. Avery, like a doubting cleric, was desperate "to abdicate his conscience in order to discover God" (103).

22. Like Avery, Cornwell read German at Oxford. Le Carré seems fond of this quotation from Goethe indicating that actions speak louder than words. For example, he has Leamas repeat the phrase he had heard from Smiley in *The Spy Who Came in from the Cold*. In *The Russia House* (109), a minor character named Walter creates a variation on the theme: "In the beginning is not the word, not the deed, not the silly serpent. In the beginning was *why?*" He is after the motive.

23. I discuss this, among other aspects of tradecraft, in chapter 7.

24. Wolfe (1987:142), with considerable understatement, concludes: "Spying appeals to motives deeper than reason or common sense can ever probe."

25. Wolfe (1987:144) incorrectly identifies him as "West German Chancellor." Had he succeeded in achieving this high office, it would have given a very different tone to the plot. Karfeld is like the French right-wing populist leader le Pen, except that Karfeld had committed crimes against humanity during the Nazi era.

26. Lumley then asks Turner about his wife and suggests he forgive her—implying that she had been unfaithful, which we learn, much later, she has been repeatedly, like Smiley's Ann.

27. This is reminiscent of a comment attributed to George Bernard Shaw—that a man who has never been a socialist by the time he is twenty has no heart, but if he remains one after forty he has no brain.

28. This links him with romantics like Leamas, Leiser, Prideaux, Westerby, and Blair. But his strong absolutist tendencies linked him to Turner and with the likes of Frey, Elsa Fenan, Karla, Goethe, and Pettifer.

29. Haydon is a prototype of the personality type that le Carré characterizes as the hollow man, the fragmented personality, and the chameleon. This prototype is more fully elaborated in Pym, *A Perfect Spy,* and in Pendel, *The Tailor of Panama.*

30. I remind the reader that Philby was the real-world model for the fictional Haldane. It is noteworthy that le Carré declined to meet with Philby when he was in Russia because he was disgusted with Philby's "monstrous treason" (Kucherawy, 1989:55).

31. Wolfe (1987:147) suggests that many of le Carré's characters suffer an ontological dislocation: "Knowing *where* you are means nothing unless you know *who* you are."

32. This concentration on personalities is strongly criticized by some (e.g., Clive James, 1977), and praised by others (e.g., Lewis, 1985), who quotes several rave reviews of it, and especially Wolfe (1987:227), who calls it le Carré's "most ambitious and perhaps best book."

33. Barley (1986:125) provides excellent insight into this relationship. Beene (1992:101) notes: "Whereas Leamas falls victim because he knows neither parents nor viable love, Westerby falls because he knows, through his father, only bankrupt love. . . . Left emotionally adrift and isolated by this shiftless father, young Westerby cannot sustain himself."

34. Wolfe (1987:201).

35. Wolfe (1987:213) observes: "A woman with whom he has spent only four hours, which she filled with lies, evasions, and transparent pseudochic; a woman, moreover, so vacuous that, since coming to the Orient, she has passed from hand to outlaw hand. . . . He never judges her accurately at all." This is an extreme manifestation of the maxim that love is blind.

36. Edwards (1988:54) claims that Westerby, as well as Jim Prideaux, are superior in their ethical decisions to Smiley. Since Jim murdered Haydon, preventing Smiley from trading him for British agents held by the Soviets, his act condemned fellow agents to many years of imprisonment. In the text and in note 39 I compare the ethical implications of Jerry's and Smiley's actions.

37. As Lewis (1985:146–7) points out, because he served as an officer in World War II, he must have been a least fifty when the action in the novel takes place.

38. To be fair, Jerry is obviously a much more complicated character. For example, he explains why he faces danger: "Sometimes you do it to save face, . . . other times you do it because you haven't done your job unless you've scared yourself to death. Other times again, you go in order to remind yourself that survival is a fluke. But mostly you go because others go—for machismo—and because in order to belong you must share" (341).

39. Panek (1987:45) even claims that Smiley wins through Westerby: "Jerry's quixotic love for Lizzie and his attempts to protect the Ko brothers define him . . . [as he] acts to protect the ideal." In other words, Smiley, the teacher, succeeds because Jerry, his student, surpasses him. In this reader's eyes, the student still falls far short of the teacher. Rather, I agree with Beene (1992:103) that Westerby ends "as an adventure hero flawed by dubious commitment and a misguided, immature honor. He disappoints; le Carré gives him opportunities for growth, only to have Jerry sidestep them."

40. James Boyd White (1994:213) describes a character in Jane Austin's *Mansfield Park* as lacking "a central self, capable of attachment, feeling, and judgement. He lacks reality and depth as a person."

41. I place Palfrey in this category because he became a double agent operating as a spy for Darker, his boss in Intelligence, as well as for Rex Goodhew, the high-ranking civil servant who is attempting to curtail the power of his intelligence agency.

42. The main cause of her suicide, an overpowering sense of guilt (tragically common among survivors), does not easily fit into any of the categories.

43. Hugh McIlvaney (1983:21), who spent two days interviewing him, sums up the consensus of those who know him well that "David Cornwell . . . is a fascinating and, above all, an intricate personality."

44. "According to attachment theory, there is no direct link between parents' early attachment experiences and their parenting behavior. Past attachment experiences are always filtered through the current mental representation of attachment in influencing parenting behavior and the construction of new attachment relationships. The current attachment representation is formed not only on the basis of the early attachment experiences, but also influenced by later relationships" (Marinus H. van Ijzendoorn and Marian J. Bakermans-Kranenburg, (1997).

45. Frank Wisner served as the first head of covert operations from 1948 to 1958, when he was committed for psychotic mania to a psychiatric hospital. He committed suicide in 1965 (Fromkin, 1996:171). Additional real world examples are discussed in chapter 8.

46. Interview with Truehart (1989:D3).

47. They do not express multiple personality syndrome, in which individuals reputedly switch back and forth between two or more established personalities. See David Cohen (1996).

48. The exceptional chameleon who seems to have a genuine chance to survive coming to terms with life is Charlie.

49. Hugh McIlvanney (1983:21).

50. Charlotte told McIlvanney: "We didn't speak for two years after he refused to attend father's memorial services. But now I realise that what he did then was honest and right. I've become tremendously fond of him."

51. "Spying on My Father" (1986:33; emphasis added). He admits that another mistake was "to separate my relationship with Ronnie from my involvement in the world of intelligence to which, by my mid-20s, I had escaped. Not only did I omit this side of the story, I was even stupid enough not to recognise that my shadowy struggles with the demons of communism might, at least in part, be the continuation of my secret war with Ronnie by other means" (33–34).

52. Ibid.

53. Le Carré puts similar fantasies of killing his father in the thoughts of his surrogate, Magnus Pym in *A Perfect Spy*.

54. "Spying on My Father" (1986:34). In a later interview with Thom Schwarz (1987:21), le Carré says, "I was prepared to release parts of my life, . . . because I don't want to draw on those resources any more. I was prepared to spend that amount of capital, if you will. What I've blown I

suppose I've done with calculation, but I certainly haven't finished my armory." As Gary O'Connor says in his revised biography *Ralph Richardson: An Actor's Life* (1997), "He wants to hoard all of himself, for that is the power of his acting. It is like Philoctetes and his bow. He mustn't give away the source of his power, for if he does, one of the arrows will leap out and wound his own flesh. (quoted in the *New York Times* October 26, 1997, 4.)

55. Personal communication, August 17, 1997.
56. One could hardly expect him to take the time to engage in the self-analysis an answer to this question would require, even if he were inclined to do so, while "in the middle of a new book."
57. See Hayes (1990:113–39).

Chapter 6

1. This book was a particularly useful reference work in writing this chapter. All references to Monaghan in this chapter are to this volume unless otherwise noted.
2. The Circus also ironically refers to the aura of unreality that characterizes much of its activities—a circus represents a world quite apart from everyday reality.
3. This description is by Steed-Aspery *(Call For the Dead,* 13). Another of the old guard, Jebedee, calls Maston the first man "to play power tennis at Wimbleton" (12). Sauerberg (1984:122) points out how Maston's "desk implies superficiality of values and domination by trivia."
4. The works of Morton Halpern, particularly *Bureaucratic Politics and Foreign Policy* (1974), and of Graham Allison, particularly *Essence of Decision* (1971), are instructive on bureaucratic politics as they relate to foreign policy.
5. This is similar to Graham Allison's distinction among types of bureaucratic politics. He differentiates the failure of bureaucracies to implement policy because of inadequate procedures from a failure caused by competition among bureaucrats. My thanks to Yael Aronoff for drawing my attention to this point.
6. Pat M. Holt (1995:31); Leslie Susser (1980:10–14).
7. Control is characterized by Leamas in *The Spy Who Came in from the Cold* by his "affected detachment . . . fusty conceits . . . milk and water smile . . . elaborate diffidence . . . [and] banality" (21).
8. Loch K. Johnson (1989:263) quotes Deputy Director of the CIA John McMahon's remarks at CIA headquarters on June 12, 1984: "Only four to five out of 160 U.S. embassies around the world are supportive of the CIA mission."
9. John Atkins (1984:176).
10. Atkins (1984:184) also suggests that "Leclerc is possibly clinically insane."
11. Dobel (1988:202) sums him up: "Percy Alleline, the head of the Circus after Control, represents the quintessential distortion of the craft by careerism. A consummate egoist, he lacks Haydon's genius or commitment.

A Maston protégé with a perpetual sense of undervalued worth, he succeeded primarily by his social ease in 'smart set' and a blunt and vigorous style that periodically produced results."

12. A similarly radical restructuring of the CIA by William Casey during the first administration of President Ronald Reagan is discussed in chapter 8.

13. A slightly different slant on this period of factional infighting in the Circus is given by Ned in *The Secret Pilgrim* (100).

14. Lacon says, "The Minister would rather live with a damp roof than see his castle pulled down by *outsiders*" (73; emphasis added). The rivalry between British Internal Security Service (MI5) and the external Secret Intelligence Service (MI6) is analogous to that between the United States Federal Bureau of Investigation (FBI) and the Central Intelligence Agency (CIA). Israel's Shin Bet (internal security) and the Mossad (intelligence) have had similar rivalries.

15. Control posts Alleline to the mundane job of directing the Nursery, where young spies were trained. Alleline builds political alliances, however, by playing golf with Conservative parliamentarians, including Miles Sercombe, who becomes the minister responsible for the Circus. Control's opinion of Alleline's opportunism is that "Percy Alleline would sell his mother for a knighthood and this service for a seat in the House of Lords" (133). Whereas Control is hardly an impartial observer, several of his colleagues (and it would seem le Carré) share his opinion.

16. Wolfe (1987:199) points out that the reference in the first chapter of the novel to "the shotgun marriage with the cousins" "alludes to the Circus's loss of options."

17. I emphasize the pervasiveness of the use of *balance* by Smiley and other heroes whom le Carré intends to represent a moral center in his novels. In this case, it is instructive because it refers to his political tactics rather than his ethical position. It would seem that the two are not unrelated, however.

18. Lacon, as the link between the Circus and the government, was determinant in shifting support from Smiley to Enderby. A self-effacing prig, Lacon is pompous, deceitful, but effective. He supports Smiley's hunt for the mole and efforts to rebuild the Circus, only to betray him through his alliance with Enderby. Dobel (1988:203) seems to bend over backward to be fair in concluding that "in that strange borderland between professionals and elected representatives, Lacon did well." Dobel's (1988:203–4; emphasis added) evaluation of Saul Enderby is only slightly harsher: "He represents the *triumph of bureaucratic rationalization over craft and art.* . . . Enderby represents the future. His ideals are manufactured and self-serving, his vision cramped, and he possess little sensitivity to the nuance of craft."

19. Sauerberg (1984:125) points out that Lacon in *Smiley's People* "develops into a figure who has begun to doubt the values of which he is supposed to be the incarnation . . . and the reader's impression of the crumbling Establishment is thus reinforced."

20. Two incidents with tape recordings are reminiscent of Richard Nixon's White House. Lauder Strickland, a singularly unpleasant member of the Circus who is a sycophantic aid to Lacon in this case, erases the taped conversation in which Vladimir, the murdered agent, had urgently requested an emergency meeting with Max, Smiley's code-name. In the other incident, the hidden microphones in the safe house where Smiley met Lacon and Strickland (unbeknownst to them) had been turned on by the very young and inexperienced Mostyn. Mostyn had been on duty during the lunch break of the desk officer when Vladimir's call came in. He turned on the recorder because he had been expecting to meet Vladimir. Consequently, the transcripts of the meeting were inadvertently transcribed and circulated in the Circus.

21. Le Carré also hints at the Soviet-style bureaucratic politics with which Karla, Smiley's nemesis, must contend: "Karla is known as a comrade of high standards of integrity, and for this reason has many enemies among the ranks of the self-indulgent" (264). Enderby, glancing at Smiley, says with irony: "We all spin the ropes that hang us, right, George?" (264). Le Carré also vividly portrays the political constraints with which Kurtz must contend in *The Little Drummer Girl*. For example, his relationship with his Chief, Misha Gavron, "was more that of a gruffly tolerated outsider than of a trusted equal. He had no tenure, but mysteriously sought none. His power base was rickety and forever shifting, according to whom he had last offended in his quest for expedient allegiance" (28). See 30, 39, 47, 254, 350, and 382 for additional examples of how he circumvented rivals, negotiated political support, and formed alliances within the German secret service.

22. Chapter 8 picks up this theme in a discussion of the CIA.

23. Anyone who has ever sat on such a committee (and anyone who has worked in any bureaucratic institution long enough is bound to have done so) will immediately recognize the astuteness of this observation.

24. Except Gadi Becker.

25. "There was a time when Langley had a lot of Bob's sort, and was the better for it" (94).

26. We are told that "Clive considered nothing on its merits. He considered who was in favour of something and who was against it. Then he considered who was the better ally" (152).

27. Perhaps Clive heard Walter's comparison of Clive to a Russian: "A verifiable fully paid-up, spineless arse-licking toady, meeting his norms and earning his medals and privileges. Who does that remind us of? No one. Certainly not our own dear Clive" (189).

28. Characterizing the Americans, the narrator says: "And my goodness, were they industrious! If numbers, money and sheer endeavour alone could have produced intelligence, the Agency would have had it by the cartload—except that, alas, the human head is not a cart, and there is such a thing as unintelligence as well. And how deeply they yearned to be loved!" (231).

29. Russell Sheriton, who had been promoted six years previously to head of Soviet operations, is the only American and CIA officer portrayed by le Carré who might be categorized as a skeptic, as I have defined the term.

30. He expands on these views in his interview with Viktor Orlik (1989:28), comparing the current experiment in the Soviet Union on a scale with 1917: "Great and wonderful changes can take place." He says, "My last, beautiful love is *glasnost* and *perestroika.*" (30). His optimism is eloquently expressed by the statement that "for the first time in my life I have felt that, together, *we can change the way people think*. . . . It is you [Russia led by Gorbachev] who are leading in the race to eliminate the enemy image. It is a brilliant diplomatic initiative, which excites and thrills the imagination of mankind" (31; emphasis added).

31. This is one of the few exceptions in which a "bad guy" loses and a "good guy" wins in bureaucratic political infighting in le Carré's work.

32. My thanks to Eric Aronoff for this observation.

33. It reminds me of F. M. Cornford (1908). Gordon Johnson (1994) provides full commentary and explanations in addition to the original text.

34. He is a top civil servant, similar in rank and function (although not in character) to Lacon in earlier novels.

35. The religious imagery in le Carré is associated with specific personality characteristics. For example, in *The Night Manager,* Burr refers to Ned's "Calvinist disposition," meaning his tendency to moralize and search his conscience. In the above quotation, Goodhew's Anglican high-minded zeal for reform implies a quality of religious crusade.

36. Tim Weiner (1995:80) quotes the uneasiness of senior Justice Department officials in liaisons with the CIA: "The agency usually has another agenda. When we don't know if we're getting the whole truth, it's a little unsettling." He quotes CIA deputy general counsel, Dawn Eilenberger, as saying that sharing secrets creates "a constant tension. That tension is never going to go away."

37. "The River House is represented by an enormous Englishwoman in perfect curls and Thatcherite twin set, known universally as Darling Katie and officially as Mrs. Katherine Handyside Dulling, Economic Counselor of the British Embassy in Washington. For ten years Darling Katie has held the golden key to Whitehall's special relationship with America's numberless intelligence agencies . . . —from the sane to the harmlessly mad to the dangerously ridiculous—the secret overworld of American might is Katie's parish, to explore, bludgeon, bargain with and win to her celebrated dinner table" (108). She feigns outrage at Goodhew's having called her a femagogue. "Me! A *femagogue!* Isn't that the most politically incorrect thing you ever *heard?* I'm a mouse, you beast. A wilting violet! And calls himself a Christian!" (108–9).

38. The composition of this committee is similar to the smaller Planning and Application Committee, which is responsible for launching the operation

that eventually leads to the second American invasion of Panama in *The Tailor of Panama*.

39. Goodhew reports: "But he did rather imply there was a knighthood at the end of the rainbow, which will be nice for Hester" (328). It is doubtful, given his actions until then, that Goodhew was actually bribed by the promise of knighthood to sell out Burr. He clearly lost his battle with Darker and rather than resign on principle, which was an option, probably rationalized that he could do more good in the new post than in retirement.

40. Since Burr had already lost control of the operation, his "sacrifice" was meaningless. Yet, le Carré enigmatically writes that Burr hates himself when he strikes the deal that saves Pine's life (401). Cornwell declined my request to explain why.

Chapter 7

1. He told Plimpton (1997:60), "What we want is not authenticity; it is credibility. In order to be credible, you have to dress the things in the clothes of authenticity." Homberger (1986:28) notes that "in the grey world of espionage the yardstick of 'plausibility' was itself problematic."

2. Peter Mass notes that among his informants in the world of espionage, most of whom are inveterate readers of spy fiction, "Notably absent on this select best-seller list was John le Carré. When I asked all my informants about him, I received mumbled, evasive replies. I suspect it's because he perhaps comes too close to the actuality of their experience." On the other hand, Miles Copeland is quoted as saying that le Carré is the favorite writer of British spooks: "They like the way he captures the mood of their world, its internal rivalries and the personal problems that get tangled up with their professional lives." Cited in Donald McCormick and Katy Fletcher (1990:66). Unfortunately, they give no source for the quotation from Copeland.

3. Homberger (1986:25) reports that the "head of Israeli Military Intelligence once said that the books of John le Carré were virtual textbooks for their agents."

4. W. T. Bartoszewski (1989).

5. In dramatic contrast, MI5 advertised in the *Guardian* and other leading British newspapers in May 1997 for new recruits. Sergei Bogdanov, head of press relations for the Russian Federal Security Service (FSS, formerly the KGB) was intrigued by this innovation. The FSS has a new innovation as well: it has established a new hotline for people to phone in tips (David Hearst, 1997:3).

6. Markus Wolf, head of East German foreign intelligence for thirty-three years, was the master of the "honey-trap," le Carré's term for the use of blackmailing individuals after trapping them in sexually compromising situations (Markus Wolf with Anne Mc Elvoy, 1997).

7. Homberger (1986:93) points out that Charlie had three families: the radical acting troupe, the Mossad team, and the Palestinians: "Each offers to Charlie an identity, a place within, and a role to play in the real world designed to fill the nothingness which was her self-identity."

8. Perhaps that is the reason that one Israeli intelligence agency is rumored to use attractive young women in the initial interviewing of potential young male recruits.

9. "A man who lives a part, not to others but alone, is exposed to obvious psychological dangers. In itself, the practice of deception is not particularly exacting; it is a matter of experience, of professional *expertise,* it is a facility most of us can acquire. But while a confidence trickster, a play-actor or a gambler can return from his performance to the ranks of his admirers, the secret agent enjoys no such relief. For him, deception is first a matter of self-defense. He must protect himself not only from without but from within, and against the most natural of impulses" (149).

10. One of my former students, a retired New York City policeman who spent most of his career under cover investigating allegations of police corruption, suggested this accounts for the high rate of alcoholism, divorce, and suicide among policemen in general but particularly among those involved in internal intelligence.

11. "We're the dead clerk from Dorking. Saint George, that's who we are. . . . there's a part of her knew damn well it was all baloney. That's where *you* come in. That's where your fieldman is ever at the ready. Oh, yes! We're keepers of the faith, lads. When it shakes, we stiffen it. When it falls, we've got our arms stretched out to catch it. . . . Be the faith ever so crackpot, Your Graces, never despise it. We've precious little else to offer them these days. Amen" (196).

12. Some critics have concluded that Smiley is a snob because of this and other related passages. I think not. He is simply irritated because Rode pretends to be what he isn't. Smiley does not respect those who attempt to hide their backgrounds.

13. For his interview with Worthington, Smiley permits himself the fiction of being happily married but does not go so far as to create fictional children (211).

14. Drake Ko had given Elizabeth Worthington, a.k.a. Lizzie Worth, the name of his beloved foster mother.

15. The narrator relates: "At heart di Salis was a loner: no one knew him, except Connie perhaps; and if Connie didn't care for him, then no one liked him either. Socially, he was discordant and frequently absurd. But neither did anyone doubt his hunter's will" (253).

16. Clive informs Palfrey that "*Langley* are taking over the case." When Palfrey asks if Ned knows "you've made them a present of his joe?," Clive replies he'll be told later (265).

17. In Martin Buber's (1958) terms, these are "I-It" rather than "I-Thou" relationships.

Chapter 8

1. Helms was director of the CIA under Presidents Lyndon Johnson and Richard Nixon. Quoted by Tim Weiner, 1995:66–7.

2. An excellent example is the use of videos and scripts of the British television political satire *Yes Minister* to educate visiting European civil servants in courses designed to familiarize them with the British civil service during the 1980s and early 1990s. I am grateful to Anne Stevens, professor of European Studies at the University of Kent at Canterbury, for this information, provided in a personal communication to her brother, Robert Ross (my colleague from Leiden University at NIAS) on June 9, 1997.

3. Burridge (1992:16) says le Carré "is to intelligence as the 19th-century Luddites were to the industrial—revolution—a rabid foe of technology. . . . He portrays intelligence technologies as peculiarly—and offensively—American." The article was originally published in *Cryptology,* a journal of the National Security Agency responsible for SIGNET in the United States. It was later reprinted in *Studies in Intelligence,* published by the CIA. Significantly, Loch K. Johnson (1989:261), a leading academic expert on intelligence, recommends among his suggested reforms: "Less fascination with intelligence hardware and more emphasis on HUMINT."

4. He says, "In my view, Markus Wolf knowingly served a completely corrupt and disgusting regime, and there was no justification whatever for the methods he used" (George Plimpton, 1997:74).

5. My own translation from Bik's review of the Dutch edition of Wolf (1997:37).

6. I do not mean to imply that citizens of countries lacking democratic structures, procedures, and cultures should not be concerned with these issues. Le Carré, however, premises these key dilemmas in a democratic context. To the extent that citizens aspire for their states to become democratic (or more democratic), they will also share these concerns.

7. Pat M. Holt (1995:35) suggests that for some, this crusade became "a western counterpart of an Islamic *jihad* or holy war."

8. "People in this directorate do want a sense of direction, a sense of what the mission is, and I need to work hard to give it to them. . . . How do you take this supertanker and get it in the direction you want to put it?" (Weiner, 1995:84).

9. "I learned about *fabulation*—how to make reality fit our script . . . in watching the Russian Navy, how we made everything they did fit our script—not because we were dishonest but because we did not know that they had a different scenario. Not many of us had read Dostoevsky" (viii; emphasis added). Bathurst, a former U.S. Naval intelligence officer, has written the only book of which I am aware devoted to developing a theory of the role culture in shaping perception in intelligence analysis. Although an important pioneering work, it is marred by his tendency to reify the notion of culture.

10. "Rarely has the equivalent between secret service and the health of the society as a whole been so aggressively asserted" (Homberger, 1986:58). The current sad state of the CIA may reflect similarly on the American condition.

11. Sauerberg (1984:175).

12. Many critics consider le Carré to have a strong anti-American bias. He has consistently denied this. My reading is that many of his anti-American characters in British intelligence accurately reflect the jealousy and resentment against Americans that was fairly widespread among the British public in the middle and late sixties when I lived in England as a graduate student. Such sentiments do not necessarily reflect the author's feelings, which appear to have become more appreciative of the positive aspects of American society, particularly after two of his sons moved to the United States, which he now frequently visits.

13. Bathurst (1993:33) argues that "U.S. time tends to be solidly in the present."

14. Tim Weiner (1997:1) reports that "two successive directors of Central Intelligence, Robert Gates in 1992 and James Woolsey Jr. in 1993, publicly pledged that the Iran records would be made public . . . But they did not know there was virtually nothing left to open: almost all of the documents were destroyed in the early 1960s."

15. Lewis (1985:48) notes: "Le Carré certainly presents the English devotion to tradition as the opposite of life-enhancing, perhaps even a form of the death wish."

16. Bathurst (1993: 31–5).

17. For example, Anthony Lewis (1997:11) quotes former governor (of New York) Mario Cuomo's speech to the American College of Trial Lawyers: "Isn't America searching for something? . . . There's no hero, no heroine, no great cause, no soaring ideology. We are riddled with political answers that seem too shallow, too short-sighted, too explosive, too harsh. We need something real to believe in, to hold onto. Something deeper, stronger, grander that can help us deal with our problems by making us better than we are, instead of meaner, that can lift our aspirations instead of lowering them."

18. Uri Bar-Joseph (1995, chapter 6).

19. Tim Weiner (December 9, 1995:5).

20. Arthur S. Hulnick (1996:145–57).

21. David M. Barrett (1996), examining the central role of Senator Richard Russell (D-Ga.) during the Era of Trust, claims the contention that no effective Congressional oversight of the CIA existed in this period has not been proven. His preliminary findings suggest a highly individualized informal relationship between Russell, very few other congressmen, and various presidents and directors of the CIA during this era. Although Barrett's research suggests that Russell and isolated other individuals did provide a check of sorts on the CIA, he has yet to establish convincing evidence of

their effectiveness. In chapter 7 of his classic study, Harry Howe Ransom (1970) discusses the development of surveillance by Congress and the key role played by Russell in preventing expansion of this role during his long congressional career.

22. Amos Yoder (1996).

23. U. S. Senate, Select Committee to Study Governmental Operations with Respect to Intelligence Activities, *Alleged Assassination Plots Involving Foreign Leaders.* (Washington D.C.: U.S. Government Printing Office, November 20, 1973); Cited in Yoder (1996; emphasis added).

24. From his remarks during a presentation at a panel entitled "The New Intelligence: The Inner Workings of Reform," Convention of the International Studies Association, San Diego, April, 16–20, 1996. For his proposal for reforms of covert action and counterintelligence, see Johnson (1989:261–3).

25. Scholars in the field of international relations, when they concern themselves with such issues at all, tend to translate (and reduce) culture to psychological terms.

26. A major CIA success was the recruitment of Colonel Chang Hsien-Yi in the 1960s. He became deputy director of Taiwan's nuclear energy research institute. Chang defected with evidence of Taiwan's progress in building a bomb, which enabled the U.S. government to pressure Taiwan into halting its program to develop nuclear weapons (Tim Weiner, 1997:A7).

27. American embassies abroad have also become terrorist targets—most recently in Kenya and Tanzania—prompting a U.S. declaration of war against terrorism.

28. George Plimpton (1997:64).

29. Jim Hoagland (1997:8). Hoagland notes that the Senate missed a golden opportunity to question George J. Tenet, who played a significant role in these efforts in his role as a member of President Clinton's National Security Council staff and then as deputy director of the CIA, in his confirmation hearings for the directorship of the agency.

30. Ash (1997:14).

31. Pitt was sentenced to twenty-seven years in federal prison. The other FBI agent, Richard Miller, is presently serving a twenty-year sentence in prison.

32. His wife, who was an FBI employee at the time, cooperated in the sting operation.

33. David Johnston and Tim Weiner (1996) report that he was tailed driving with men in a car bearing diplomatic license plates registered to the Russian embassy, spent money lavishly ($32,000 in cash in a single day), and copied secret documents on his notebook computer, which he failed to delete from the hard drive, thereby leaving concrete evidence of his treason. His final assignment was as head instructor at the CIA training camp outside Williamsburg, Virginia, and he betrayed the names of his trainees to the Russians. He only came under suspicion after failing a routine lie-detector test in October and December 1995.

34. This was symbolized by the unprecedented joint press conference given by the director of the CIA, John Deutch, and the director of the FBI, Louis Freeh. Deutch emphasized that "the Russian intelligence services remain active in targeting not only the CIA but other U.S. national security organizations" (Brian Knowlton [1996]).

35. Reprinted in the *International Herald Tribune,* November 21, 1996, 8.

36. "Killers, Scoundrels and Spies," August 27, 1995, 14E.

37. Reprinted in the *International Herald Tribune,* December 19, 1996, 8.

38. Ransom (1970, chapter 5) discusses seventeen other agencies in his classic study. Johnson (1989:15) quotes a former deputy director of the CIA, Adm. Rufus Taylor, who referred to the various intelligence agencies as a "tribal federation."

39. Reported by Tim Weiner (May 16, 1996: A17).

40. Another trend in the intelligence community, which has become more pronounced in the aftermath of the Persian Gulf War, has been a shift in focus away from strategic intelligence servicing of the highest level of national political and military leaders to serving the tactical level of the military. Dave Aidekmann (1996), after a thoughtful consideration of the trend, concludes with concern: "The strategic intelligence capabilities that have been diminished through tacticalization should be maintained."

41. Ransom (1970:253) summarizes his prescriptions: "(a) organizational mistakes which have combined foreign information gathering and political action need to be repaired by surgery; (b) covert political operations should only be undertaken to prevent a direct threat to national security and as an alternative to overt military action; and (c) the President and State Department should exert effective political control over secret foreign operations at all times. Put another way, the President and the National Security Council must effectuate their authority to know what the intelligence establishment is doing and to control it."

42. Quoted as the epigraph to the Preface to this book.

43. Among the most frequently adduced causes of intelligence failure, Laqueur (1998:308) suggests that bias has been exaggerated, whereas ignorance, lack of political sophistication and judgement, lack of training and experience, "lack of imagination and the assumption that other people behave more or less as we do," the politicization of intelligence, bureaucratic thinking, incompetence, and self-deception are far more serious. Laqueur recommends "the recruitment of promising individuals, careful personnel evaluation, thorough assignment processes, extensive and systematic training in relevant subjects, a constant search for better means of collection, and the pursuit of efficiency with a minimum of bureaucratic procedure" (309).

44. Holt served on the staff of the U.S. Senate Foreign Relations Committee for twenty-seven years, including three as director. He is presently in charge of the committee's activities relating to intelligence.

45. "The most important checks on the abuse of power in a democracy are, in the end, the attitudes held by people in office and across the land." In

chapter 12 of his book, entitled *Pathways of Reform,* Johnson prescribes remedies for what he terms the "seven sins" of American intelligence: biased intelligence, disregarded intelligence, indiscriminate covert action, inadequate protection, misused counterintelligence, inadequate accountability, and indiscriminate collection. He observes that the first two are heavily influenced by personality factors. Johnson attributes the indiscriminate use of covert action to historical factors, particularly the tendency to see the Cold War in zero-sum terms (i.e., all or nothing—victory or defeat). The other "sins" are primarily influenced by bureaucratic factors and therefore susceptible to improvement through organizational reform. He gives an extended analysis of William Casey, director of Central Intelligence under President Reagan, as a negative example.

Chapter 9

1. Reprinted in Bloom (1987:17).
2. Although there are clearly roots in Greek tragedy, contemporary notions of self-consciousness and freedom of choice alter the nature of such dilemmas.
3. In a much earlier essay, "Wrong Man on Crete," le Carré expresses his frustration and lack of optimism with another intractable conflict: "I hated the political feeling about Cyprus because there was no bridge of reason on which to meet" (*Holiday,* 38, December 1965; 74–5).
4. The metaphor of the Israelis and Palestinians as Siamese twins was, to the best of my knowledge, first used by Arie "Lyova" Eliav, a pioneer of reconciliation between the two peoples. Unfortunately, they share a common heart, Jerusalem, which makes separation as dangerous as living together. See Aronoff and Aronoff (1998) for a brief discussion of Eliav's pioneering role in the peace process.
5. Le Carré told Robert McNeill (1989; emphasis added) that to survive, literature needs to "give us pleasure, and to give us relevance, and to provoke us, [and] must surely *promise some changes in its own time.*"
6. Barley (1986:22–3) makes this point particularly well.
7. One can detect the influence of the tradition from Locke to Mill (through Hume, Fergusson, Smith, and Bentham) in le Carré's liberalism.
8. Ash (1997:16) refers to Markus Wolf's "grandiose delusion" through which he excused his life's work in the infamous East German Stasi in terms of romantic rationalization: "It was all done for the good of the great cause."
9. Walter Laqueur (1993:6) observes: "Intelligence is not just the story of individual spies and defectors, it is the sum total of our knowledge about political, economic, and military trends in the outside world."
10. See, for example, Loch K. Johnson (1989). Betts (1978:78) recommends: "For the sake of clarity and acuity, the intelligence bureaucracy should be streamlined."

11. Unfortunately, almost immediately after taking office, the new government decided to postpone legislation on this most important issue. In the 1997 British election, le Carré endorsed the candidacy of the independent candidate Martin Bell, who ran on an anti-corruption platform. Bell's campaign diary, published as "The Accidental Hero" *The Guardian,* May 6, 1997, G2, 2–5, reveals him to be the kind of independent liberal spirit struggling against the Establishment who le Carré admires. Bell, a former correspondent for the BBC, became the first independent candidate elected to Parliament in nearly fifty years.

12. Uri Bar-Joseph (1996). See also Bar-Joseph (1995) and Susser (1998).

13. Cornwell writes "my grandfather A. E. F. Cornwell was a keen lay-preacher in the Baptist cause, my mother's elder brother Alec Glassy M.P. preached, I think in the Congregationalist cause, and all three husbands of my father's sisters dispersed themselves among the non-conformist pulpits of Parkstone and Poole" (personal communication to the author, May 29, 1997).

14. White (1994:304) writes: "the task of the writer is not so much to use words with preexisting meanings as to create a text that gives new meanings to the words within it; this in turn means that a text about authority does not simply point to the authority it invokes or resists but partly creates it."

15. Joseph Gochal, "The Myth of Smiley: Politics and the Writings of Albert Camus and John le Carré" (unpublished paper), astutely compares Smiley with Camus' absurd man.

Appendix

1. When a character has appeared in *Tinker, Tailor, Soldier, Spy; The Honourable Schoolboy;* and *Smiley's People,* the entry will be listed as the *Karla Trilogy.* For more extensive descriptions of some of these characters as well as a detailed history of the Circus, chronology of its operations, and definitions of some of le Carré's special spy jargon (which constitutes more than two hundred words and phrases), see Monaghan (1986).

References: Work Cited

Works by John le Carré, by Year of Publication

Novels

1961. *Call For the Dead.* Harmondsworth: Penguin.
1962. *A Murder of Quality.* New York: Bantam Books.
1963. *The Spy Who Came in from the Cold.* New York: Coward-McCann, Inc.
1965. *The Looking Glass War.* London: Heron Books.
1968. *A Small Town in Germany.* New York: Dell.
1972. *The Naive and Sentimental Lover.* New York: Alfred A. Knopf
1974. *Tinker, Tailor, Soldier, Spy.* New York: Bantam Books.
1977. *The Honourable Schoolboy.* New York: Alfred A. Knopf.
1979. *Smiley's People.* New York: Alfred A. Knopf.
1983. *The Little Drummer Girl.* New York: Alfred A. Knopf.
1986. *A Perfect Spy.* London: Hodder & Stoughton.
1989. *The Russia House.* New York: Alfred A. Knopf.
1990. *The Secret Pilgrim.* New York: Alfred A. Knopf
1993. *The Night Manager.* New York: Alfred A. Knopf.
1995. *Our Game.* New York: Alfred A. Knopf.
1996. *The Tailor of Panama.* London: Hodder & Stoughton.

Short Stories

1964. "You Can't Sack a College Boy." *Spectator,* 27 November: 699–700.
1967. "Dare I Weep, Dare I Mourn?" *Saturday Evening Post,* 28 January: 54, 56, 60.
1968. "What Ritual Is Being Observed Tonight?" *Saturday Evening Post,* No. 22, 2 November: 60, 62, 64–5.

Autobiographical Essays

1977. "In England Now." *New York Times Magazine,* 23 October, 34–5, 86–7.
1977. "England Made Me." *Observer,* 13 November, 25.
1986. "Spying on My Father." *Sunday Times,* 16 March, 33–5.

Nonfiction

1965. "What Every Writer Wants." *Harper's,* November, 142–5.

1965. "Wrong Man on Crete." *Holiday,* Vol. 38, December, 74–5.

1966. "To Russia, with Greetings: An Open Letter to the Moscow '*Literary Gazette.*'" *Encounter,* Vol. 26, No. 5, May, 3–6.

1966. "The Spy to End Spies: On Richard Sorge." *Encounter,* November, 88–9.

1968. "A Writer and a Gentleman." *Saturday Review,* 30 November, 4, 6.

1968. "Introduction." Bruce Page, David Leitch, and Phillip Knightley, *The Philby Conspiracy.* Garden City, NY: Doubleday.

1970. "Vocation in a World of Pain." *Sunday Times,* 25 October, 27.

1971. "Well Played, Wodehouse." *Sunday Times,* 10 October, 25.

1979. "An American Spy Story." Review of Thomas Powers, *The Man Who Kept Secrets. New York Times Book Review,* 14 October, 1, 46–8.

1979. "At Last, It's Smiley." *Sunday Telegraph Magazine,* No. 161, 21 October, 105, 108, 111, 114.

1980. "Siege." *Observer Review,* 1 June, 25.

1980. "Introduction." In Don McCullin (photographs), *Hearts of Darkness,* 9–21. London: Secker & Warburg.

1981. "Unlicensed to Quote." Letter to *The Times of London,* 17 March: 13.

1981. "World Service." Letter to *Times,* 1 July, 15.

1982. "Optical Illusion." Letter to *Times,* 22 March, 11.

1982. "Memories of a Vanished Land." *Observer Review,* 13 June, 9–10.

1983. "Exiles in the White Hotel." *Observer Review,* 26 June, 25–6.

1983. "The Betrayal." *Observer Review,* 3 July, 23–4.

1984. "Hughes of Hong Kong. *Sunday Times,* 8 January, 9.

1986. "Don't Be Beastly to Your Secret Service." *Sunday Times Review,* 26 March, 41–2.

1986. "The Clandestine Muse." *Johns Hopkins Magazine,* August, 11–16.

1989. "Why I Came in from the Cold." *New York Times,* 29 September, OP-ED.

1993. "Tinpots, Saviors, Lawyers, Spies." *New York Times,* 4 May, OP-ED.

1996. "Quel Panama!" *New York Times Magazine,* 13 October, 52–55.

1996. "The Tailor of Panama." Letter to the editor, *New York Times Book Review,* 3 November, 4, 22.

Interviews of John le Carré

Anonymous. 1996. "Running away from the Circus: Profile John le Carré." *Sunday Times,* 27 October.

Assouline, Pierre. 1986. "John le Carré: Spying on the Spymaster." *World Press Review,* August, 59–60.

Barber, Michael. 1977. "John le Carré: An Interrogation." *New York Times Book Review,* 25 September, 9, 44–5.

Blades, John. 1989. "Spy Novel Superpower." *Chicago Tribune,* 19 June, 1–2.

Bonfante, Jordan. 1964. "The Spy-Master Unmasked." *Life,* 28 February, 39–40, 42.

Boucher, Anthony. 1963. "Criminals at Large." *New York Times Book Review,* 8 September, 45.

Bragg, Melvyn. 1976. "The Things a Spy Can do—John le Carré Talking." *The Listener,* 27 January, 90.

———. 1983. "A Talk with John le Carré." *New York Times Book Review,* 13 March, 1, 22.

———. 1988. "*The Little Drummer Girl:* An Interview with John le Carré." In *The Quest For le Carré,* edited by Alan Bold, 129–43. New York: St. Martin's.

Cameron, James. 1974. "The Case of the Hot Writer." *New York Times Magazine,* 8 September, 55, 57, 59, 61, 64, 66, 68.

Chiu, Tony. 1980. "Behind the Best Sellers: John le Carré." *New York Times Book Review,* 6 January, 30.

Crutchley, Leigh. 1966. "The Fictional World of Espionage." *Listener,* 14 April, 548–9.

Davis, Douglas. 1997. "Smiley's Person." *Jerusalem Post Magazine,* 21 November, 19.

Dean, Michael. 1974. "John le Carré: The Writer Who Came in from the Cold." *Listener,* 5 September, 306–7.

Gelber, Alex, and Edward Behr. 1983. "A Stellar Spymaster Returns." *Newsweek,* 7 March, 40, 42–4.

Gross, Miriam. 1980. "The Secret World of John le Carré." *Observer Review,* 3 February, 33, 35.

———. 1980. "A Labyrinth of Espionage: On the Trail of a Master Spy Novelist." *World Press Review,* Vol. 27, No. 5, 62.

Hodgson, Godfrey. 1977. "The Secret Life of John le Carré: *Book World* Interview." *Washington Post Book World,* 9 October, E1, E6.

Isaacson, Walter, and James Kelly. 1993. "We Distorted Our Own Minds." *Time,* 5 July, 32–3.

Kanfer, Stefan, with Dean Fischer. 1977. "The Spy Who Came in for the Gold." *Time,* 3 October, 48–53.

King, Larry. 1995. "Interview With John le Carré." *Larry King Live,* CNN, August.

Kuchery, Dennis. "Romance in Russia: A Spy Novelist Comes in from the Cold." *Maclean's,* 19 June, 55.

Leitch, David. 1987. "The Ultimate Spy." *Sunday Times Magazine,* 13 September, 50–1.

Lelyveld, Joseph. 1986. "Le Carre's Toughest Case." *New York Times Magazine,* 16 March, 40, 42–6, 79, 90–1.

Mathews, Tom. 1989. "In from the Cold." *Newsweek,* June 5, 52–7.

McIlvanney, Hugh. 1983. "The Secret Life of John le Carré." *Observer,* 6 March, 18–19, 21–22.

McNeill, Robert. 1980. Interview of John le Carré. *McNeill-Lehrer Report,* 16 August.

———. 1989. Interview of John le Carré. *McNeill-Lehrer Newshour,* May.

O'Connor, John J. 1985. "Le Carré, on Channel 13, Discusses Himself and His Writing." *New York Times,* 12 July, C26.

Orlik, Viktor. 1989. "Spies Who Come in from the Cold War: A Session between John le Carré and the Soviets." *World Press Review,* Vol. 36, No. 10: 28 October, 30–1.

Osnos, Peter. 1983. "Le Carré's Drumbeat: Defending His 'Equation' on the Palestinians." *Washington Post,* 6 April, B1, B4.

Phillips, Mark. 1996. "In From the Cold." *CBS Sunday Morning,* CBS News, 17 November, transcript by Burrelle's Information Services, 21–5.

Plimpton, George. 1997. "John le Carré: The Art of Fiction CXLIX." *The Paris Review,* No. 143, summer, 50–74.

Rodgers, Byron. 1982. "Closing the File." *Radio Times,* 18–24 September, 90.

Ross, Andrew. 1996. "Master of the Secret World: The *Salon Interview/* John le Carré." http://www.salon 1999.com/weekly/lecarre961021.htm.

Sanoff, Alvin P. 1989. "The Thawing of the Old Spymaster." *U.S. News and World Report,* 19 June, 59–61.

Schiff, Stephen. 1989. "The Secret Life of John le Carré." Condensed from *Vanity Fair. Reader's Digest-Canadian,* November, 63–7.

Schwarz, Thom. 1987. "Inside Books: John le Carré on Perfect Spies and Other Characters." *Writer's Digest,* February, 20–1.

Simon, Scott. 1996. "Interview With John le Carré." *National Public Radio,* 14 November, fdch@npr.org (Federal Document Clearing House).

Streitfeld, David. 1992. "Debriefing John le Carré." *Book World,* 8 November, 15.

Truehart, Charles. 1989. "John le Carré, the Spy Spinner after the Thaw." *Washington Post,* 25 May, D1–3.

Vaughan, Paul. 1979. "Le Carré's Circus: Lamplighters, Moles, and Others of That Ilk." *Listener,* 13 September, 339–40.

Wapshott, Nicholas. 1982. "Tinker, Tailor, Soldier, Novelist." *Times,* 6 September, 7.

Watson, Jonathan. 1969. "Violent Image." *Sunday Times,* 30 March, 55, 57.

Literary Analyses of the Work of John le Carré

Books

Barley, Tony. 1986. *Taking Sides: The Fiction of John le Carré.* Philadelphia: Open University Press.

Beene, LynnDianne. 1992. *John le Carré.* New York: Twayne.

Bloom, Clive, ed. 1990. *Spy Thrillers: from Buchan to le Carré.* New York: St. Martin's.

Bloom, Harold, ed. 1987. *John le Carré.* New York: Chelsea House.

Bold, Alan, ed. 1988. *The Quest for le Carré.* New York: St. Martin's.

Cobbs. John L. 1998. *Understanding John le Carré.* Columbia, S.C.: University of South Carolina Press.

Homberger, Eric. 1986. *John le Carré.* New York: Methuen.

Lewis, Peter. 1985. *John le Carré.* New York: Frederick Ungar.

Monaghan, David. 1985. *The Novels of John le Carré.* Oxford: Basil Blackwell.

————. 1986. *Smiley's Circus: A Guide to the Secret World of John le Carré.* New York: Thomas Dunne Books, St. Martin's.

Sauerberg, Lars Ole. 1984. *Secret Agents in Fiction: Ian Fleming, John le Carré, and Len Deighton.* London: Macmillan.

Wolfe, Peter. 1987. *Corridors of Deceit: The World of John le Carré.* Bowling Green, Oh: Bowling Green University Press.

Articles and Book Chapters

Adams, Michael. 1989. "John le Carré/David John Moore Cornwell." In *Critical Survey of Mystery and Detective Fiction Authors,* edited by Frank N. Magill, 1041–7. Englewood Cliffs, NJ: Salem.

Atkins, John. 1984. "16: The World of John le Carré and 17: Le Carré's People." *The British Spy Novel.* New York: Riverrun Press, 170–90.

Bell, Pearl K. 1974. "Coming in from the Cold War." *New Leader,* 24 June, 15–16.

Bloom, Harold. 1987. Introduction. In *John le Carré,* edited by Harold Bloom, 1–6. New York: Chelsea House.

Bold, Alan. 1988. Introduction. In *The Quest for John le Carré,* edited by Alan Bold, 9–24. New York: St. Martin's.

Brady, Charles. 1985. "John le Carré's Smiley Saga." *Thought,* Vol. 60, Sept., 275–296.

Bradbury, Richard. 1990. "Reading John le Carré." In *Spy Thrillers,* edited by Clive Bloom, 130–9. New York: St. Martin's Press.

Cawelti, John G., and Bruce A. Rosenberg. 1987. "The Complex Vision of John le Carré." In *The Spy Story,* 156–86. Chicago: University of Chicago Press.

Crechan, Stewart. 1988. "Information, Power, and the Reader: Textual Strategies in le Carré." In *The Quest for le Carré,* edited by Alan Bold, 103–28. New York: St. Martin's.

Diamond, Julie. 1984. "Spies in the Promised Land: A Review Article." *Race & Class,* Vol. 25, No. 4, 35–40.

Dobel, J. Patrick. 1988. "The Honourable Spymaster: John le Carré and the Character of Espionage." *Administration & Society,* Vol. 20, No. 2, 191–215.

East, Andy. 1983. "CWF 41: Le Carré, John." In *The Cold War File,* 169–78. Metuchen, NJ: Scarecrow.

Edwards, Owen Dudley. 1988. "The Clues of the Great Tradition." In *The Quest for le Carré,* edited by Alan Bold, 41–68. New York: St. Martin's.

Gadney, Reg. 1974. "Triple Agents?" *London Magazine,* October-November, 73–7.

Garson, Helen. 1988. "Enter George Smiley: Le Carré's *Call for the Dead.*" In *The Quest for le Carré,* edited by Alan Bold, 73–80. New York: St. Martin's.

Geoghegan, Jack. 1988. "The Spy Who Saved Me: A Thriller Starring John le Carré." *New York Times Book Review,* 4 December, 16.

Giddings, Robert. 1988. "The Writing on the Igloo Walls: Narrative Technique in *The Spy Who Came in from the Cold.*" In *The Quest for le Carré,* edited by Alan Bold, 188–210. New York: St. Martin's.

Green, Vivian. 1988. "*A Perfect Spy:* A Personal Remembrance." In *The Quest for le Carré,* edited by Alan Bold, 25–40. New York: St. Martin's.

Grella, George. 1976. "Murder and Loyalty." *New Republic,* 31 July, 23–5.

Halperin, John. 1980. "Between Two Worlds: The Novels of John le Carré." *South Atlantic Quarterly,* Vol. 79, Spring, 17–37.

Hayes, Michael J. 1990. "Are You Telling Me Lies David? The Work of John le Carré." In *Spy Thrillers,* edited by Clive Bloom, 113–29. New York: St. Martin's Press.

Hughes, Celia. 1981. "Serious Reflections on Light Reading: The World of John le Carré." *Theology,* Vol. 84, July, 274–9.

Jeffares, A. Norman. 1976. "John le Carré." In *Contemporary Novelists,* 21st ed., edited by James Vinson, 793–5; 22nd ed., 381–2. New York: St. Martin's.

Johnson, Douglas. 1977. "Three Cards of Identity." *New Society,* Vol. 42, 3 November, 247–8.

Kakutani, Michiko. 1984. "Mysteries Join the Mainstream." *New York Times Book Review,* 15 January, 1, 36–7.

Kanfer, Stefan. 1987. "'Our Impudent Crimes': The Honourable Schoolboy." In *John le Carré,* edited by Harold Bloom, 7–12. New York: Chelsea House.

King, Holly Beth. 1987. "Child's Play in John le Carré's *Tinker, Tailor, Soldier, Spy.*" In *John le Carré,* edited by Harold Bloom, 65–72. New York: Chelsea House.

Kirk, John. 1964. Introduction to John le Carré, *The Incongruous Spy,* a republished double edition of *Call for the Dead* and *A Murder of Quality.* New York: Walker & Co.

Laity, Susan. 1987. "'The Second Burden of a Former Child': Doubling and Repetition in *A Perfect Spy.*" In *John le Carré,* edited by Harold Bloom, 137–64. New York: Chelsea House.

Lasseter, Victor. 1982. "John le Carré's Spy Jargon: An Introduction and Lexicon." *Verbatim,* Vol. VIII, No. 4: 1–2.

Maddox, Tom. 1986. "Spy Stories: The Life and Fiction of John le Carre." *Wilson Quarterly,* Vol. X, No. 4:158–170.

Masters, Anthony. 1987. "John le Carré: The Natural Spy." In *Literary Agents: The Novelist as Spy,* 229–65. New York: Basil Blackwell.

McCormick, Donald, and Katy Fletcher. 1990. "David John Moore Cornwell." In *Spy Fiction: A Connoisseur's Guide,* 63–6. New York: Facts on File.

McWilliams, Wilson Carey. 1980. "Contending With God, Fidelity, and Freedom." *Worldview,* March 1980, 30–1.

Monaghan, David. 1983. "John le Carré and England: A Spy's-Eye View." *Modern Fiction Studies,* Vol. 29, Autumn, 569–82.

———. 1987. "A World Grown Old and Cold and Weary: Description as Metaphor." In *John le Carré,* edited by Harold Bloom, 117–36. New York: Chelsea House.

Moritz, Charles, ed. 1974. "John le Carré." *Current Biography,* 232–5. New York: H. W. Wilson.

Most, Glenn W. 1987. "The Hippocratic Smile: John le Carré and the Traditions of the Detective Novel." In *John le Carré,* edited by Harold Bloom, 81–102. New York: Chelsea House.

Neuse, Steven M. 1982. "Bureaucratic Malaise in the Modern Spy Novel: Deighton, Greene, and Le Carré [sic]." *Public Administration,* Vol. 60, Autumn, 293–306.

O'Neill, Philip. 1988. "Le Carré: Faith and Dreams." In *The Quest for le Carré,* edited by Alan Bold, 169–87. New York: St. Martin's.

Panek, Leroy L. 1987. "Espionage Fiction and the Human Condition." In *John le Carré,* edited by Harold Bloom, 27–48. New York: Chelsea House.

Rao, K. Bhaskara. 1984. "John le Carré." In *Critical Survey of Long Fiction: English Language Series,* edited by Frank N. Magill, 1606–19. Englewood Cliffs, NJ: Salem.

Rowe, Margaret Moan. 1988. "Women's Place in le Carré's Man's World." In *The Quest for le Carré,* edited by Alan Bold, 69–86. New York: St. Martin's.

Rothberg, Abraham. 1987. "The Decline and Fall of George Smiley: John le Carré and English Decency." In *John le Carré."* Edited by Harold Bloom, 49–63. New York: Chelsea House.

Royle, Trevor. 1988. "Le Carré and the Idea of Espionage." In *The Quest for le Carré,* edited by Alan Bold, 87–102.

Rutherford, Andrew. 1978. "The Spy as Hero: Le Carré and the Cold War." In *The Literature of War: Five Studies in Heroic Virtue.* New York: Barnes & Noble. Reprinted in *John le Carré,* edited by Harold Bloom, 13–26. New York: Chelsea House, 1987.

Sauerberg, Lars Ole. 1987. "Fear of Extremes: England's Relationship with German and America." In *John le Carré,* edited by Harold Bloom, 103–12. New York: Chelsea House.

Scanlan, Margaret. 1990. "Philby and His Fictions." In *Traces of Another Time: History and Politics in Postwar British Fiction,* 87–115. Princeton: Princeton University Press.

Seed, David. 1990. "The Well-Wrought Structures of John le Carré's Early Fiction." In *Spy Thrillers,* edited by Clive Bloom, 140–59. New York: St. Martin's.

Silver, Brenda R. 1987. "Women as Agent: The Case of Le Carré's Little Drummer Girl." *Contemporary Literature,* Vol. 28, No.1, 15–40.

Symons, Julian. 1974. "Criminal Activities." *New Review,* Vol.1, 4 July, 60–1.

Smith, Myron J., Jr. 1976. "Introduction" and "le Carré, John." *Cloak-and-Dagger Bibliography: An Annotated Guide to Spy Fiction, 1937–197, v-xi, 105–6.* Metuchen, NJ: Scarecrow.

Snyder, John. 1980. "John le Carré." In *Twentieth Century Crime and Mystery Writers,* edited by John M. Reilly, 933–35. New York: St. Martin's.

Steinbrunner, Chris, and Otto Penzler. 1976. "John le Carré." In *Encyclopedia of Mystery Detection,* 242–3. New York: McGraw Hill.

Wakeman, John, ed. 1975. "John le Carré." *World Authors: 1950–1970,* 841–2. New York: H. W. Wilson.

Walker, Christopher. 1987. "Le Carré Dodges the Glasnost Grilling." *Times,* 20 May, 7a.

Wallace, Douglas. 1985. "John le Carré: The Dark Side of Organizations." *Harvard Business Review,* Vol. 63, January-February, 6, 7, 10, 12, 14.

Reviews

Anonymous. 1974. "Hunt the Sleeper." *Times Literary Supplement,* 19 July, 761.

Adams, Robert M. 1964. "Couldn't Put It Down." *New York Review of Books,* 5 March, 13–4.

Alvarez, A. 1980. "Half-angels versus Half-devils." *Observer,* 3 February, 39.

Annan, Noel. 1986. "Underground Men: A Perfect Spy." *New York Review of Books,* 29 May, 3,4,6,7.

Bannon, Barbara A. 1987. "Generations of Intrigue." *Commonweal,* 113, 23 May, 308–9.

Behr, Edward. 1986. "The Making of a Double Agent: The Thriller as Psychological Case Study." *Newsweek,* 7 April, 1986.

Binyon, T. J. 1977. "A Gentleman among Players." *Times Literary Supplement,* 9 September, 1069.

———. 1983. "Theatre of Terror." *Times Literary Supplement,* 25 March, 289.

Boyd, William. 1991. "Oh, What a Lovely Cold War." *New York Times Book Review,* 6 January, 3.

Broyard, Anatole. 1982. "Le Carré's People." *New York Times Book Review.* 29 August, 23.

———. 1983. *New York Times,* 25 February, 21.

Buckley, William F. 1983. "Terror and a Woman." *New York Times Book Review,* 1, 23. Reprinted in *John le Carré,* edited by Harold Bloom, 113–16. New York: Chelsea House, 1987.

Burges, Anthony. 1977. "Peking Drugs, Moscow Gold." *New York Times Book Review,* 25 September, 9.

Buruma, Ian. 1991. "After the Fall." *New York Review of Books,* 28 March, 8–9.

Caute, David. 1980. "It Was a Man." *New Statesman,* 8 February, 209.

Conroy, Frank. 1986. "A Perfect Spy." *New York Times Book Review,* 13 April, 1, 24.

Corney, Hyam. 1983. "Drum Beats." *Jerusalem Post Magazine,* 1 April, 6.

Daleski, H.M. 1997. "A Loveable Jew." *Jerusalem Report,* 23 January, 46–7.

Edwards, Thomas R. 1986. "Father, Son, Soldier, Spy." *New Republic,* 19 May, 32–4.

Elliott, George P. 1965. "It's Spying Who Counts." *New York Times Book Review,* 25 July, 8.

Fenton, James. 1977. "Le Carré Goes East." *New Review,* Vol.4, October, 3–4.

Finger, Louis. 1977. "The Manly One." *New Statesman,* 23 September, 414–15.

Galnoor, Yitzhak. "Teatron l'lo Bidur" (Theater Without Entertainment). *Ha'Aretz,* 28 October, 18, 19.

Gray, Paul. 1989. "A Master Hits His Old Pace." *Time,* 29 May, 50.

James, Clive. 1977. "Go Back to the Cold!" *New York Review of Books,* 27 October, 29–30.

Jensen, Kurt. 1996. "The Play of Story in the Human Heart." *Boston Sunday Globe,* 27 October.

Kaplan, Fred. 1996. "Fantasies That Never Happened" (Sipurei Habedim Shel Lo Kara). *Ha'Aretz,* 24 November, 5 B.

Kaufman, Gerald. 1983. "John le Carré's Israeli Thriller." *Jewish Chronicle,* 1 April, 17.

Knegtmans, Hans. 1996. "A Manufactured Revolution" (Een versonnen revolutie). *HP/De Tijd,* 22 November, 102.

Laqueur, Walter. 1983. "Le Carré's Fantasies." *Commentary,* June, 62–67. Responses by Jacques Barzun, Gideon Rose, and Thomas B. Windholz, 15–18. Laqueur reply, 18.

Lekachman, Robert. 1980. "Good Boys, Bad Boys, Old Boys." *The Nation,* 26 April, 504–6.

Lehmann-Haupt, Christopher. 1995. "In Pursuit of Memory, and a Double Agent." *New York Times,* 2 March.

Locke, Richard. 1974. "The Spy Who Spies on Spies." *New York Times Book Review,* 30 June, 1–2.

Marcus, Steven. 1965. "Grand Illusions." *New York Review of Books,* 5 August, 20–21.

Menand, Louis. 1995. "Under Western Eyes." *New York Review of Books,* 20 April, 4–5.

Miller, Karl. 1974. "Gothic Guesswork." *New Republic,* 18 July, 24–7.

Mitgang, Herbert. 1993. "New Evil, New Empire, Same Fun." *New York Times,* 23 June.

Morrison, Blake. 1986. "Love and Betrayal in the Mist." *Times Literary Supplement,* 14 March, 380–1.

O'Brien, Conor Cruise. 1989. "Bad News for Spies." *New York Times Book Review,* 21 May, 3.

Paulin, Tom. 1980. "National Myths." *Encounter,* Vol. 54, June, 58–60.

Prawer, S. S. 1980. "The Circus and Its Conscience." *Times Literary Supplement,* 8 February, 131–2.

Prescott, Peter S. 1983. "In the Theater of the Real." *Newsweek,* 7 March, 42.

Pritchett, V. S. 1980. "A Spy Romance." *New York Review of Books,* 7 February, 22–4.

Pryce-Jones, David. 1983. "A Demonological Fiction." *New Republic.* 18 April, 27–30.

Remnick, David. 1993. "Le Carré's New War." *New York Review of Books,* 12 August, 20–3.

Rohter, Larry. 1996. "In the Land of the Big Ditch, le Carré's in Hot Water." *New York Times International,* 19 November, A 4.

———. 1996. "Le Carré's Latest Has the Locals Shaking Their Head." *International Herald Tribune,* 20 November, 2.

Rush, Norman. 1996. "Spying and Lying." *New York Times Book Review,* 11.

Scammell, Michael. 1995 "Still Out in the Cold." *New York Times Book Review,* 26 March, 13.

Schiff, Stephen. 1989. "The Secret Life of John le Carré." *Vanity Fair,* June, 146–50, 152, 154, 188–89. Condensed version, *Reader's Digest,* November, 63–67.

Stern, Laurence. 1977. "The Secret World of George Smiley." *Washington Post Book World,* 9 October, E1, E6.

Streitfeld, David. 1996. "John le Carré: Lies, Damn Lies and the Spy Game." *International Herald Tribune,* 7 November, 24.

Symons, Julian. 1993. "Our Man in Zurich." *New York Times Book Review,* 27 June, 1.

Wolcott, James. 1983. "The Secret Sharers." *New York Review of Books,* 14 April, 19–21.

Wood, Michael. 1980. "Spy Fiction, Spy Fact." *New York Times Book Review.* 6 January, 1, 16, 17.

———. 1996. "The Lying Game." *New York Review of Books,* 28 November, 16–17.

Works on Spy Fiction, Espionage and International Relations

Aidekman, 1996. "The Tacticalization of American Intelligence: A Misdirection of Mission?" Paper presented at the 1996 meeting of the International Studies Association, 16–20 April, San Diego.

Allison, Graham T. 1971. *Essence of Decision: Explaining the Cuban Missile Crisis.* Boston: Little, Brown.

Aronoff, Myron J., and Yael Aronoff. 1996. "Explaining Domestic Influences on Current Israeli Foreign Policy: The Peace Negotiations." *Brown Journal of World Affairs,* Vol. 3, No. 2, Summer-Fall, 83–101.

———. 1998. "Domestic Determinants of Israeli Foreign Policy: The Peace Process from the Declaration of Principles with the PLO to the Oslo II Interim Agreement with the Palestinian Authority." In *The Middle East and the Peace Process: the Impact of the Oslo Accords,* edited by Robert O. Freedman, 11–34. Gainesville: University Press of Florida.

Aronoff, Myron J., and Pierre Atlas. 1998. "The Peace Process and Competing Challenges to the Dominant Zionist Discourse." In *The Israel-Palestinian Peace Process,* edited by Ilan Peleg, 41–60. Albany: State University of New York Press.

Ash, Timothy Garton. 1997. "The Imperfect Spy." *New York Review of Books,* 26 June, 12, 14, 16.

Bar-Joseph, Uri. 1995. *Intelligence Intervention in the Politics of Democratic States: The United States, Israel, and Britain.* University Park, PA: Pennsylvania State University Press.

———. 1996. "From the Tobianski Affair to the Law of the GSS: State-Intelligence Relations in Israel, 1948–1996." Paper presented at the 1996 meeting of the International Studies Association, 16–20 April, San Diego.

Barret, David M. 1996. "Researching a Black Hole: Sen. Richard Russell (D-Georgia), Congress, and the CIA in the 'Era of Trust.'" Paper delivered at the 1996 meeting of the International Studies Association, 16–20 April, San Diego.

Bartoszewski, W. T. 1989. "The Myth of the Spy." *JASO: Journal of the Anthropological Society of Oxford,* Vol. 20, No.1, 27–35.

Bar-Zohar, Michael. 1972. *Spies in the Promised Land.* Boston: Houghton Mifflin.

Barzun, Jacques. 1965. "Meditations on the Literature of Spying." *American Scholar,* Vol. 34, 167–78.

Bathurst, Robert. B. 1993. *Intelligence and the Mirror: On Creating an Enemy.* Oslo: International Peace Research Institute and Newbury Park (London): SAGE.

Betts, Richard K. 1978. "Analysis, War, and Decision: Why Intelligence Failures Are Inevitable." *World Politics,* Vol. 31, No. 1, October, 61–89.

Bik, J. M. 1997. "Three Rubles for a Double Spy: Memoirs of Markus Wolf" (Drie roebels voor een dubbelspion: Herinnerngen van Markus Wolf). *NRC Handelsblad,* 6 June, Boeken 6, 37.

Black, Ian, and Benny Morris. 1991. *Israel's Secret Wars: A History of Israel's Intelligence Services.* New York: Grove Weidenfeld.

Blake, George. 1990. *No Other Choice: an Autobiography.* London: Jonathan Cape.

Bower, Tom. 1995. *The Perfect Spy: Sir Dick White and the Secret War, 1935–90.* London: Heinemann.

Boyle, Andrew. 1979. *The Climate of Treason.* London: Hodder and Stoughton.

Brock, David. 1986. "Spies Are Back in U.S. Arsenal." *Washington Times,* 23 June, 6,8–15.

Brown, Charles W. 1989. *Nathan Hale: the Martyr Spy.* New York: J. B. Oglive.

Buchan, John. 1915. *The Thirty-Nine Steps.* Reprint. New York: Popular Library, 1974.

Burridge, James. 1992. "SIGINT in the Novels of John le Carré." *Crotolog* (National Security Agency) reprinted in *Studies in Intelligence* (Central Intelligence Agency), 11–18.

Carr, E. H. 1947. *International Relations between the Two World Wars, 1919–1939.* London: Macmillan.

Clements, Frank A. 1995. *Israeli Secret Services: An Annotated Bibliography, International Organizations,* Vol. 12.

Copeland, Miles. 1974. *The Real Spy World.* London: Weidenfeld and Nicholson.

Cram, Cleveland C. 1995. "Of Moles and Molehunters." *Studies in Intelligence,* Vol.38, No.5., 129–37.

Eisenberg, Dennis, Uri Dan, and Eli Landau. 1978. *The Mossad.* New York: Signet.

Elshtain, Jean Bethke. 1992. *Just War Theory.* New York: New York University Press.

Epstein, Edward Jay. 1994. "Why Spy?" *New York Times Magazine,* 22 May, 42–3.

Fest Joachim. 1996. *Plotting Hitler's Death: The Story of German Resistance.* New York: Metropolitan Books/ Henry Holt & Co.

Fromkin, David. 1996. "Daring Amateurism: The CIA's Social History." *Foreign Affairs,* Vol. 75, No. 1, January-February, 165–72.

Gilbert, Martin. 1991. *Churchill: A Life.* London: Heinemann.

Gillespie, Robert. 1970. "The Recent Future: Secret Agents and the Cold World War." *Salmagundi,* Vol. 13, 45–60.

Godfrey, E. Drexel, Jr. 1978. "Ethics and Intelligence." *Foreign Affairs,* Vol. 56, No. 3, April, 624–42.

Halperin, Morton H. 1974. *Bureaucratic Politics and Foreign Policy.* Washington, D.C.: Brookings Institution.

Hearst, David. 1997. "Moscow Hot-Line Seeks Spies to Turn." *Guardian,* 5 June, 3.

Hoagland, Jim. 1997. "Mission Impossible: The Make-Believe World of Today's CIA." *International Herald Tribune,* 15 March, 8.

———. 1997. "CIA's 'Zipless Coup' in Iraq Is a Matchless Flop." *International Herald Tribune,* 9 May, 8.

Holt, Pat M. 1995. *Secret Intelligence and Public Policy: A Dilemma of Democracy.* Washington, D. C.: Congressional Quarterly.

Hulnick, Arthur S. 1996. "US Covert Action: Does It Have a Future?" *International Journal of Intelligence and CounterIntelligence,* Vol. 9, No. 2, Summer, 145–57.

International Herald Tribune. 1996. "Editorial: Yesterday's Scoundrel." 19 December, 8.

———. 1996. "Editorial: Spy Game Continues." 21 November, 8.

Hunter, Evan. 1982. "Spies and Moles and Other Entertainers." *New York Times,* 24 January, 12,17.

Johnson, Loch K. 1989. *America's Secret War: The CIA in a Democratic Society.* New York: Oxford University Press.

Johnston, David, and Tim Weiner. 1996. "Sloppy Tradecraft in Singapore Betrayed Suspected CIA Traitor." *International Herald Tribune,* 22 November, 3.

Karalekas, Anne. 1985. "History of the Central Intelligence Agency." In *The Central Intelligence Agency: History and Documents,* edited by William Leary. University, AL: University of Alabama Press.

King, Robert D. "Treason and Traitors." *Transaction/SOCIETY,* Vol.35, No.2, January-February, 329–50. Originally published in 1989.

Knightly, Philip. 1986. *The Second Oldest Profession: Spies and Spying in the Twentieth Century.* London: A. Deutsch.

Knowlton, Brian. 1996. "U.S. Charges CIA Official as Paid Spy for Russia." *International Herald Tribune,* 19 November, 1.

———. 1996. "FBI Agent Is Charged with Spying for Moscow: Wife Aided Sting Operation against Him." *International Herald Tribune,* December, 1.

Laqueur, Walter. 1993. "Intelligence and Secrecy: Sovietology Redux." *Transaction/SOCIETY,* Vol. 30, No. 2, January-February, 4, 5, 7–13.

———. 1998. "The Future of Intelligence," *Transaction/SOCIETY,* Vol. 35, No. 2, January-February, 301–11. Originally published in 1985.

Lekachman, Robert. 1984. "Super Thrillers and Superpowers." *New York Times Book Review,* 19 February, 1,32.

Lowenthal, Mark M. 1992. "Tribal Tongues: Intelligence Consumers, Intelligence Producers." *Washington Quarterly,* Winter, 157–68.

Mauerer, Alfred C., Marion D. Turnstall, and James M. Keagle, eds. 1985. *Intelligence: Policy & Process,* Boulder: Westview.

McCormick, Donald, and Katy Fletcher. 1990. *Spy Fiction: A Connoisseur's Guide,* New York: Facts on File (1990:66).

Menger, Truus. 1982. *Toen niet, nu niet, nooit (not then, not now, never).* Den Haag: Leopold.

Nelson, John S. 1996. "Talking International Relations: Nature and Reality Versus Honor and Anger (or What Spy Stories Can Tell Us about the Modern Paradigm from Thomas Hobbes)." Paper delivered at the annual meeting of the American Political Science Association, Chicago.

New York Times. 1995. Editorial. "Killers, Scoundrels and Spies." 27 August, 14.

———. 1995. Editorial. "The Keys to the Spy Kingdom." 19 May, 14.

Nicholl, Charles. 1992. *The Reckoning: The Murder of Christopher Marlowe.* Chicago: University of Chicago Press.

Oseth. John M. 1985. *Regulating U.S. Intelligence* Operations. Lexington: University Press of Kentucky.

Pfaff, William. 1996. "Spooky Question: Does the CIA Obey the Law?" *International Herald Tribune,* 21 November, 9.

Pincus, Walter. 1996. "Crisis at CIA: Why Are Its Young Officers Resigning?" *International Herald Tribune,* 28 November, 7.

Pincher, Chapman. 1984. *Too Secret Too Long.* New York: St. Martin's.

———. 1987. *Traitors: The Anatomy of Treason.* New York: St. Martin's.

Political Notes. 1997. "Sorry, That's Classified." *International Herald Tribune,* 14 May, 3.

Powers, Thomas. 1995. "No Laughing Matter." *New York Review of Books,* 10 August, 4–6.

Ransom, Harry Howe. 1970. *The Intelligence Establishment.* Cambridge, MA: Harvard University Press.

Raviv, Dan, and Yossi Melman. 1990. *Every Spy a Prince: The Complete History of Israel's Intelligence Community.* Boston: Houghton Mifflin.

Schmitt, Eric. 1992. "Spy-Satellite Unit Faces A New Life in Daylight." *New York Times,* 3 November, A16.

Stafford, David. 1998. *Churchill and the Secret Service.* Woodstock, N.Y.: The Overlook Press.

Steiner, Zara. 1998. "A Question of Intelligence" (Review of Stafford, 1998). *New York Times Book Review,* February 22, 10.

Susser, Leslie. 1998. "Can the Mossad Bounce Back?" *Jerusalem Report,* 8 January, 10–14.

Teveth, Shabtai. 1996. *Ben-Gurion's Spy: The Story of the Political Scandal That Shaped Modern Israel.* New York: Columbia University Press.

Trahair, Richard C. S. 1994. "A Psychohistorical Approach to Espionage: Klaus Fuchs (1911–1988)." *Mentalities/Mentalités,* Vol. 9, No. 2, 28–49.

———. (unpublished). "A Q-Method Study in Espionage: George Blake, Superspy."

Traynor, Ian. 1997. "Bridge of Spies." *Guardian,* 26 March, 2–3.

Waltzer, Michael. 1992. *Just & Unjust Wars,* 2nd. ed. New York: Basic Books.

Weiner, Tim. 1994. "A Traitor, Yes, But Maybe He Has a Point," *New York Times,* May 1, 4E.

———. 1995. "C.I.A. Chief Says Moscow, with Help from Double Agent, Warped U.S. Perceptions." *New York Times, International,* 9 December, 5.

———. 1995. "The C.I.A.'s Most Important Mission: Itself." *New York Times Magazine,* December 10, 64–7, 80, 82, 84, 104, 106.

———. 1996. "A Spy Agency Admits Accumulating $4 Billion in Secret Money." *New York Times,* 16 May, A17.

———. 1996. "A Swift Rise at the CIA, a Swift Fall." *International Herald Tribune,* 20 November, 1, 10.

———. 1997. "CIA Memory Goes Blank: Secret Files on Iran Destroyed Decades Ago." *International Herald Tribune,* 30 May, 1, 7.

———. 1997. "How a Spy Left Taiwan in the Cold," *New York Times, International,* December 20, A7.

Weiner, Tim, David Johnston, and Neil A. Lewis. 1995. *Betrayal: The Story of Aldrich Ames, an American Spy.* New York: Random House.

West, Nigel. 1982. *The Circus: MI5 Operations, 1945–1972.* Briarcliff Manor, NY: Stein and Day.

Winterbotham, F. W. 1974. *The Ultra Secret.* New York: Dell.

Wiseman, Carter S. 1975. "Who's Really Who in Espionage." *Newsweek,* 15 December, 26–27.

Wolf, Markus, with Anne Mc Elvoy. 1997. *Man Without a Face: The Autobiography of Communism's Greatest Spy.* New York: Time Books.

Wright, Peter. 1987. *Spy Catcher.* New York: Viking.

Yoder, Amos. 1996. "CIA Covert Actions—Were They Worth It?" Columbus, Oh: Mershon Center, Ohio State University.

Zeiger, Henry. 1965. *Ian Fleming: The Spy Who Came in with the Gold.* New York: Duell, Sloane, and Pearce.

General References

Aronoff, Myron J. 1989. *Israeli Visions and Divisions: Cultural Change and Political Conflict.* New Brunswick, NJ: Transaction.

Bandura, Albert. 1990. "Selective Activation and Disengagement of Moral Control." *Journal of Social Issues,* Vol. 46, No.1, 27–46.

———. 1996. Claudio Barbaranelli, Gian Vittorio Caprara, and Concertta Pastorilli. "Mechanisms of Moral Disengagement in the Exercise of Moral Agency." *Journal of Personality and Social Psychology,* Vol. 71, No. 2, 364–74.

Bell, Martin. 1997. "The Accidental Hero: Exclusive-My Campaign Diary." *Guardian,* 6 May, 3–5.

Berger, Peter, and Thomas Luckmann. 1966. *The Social Construction of Reality.* Garden City, NY: Doubleday. Reprint. Harmondsworth: Penguin, 1991.

Bloom, Harold. 1973. *The Anxiety of Influence: A Theory of Poetry.* New York: Oxford University Press.

Buber, Martin. 1958. *I and Thou.* New York: Charles Scribner's Sons (second edition).

Buruma, Ian. 1997. "Artist of the Floating World." *New York Review of Books,* 9 January, 8, 9, 11.

Chapman, H. Perry. 1996. "Jan Steen, Player in His Own Paintings." In *Jan Steen: Painter and Storyteller,* edited by Chapman, et al. New Haven: Yale University Press.

Cohen, David. 1996. *Alter Egos—Multiple Personalities.* London: Constable.

Concise Oxford Dictionary. 1995. 9th ed., edited by Della Thompson. Oxford: Clarendon Press.

Cornford, F. M. 1908 (1994). *Microcosmographia Academia.* Reprinted in Gordon Johnson, *University Politics: F. M. Cornford's Cambridge and his Advice to the Young Academic Politician.* Cambridge: Cambridge University Press.

Dexter, Louis Anthony. 1993. "Complexities of Corruption." *Society,* Vol. 30, No. 4, May-June, 64.

Dobbs, Michael. 1996. "A New, Disturbing Chapter Emerges in Holocaust History." *International Herald Tribune,* 11 November, 1,12.

Edelman, Murray. 1995. *From Art to Politics.* Chicago: University of Chicago Press.

Eliot, George. 1895. *Felix Holt: The Radical.* Edinburgh: William Blackwood.

Forster, E. M. 1951. *Two Cheers for Democracy.* London: Edward Arnold.

Garber, Marjorie. 1995. "Back to Whose Basics?" *New York Times Book Review,* 29 October, 55.

Geertz, Clifford. 1973. *The Interpretation of Cultures.* New York: Basic Books.

———. 1980. *Negara: The Theatre State in Nineteenth-Century Bali.* Princeton: Princeton University Press.

———. 1983. *Local Knowledge.* New York: Basic Books.

———.1995. *After the Fact.* Cambridge, MA: Harvard University Press.

Gerth, H. H., and C. Wright Mills, eds. 1946. *From Max Weber: Essays in Sociology.* New York: Oxford University Press.

Gluckman, Max, ed. 1964. *Closed Systems and Open Minds: The Limits of Naivety in Social Anthropology.* Chicago: Aldine.

Goffman, Erving. 1982. *Interaction Ritual: Essays in Face-to-Face Behavior.* New York: Pantheon.

Herford, R. Travers. 1962. *Pirke Aboth, The Ethics of the Talmud: Sayings of the Fathers.* New York: Schocken.

Howe, Irving. 1992. *Politics and the Novel.* New York: Columbia University Press.

Ijzendoorn, Marinus H., and Marian J. Bakermans-Dranenburg. 1997. "Intergenerational Transmission of Attachment: State of the Art in Psychometric, Psychological, and Clinical Research." In *Attachment and psychopathology,* edited by L. Atkinson and K. J. Zucker. New York: Guillford.

Keegan, John. 1996. "Early Holocaust Reports and a Code of Silence." *International Herald Tribune,* 27 November, 9.

Lehmann-Haupt, Christopher. 1996. Review of *Plotting Hitler's Death* by Joachim Fest. *International Herald Tribune,* 28 October, 9.

Lewis, Anthony. 1997. "America Is Searching: Is It for Mario Cuomo?" *International Herald Tribune,* 25 March, 11.

Lockard, Joan S., and Delroy L. Paulhus, eds. 1988. *Self-Deception: An Adaptive Mechanism.* Englewood Cliffs, NJ: Prentice-Hall.

McWilliams, Wilson Carey. 1995. "Ambiguities and Ironies: Conservatism and Liberalism in the American Political Tradition." In *Moral Values in Liberalism and Conservatism,* edited by W. Lawson Taitte, 175–212. Dallas: University of Texas Press.

———. 1995. "Poetry, Politics, and the Comic Spirit." *PS (Political Science),* Vol. 28, No. 2, June, 197–200.

Mulisch, Harry. 1982. *De Aanslag* (The Assault). Amsterdam: De Bezige Bij.

Orwin, Clifford. 1994. *The Humanity of Thucydides.* Princeton: Princeton University Press.

Oxford Dictionary of Quotations. 1977. 2nd ed. Oxford: Oxford University Press.

Quinton, Anthony. 1984. "Moral Minefields." *New Republic,* 26 November, 30–32.

Ricoeur, Paul. 1986. *Lectures on Ideology and Utopia.* New York: Columbia University Press.

Shakespeare, William. 1988. *William Shakespeare: The Complete Works, Compact Edition. Hamlet* and *As You Like It.* Oxford: Clarendon Press.

Shklar, Judith N. 1984. *Ordinary Vices.* Cambridge: Belknap Press of Harvard University.

Shils, Edward A. 1956. *The Torment of Secrecy.* Glencoe, Il: The Free Press.

Shaw, George Bernard. 1903. *Man and Superman.* London: Constable

Stephen, Sir Leslie, and Sir Sidney Lee, eds. 1968. *Dictionary of National Biography.* Oxford: Oxford University Press.

Vernon, John. 1995. "The Black Face of Freedom." *New York Times Book Review,* 29 October, 12.

Weisell, Elie. 1976. *Messengers of God.* New York: Random House

White, James Boyd. 1994. *Acts of Hope: Creating Authority in Literature, Law, and Politics.* Chicago: University of Chicago Press.

Zerubavel, Eviatar. 1991. *The Fine Line: Making Distinctions in Everyday Life.* New York: Free Press.

Zuckert, Catherine. 1995. "Why Political Scientists Want to Study Literature." *PS (Political Science),* Vol. 28, No. 2, June, 189–90.

Personal Communications and Unpublished Sources

Cornwell, David. 1996. Correspondence of 17 August and 11 November.

———. 1997. Correspondence of 29 May and 23 June.

Gochul, Joseph. 1997. "The Myth of Smiley: Politics and the Writing of Albert Camus and John le Carré. Unpublished junior seminar paper, December.

Horowitz, Irving Louis. 1993. Correspondence of 7 July.

McWilliams, W. Carey. 1994. Undated correspondence.

Stevens, Anne. 1997. Email of 9 June to Robert Ross.

Trahair, Richard C. S. 1995, Correspondence of 19 July.

———. 1996. Email of 3 December.

Subject Index

Name Index